Music an
Traditions

Music and Dance Traditions of Ghana

History, Performance and Teaching

Paschal Yao Younge

Forewords by
Daniel Avorgbedor,
Komla Amoaku *and*
Francis Nii-Yartey

McFarland & Company, Inc., Publishers
Jefferson, North Carolina, and London

LIBRARY OF CONGRESS CATALOGUING-IN-PUBLICATION DATA

Younge, Paschal Yao.
Music and dance traditions of Ghana : history, performance and
teaching / Paschal Yao Younge ; forewords by Daniel Avorgbedor,
Komla Amoaku and Francis Nii-Yartey
p.   cm.
Includes bibliographical references and index.

ISBN 978-0-7864-4992-7
softcover : 50# alkaline paper ∞

1. Folk music — Ghana — History and criticism.
2. Folk dance music — Ghana — History and criticism.
3. Folk dancing — Ghana.   I. Title.
ML3760.Y68   2011   781.62'960667 — dc23   2011027082

BRITISH LIBRARY CATALOGUING DATA ARE AVAILABLE

Front cover image: Tɔra women's recreational dance-drumming ceremony,
performed by the Tamale Youth Home Cultural Group (2009)

Manufactured in the United States of America

McFarland & Company, Inc., Publishers
Box 611, Jefferson, North Carolina 28640
www.mcfarlandpub.com

Affectionately dedicated to my parents,
Augustine Kwasigah Younge and Catherine Afiwor Younge,
and to my beloved wife, Zelma C.M. Badu-Younge.
Old man and old lady, rest in peace. Metrova, thank you.

N

Map of Africa — Countries and Capitals

Source: ESRI DATA

| 0 | 550 | 1100 | 2200 | 3300 |

Kilometers

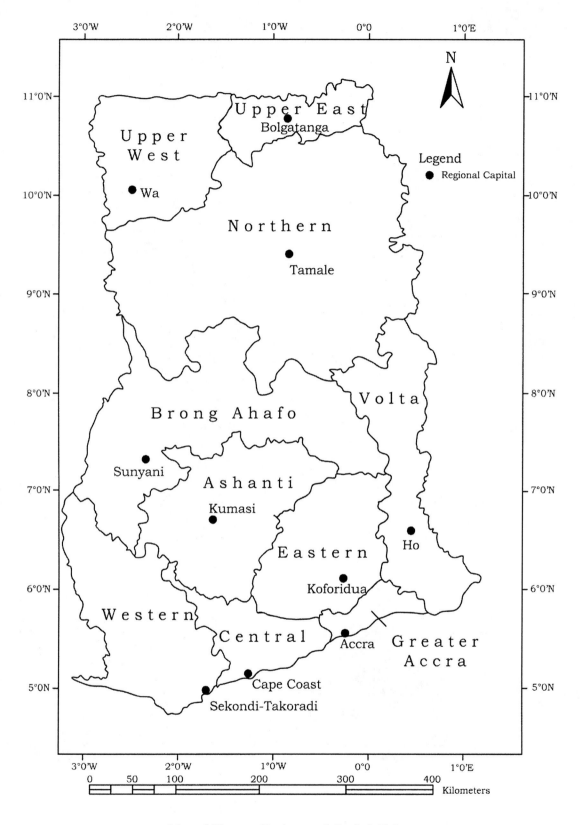

Map of Ghana — Regions and Capital Cities

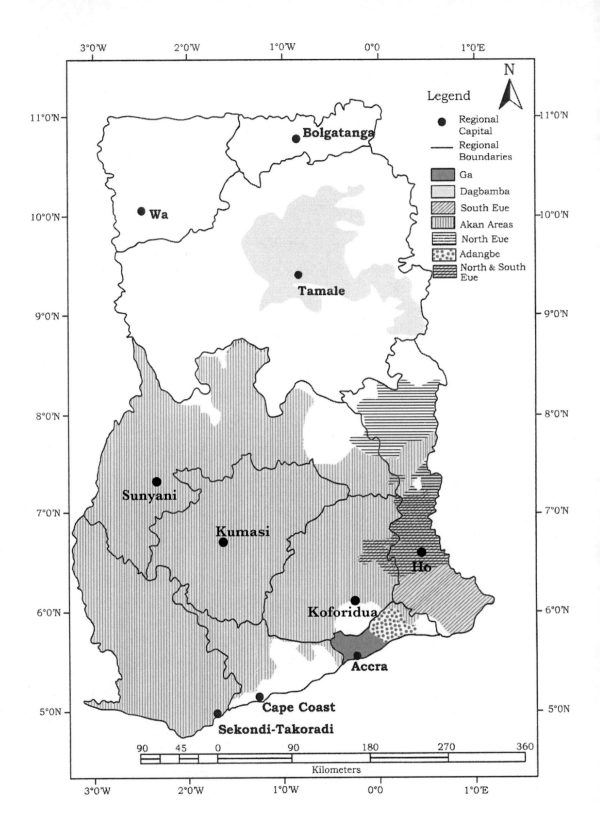

Map of Ghana — Akans, Ga/Dangmes, Eves, and Dagbama Areas

Table of Contents

Between pages 166 and 167 are 16 color plates containing 25 images

Acknowledgments

My special thanks go to all the following traditional artists, performing groups, chiefs, and elders who provided useful information during my 15 years of research: Von Abubakari Salifu "Dunyin La Na," Adade Foli, Atsu Atsiatorme, Francis Kofi, Wisdom Agbedanu, Kassah Kini Teyi, Dasoshie Seku, Agbade Kassah, Openo Yao, Killer Fiebor, Johnson Kemeh, Agbo Setsoafia, Bokor Yibor Setsoafia, Akakpo Doamekpor, Adegbedzi Kamasa, Bertha Ahiable, Theresa Dzila, Awunyesede Dzila, Mana Bedzra, Agbokpa Wordui, John Dedzo, Samuel Doe Aʋudi, Dollar Sedzro, Connie Ahiawortor, Joseph Young, Rocky Atsu Kpɔha, Agbade Kassah, Seth Gati, Gbolo Kɔsi, Ata Nyawuto, Bright Quarshie, Osei John, Merigah Abukari Salifu, Kwasi Asare, Ali Benedict Kolaan, Solomon Amonquandoh, Alhassan Iddrisu, Jane Aba Yankey, William Diku, the late Prof. Mawere Opoku, Haroon Abdulai, Cecilia Mensah, Sulley Moro, Gogo Amoah, Francis Nii Yartey, Nii Kwaku Mensah III, David Amoo, Ewomenyo Ofori, Isaac Felbah, Nii Kwei Sowah, Sam Thompson, Anyeitei Robin, David Nyarko, Laryea Amoah, James Nii Aryetey Tetteh, Kumordzi Ofori, Robert Ansah Nunoo, Adjei Mensah, Grace Tetteh, Alhassan Iddrisu Damankung, Ibrahim Haruna, Abukari Imoro, Abukari Adam, Azaratu Alhassn, Pagkpemah Alhassan, Napari Mahama, Napari Nabila, Zubeiru Alhassan, Nabila Alhassan, Mahami Wumbei, Fuseini Iddrisu, Baba Amidu, Mac-Abubakar, Mohammed Abdul-Rahaman, Alavanyo Uudidi Adeʋu, Alavanyo Uudidi Gbolo, Alavanyo Uudidi Egbanegba, Dzogadze Atsiagbekɔ, Dzodze Atibladekame, Dzodze Apetepe Akpoka, Dzodze Apetepe Atrikpui, Anlɔ Afiadenyigba Gadzo, Anlɔ Afiadenyigba Akpoka, Tadzeʋu Gahu, Aflao Mawulikplimi Adzogbo, Ho Agbenya Bɔbɔɔbɔ, Abodzentse Gome Group, Emashie Kpanlongo Group, Ghana Dance Ensemble, University of Ghana, Ghana Dance Ensemble, National Theater of Ghana, Tamale Youth Home Cultural Group, Jakpahi Dang Maligu Bla, and Kpeju Jera Group. This publication would not exist without their useful cultural perspectives.

I wish to thank my research and field assistants and also my language specialists, Joseph Younge, Philip Kassah, David Amoo, Mohammed Abdul-Rahaman, Benedict Kolaan Ali, Brigit Tetteh-Batsa, Augustine Mikado, Yusif Mahama, Michael Ofori, and Ephraim Kotey Nikoi. I would like to extend my special gratitude to Professor Komla Amoaku, Dr. Daniel Avorgbedor and Professor Francis Nii-Yartey for their forewords about music, dance and dance-drumming traditions in Africa.

I am very grateful to the Ohio University vice president of research, Baker Fund, and director of African Studies, Dr. Steven Howard, for their various contributions to this project. I thank former and current deans and directors of the College of Creative Arts, Philip Faini and Dr. Burnie Schultz, and the Office of the Provost at West Virginia University for their initial financial support, as well as members of the Azaguno African Drumming and Dance Ensemble for their encouragement during the various stages of this work.

My gratitude also goes to directors of the Ghana dance ensembles, the national dance companies of Ghana at the National Theater and University of Ghana, and all named and unnamed artists who contributed their time and knowledge to this work. My thanks go to readers and typists and others who provided helpful criticisms and suggestions—especially Leslie Greene for typing the bibliography, Betsy Jordan for photography, Maria Billings Jameau for preliminary editing, Kristofer Olsen for musical transcriptions, and Patrick Ryan Giguere, James Younge and Andrea Otto for audio, video recording and video editing, respectively.

My special thanks goes to Zelma Badu-Younge for her love, encouragement, support, dance demonstrations, descriptions of dance movements, typing of the glossary and video recording, and to my other family members, Joseph, Larry, Blandina, James, Benedicta and Rita. I thank you all.

Forewords

African Arts in Education: Theory and Practice
by Daniel Avorgbedor

One of the challenges facing curricular revisions and inventions in the academy concerns the teaching and learning of music and dance traditions outside of mainstream Western music and ballet. There are several components of this challenge, which are significant:

   i. The Western approach tends to approach definitions and practices of music from limited conceptions and resources. For example, the origin of the word "music," the Greek term *mousikes*, carried a broader perspective: it included poetry, instrumental music, song and movement.

   ii. In many world music and dance traditions, the visual-plastic, tactile, olfactory, mime, gesture and gesticulation, as well as a whole range of performance events, fall within the song-speech continuum but defy definition as "song" or "speech"—these definitions are integral to the local definitions and practices of music-dance.

   iii. Despite the numerous texts that exist on music and its dialectical relationships to emotion and affect, individual stories and biophysiologies, cultural contexts, histories, localities, and the current rapid diffusion of music and cultural practices on a global scale complicate the challenges facing the teaching and learning of music in the classroom.

   iv. African culture continues to be grossly misunderstood and continues to challenge, willy-nilly, the claims of contemporary scholarship. Even when attempts are made today on the part of some scholars who position themselves as "sensitive" and thus "knowledgeable," these attempts are often subtly disguised political acts of great convenience and of significant ideological and material advantage to these scholars.

   v. The relatively complex nature of music and dance practices in Africa also imposes an additional challenge for the music educator of today, especially concerning selection, re-interpretation, grading, and teaching methods.

   vi. The recontextualization of performance traditions that emanate from and exemplify the essential oral, aural, and written features of the host cultures being studied also challenges our long-held beliefs about music education, including our belief in the very nature of the cloistered space known as the classroom.

The outlines above are just a small part of the catalog of problem and prospect areas that should be considered in the context of any music education curriculum initiative. A serious consideration of these six general points will make a significant advancement in the philosophical background, the raw materials, and the teaching strategies that are used to make a meaningful integration of African music and dance materials into the classroom.

Paschal Younge's *Music and Dance Traditions of Ghana* is highly commended here for two main reasons: Paschal is one of the few educators who consistently explore the issue of African arts in education from both theoretical and practical viewpoints. He is well-qualified professionally, both in the subject matter of African music and dance, and as a music educator. A third factor which adds significantly to his range of expertise, qualifications and cultural sensitivities regards his early active experiences with the performance traditions of his hometown or cultural area in Ghana. A fourth expertise and background resource concerns his continuing experience with the American, European and Asian classroom settings. In the United States, for example, he has led and taught several study abroad groups. Thus, Paschal is uniquely positioned and privileged in multiple ways that inform his critical, resourceful, and innovative approaches to the teaching of the African performing arts in the Western classroom.

As indicated in the very scope of the book, there is balanced emphasis on multimedia, which is necessary and consistent with the general philosophical foundations, the basic ontological statuses of the African materials, contemporary media technologies, and the target audiences' backgrounds and needs. Thus, the video examples, notations or visual representations, and the practical involvement of students, are all well-envisioned to support the basic premises of this project, no matter how difficult it is for one group of people to appreciate or understand the long-held traditions of another, especially where meaning is crucial.

Although the materials are limited to specific ethnic traditions of Ghana, they nevertheless encapsulate the core of the sites of significance and meaning in African performance arts and their various implications for contemporary music education. Even so, the Ghana materials may present specific challenges—they may even be considered too "rich" for certain Western classroom situations. However, the avant-garde techniques, sound premises, and the systematic (according to Western classroom practices) approaches and innovative strategies will mitigate many of these challenges. The tradition of a conference on the African performing arts (held seasonally at Ohio University–Athens), started by Paschal, is further demonstration of his firm commitment to the scholarly study of African performing arts and the inter- and multidisciplinary challenges they pose to music education in our time. *Music and Dance Traditions of Ghana*, therefore, represents a significant step in the current search for the tools, materials, and perspectives that would serve the needs of demographically diverse school contexts.

Daniel Avorgbedor received his Ph.D. from Indiana University in 1986 and has since taught at the University of Ghana (Legon), Bretton Hall College (UK), City College of New York, and Ohio State University from 1995 to 2009. He served as editor of RILM Abstracts of Music Literature *from 1990 to 1994 and his research and teaching specializations include world music theories and pedagogy.*

Perspectives on Ghanaian Music
by Komla Amoaku

A foreign student who was visiting Africa for the first time made an observation during a class discussion on his experience in Ghana:

I was told a lot about culture shock upon our arrival in Ghana. Yes, I admit I had a shock but it was not the kind driven by differences in cultures. Strangely, it was the similarities between our cultures and the transplantation of America in Ghana that shocked the hell out of me — the electronic media, DJs, the incredibly numerous churches and the mode of dressing among the young and the old. I find these intriguing. What hope do you have for the survival of your cultures and traditional music — especially since they are orally transmitted and not largely documented?

The above observation, made by a student of San Diego State University during a summer study-abroad program in 2005, succinctly addresses an inescapable issue that confronts not only Ghana but also the entire continent of Africa in this era of globalization. Additionally, it underscores the importance and relevance of Paschal Yao Younge's relentless efforts to answer some of the questions posed by this very important observation.

The institutionalized approach to the study and teaching of traditional African music has had quite a long track record in Ghana. The Christian missionaries were inevitably in the vanguard of this process. They established mission schools and churches, and, for the handful who had access to formal education, there were no other alternatives than these. As one looks back, one may remember such missionary-established teacher training colleges as the Presbyterian training colleges in Akropong and Amedzofe, where most of Ghana's music luminaries were educated, not to mention Achimota, which similarly played a major role in music education in Ghana during and after the pre-independence years.

But, who were the teachers of African music and how was the subject taught? What sort of theoretical framework formed the basis of instruction and did it adequately articulate the complexities of African music? Given the fact that among the major objectives of these missionaries and colonial masters was the total conversion of the traditional African to Christianity, to what extent were cultural and social contexts used as a basis for instruction?

The relevance of, and answers to, these questions may be found in the *Music and Dance Traditions of Ghana*. Intended as a handbook for music educators, teachers, world music percussionists, and others, this study has certainly come at a critical time in this era of globalization when the concept of multiculturalism has become a stark reality with serious global underpinnings and implications.

The content layout of this study, in itself, is a true reflection of the diversity of cultures presented here. Whoever may choose to use this handbook and its audio-visual support aids will be embarking on a fascinating journey though time and space into the most complex realm of the collective consciousness and psyche of the communities represented.

It is clearly articulated that music and dance are situational and function as the most potent cohesive forces in traditional societies. The traditionalists actually make no distinction between music and dance or between music and dance and visual art. To them, they are all inseparable.

As the mirror that reflects the totality of traditional life, it is imperative that music in these communities be studied in a holistic way. It must be understood that notwithstanding the loose compartmentalization of music into functional areas, there is that traditional concept of the universe which permeates every level of community life from the highly sacred to the recreational. Therefore, ultimate artistic experiences, whether they are on an occasion of birth, puberty, marriage, death, or even ceremonial or recreational, are guided by a belief in the presence of the supernatural. This is often acknowledged through the primordial repetition of an archetype, which may be in the form of a ritual, usually a libation.

My personal experiences from field explorations enable me to place this handbook in context, as modern technology is creating avenues for the development of all sorts of theories that research scholars hope may help unravel the incomprehensible underlying factors that bind the body and soul of traditional African music together. There are now theories that proclaim an understanding of the brain activity of master drummers in performance situations and can pretty much predict the rhythmic sequences they may play in various given circumstances. What this means is that computerized analyses of transcribed rhythmic patterns of selected dance forms reveal that there is a limitation in choice of patterns, and the master or lead drummer simply shifts and places them at different points with each repeat of the cycle. It has also been suggested that lead or master drummers make mistakes by deviating from pre-conceived rhythmic patterns.

As a drummer myself, I have great difficulty subscribing to the above theory. Furthermore, the master or lead drummer does not play in isolation. He is invariably prompted by supporting drums on one hand, and the occasion of the performance on the other hand. There is additionally a close relationship between the dancer(s) and drummers as they take cues from each other: It is often said that a bad dancer makes a good drummer a bad drummer while a good dancer makes a bad drummer a good drummer.

During one of my field explorations at a Yeʋe shrine located along the Volta Lake in Ghana, there was a five-hour non-stop performance of a ritual, which, for me, defied every existing theory. The drummers were virtually directed and dictated to by the divinities through their mediums. The versatility of the drummers was incredibly impressive as they switched instantaneously from one dance to another—from brekete, afa, asafo, adeʋu, yeʋe and so forth—as the divinities demanded. The intensity of the performance remained so uncompromisingly high that as the kɔkusiwo, the mediums of the divinity kɔku, finally entered into their state of possession, the atmosphere became so frighteningly charged that some passive observers had to seek shelter.

I consider it necessary to share the above experience as a proof that one should approach the study of traditional African music with an open mind. Any theory that one may choose to use as a basis should not be absolute, for if one experiences a typical non-recreational performance situation in our African community, no computerized theory can explain the underlying psychic phenomenon that drives it and those involved in its process. The organization of music in traditional societies carries with it all sorts of responsibilities without which the communities can derive no satisfaction or meaning from the occasion.

First of all, the occasion should be defined by the type of music being organized. Secondly, what is the purpose of the occasion? Is it a funeral? If it is, whose is it? If it is the funeral of a traditional ruler, then certainly the performance must go hand-in-hand with specific rituals. Or is it any other occasion than a funeral? Each occasion is identified with its own type of music and dance.

Thirdly, who are the intended participants? Some communities restrict involvement of participants in certain types of music to indigenes only.

Fourth, there are types of music that can only be performed on specific days that may be prescribed by the number of days within each market-day cycle. In some communities, each day of the cycle may be reserved for certain rituals. Therefore, in addition to the conventional calendrical year, there is also a calendar prescribed by community events and other factors.

Fifth, the symbolic and psychological parameters that guide performance situations constitute the contextual norms that define the significance of the situation in the community.

The list can go on and on. However, the thrust of all of these is that music-making occasions in traditional African societies are the total embodiment of the collective consciousness of life. The individual lives and experiences these events from conception to the grave and thereafter, where, it is believed, life continues.

The interactive learning processes throughout one's lifespan are shaped by the devices inherent in the art forms. In song texts there are didactic elements from which the child or individual acquires linguistic skills. Proverbs, riddles, tongue twisters, and so on, are pastimes enjoyed by the fireside, highlighted by storytelling sessions which combine music, dance and drama. Spontaneity and creativity are the hallmark of these activities and children particularly are thrilled by the challenge to create on such occasions.

The luminaries of the arts in Africa have blazed the trail for ensuing generations. Many of them suffered consequences for being too traditional in their artistic expressions. There were no reliable documented points of reference as we experience today. They tried to create and develop instrumental resources that could interpret their music. There were no teaching aids specifically designed for the teaching and learning of African music. In fact, if these luminaries had had just a bit of the technology prevalent today, their legacies would have been more far-reaching than they are. One can imagine just how many years each one spent collecting data and drawing inspiration from field explorations. This is why they were able to combine scholarship with artistry so effectively.

During the days of the old school, such names as Dr. Ephraim Amu, Pappoe Thompson, J.H. Kwabena Nketia, N.Z. Nayo, Phillip Gbeho, Ndor, Riverson, Fela Sowande, Ekweme, Augustine Young, and others, immediately brought to mind their excellent teaching skills, scholarship, first-class artistry, and discipline.

Today's generation will tread a much easier path. The indignities and prejudices are much less now as the study of the diverse cultures of Africa has become more and more exciting and attractive. Here, in a nutshell, is a road map to the body and soul of Africa. In all, 22 different musical types, representing the Akan, Dagbamba, Southern Eʋe, Central and Northern Eʋe, the Ga and the Dangme, have carefully been selected for this handbook. The musical types cover the essential traditional institutions that serve as repositories for them; the ritual, ceremonial, social and recreational activities are represented by these 22 selections.

The relevance of Younge's work to current preservation interventions and to the systematic documentation of these rapidly disappearing musical traditions is a major boost for music education — not only in the outside world but, most importantly, also in Ghana, where such teaching aids are non-existent.

Finally, Younge adequately addresses the concerns of the impact of globalization, which may result in total assimilation of lifestyles that have been driven by oral traditions for centuries without the imposition of esoteric theories and terminologies. There is, indeed, hope for the survival of Africa's traditional musical cultures.

Komla Amoaku is an internationally renowned research scholar, a performing and recording traditional and contemporary artist, composer, educator and arts administrator. He is a product of the universities of Ghana, Legon, Illinois and Pittsburgh, where he received his Ph.D. in ethnomusicology. He also studied at the Akademie Mozarteum–Salzburg with the legendary Professor Carl Orff. He is the former executive director of the National Theatre of Ghana and is currently the executive director of the Institute for Music and Development in Ghana.

Perspectives on Ghanaian Dances
by Francis Nii-Yartey

In Ghana, the role of dance is vital to the fundamental cultural expression of the people. Through traditional genres like the Agbekɔ of the Eʋe, the Kple of the Ga-Dangbe, the Adowa of the Akan, the Kundum of the Ahanta, the Baamaaya of the Dagbamba, the Bawaa of the Dagarti and others, opportunities are created for the renewal of social and religious bonds. These dances also provide important educational and physical activity for the community. Additionally, dance helps to provide contextual meaning to the various rituals, ceremonies and festivals organized in almost every major community, which take place throughout the year.

However, the socio-economic and cultural conditions that nourished these dance forms have changed significantly due to the occurrence of slavery and colonization and the subsequent introduction of a foreign system of education and the introduction of communication technology. Artistic and other social affiliations through participation in international, national and regional arts festivals, workshops, seminars and other cultural and artistic activities, have created unprecedented opportunities as well as challenges in the way Ghanaian dance is practiced today.

This situation, in addition to internal social and cultural dynamics stemming from the accelerated mobility of people, goods, services and artistic ideals across ethnic borders, has increased the incidence of intercultural tolerance and the borrowing of ideas. Today, for example, there are more non–Akan or non–Eʋe Ghanaians who understand and appreciate the Adowa dance of the Akan or the Agbadza dance of the Eʋe. Hopefully, this inter-textuality will steadily advance and stimulate the creation of national dance forms, which may eventually replace the present ethnic forms. One may even see the future creation of continental African dance forms.

The seeds for this are already germinating as a dance phenomenon referred to as "contemporary African dance," which is sweeping across Africa today, Ghana included. Contemporary African dance explores artistic and cultural elements of both the African past and the experiences of the present. New discoveries and approaches to dance practice, through the establishment of teaching and research institutions for dance and other formal educational facilities (the Institute of African Studies, the Ghana Dance Ensemble, and the School of Performing Arts at the University of Ghana), have helped dance to grow beyond its traditional context in the wake of Ghana's independence from Britain.

The good work of these institutions and informed individuals, through the formal training of dance practitioners, research and writing, has enabled Ghanaian dance practice to follow a path of development that allows the vitality and unique impulses of Ghanaian dance and "[makes] allowances for new constructions, meanings and a richer and more extended vocabulary" ("with an eye towards clarity in the creation of the salient qualities of the repertory of dances from many regions and stages" Opoku, 1969, pp. 85–89). Out of these experiences, two phases of dance development have merged alongside the traditional classical forms: the neo-traditional and the contemporary. The language, inspiration, content and symbolisms of these new genres are drawn from the traditional setting.

In Ghana, as in most parts of Africa, dance and the related arts of music, drama and the visual arts continue to permeate all activities of the life cycle. Over the years however, through contact with the outside world and within the continent itself, Ghanaians have acquired new ways of addressing the many issues confronting them today. Foreign values as well as dynamic internal changes have had a tremendous impact on the arts.

The challenge for Ghanaian dance today is, therefore, for its practitioners (both within the traditional setting as well as those trained in the school system) to find efficient ways of preserving the classical dance heritage as well as to help to push the spatial, stylistic, creative and technical boundaries beyond their present limitations. They must also formalize and codify the results of their creative energies through the publication of well-researched findings inspired by criteria and processes accepted by most in the artistic world. Clearly, Dr. Paschal Yao Younge's book *Music and Dance Traditions of Ghana* is a major contribution to this effort.

Francis Nii-Yartey has been in the forefront of contemporary African dance development in Ghana for many years. He is an associate professor of dance at the School of Performing Arts, University of Ghana–Legon, and director of Noyam African Dance Institute, which he founded in 1998. He was the artistic director of the Ghana Dance Ensemble at the University from 1976 to 1993, and of the National Dance Company of Ghana at the National Theatre of Ghana from 1993 to 2006. He was awarded the Grand Medal (Civil Division) by the head of state of Ghana in 2000, for his contribution to choreography and dance development.

Preface

The transmission of a "society's cultural heritage of ideas, beliefs, modes of thought, values, forms of knowledge and skills as well as its work of art in the plastic, visual and sound medium" has been the primary objective of education for ages (Nketia 1983, 1). This philosophy of education, although limited in scope, encouraged the development of the potential of individuals in a realistic relation to their heritage of music. In this light, music education encouraged cultural alienation rather than integration. Global, multicultural and intercultural music education, and aspects of contemporary philosophy of education seek to change this trend.

Music education programs are now a means of promoting cultural integration and cultural assertion. Most importantly, they

> provide not only deliberately instituted procedures designed to shape the musical skill, knowledge and taste of the learner in relation to his own culture but also other materials that will expose him to a wider variety of musical concepts, sound materials, structures and techniques that will enhance and shape his musicality without alienating him [Nketia 1983, 14].

This new approach is largely due to intercultural and cross-cultural activities being incorporated into the education curriculum at all levels.

Although ethnomusicologists have done substantive research into so-called African music and dance traditions for the past four decades, unfortunately, much of their work remains to be clearly understood and utilized by music educators and others. Efforts by the Society of Ethnomusicology's Education Committee (SEM), the College Music Society, the International Society for Music Education, and the Music Educators National Conference (MENC), through several projects such as Music in World Cultures Project (Music Educators National Conference 1972), Multicultural Imperatives (Music Educators National Conference 1983), Multicultural Approaches to Music Education Symposium of 1990 (W. Anderson 1990, vii), Teaching Music Globally (Shehan Campbell 2004), and Thinking Musically (Wade 2004), have provided new ideas and materials for use by educators and teachers in this direction. However, there is a need for more to capture the concepts and philosophy of African musical traditions.

Music and Dance Traditions of Ghana is written to provide educators with more resource material to enhance their intercultural teaching. This book is useful for cultural, social, ethnological and integrated teaching and learning within a liberal studies program since the book looks at music as a concept quite different from western classical aesthetics.

There are six types of so-called music created in Ghana today: traditional Ghanaian music, neo-traditional Ghanaian music, western art music, new–Ghanaian art music, western popular music, and neo–Ghanaian popular music. This book focuses only on the traditional musical expressions.

The book discusses 22 traditional musical types as performed by the Akan, Dagbamba, Eʋe and Ga-Dangbe ethnic groups in Ghana. Since this work aims at teaching about the social and cultural backgrounds of the people and their so-called music, the author has used mostly traditional sources in his data collection process, in addition to various research materials by past students and instructors from the Institute of African Studies and School of Performing Arts at the University of Ghana, most of which have become archival materials.

Collection of data for this project took well over 15 years, during which period the author conducted interviews, recorded video and audio performances, participated in traditional performances, and learned the drumming, dance and several songs of the selected musical types. Discussed under each musical type are:

  i. historical background and development;
 ii. occasions of performance;
iii. musical instruments/percussion ensemble;
 iv. organization of dance-drumming;
  v. form, structure and performance practices and roles;
 vi. movement, dance and dramatic enactment; and
vii. objects of art and other visual art forms, etc.

In parts one and two, the author discusses dance-drumming ceremonies of the Southeastern, Central and Northern Eʋe, respectively, with an emphasis on their historical, geographical, cultural, and social backgrounds. Selected musical types include Adzogbo, Agbadza, Atibladekame, Atrikpui, Atsiagbekɔ, Gahu, Gadzo, Adeʋu, Bɔbɔɔbɔ, Egbanegba and Gbolo. Parts three, four and five focus on the dance-drumming ceremonies of the Ga-Dangbe, Akan and Dagbamba ethnic groups. Dance-drumming ceremonies discussed include Gome, Kpanlongo and Kolomashie of the Ga-Dangbe, Adowa, Asaadua, Sikyi, Kete of the Akan and Baamaaya, Bla, Jɛra and Tɔra of the Dagbamba.

Transcriptions and analysis of songs with pronunciation guides and a feel of the percussion ensembles are included in Part Six. In Part Seven, "Teaching African Music and Dance-Drumming," the author discusses the components of an African music dance-drumming curriculum, which include: appreciation, focused and guided listening, drumming, singing, movement and dance, interactive storytelling, games and physical education, social studies, visual arts, drama, pantomime and other theatrical activities.

The section also gives a profile of Ghana: history, government and the people, religion, climate, economic activities, culture, education, performing art traditions, and sample lesson plans for teaching the Bɔbɔɔbɔ dance-drumming ceremony.

Appendix A shows photographs of performing groups and descriptions of accompanying DVDs. Glossary, bibliography and other recommended reading sources on Ghanaian history, culture and musical traditions are also provided.

Complimentary materials described in Appendix A include ten 120-minute DVDs. DVDs 1 to 6 focus on the dance-drumming ceremonies of the Southeastern, Central and Northern Eʋes. DVD 7 focuses on the Ga-Dangmes with DVDs 8, 9 and 10 focusing on the dance-drumming ceremonies of the Akans and Dagbamba ethnic groups.

Comprehensive instructional videos, CD/Roms and DVDs on how to teach the various phases of the dance-drumming types, including dance movements, are also being developed.

Another unique feature of this book is the deliberate use of non–English characters such as the vowels ɛ and ɔ, the consonants ɖ, ƒ, ŋ, ʋ, ɣ, and x, and the diagraphs *ts, tsw, tsy, tw, sh, shw, dz, dw, gb, gw, gy, hw, hy, nw, ny, Ŋm, kp, kw,* and *ky.* In most published texts about Ghana, these non–English characters are substituted with English ones. Although most of these substitutes are accepted and used in Ghana today, it is very important that the language of the ethnic groups be respected — hence, the need to use these indigenous characters in this book. For example, *ʋ,* as in Eʋe, is often written Ewe, and *ɔŋ,* as in Dagbɔŋ, as Dagbon. An orthography is provided at the beginning of each cultural section to help the reader with these pronunciations.

Introduction: Ghana in Perspective

Somewhere along the West Coast of Africa, along the Gulf of Guinea, in the Atlantic Ocean, there is a land. This land abounds in cocoa, timber, gold, diamond, manganese, bauxite, and sunshine. Its people are identified by their warmth and their hospitality, its festivals marked with pomp and pageantry, and its climate offers a haven for sun-seekers. This is Ghana [Ghana Tourist Board 1989, 7].

History, Government, and the People

On March 6, 1957, Ghana, then referred to as the Gold Coast, gained her independence under the late Dr. Kwame Nkrumah, who became the first prime minister of the country in 1961 when it became a republic within the Commonwealth of Nations. With a current population of nearly 20 million people and a growth rate of 2.7 percent, Ghana is comprised of over 46 different ethnic groups. Each ethnic group has its own distinct language; some of the major ones are: *Twi, Ewe, Hausa, Dagari, Dagbaŋli, Nzema, Ga, and Fante.* The great diversity of languages spoken, along with British colonization, has resulted in the adoption of English as the official language.

Administratively, the country is divided into ten regions and 130 districts. The capital city of Ghana is Accra, which is located in the Greater Accra Region. Ghana's link with the outside world dates as far back as the 14th century when the Portuguese, and later the Danes, Dutch, British and other Europeans, came to the country for trade. Prior to this era, however, the country had contact with traveling merchants from the Middle East. The existing castles, forts, and schools are evidence of some of the European legacies that have touched the land and culture of Ghana.

Religion

Missionary activity, which began around the early 17th century, fostered the development of several Orthodox and Pentecostal Christian churches in addition to other Islamic and eastern religious institutions. Traditional African religion, however, is still practiced by almost 45 percent of the population. Ghanaians, like most other Africans, believe in one supreme God, who they regard as the creator and father of the universe.

This God is seen to be highly enigmatic and is therefore accorded the highest reverence in all activities of the people. The various names attributed to God by the different ethnic groups include: the Creator, the Comforter, the Great One, the Great Spirit, the Grand Ancestor, and

This chapter originally appeared in the author's CD booklet, "Ghana: Rhythms of the People, Traditional Music and Dance of the Ewe, Dagbamba, Fante, and Ga People," published under Music of the Earth Series-CD by Multicultural Media, MCM 2000, 3018, ISBN 002930132. It is printed here with the permission of the publisher.

the Dependable One. It has become a common practice for parents to name their children based on the virtuous attributes of God, since many believe that babies are born out of divine intervention.

Climate and Economic Activities

Ghana experiences two climatic seasons: the wet or rainy season from April or May to October, and the dry or harmattan season from November to March. Agriculture, with cocoa as the main cash crop, accounts for over 50 percent of the gross domestic product. Also produced for export are maize, cassava, plantain, coffee, shea butter, timber, and minerals—including gold, diamond, bauxite, manganese, and salt.

Other than farming, the principal economic activities include pottery, handicrafts, metal work, beadwork, basketry, leatherwork, tie-dye, and textiles. Fishing is common along the coastal belt and inland rivers, especially along the Volta River, the largest and longest in the country.

Culture and Education

Although European, American, and Arabic cultures have altered the lives of the Ghanaian people, the majority still retain their traditional customs. Festivals, which are celebrated to recognize landmarks in history, religious beliefs, and reflections of life, are essential aspects of Ghanaian culture. Some of the popular festivals include: *Hogbetsotso* (Aŋlɔ Eʋe), *Adae* (Akan), *Damba* (Dagbamba), and *Homɔwɔ* (Ga).

Although formal education has undergone several changes since Ghana's independence, schools, from preschool to university levels, continue to thrive. Acquisition of knowledge is seen as a tool to safeguard the continuous growth and development of the country, and thus there is a tremendous amount of importance placed on the education of young people through traditional methods as well as the Western formal system.

In the traditional method, education is seen as a socialization process through which the individual acquires the necessary tools for a successful life. This approach to education involves experiential learning through direct observation and participation of the young, guided by the adults.

Ghanaians are noted for their special cultural traits: respect for authority, old age, the mysterious and the spiritual; honor toward the sexes and status in society; hospitality toward visitors or strangers; national pride; a sense of gratitude; and moral values—all of which are inculcated in children through the socialization process.

Musical Events

Like cultural traits, traditional music education is taught through the process of socialization. In most Ghanaian languages there are no words to represent music, rhythm, or singing as separate activities; music-making is a broad, encompassing activity that is part and parcel of daily life. Newborns inherit a keen sense of rhythm and musicality as they are carried around on the backs of their mothers, sisters, aunts, or cousins as they dance, work, and play.

Children learn to dance and play instruments through observation, imitation, and participation at frequent social occasions. As it is in all African societies, traditional music-making in Ghana is a social and communal effort.

Musical events in contemporary Ghana serve various functions. Many new artistic creations that have resulted from Western influences (including the popular highlife music), and from sacred and instrumental art music, are made for leisure and entertainment. Traditional music activities may also serve recreational purposes, but traditional music is more greatly appreciated for its specific functionality and symbolism for a specific event. Each ethnic group has its own unique forms of music that permeate the culture at all levels: life-cycle events such as birth, initiation, adulthood, death, and marriage; economic activities; political activities; and recreational activities.

Aesthetic values placed on any musical performance include the quality and authenticity of the medium, specific style and form, appropriateness of relation with objects of art, audience and participant interaction, and symbolic usages.

PART ONE.
Dance-Drumming of the Southeastern Eʋes

"One does not refuse to sleep because of death."— Eʋe Proverb

Orthography of Eʋegbe

- (a)   sounds like a in cat
- (e)   sounds like a in gate
- (ɔ)   sounds like o in cost
- (u)   sounds like oo in cool
- (ɛ)   sounds like e in men
- (i)   sounds like ee in feet
- (o)   sounds like o in goal
- (ɖ)   slightly softer than d, and is pronounced farther back in the throat
- (ƒ)   a bilabial f pronounced as if you are blowing a candle
- (ɣ)   like a soft h in English
- (x)   a voiceless velar fricative, like a voiceless h
- (ŋ)   like ng in sing
- (ʋ)   like an English v, pronounced with both lips
- (ts) sounds like ts in hits
- (tsy) sounds like in ch in chair
- (dz) sounds like ts in hearts but softer
- (kp) position the velum as fork, the lips as for p, and then release the two, closing simultaneously
- (gb) sounds like kp but heavier
- (ny) sounds like n in onion
- (')   high tone
- (˜)   nasal sound

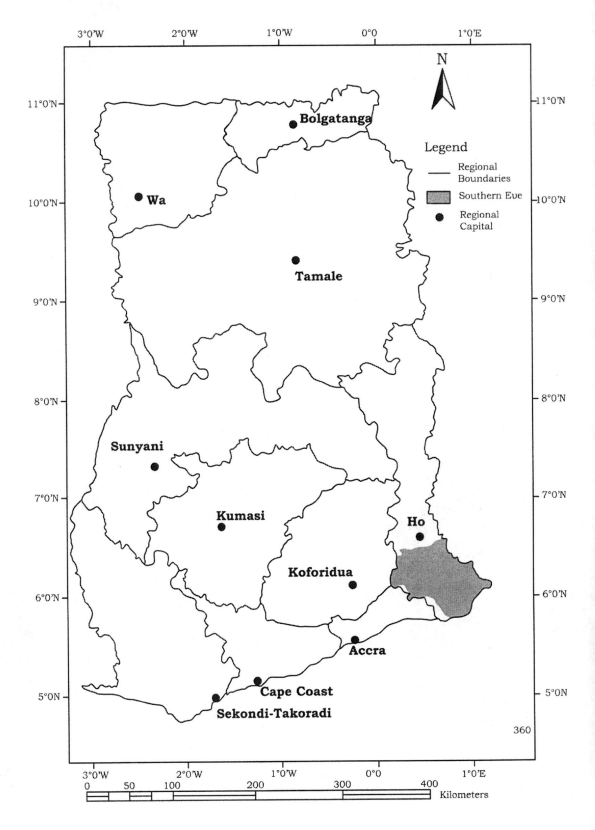

FIGURE 1.1: Map of Ghana showing southeastern Eʋe territories.

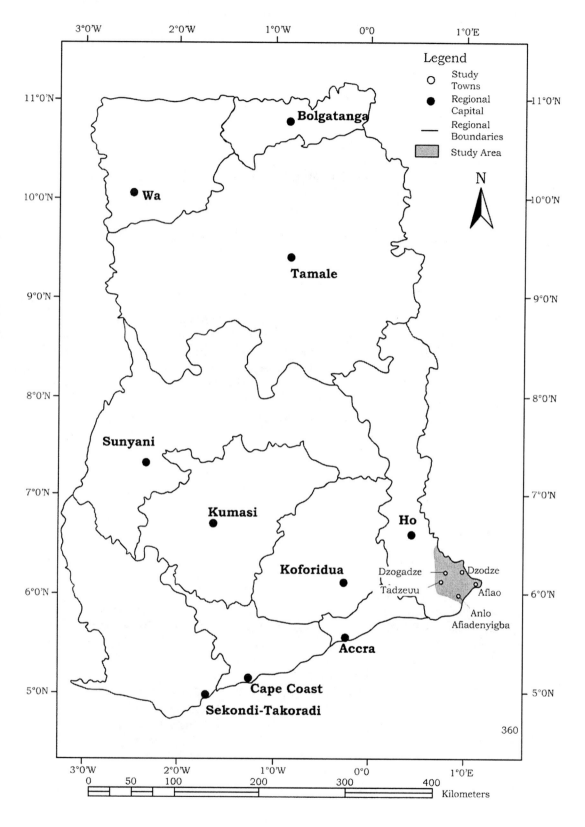

FIGURE 1.2: Map of Ghana showing research area.

1. Historical, Geographical, Cultural, and Social Background of the Southeastern Eʋes of Ghana

The Land and the People

The southeastern Eʋe of Ghana were once part of one culturally close body of people with autonomous tribal groupings, whose spiritual leaders were called *trɔnuawo*.

Western countries that colonized Africa in pursuit of commercial gains divided the entire region, and as a result there are southern Eʋe settlements in various parts of West Africa today. The southeastern Eʋe, who have common customs, beliefs and traditions, are today living in separate regions and countries, under different systems of government.

The Eʋe can be found presently in four West African countries: Ghana, Togo, Benin, and Nigeria. The majority of the Eʋe are located in the southern corner of the lower Volta River in Ghana, the southern half of Togo, and in Benin up to latitude 8 degrees north (Mamatah 1978).

In Ghana, the southeastern Eʋe area covers the Keta, Ketu (north and south), Akatsi, and parts of the north and south Tɔngu administrative districts, which comprise Anlɔ, Ave, Avenɔ, Klikɔ, Some, Flawu, Dzodze, Ueta and Abor traditional areas.

In the Republic of Togo, the Eʋe can be found at the following major settlements: Lome, Anexɔ, Genyi, Noefe, Voga, Kpalime Agbedrafɔ, Badzida, Adzanu, Atando, Togoville and Ziɔ.

The southeastern Eʋe, who speak a common Eʋe dialect called Fɔgbe (Fɔn), can be found at: Allada, Adza, Agbome, Agoe, Fla, Kome, Glefe, Kutɔnu, and Fɔgbonu (Xɔgbonu) in the Republic of Benin. The Eʋe are located in scattered areas in Lagos, Badagri, and their suburbs in the Federal Republic of Nigeria.

These southeastern Eʋe settlements, although believed to be of a common ancestry, speak a variety of dialects of the Eʋegbe, Eʋe language. The characteristic unifying factors that help to identify these people as one major ethnic block are their cultural practices, social activities and values, religious beliefs, and their traditional musical activities.

The nature of rainfall and the various topographical features that cover the entire southeastern Eʋe region in Ghana give rise to variety in vegetation. The coastal belt supports thorny creeper species locally called a *fla* or *be* (a species of thatch) (*Imperetus cylindrical*).

Coconut trees abound on the coastal belt and around the numerous lagoons; *amuti*, a typical lagoon tree (*Avicennia germinanus*), and *gbleke*, a short grass (*Paspalum vaginatum*), constitute the typical vegetation. Deep inland, the vegetation gives rise to shrubs, palm and baobab trees.

The various economic activities of the people are influenced by varieties in ecology. Those around the coast and lagoons depend on fishing for their livelihood, with shallot and onion farming, poultry, and the production of copra and coconut oil as support.

Further inland, basketry, mat-making, cultivation of vegetables and other cash crops, such as cassava and maize, are the main sources of income. Petty trading is now a dominant economic activity in all southeastern Eʋe settlements.

Historical Background

The history of the southeastern Eʋe, like the histories of most sub–Saharan African countries as documented by early explorers, missionaries, and ambassadors of Islam, is not always reliable. Through oral tradition, linguistic data, ethnological and archaeological and other documentary sources, southeastern Eʋe history is being rewritten (Merriam 1968 and Nketia 1972).

Much of the history today depends mostly on legends, folktales, song texts, riddles and poetry referred to as xotutuwo, the historical tales/stories of the elders (Kove 1978). These xotu-tuwo, supported by some tenable documentaries by Ellis Burdon (1890 and 1893) and J.D. Fage's *An Atlas of African History*, help to streamline the history of the southeastern Eʋe.

Tradition has it that the southeastern Eʋe, together with the Ibo of present Nigeria, Ga/Dangme and Akan of Ghana and other West African people, crossed the Sahara from the Far East to set up the Sudanese empires of history: Mali, Ghana, and Songhai. There was a major exodus from these empires in the 11th and 12th centuries, which some historians attributed to political upheavals as well as population pressures.

The southeastern Eʋe, together with the Yoruba, initially settled in Oyo, Ayo in Nigeria, but later migrated to Ketu in present-day Benin. The Eʋe culture and civilization as we know it today has since been significantly influenced by the Yoruba, Ibo and other ethnic groups from Benin and Nigeria.

Further migration led the Eʋe through Adzawere, Tado, Saligbe, Azɔvee, Mɔnɔto, Tsagbe, Dzemeni, Dogbonyigbo, Akplaxoe and Nɔtsie to their present settlements in Ghana in the early 13th century. There are various conflicting historical accounts about the southeastern Eʋe up to their Ŋɔtsie settlement, but the history becomes clearer and more substantiated with their settlement in Ŋɔtsie and further movements to their present-day habitations in Ghana.

At Ŋɔtsie, also called Hogbe, Glime or Agbogbome, the southeastern Eʋe, along with other ethnic groups, lived in three separate divisions: Tado, Dogbonyigbo and Central Ŋɔtsie. The southeastern Eʋe, together with the Bɛ̃ and Agu people, formed the Dogbonyigbo group (Gaba 1969).

Although all three divisions had clan heads, a supreme king of Ŋɔtsie with the stool name Agɔkɔli ruled over them. The king was worshipped as a god or an earthly potentate to whom they voluntary surrendered service. All the kings ruled wisely until the rule of a tyrant, Agɔkɔli I, the son of Togbui Afɔtse, whose despotic rule led to the disintegration of the kingdom around the latter part of the 12th or the beginning of the 13th centuries.

The Eʋe escaped and traveled together with the Ga, Dangme and the Akwamus during the chaos in Ŋɔtsie under Agɔkɔli's rule. The southeastern Eʋe "had been where they are now when the Portuguese set foot on the Gold Coast, now Ghana in 1471" (Fianu 1986).

Social and Cultural Profile

Political Authority. Traditional authority governs the entire southeastern Eʋeland. Chiefs and elders such as *dufiawo* (town chiefs), *tokɔmefiawo* (clan heads), *dumegãwo* (elders), and *avadadawo* (military commanders), rule over the people.

Special traditional arbitration courts and intermediary spirits and powers administered by traditional religions resolve disputes, conflicts and problems when they arise.

Major festivals celebrated under the auspices of the chiefs and elders are those derived from ancient harvest festivals, which every settlement celebrated in Ŋɔtsie. Unlike the past, when the festivals were aimed at thanking Mawu, the Almighty God, for the good harvest, good health and peace, present-day celebrations seek to create opportunities for family reunions, platforms for purification rites and to plan development projects.

Some of the festivals still observed include: Anlɔ-Hogbetsotsozā, Agbozume-Sometutuzā, Aflawu-Godigbezā, Avernopedo-Agbelizā, Voga-Adzinukuzā and Adekpoezā, Sokpe-Tɔtsotsozā, Akatsi-Denyazā and Anecho-Tugbazā (Younge 1992).

RELIGION. The southeastern Eʋe have great reverence for the Supreme Being, whom they call *Mawu*. *Mawu* is conceptualized as a male and is thus regarded as father and sustainer of the universe. Many theophorous names are used to show God's greatness: *Mawuenyega* (God is the greatest one), *Mawunyo* (God is kind), *Mawuli* (God is near/exists), and *Mawusi* (in the hands of God).

During daily prayers, the praise names of the Great One are mentioned: *Mawu Segbolisa* (the Father), *Mawu Kitikata* (the Source of Life), and *Mawu Aɖanuwɔtɔ* (the Blessed Trinity who is omnipotent, omnipresent and omniscient). If prayers constitute worship, then the Eʋes give God direct worship (Gaba 1964).

The Supreme Being, *Mawu*, is worshipped through intermediaries such as priests and other mediums since the God is so nebulous and invisible. Worship is perpetuated through lesser gods known as *trɔwo* (deities), *se* (supreme beings), and *lēgba* (idols).

The Eʋe also worship ancestral spirits, who, they believe, inhabit the world and intercede on their behalf. These spirits are deified in sacred ancestral stools, *Tɔgbuizikpuiwo*. The pouring of libation further strengthens this bond between the living and the dead. Ritual officials in various degrees also exist for magic, witchcraft, healing, divination and sooth saying (Younge 1992).

Apart from the above traditional forms of worship, the southeastern Eʋe have embraced different Christian religions. There are thousands of Catholic, AME Zion, Evangelical Presbyterian and Pentecostal churches scattered all over the area.

Perspectives and Musical Concepts

The southeastern Eʋe have unique sociocultural perspectives on music and other performing arts. Any musical activity is seen as a performance and a play activity, which combines other art forms. Musical activities are viewed as emanating from the physical as well as the spiritual worlds.

These perspectives guide the development of concepts and structures that the people utilize in every performance situation. Music is regarded as a multifaceted activity that includes music, dance, drama, storytelling, miming, acrobatics, and other performing arts.

Music and other performing arts are organized generally as *nukpɔkpɔ*, a public spectacle. A public spectacle refers to any performance or production of music, dance, drama or a combination of all performing and visual art forms.

VOCAL VS. INSTRUMENTAL MUSIC. The concept of music includes both vocal and instrumental activities (Agbodeka 1997; Fiagbedzi 153). There is no specific word or term for "music" among the southeastern Eʋe. The notion of vocal and instrumental music can only be inferred from a group of terms and practices, concepts, and musical instruments among the southeastern Eʋe.

Hādzidzi, the art of singing, stands for the vocal form of music, but there is no specific word for instrumental music. Vocal music is the most celebrated activity among the Eʋe. Instrumental music is considered an extension or adjunct to vocal music. It is used mainly to accompany dancing and singing or both.

There are instances where instrumental music may be used in contemplative modes such as performance at the courts of chiefs, at funerals, or at storytelling sessions. Instrumental music, as perceived and used in western art music, is not prevalent among the southeastern Eʋe.

In instrumental or drum music, *vugbe*, rhythmic patterns of drumming are quite often "text-bound" and may be understood in terms of translatable words. They may also be understood by mnemonic or nonsense syllables with which the drummer creates or identifies patterns or drum rhythms. This is the main form of musical notation that the people use to teach, remember, learn and interpret rhythmic patterns (Fiagbedzi in Agbodeka 1997, 153).

ORGANIZATION OF "MUSICAL" DANCE-DRUMMING ACTIVITIES. Traditional "music" dance-drumming activities are organized in two ways among the southeastern Eve: (i) free musical performances with no specific ritual or ceremony, and (ii) controlled musical performances that are contextually-bound.

The first category of musical types caters to pleasure, entertainment, or artistic experience as an end in itself. These are leisure time, boredom-killing dance-drumming and song types that are referred to as *modzakadevuwo*— entertainment music. Most of these types may also function at funerals or any festival.

The second category of musical types is seen as part of the traditional ceremony, the ritual, or the special event to which they are connected. Dance-drumming types in this category are performed at specific points in time during the ceremony, either as a prelude, interlude, or postlude. Most of these musical types are linked with political activities, religious activities, occupational activities and life-cycle events.

Dance-drumming among the southeastern Eve is organized as a social event, and is principally a group activity. Groups are organized within the framework of the *kɔfe* (village), *to* (ward/division) or *du* (town). There are musical groups or bands found in almost every community, in addition to the more general performances, which are open to everybody in the community.

There are certain traditionally-accepted roles assigned to special people in the communities for effective and high-standard musical presentations:

i.	*hakpala*	the composer of songs;
ii.	*henɔ/hadzitɔ̃/hãglã*	the lead singer or cantor;
iii.	*hatsola*	special assistant to the *henɔ*;
iv.	*hatsovi*	usually two assistants to the *henɔ* and *hatsola*;
v.	*azagunɔ*	the master/lead drummer;
vi.	*azagunɔkpewo*	players of supporting instruments;
vii.	*vumegã*	the male patron of a group;
viii.	*vudada*	the female leader or queen mother of the group;
ix.	*kpɔnkuitɔwo*	special assistants to the *vumega* and *vudada*; and
x.	*atinua or kadaa*	the disciplinarian of a group at a performance (Kovey 1998).

CONTEXT OF "MUSICAL" DANCE-DRUMMING ACTIVITIES. Music-making occurs at all levels of the social and cultural life of the southeastern Eve. Generally, music and dance exists for life-cycle events, work, political institutions, religion and leisure.

MUSIC AND LIFE CYCLE EVENTS. In addition to *vihehedego*, a naming or outdooring ceremony for newborns which is usually organized eight days after a child's birth when singing, clapping and sometimes dance can be only seen on a limited scale, there are musical performances reserved for *vewɔwɔ* (twin rites) and funeral celebrations.

The southeastern Eve do not have specific traditional musical performances for marriage ceremonies. Christian marriages and weddings, however, are musical occasions.

Funeral music includes the singing of dirges, choral laments and the performance of social and religious dance-drumming types depending on the status of the dead or the bereaved family. Performances at the funeral start at *ŋudɔdɔ* (wake), continue through *amedidi* (burial), and end with *yɔfofo/tsyɔga* (grand funeral) and *tsyɔlɔlɔ* (final rites).

MUSIC FOR WORK AND LEISURE. Economic activities call for music-making. Girls, hawking commodities such as fish, fruits, and foodstuffs, sing as they sell their goods. Sea fishing in the coastal towns, which is organized as a group activity, uses songs for the collective effort of pulling the net and rowing the boat.

Farming activities, such as weeding, sowing and harvesting, are accompanied by songs. *Kente*-weaving, carpentry, blacksmithing, carving, and pottery are all activities for music-making.

During leisure periods, especially in the evening after the day's work, *glitoto* (storytelling of folktales) and *xotutuwo* (stories of the past by elders) are occasions for music-making.

MUSIC AND POLITICAL INSTITUTIONS. In the political arena, especially at the courts of chiefs, music serves as the main uniting force, and it brings life to the entire *fianɔfe*, the chief's abode. *Zizihawo*, songs of old, *atrikpui, gadzo, gabla, atamga* and *kpegisu*, all *blēmaʋuwo*, ancient music and dance types, are performed during the installation of chiefs, the ceremony of presenting a new chief to the *awɔmefia* (the paramount chief of the Eʋe in Aŋlɔgã), *tɔgbuizikpui kɔklɔ*, cleaning of ancestral stools, and at state festivals.

Instruments such as *lāklēʋu, agblɔʋu, ʋuga* and *atopani*, feature prominently at the courts of chiefs and their sounds are often used as surrogates for speech.

MUSIC AND RELIGION. Musical pieces for religious ceremonies are named after the deities from whom a particular music is believed to have originated. The music of the *Afa, Yeʋe, Brekete,* and *Kɔku* cults are therefore called *Afaʋu, Yeʋeʋu, Brekete,* and *Kɔkuʋu,* respectively. Music from each can therefore be distinguished by name.

Music and dance for deities are organized as part of ritual worship. Some of the deities call for music before, during, or after the rites, as instructed by the particular god.

Songs sung during the rites may be by an individual or a chorus, according to the specific instructions of the god. Accompaniment for songs ranges from a single *gakogui* (double bell) or *axatse* (rattle), to a complex combination of drums and other instruments.

The southeastern Eʋe presently enjoy a variety of music apart from traditional music, which includes: western classical art music, western popular music, and neo–African art music and neo–African popular music.

MUSIC EDUCATION. Music education at the traditional level involves several methods, including:

  i. the socialization method, which involves slow absorption through exposure to musical situations;
  ii. experiential learning through games, storytelling sessions and aural engagements;
  iii. direct observation and participation through a form of apprenticeship to a master musician, drummer or singer; and
  v. individual participation in musical activities through imitation — all of which are connected to some kind of physical movement.

MUSICAL SOUND SOURCES. Musical sound sources are derived from four areas among the southeastern Eʋe:

  i. the voice, the most important sound source;
  ii. instruments that may be specifically of Eʋe origin: idiophones such as *gakogui* (double bell), *adodo* (multiclapper bell), *axatse* (rattle), *akpe* (hand-clapping), membranophones or drums such as *atsimeʋu, sogo, kidi, kagan, kroboto, gboba,* etc., chordophones such as *tsafulegede* (bow-harp), and aerophone, such as *kpe* (horn);
  iii. instruments that are borrowed from other Ghanaian/West African cultures: *dondo* (hourglass-shaped drum) and *blekete*, "*guŋgoŋ* of Dagbamba origin" (cylindrical drum), etc.; and

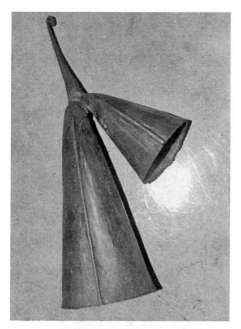

FIGURE 1.3: *Gakogui/Tigo/Gakpevi*

iv. instruments acquired as a result of contact with Western European agents: *sanku* (harmonica) and *biglo* (bugle), etc.

Any of the above sound sources may be combined during a performance depending on the particular type of music/dance-drumming or ritual. Membranophones or drums, and idiophones, bells and rattles, remain the main sound sources used by the Eve in their music-making — apart from the voice.

Instruments favored in most traditional musical types and used in the selections are: agblɔvu, atoke, atsimevu, atopani, axatse, gakogui, gboba, kagan, kidi, kroboto, sogo and totodzi.

INSTRUMENTS. Gakogui. This instrument serves as the foundation for all Eve percussion ensembles. Its rhythmic framework or patterns guides almost all performances.

The *gakogui*, or the double bell, is constructed from iron pipes or tire rims by experienced blacksmiths. Sound is produced by striking the two attached bells with a wooden stick about 30.5 cm or 12.5 inches in diameter.

It is a self-sounding, non-melodic idiophone, but when properly made or tuned, its two bells produce pitch levels an interval of about a fourth. The lower and bigger bell is vocalized as *ti* and the smaller bell as *ko*. These vocable syllables are used in the teaching and learning of various rhythmic patterns on the *gakogui*. *Tigo* is another name for this instrument, which is derived from the two syllables *ti* and *ko*.

The bigger bell, "lower in pitch," is referred to as the mother and the smaller bell, "higher pitch," is referred to as the child. Hence the maiden name of this instrument, *gakpevi*, which symbolizes a mother carrying her baby on her back or the mother protecting her infant child.

Atoke. Atoke or toke, a boat-shaped or slit bell, is another self-sounding idiophone which is constructed from flat iron materials. Sound is generated by striking the top outer side ("almost the middle" of the slit of the bell), held

FIGURE 1.4: Playing technique on the *gakogui* as illustrated by Killer Fiebor of Aŋlɔ Afiaɖenyigba *Gadzo* Group (2006).

FIGURE 1.5: *Atoke*

FIGURE 1.8: Playing technique on *axatse* as illustrated by Kɔku Alɔmene and Emmanuel Azumah of the Aŋlɔ Afiadenyigba *Gadzo* Group (2006).

FIGURE 1.6: Playing technique on the *atoke* as illustrated by a member of the Ghana Dance Ensemble, University of Ghana, Legon (2009).

loosely in the left palm with a piece of straight iron held in the right hand.

Atoke is used mostly to emphasize or embellish the *gakogui*, though it may also take the role of *gakogui* in some performances. It is significantly featured during *Hatsiatsia*, song cycle phases of dance drumming. When two or three *atoke* are combined, they are tuned to different pitches.

Axatse. *Axatse* is classified as a shaken, non-melodic idiophone. It is made of beads woven around a hollowed gourd or a gourd wrapped in strings of seeds or beads. It emphasizes the rhythmic

Right: FIGURE 1.7: *Axatse*

patterns played by the *gakogui* in most percussion ensembles. Sound is produced on an *axatse* by holding the neck with one hand and striking the beaded part on the thigh and the palm of the second hand. *Axatse* is played by striking against the palm during processional phases of performances or when standing.

Agblɔʋu. The *agblɔʋu* serves as a speech surrogate (apart from its function as a supporting drum) in most Eʋe percussion ensembles. It announces the arrival of chiefs at functions and plays messages related to the cultural values of the people. The *agblɔʋu* used to be one of the main drums used during wars to transmit messages.

The *agblɔʋu* is now featured exclusively at the courts of chiefs and also during some religious festivals, such as *Tɔgbuizikpuikɔklɔ*, pacification or cleansing of ancestral stools in the absence of intertribal wars. No southeastern Eʋe chief will travel for any official duties in full regalia without the accompaniment of *agblɔʋu* sounds. The *agblɔʋu* is played in front of chiefs during state ceremonies, such as festivals.

Sound is generated on this drum by the player hanging it by the left side of the body with a sling attached and hitting the center of the membrane with two curved or straight sticks. See Figure 1.10 on page C-1 of color insert.

Atsimeʋu. The *atsimeʋu* is one of the largest and tallest drums in any Eʋe percussion ensemble. It is

FIGURE 1.9: *Agblɔʋu*

modeled after the *agbomlɔanyi,* a similar drum used in Yeʋe religious ceremonies and other ancient dance-drumming types. The *atsimeʋu* is featured as a lead drum in most ensembles.

The Eʋe use two methods in the construction of *atsimeʋu* and other drums: *ʋutoto* and *ʋubabla.*

Uutoto involves the carving of a drum from a solid wood such as *logo* or *efɔ,* which are special species of the cedar tree. Drums in the olden days were all constructed using this method and were comparatively smaller and lighter in weight when compared to present ones because of incessant wars, which prompted the frequent movement of the people.

The Eʋe believe in one Supreme Being, *Mawu,* who looks over them as the father of all other gods. The countless deities operate as nature gods, sky gods and water gods. They believe that trees, especially *logo* and *efɔ,* possess spirits that have to be pacified before they are felled for drum construction.

Accordingly, before the tree is felled, *dzatsi,* a mixture of corn flour and water, is prepared, and after prayers to the gods of the forest, it is offered in addition to seven cowries at the base of the tree as sacrifice to the spirit of the tree, the ancestors and all the drummers who have passed.

The tree is then cut for the *ʋutoto* to begin. In the olden days, the drum-maker would use an axe to cut down the tree. Today, a handheld chain saw is used for this purpose.

After the tree has fallen, the drum-maker will measure the trunk to the specific lengths of the drums he is going to make from the tree. Smaller limbs are used for firewood or drumsticks. The sectioned parts of the tree are then transported to the drum-maker's workshop.

The *ʋutoto* process begins by marking the top circumference of the drum to be carved. An axe and two different types of spades are used to create the mouth of the drum. A cutlass is used to make the outer shape of the drum shell.

Once this is completed, a manual drill is used to make a hole in the base to meet the top cavity. A handle blade is then used to smooth the outside of the shell. The unique designs carved on the drum shell are the personal markings of each drum carver.

While some designs are purely acts of artistic expression, others have historic and symbolic significance. A chisel is used for this purpose. After a final smoothing of both the inside and outside of the shell, peg holes are measured and drilled.

Now it is time to prepare the drumhead to cover the shell. First, a bush twine ring is made the size of the mouth of the drum shell. Wooden pegs are then carved out of a local hardwood called *nyatse.*

The skin is prepared by removing the fur with the help of ash from the fireplace. It is soaked in water for 30 minutes to one hour, depending on its toughness of the skin, to soften. Different types of skin may be used for the drumhead, but the skin of the antelope or deer is preferred because of their resonance and durability.

The final stage involves the attachment of the skin to the drum shell. The skin is fastened onto the ring of twine with *adzɔka* (a bush rope) or nylon string and, in some cases, wire cables (due to social changes affecting musical practices in Ghana). The pegs are then hammered into place for the fine-tuning of the drum. It takes four to six days to complete one drum.

Once a drum is completed, the buyer provides a bottle of the local gin, *akpeteshie,* with which the drum-maker pours a libation before the drum is removed from the shop.

Uutoto is still used for specific drums associated with religious and political institutions such as *atopani, abudu, agblɔʋu, adaʋatram* (also known as *lakleʋu*), and *agbomlɔanyi.*

Uublabla is by far the most common method of making drums among the Eʋe. The process can be divided into three stages.

[Stage One:] A template is made by cutting wooden staves to size from a 365.8cm by 30.5cm "12 feet by 1 foot" "*Odum*" board. The type of drum determines the size of the stave. The diagram below shows the design of the stave. As illustrated below, one end of the stave is wider than the other and the widest section at the middle section results to a more bulged stem or frame of the finished drum.

Right: FIGURE 1.11: Stage Two: At this stage, the individual staves are fastened together.

A   B   C

These staves are arranged side by side between two concentric iron hoops, very much like those found on wine casks. The hoops are held a few feet above the ground with the other end of each stave resting firmly on the ground. The inner hoop is removed after several larger ones are added at the outside and hammered into position to press the staves more closely together.

At this point, the staves are close-knit at one end and all the other ends stick out. The staves are forced together by pulling fast a rope tied to a tree and looped around the staves to fasten the other loose ends together.

Iron loops of suitable sizes are added and ringed round them to keep them close before the peg holes are bored. The pegs are cut and shaped from the same *Logo* or *Efɔ* tree or other hard wood found in the area and notched to hoop the tension twine in place.

Stage Three: The final stage consists of attaching the membrane of an antelope or deerskin to the head and tuning. The skin is laced to the loop and knotted round the peg in six vertical throngs that show a combined pattern of a "W" and "N," the latter pattern strengthening the first. The skin is then trimmed close to the *Adzɔka,* bush twine hoop and the pegs are driven in evenly to roughly tune the drum [Fiagbedzi 1971].

The *atsimeʋu* is played tilted forward towards the dance or performance arena supported by a stand, *ʋuglãtsi or ʋudeti.* Two playing techniques are employed on the *atsimeʋu:* the one

FIGURE 1.12: *Atsimevu*

FIGURE 1.13: *Atsimevu*

FIGURE 1.14: *Atsimevu* technique as illustrated by S.K. Agudzamega of the Dzogadze *Atsiagbekɔ* Group (2008).

FIGURE 1.15: *Atsimevu* technique as illustrated by Agbo Setsoafia of the Aflao *Adzogbo* Group (2006).

FIGURE 1.17: *Atopani* technique as illustrated by Prosper Kɔku Dokli of the Aŋlɔ Afiaɖenyigba *Gadzo* Group (2006).

FIGURE 1.18: *Gboba*

stick supported by hand technique, and the two sticks technique. In the hands of a master drummer, manipulation of the membrane with dexterity produces at least 11 tones or sounds, such as: *ga, gi, ki, te ge de, tsi to ka, dza dzi.* The approach to the realization of these tones is shown in Part Six of the book about percussion scores.

Atopani. The *atopani* is believed to be of Akan origin, a fact that cannot be disputed since most of the speech patterns or drum languages (*ʋugbewo*), as played today, have traits of the Akan language in them. *Atopani* is mostly featured at the courts of chiefs and in limited dance-drumming performances such as *Atrikpui, Afli, Uugā, and Kete.*

The *atopani* is a bottle-shaped drum carved from *logo-azagu*, a species of cedar, using the *ʋutoto* method. It is played in pairs with two curved sticks as shown in Figure 1.16 (page C-1 in color section).

Atopani, unlike other Eʋe instruments, are reserved solely for political events. Every community under the control of the chief owns this drum. It is kept alongside the stool and other sacred objects as part of the chief's regalia in a secured "stool room" for security and religious reasons. Special prayers and sacrifices are made before the *atopani* is removed from the stool house for any performance.

FIGURE 1.20: *Sogo*

Gboba. Originally called *gbaba* ("wide"), because of its wide playing area or head, the *gboba* is used mainly for two dance-drumming types: *kinka* and *gahu*.

The *gboba* is a low-pitched, single-headed drum with an opening at one end. It is described as a barrel drum constructed using the *vubabla* method. It is played with either two straight sticks or hands, depending on the context. The drum is held in place, tilted forward between the drummer's legs or by a wooden stand similar to the one used for the *atsimevu*.

Sogo. *Agbobli* is another name for the *sogo* drum. *Sogo* symbolizes the father (with *kidi* and *kagan* as

Left: FIGURE 1.19: *Gboba* technique as illustrated by S.K. Agudzamega of the Dzogadze *Atsigbekɔ* Group (2008).

mother and child, respectively) in Eʋe percussion ensembles. The concept of family unity is thus reinforced in performance situations.

Sogo is a single-headed closed drum. Three basic playing techniques are employed: the two stick technique, the stick and one hand technique, or the two hands technique. Four basic pitch levels or tones can be derived by agitating the membrane: high, medium, low and muted tones.

Striking or hitting the center of the membrane with the palm obtains the low pitch. This tone is vocalized as *ga* or *da*. The medium pitch level or open tone is realized by hitting the membrane halfway to the center of the membrane. The tone is vocalized as *te, ge, be,* and *de.*

A muted, or dead, tone is obtained by pressing the center of the membrane with one hand or stick and hitting the same area with the second hand or stick. This is vocalized as *to.* The high pitch level is obtained by playing close to the rim, sounding *gi.*

During a performance, the player sits upright and holds the drum between the thighs. The *sogo* can be used as a supporting as well as lead drum.

Kidi. *Kpetsi, asiʋui* and *ʋuʋi* are other names for the *kidi.* The *kidi* is a single-headed closed drum. The *kidi* has all the features of the *sogo* except for its size, timbre and function in the percussion ensemble.

FIGURE 1.21: *Sogo* technique as illustrated by Kɔku Azumah of the Aŋlɔ Afiaɖenyigba *Agbadza* Group (2006).

FIGURE 1.22: *Kidi*

The *kidi* functions mainly as a supporting drum in most percussion ensembles. It usually plays in dialogue with a *sogo* and also doubles up with a *sogo* in some ensembles as a supporting drum.

The player sits and keeps the drum firmly in front — almost between the thighs — during a performance. Hitting the center of the membrane using the two-stick technique derives two basic tones: open and closed/muted.

Open tones or bounce-strokes are realized by bouncing the sticks alternately at the center of the membrane. Pressing the sticks at the center of the membrane generates closed tones or press strokes.

Kagan. The *kagan* is the smallest

FIGURE 1.23: *Kidi* technique as illustrated by Kɔku Azu-mah of the Aŋlɔ Afiaɖenyigba *Agbadza* Group (2006).

FIGURE 1.24: *Kagan*

and highest-pitched drum in any Eve percussion ensemble. *Kpetsigo, kpakpanu* and *kagaŋ* are other names for this drum. It is a single-headed open drum played with two straight sticks. Open tones or bounce-strokes are the basic tones generated on this drum, and they are made by striking across the rim to the center of the membrane.

The *kagan* assists the *gakogui* to establish time in dance drumming percussion ensembles, by playing a basic ostinato pattern. It is played in a seated position with the drum slightly tilted away and held between the knees of the player

Kroboto/Totodzi. *Kroboto* and *totodzi* were the main instruments used as signal drums during wars. *Kroboto* functions as the male principle and *totodzi* as the female principle.

The playing technique used for both the *kroboto* and the *totodzi* is similar to that used for the *kidi*. The only difference is that the drums are to be tilted forward from the player. As with the *kidi*, hitting the center of the membrane using the two-stick technique derives two basic tones: open and closed/muted.

FIGURE 1.25: *Kagan* technique as illustrated by Kɔku Azumah of the Aŋlɔ Afiaɖenyigba *Agbadza* Group (2006).

FIGURE 1.26: *Kroboto*

FIGURE 1.27: Varieties of *kroboto* and *totodzi*.

Open tones or bounce-strokes are realized by bouncing the sticks alternately at the center of the membrane. Pressing the sticks at the center of the membrane generates closed tones or press strokes. Both curved and straight sticks are used on these drums.

Rhythmic patterns performed on these drums retain some of the unique original *υugbewo* (drum texts), relating to wars. In Atsiagbekɔ, for example, the *kroboto* plays, "*Gbedzi ko madɔ,*" which means, "I will only die on the battlefield." The *totodzi* plays, "*Kpla kpla midzo,*" meaning, "Hurry, let's go to war." All these texts remind the people of their history whenever Atsiagbekɔ, a warrior's dance, is performed.

The *kroboto* and the *totodzi* are used today mainly in the Atsiagbekɔ and Kpegisu warrior dance ceremonies among the southeastern Eυe in Ghana.

Taυugā. The *taυugā,* the Eυe version of the Akan *bɔmma* or *fɔntɔmfrɔm,* like the *atopani,* is reserved solely for political institutions and events. *Taυugā,* also known as *υugā* or *abuḍu,* are usually dressed in white cloths, a symbol of their sacredness and purity.

Taυugā is kept alongside the stool and other sacred objects as part of the chief's regalia in a secured stool room for security and religious reasons. Every traditional area ruled by a chief owns one of these drums.

FIGURE 1.28: *Kroboto* technique as illustrated by Killer Fiebor of the Aŋlɔ Afiaḍenyigba *Gadzo* Group (2008).

The *tavugā* may be used during funerals of elders and also in some religious and warrior dance-drumming rituals for state deities. During state assemblies or festivals, the presence of *tavugā* symbolizes the chief's majesty and power.

Two curved or straight sticks are used on this drum to generate two tones: open and closed. Rhythmic patterns played on the *tavugā* are mostly interpreted as "nonsense syllables" with no verbal basis.

The rhythmic patterns in a dance-drumming ceremony emphasize dance movements and other patterns performed especially on *atopani*. Specifically, the *tavugā* echoes the walking and other symbolic movements of the chief during such festive occasions. See Figure 1.31 on page C-2 of color section.

FIGURE 1.29: *Totodzi* technique as illustrated by S.K. Agudza-megah of the Dzogadze *Atsigbekɔ* Group (2008).

Right: FIGURE 1.30: *Tavugā*

2. *Adzogbo* Ritual Dance-Drumming Ceremony

Historical Background and Development

Adzogbo is one of the religious music and dance forms introduced to Ghana by the southeastern Eʋe in the late 19th century from Benin. This music and dance was popular during the reign of Tɔgbui Kundo, the last great king of ancient Fɔn of Benin (formerly Dahomey). During that period in history, the music and dance was associated with their war god, *Adzo,* considered one of the most powerful among the Eʋe.

This religious music and dance ceremony known as *Adzoʋu* was then performed prior to going into battle, an opportunity for the warriors to commune with *Adzo.* It was mainly performed in the night to summon the warriors to take up arms and get ready for impending battle. The music and dance was performed in honor of the gods and goddesses of war, since the Eʋe believed in their spiritual efficacy.

The young warriors would be put in seclusion before an impending battle, where they were bathed with protective herbs and, most importantly, trained in the esoteric lore of the war god amidst *Adzo* music and dance. It was believed that during these ritual ceremonies, the war god dictated the dance movements as well as the choreography. Although originally a prewar dance, in the absence of wars *Adzo* (or *Adzogbo*) has changed in context and structure.

The original ritual music and dance was first converted to *Ahiaʋu,* a love or courtship music and dance during which performance young men would display their so-called love charms, *dzoka,* to seduce the women. These young warriors supposedly misappropriated their spiritual war powers for sexual gratification.

When *Adzogbo* found its way to Ghana, it became known as *Modzakadeʋu,* an entertainment or recreational music and dance for youth. *Adzogbo* performance today still retains some of the original rituals, costumes, dance movements and choreography even in the absence of its original ritual context.

Other names used today for the same dance are: *Adzogbe* ("Let us go to war") and *Dogbo,* which is used by the Wheta people of Ghana. *Adzogbo* can be seen today among the southeastern Eʋe in present Benin, Togo and Ghana during state, harvest and historic festivals, New Year celebrations, funerals and other social occasions. *Adzogbo* groups are organized as "popular bands" specializing solely in *Adzogbo* music and dance.

Organization of the Dance-Drumming Ceremony

FORM AND STRUCTURE. *Adzogbo,* as *Modzakadeʋu,* a recreational dance-drumming, is now mainly for entertainment. It is context-free and can be performed on any occasion provided the required space is available for the dancers, instruments/instrumentalists and audience. Audience participation is somehow restricted, although it is a social performance.

Audience participation is not allowed until the second *kadodo* or *atsokla* (women's dance section), which is the last stage/phase of the performance. Audiences are not allowed to participate in the other stages of the performance because of the intricate, vigorous and well-choreographed dance movements. There are six distinct phases of *Adzogbo* performance. These are:

i.	*gbefaɖeɖe*	the announcement;
ii.	*ʋuyɔyɔ*	warm up for the musicians;
iii.	*tsi fo fodi*	purification rites;
iv.	*kadodo*	female dance phase;
v.	*atsiawɔwɔ*	men dance phase; and
vi.	*kadodo*	round off dance phase.

Figure 2.1: Aflao Mawulikplimi *Adzogbo* Agbazo

Phase One: *Gbefaɖeɖe*. There is a brief drumming at dawn by only the master instrumentalists who will be featured on a set day for any performance. This is referred to a *ʋudzradzrado* (tuning of the drums).

This performance is intended to alert all members of the group of an impending performance in order to see if all the instrumentalists are available for the performance and also to make sure the instruments are in good condition. This phase also serves as an informal rehearsal for the musicians.

Phase Two: *Uuyɔyɔ*. At the designated time for the performance, the instrumentalists gather to play. This may start with the apprentice drummers who will play after setting up all the instruments of the ensemble. The master musicians will later take over to prepare and set the mood for the male and female dancers.

The main purpose of this stage of the performance is for the musicians to retune their instruments (a process known as *adzokpaɖeɖe* or *ʋuyɔyɔ*, "calling of the drums") and also to alert the dancers that they are ready for the show.

Phase Three: *Tsifofodi*. There is a purification ceremony when all preparations are completed and the dance arena is set. This ritual ceremony has two components, *tsifofodi* (libation) and *amawuwu* (sprinkling of spiritual herbs).

The libation is performed by the *ʋumega*, president of the group, or his representative. This ritual is meant to call on the Almighty

God and His lieutenants, the smaller gods and ancestors, to come and be present and bless the celebration. The ritual involves the mixing of corn flour and water, believed by the Eʋes to be the favorite food of the gods, in a calabash; after a series of prayers, the mixture is poured on the ground.

The second component, which is performed by a "possessed" member of the group, usually the spiritual head/medicine man, *agbazo*, then follows. This ritual is similar to the Asperges Me and its sprinkling of holy water that begins the Catholic Mass.

A pot filled with medicinal herbs and water, *amaze*, is sprinkled around the dance arena for protection against any form of evil spirits. It is also an invitation to the *leshiwo* and *legashiwo* (men and women dancers) to get ready to perform. This second ritual may continue throughout the rest of the performance. See Figure 2.2 on page C-3 of color insert.

Phase Four: *Kadodo*. The dance arena is set for *kadodo* (also known as *atsokla*), the female dance phase, after the purification rites. The female dancers enter the dance arena with a short procession in two groups and perform in a semicircle in front of the drummers or form two perpendicular lines at the opposite ends of the drummers facing the audience.

Once they are positioned in their various spots, songs in free rhythm are performed without any instrumental accompaniment. The drummers begin to play when the lead singer begins to sing in a more strict rhythm.

Phase Five: *Atsiawɔwɔ*. This is an interesting theatrical display of drama, play and virtuosity of dance skills. Two women, lead cantors/dancers positioned in the dance arena, will call the male dancers through songs with a response coming from another two women stationed with the male dancers, who are at this time hidden from the spectators. This call and response exchange is repeated and then comes the *lebiala, lega, atsiayɔla or atsiadotɔ*, the lead dancer, to perform some movements and then retreat. He shows up again with his assistant and both perform another dance routine. Both retreat and return immediately to the arena with the rest of the dancers. Agbazo may also start the Atsiawɔwɔ phase.

The female dancers may now be positioned behind the drummers or retain the positions they held in the *kadodo* phase. They will support the drummers in this phase of the performance with songs accompanied by handclapping.

The lead dancer decides the dance routine/sequence. He calls out or sings the dance routine, known as *le* or *atsia* (style or display), which is then played by the master drummer on the *atsimeʋu* while he dances alone or with his assistant. The rest of the dancers spring to action after this preview.

The *atsiawɔwɔ* continues in this format until the male dancers get exhausted and retreat to their dressing room. Another *kadodo,* which is open to all, including the audience, then follows.

Phase Six: *Kadodo*. The final phase of the performance usually follows the same organizational structure and dance movements as stage four. Because of audience participation, this phase may have room for "free" dancing and may incorporate other Eʋe dances such as *Agbadza*. The male dancers may come back to participate in this round-off dance after removing their costumes.

In a typical traditional performance as practiced in Benin today, the *leshiwo* have to undergo some ritual purification before a performance. In some areas they may even have to abstain from sex a day prior to the performance. This ritual is not observed in Kedzi, Aflao, Anloga, Dzodze, and others places in Ghana where the dance is still performed.

Songs

Songs in *Adzogbo* connect the past to the present and also serve as a vehicle through which the physical and the spirit world interact. The lyrics of the songs provide avenues for communication during any performance. Themes of the songs spread across all spheres of life of the Eʋe people: love, endurance, respect, history, war, topical issues, morals, and philosophy, etc.

Most of the songs are sung using a liturgical language — a mixture of Eʋe, Fɔn, Yoruba and sometimes English, and is often difficult to understand the message being conveyed through the songs.

Tonal arrangements in *Adzogbo* songs make use of melodic modes based on both hemitonic and anhemitonic forms of the pentatonic and hexatonic scales. The songs are usually in call and response pattern and may be very short and strophic. Harmony is generally the result of males and females signing an octave apart with occasional use of sporadic fourths, fifths, thirds and sixths.

The Percussion Ensemble

Instruments of the ensemble include:

  i.   *Atsimeʋu:* As the master or lead drum, this instrument controls the dance movements and communicates directly with the dancers. Both the lead drummer and dancer determine the number of *atsia* (dance routines) to be performed in a given situation. This instrument plays various patterns known as *ʋugbewo* (drum texts). These patterns are made of lexical texts and nonsense vocable or mnemonic syllables.

  ii. *Sogo,* also known as an *agbobli,* serves as the first response and supporting drum that plays in dialogue with the atsimeʋu.

  iii. *Kidi,* also known as a *kpetsi, ʋuvi* or *asiʋui,* serves as the second response and supporting drum.

Figure 2.3: Front row from left: *axatse, sogo, kidi, kagan,* and *axatse;* back row from left: *gakogui* and *atsimeʋu.* Aflao Mawulikplimi *Adzogbo* Percussion Ensemble (2006).

iv. *Kagan*, or *kaganu*, is the third supporting drum, which plays a basic ostinato accompanying pattern.

v. *Gakogui*, or *gakpevi*, a double bell, guides the whole ensemble by playing the time line, a fundamental rhythmic pattern that serves as a reference point for all instrumentalists and dancers.

vi. *Axatse*, or *go*, a rattle, supports the *gakogui* by reinforcing the time line.

vii. *Akpe*, handclapping, is used mostly by the women to reinforce the time line during phases two, five and six of the performance.

Dance Organization

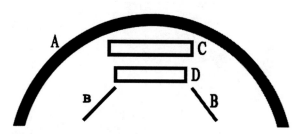

Figure 2.4: *Kadodo* performance arena A. A: audience; B: female dancers; C: elders/chorus; D: drummers.

DANCE ARENA. There are different ways to arrange the dance arena for *kadodo* and *atsiawɔwɔ* during performances. The preferred arena for a performance depends on the specific occasion. In all spatial arrangements however, the audience forms around the performers in a circular or semicircular shape. There are two arrangements for *kadodo*. In the first setup, below, the women dancers form two diagonal lines on each side of the drummers who are positioned at the center rear of the performance arena as shown in Figure 2.4.

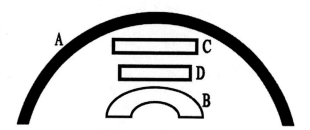

Figure 2.5: *Kadodo* performance arena B. A: audience; B: female dancers; C: elders/chorus; D: drummers.

In the second setup, as shown in Figure 2.5, the women dancers form a semicircle in front of the drummers who are positioned at the center rear of the performance arena.

The three arrangements for the *atsiawɔwɔ* phase and the rest of the performance are shown below. During the *atsiawɔwɔ* phase, the female dancers, as shown in Figure 2.6, perform behind the drummers as part of the chorus. If elders are present, they are seated behind the female dancers and chorus.

During other performances, usually festivals and special occasions, the female dancers will assume their positions as in the *kadodo* phases shown earlier.

In all the above arrangements, the instrumentalists are positioned to face the direction of the wind. It is important that they play to the wind for the sound to carry to the dancers.

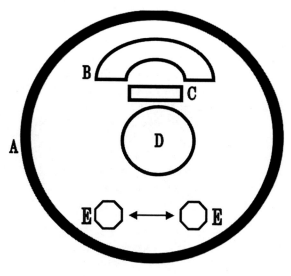

Figure 2.6: *Atsiawɔwɔ* performance arena A. A: audience; B: female dancers; C: drummers; D: male dancers; E: lead male dancer.

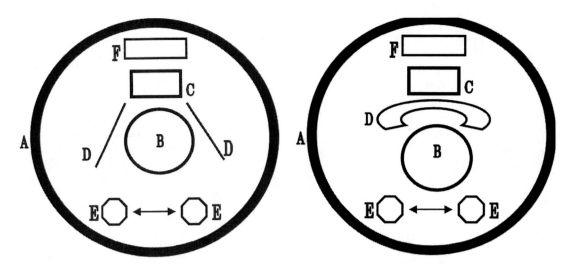

Figure 2.7: *Atsiawɔwɔ* performance arena B. A: audience; B: male dancers; C: drummers; D: female dancers; E: lead male dancer; F: elders.

Figure 2.8: *Atsiawɔwɔ* performance arena C. A: audience; B: male dancers; C: drummers; D: female dancers; E: lead male dancer; F: elders.

DANCE MOVEMENTS AND CHOREOGRAPHY. *Kadodo.* Kadodo is a "show-off" dance. The dancers use mirrors to show or bluff the male spectators and the entire audience. Some of the male dancers, *leshiwo,* may join the women in this initial performance, but without the mirrors and their elaborate costumes. The women, lined up in pairs, dance towards the performance space, in front of the drummers. They dance towards the drummers with their bodies facing in towards the center of the arena. As they pass the drummers, the dancers split, with one line going to either side of the drummers; alternatively, the dancers form a semicircle in front of the drummers.

The processional dance to the arena involves the dancers using their torsos bent forward from the hip, stepping twice with the right foot, and then immediately twice with the left, continuously, in a shuffling fashion. With bent arms and hands slightly forwards, the women swing their arms backwards and forwards in opposition to each other.

The processional dance can also be the *dzimeɲeɲe,* the main dance movement in *agbadza.* This involves strong chest contractions and releases uniquely peculiar to southern Eʋe traditions. The body is slightly tilted forward with knees bent.

After settling into two lines or a semicircle, the dance movement is changed into the basic *kadodo,* a side-to-side movement that travels right-left-right, and then left-right-left, moving rhythmically with the drums.

While in place, the dancers continue to sing, clapping at will and thereby motivating both the male dancers who are hidden in the courtyard and those who are watching. At certain moments, the music changes, signaling the dancers to change their movements. Badu-Younge best describes *kadodo*:

Using a side-to-side step, the dancers move gracefully with fluid as well as vigorous movements. The basic side-to-side movements alternate with other specialized movements that are linked to specific master drum patterns. When the first movement variation is played, two dancers move to the centre of the arena with a fast-paced shuffling walk, stepping twice with the right foot, and then twice with the left. A second variation signals the dancers to execute their "show off" style. They bend their bodies down lower and rapidly raise and drop their heels. With the torso leaning forward, it is vibrated rapidly by quickly pushing the scapula tightly downwards towards the spine and then releasing it (the chest automatically rises when the scapula is pushed downward.) As the torso arches slightly, the pelvis is released and the arms, still in position from the previous movement, swing backwards and forward at half the speed of the torso movement, hands swinging back in a relaxed manner. The music and speed of the foot-heel movement is the same as that of the torso. The dancers may rotate towards or away from each other as they wish. The basic movement and subsequent movements mentioned above are repeated by all the dancers, before returning to their original lines [Badu-Younge 2000, 165].

Figure 2.9: Aflao Mawulikplimi *Adzogbo* Group performing *Atsokla/Kadodo* (2006).

Atsiawɔwɔ. The male dancers, depending on the specific routine, utilize several movements. There are, however, three basic dance vocabularies or routines which are usually used in the choreography. These include:

   i.   entry to the dance arena;
   ii. beginning a dance routine; and
  iii. first dance routine.

Entry to the Dance Arena: The male dancers usually enter the dance arena in the same formation, using the same steps as the female dancers in the *kadodo* processional dance but with a more bold and vigorous execution. When the music changes, they all switch to the *kadodo* movements that the females perform in the center of the arena in pairs.

Beginning a Dance Routine: In preparation for a new dance routine, the dancers circle around themselves while traveling sideways. They may also walk around the arena in a circle while the lead dancer calls the next routine. Once the routine is announced, a cue from the master drummer ushers in the new routine.

On cue when *dzadza dzadza dzadza* (*ʋugbe* vocable/mnemonics syllable) is played by the master drum, the dancers jump and land with both feet—in-out, in-out, in-out, bending their knees as they swing their upper bodies left and right to correspond with the rhythm of the feet. This is repeated a number of times depending on the routine to be performed and it is then followed by the actual routine.

First Dance Routine: The first dance routine performed by most groups in Ghana is referred to as *gbedodoɖa*, a prayer or tribute to *Adzo* and the ancestors. It is also a dramatic way of asking permission from the elders to perform. It is otherwise regarded as a moment to greet the audience.

The lead dancer does not call this dance routine. One of the dancers enters the dance arena and finishes their preparatory female *kadodo* movements; the lead dancer raises his right hand as a signal to the rest of the dancers. They take two steps backwards in line in preparation for a jump that turns them in the air. Then they quickly step forward with their left feet, immediately followed by their right feet, which begins the turn and jump. When landing from the jump, they place the left and then the right feet on the ground.

After this turn, they clap their hands in a prayer position, standing erect and looking up. Then they quickly turn in the opposite direction by stepping forward with the right foot using the left foot to turn, and repeat the prayer position. Depending on the choreography, the dancers return to circling around themselves while traveling sideways and on cue repeat the movement described above, but this time they perform the beginning of a new dance routine described earlier and end up with the "prayer movement."

Costume and Other Visual Art Forms

Male dancers use an elaborate costume in *Adzogbo* performance. The most important part of the men's costume is known as an *aʋlaya*, a type of skirt made up of several layers of cloth with different designs. A cloth is folded over a cord and tied around the dancer's waist and abdomen in such a way that the cloth gathers and stands out like a tutu (Avorgbedor 1987, 12; Badu-Younge 2000, 165).

Due to the large number of pieces of cloth involved, the skirt attains a volume which allows the wearer's arms to rest on top of the skirt, at an angle of almost 90 degrees with the body. The number of cloths used in an *aʋlaya* depends on the wealth of the individual dancer and the ability to move quickly and precisely with extra bulk and weight while executing the dance movements.

A male dancer can wear as many as 20 pairs of the above-mentioned cloths, which measure approximately six yards in length. The different layers of cloth, when set in motion, emphasize the movement and the richness of the dance styles. The layers of cloth become an extension of the movement, which involves a lot of mid-torso rotation (Badu-Younge 2000, 165).

The *aʋlaya* is worn on top of an *atsaka*, a special type of knee-high dancing shorts typical of the Eʋe. Other appendages worn include *teleʋi*, secondary rattles/bells made from seashells or gourds filled with seeds, which are tied around the knee over a protective bandage. *Ala*, woven raffia skirts, are tied over the *teleʋi* to prevent it from slipping. During a performance, *teleʋi* enhances the rhythmic footwork of the dancers, and together with the *ala*, further dramatizes the dance movements.

Ala also represent the spirit of *Adzo* in contemporary performances. Male dancers believe that they are protected from any danger or injury during a performance when they wear the *ala*. They also believe that the spirit of *Adzo* directs them through the execution of the movements.

Another object of art used in the performance by the lead male dancer is a *sɔshi*-horsetail, to emphasize the text of the *atsia* that he calls or sings during his demonstrations. A foot-long straight stick may be used instead of *sɔshi* on some occasions.

Other accessories used by the male dancers include *taku*, shawls or scarves, which are wrapped around the upper torso and around both arms, creating a dazzling effect when the dancers spin. Necklaces of gold, silver or beads are worn around the neck. A *kuku or togbenya*, a floppy hat, covers the head.

White talcum powder is smeared all over the body as form of makeup. Completing the men's elaborate costume is a smaller scarf or towel, called *mafi,* which is placed around the neck and is used as decoration, as well as to wipe away perspiration.

The women's costume is less elaborate but very colorful. The female dancers use the typical traditional dress, *avɔ,* one two-yard strip of cloth which is tied under their armpits and wrapped around their body; a second is wrapped around the waist and hangs to knee-level. Each dancer selects and provides her own cloth. The richness of the cloth is dependent on the pride and wealth of the family. Jewelry is optional, and usually consists of beads worn on knees, wrists, and elbows (Badu-Younge 2000, 165).

All women dancers carry decorative hand mirrors or fans during their *atsokla* section. Makeup includes white clay or powder smeared on the body in geometrical shapes for decoration and also to show the purity of the gods. The woman may also braid their hair and wear *taku* head kerchiefs around their necks or diagonally across their bodies.

Drummers can wear their everyday clothing but must wrap an African cloth around the waist while performing the *Adzogbo* music and dance. See Figure 2.11 on page C-4 of color insert.

Figure 2.10: Aflao Mawulikplimi *Adzogbo* female dancers in action (2006).

Components of a Adzogbo Male Dancers' Costume (figures 2.12–2.24)

Figure 2.12: *Atsaka*

Figure 2.13: Front view of *atsaka*.

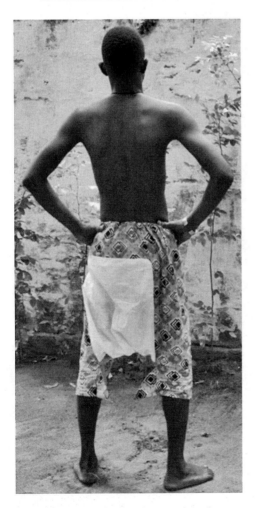

Figure 2.14: Back view of *atsaka*.

Figure 2.15: *Televi*

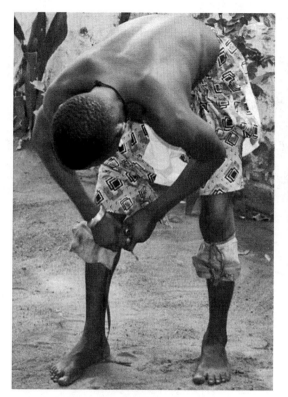

Figure 2.16: *Televi* worn on the legs.

Figure 2.17: *Ala*

Figure 2.18: *Ala* worn on left leg.

Right: Figure 2.19: Complete *ala* on both legs.

Figure 2.20: Preparing the *aʋlaya*.

Figure 2.21: Putting on the *aʋlaya*.

Right, Figure 2.22: Complete *aʋlaya*.

Figure 2.23: Wearing of the *kuku*.

Figure 2.24: Complete costume with *mafi*.

3. *Agbadza* Funeral Dance-Drumming Ceremony

Historical Background and Development

Agbadza is among the oldest musical types performed by the southeastern Eʋe of Ghana. It is a social dance performed across the entire sub-region of West Africa from Nigeria to Ghana. Every southern Eʋe town or village performs a type or variety of *Agbadza*.

Agbadza is also best described as a funeral dance — as *Adowa* is among the Akans of Ghana. It can, however, be heard on other social occasions such as festivals, visits of state dignitaries and other religious ceremonies.

It is a rather difficult undertaking to trace the origin of *Agbadza*. The only documentary evidence of its origin was an account by Da Cruz, who stated that *Agbadza* was created by King Tegbeson 1732–1775 together with other musical types like *hanhye, gokwe,* and *gbolo,* which were performed at the courts of the kings of Dahomey, now called Benin (Nketia 1971/1973). *Agbadza* was performed then only in the evenings.

Oral tradition has it that *Agbadza* emanated from an older war dance-drumming ritual, *atrikpui,* which was originally only performed by men. During that period in history, the majority of Eʋe men are believed to have been farmers, hunters, and warriors, and quite a number were also known to be musicians, specifically *hakpalawo* (composers), *henɔwo* (singers and drummers), and *azagunɔwo* (master drummers).

The Eʋe were believed to be close to nature. They lived close to the forests and were able to relate to the wild animals; as a result, they communicated with such species as gorillas, monkeys and apes.

It is no coincidence that, to this day, the people strongly believe a hunter on a hunting expedition first sighted monkeys and gorillas performing this music and dancing to mourn their dead, which he later taught other hunters on his return from the expedition.

The music was then used by men to prepare for war and also after wars to celebrate victory or defeat. *Agbadza* is performed today as recreational dance-drumming and it is open to all — males, females and children, irrespective of class or religion.

The word "*Agbadza*" has two varied interpretations to the Eʋe: i. a broad-based dance-drumming, and ii. war girdle. As a broad-based dance, *Agbadza* is open to all ("dance for all") and as a war girdle, it is performed to symbolize its original usage and subsequent development from *atrikpui,* war music, and dance drama, *aʋaʋu.*

Agbadza is known by variety of names among the southern Eʋe of today: *agbomasikui, akpoka, agba, ageshie* and *kini.* Tempo is the main distinguishing factor among the varieties mentioned above. *Agbomasikui, akpoka* and *agba* are slower as compared to *kini* and *ageshie.*

46

The various names are also attributed to the various circumstances under which the Eʋe migrated from Benin to their present settlements. These varieties of *agbadza* can be seen as one travels among the southern Eʋes from southwestern Nigeria to Ghana.

Organization of the Dance-Drumming Ceremony

FORM AND STRUCTURE. *Agbadza* traditionally has six phases:

i.	*adzotsotso*	a prewar ritual;
ii.	*banyinyi*	tribute to the ancestors and gods;
iii.	*avɔlunyanya*	tribute to the musicians who have died;
iv.	*vutsɔtsɔ*	main dance-drumming phase;
v.	*hatsiatsia*	joining of songs or song cycle; and
vi.	*vutsɔtsɔ*	main dance-drumming phase.

Phase One: *Adzotsotso*. *Adzotsotso*, which starts the performance, involves the participants converging at the center of the arena, squatting, and singing songs in free rhythm. These special songs, referred to as *asafohawo*, *kaleseye* (songs of valor), *dzidefohawo* (songs of courage), and *atamkahawo* (songs of oath), are aimed at warming up or preparing the participants for a performance.

This ritual is done to recount the preparation for wars in the past, a direct remembrance of the ancestors when the songs were used to stir the people into action, as they were believed to invoke the spiritual forces for war. This phase may be omitted during performances, especially during *kini* and *ageshie*. Those Eʋes living along the coastal areas—the Aŋlɔ Eʋes in Aflao, Keta and Aŋlɔ Afiaɖenyigba, for example—may omit *adzotsotso* and begin their performances with *banyinyi*.

Phase Two: *Banyinyi*. *Banyinyi* symbolizes *kaklanana tɔgbuiwo*, meaning "asking permission from the ancestors to perform," which most often starts almost every traditional dance-drumming of the Eʋe. It is a moment of prayers and meditation through music and dance to alert and pacify the old musicians and ancestors. This introductory performance to the gods allows for a smooth and high standard performance.

Agbadza Banyinyi involves the performance of some type of religious music such as *afaʋu*, *fofuiʋu*, or *ga*. *Afaʋu* is the preferred religious dance-drumming. This phase is very brief and it is repeated at least two times using varied tempi.

Phase Three: *Avɔlunyanya*. *Avɔlunyanya*, which serves as an introduction to the first *vutsɔtsɔ* phase, quickly follows the *banyinyi* section. *Avɔlunyanya* is performed as an invitation to the performance for the spirits of the past drummers, singers, dancers and composers.

This phase is started by the traditional call to action or performance: "*Hoɖoɖuio?*" (Are you ready?) by the main cantor asking the participants to get ready for the performance. The response, "*Hoo*," meaning "We are ready," sets the stage for the performance. The lead cantor then calls a song, which is taken over by the *hatsola* and *hatsoviwo* in free rhythm.

Towards the end of this preliminary singing by the lead singers known as *haflɔflɔ*, a group of idiophones led by the *gakogui* start the *agbadza* timeline in strict rhythm. Other supporting instruments enter with the master drum, *sogo*, dictating the mood of the performance.

Avɔlunyanya, which may be repeated, evolves into the first main dance section, *Vutsɔtsɔ*. *Avɔlunyanya* and the first *vutsɔtsɔ* phase are structurally the same section but the latter is shorter.

Phase Four: *Vutsɔtsɔ*. The *vutsɔtsɔ* phase is what most people know as *agbadza*. It is the main dance-drumming phase during which most of the dance, singing and master drum interaction with supporting instruments occur. The culmination point during this phase is when all the supporting instruments stop playing to allow the lead drum to play alone. *Gakogui, axatse* and *kagan* may be used on some occasions with the *sogo*.

Songs performed during this section of the performance — known as *adzo*, a period of relaxation when drinks are served and announcements are made — are usually short, litanical and repetitive. Dance during this section may also be more dramatic. *Adzo* can also be performed after the *hatsiatsia* section.

Phase Five: Hatsiatsia. *Hatsiatsia*, literally meaning "the joining or selection of songs," which follows, is presently not observed by most communities. During this section, songs based on topical issues and *halo*, songs of ridicule, are heard.

Hatsiatsia songs may or may not be accompanied by any instrument. *Gakogui* may be used if accompaniment is needed. So much importance is attached to *hatsiatsia* that only those who know the songs take part. *Hatsiatsia* songs are more dramatic and may involve gestures during the song performance.

The sixth or final phase of the performance is another extended *ʋutsɔtsɔ*, which can last for several hours.

Songs

Themes of *agbadza* songs relate to several topics of interest. Song texts reflect on the general behavior or social life, historical and cultural values and practices of the southern Eʋe. Historical songs in *agbadza* are usually of the *atrikpui* type, and talk about the kings, wars and migration stories of the Eʋe.

Tonal arrangements in *agbadza* songs make use of melodic fragments based on both the hemitonic and anhemitonic of the tetratonic, pentatonic, and hexatonic scales. *Agbadza* songs are usually in call and response pattern and are very short, litanical and lyrical — with the exception of *hatsiatsia* songs.

Polyphony is generally the result of males and females signing an octave apart. Crossings of parts and occasional use of fourths, fifths, seconds and thirds, underline the extent to which harmony is derived. Sixths are heard on rare occasions.

The Percussion Ensemble

Instruments of the ensemble include:

i.   *Sogo*: Theoretically, the *sogo* directs all other instruments of the ensemble, as well as the whole performance, together with the lead singer and elders. The duration of any performance is determined by the lead singer, elders and the *sogo* drummer but the *sogo* performs the end signal. *Sogo* plays various patterns known as *ʋugbewo*, drum texts, which are made of burden texts and nonsense vocable or mnemonic syllables.

ii. *Kidi*: A response and supporting drum that plays in dialogue with the *sogo*.

iii. *Kagan*: Another supporting drum that plays a basic ostinato accompanying rhythmic pattern.

iv. *Gakogui*: A double bell that plays the timeline, which serves as a reference point to all other instrumentalists, dancers and singers.

v.   *Axatse*: A gourd rattle that supports or emphasizes the *gakogui*.

vi. *Akpe*: Handclapping, with or without wooden clappers, supports and emphasizes the *gakogui*.

See Figure 3.1 on page C-5 of color insert.

Dance Organization

DANCE ARENA. *Agbadza* is usually performed in an open space with enough shade to protect the participants. In almost every Eυe community, a *υɔnu*, a designated assembly ground, is used for this performance. The *υɔnu* is also used for other social events in the community.

There are two traditional ways of arranging the dance arena depending on the specific occasion. Dance arena A, as shown below, is used mostly when the performance is staged for special guests at festivals or special events at which the drummers and dancers face their guests.

In Dance arena B, the performers form a complete circle. This is the usual arrangement for most occasions. In both arenas, it is customary for the *gakogui* and *axatse* to sit behind the *sogo*, *kidi* and *kagan* players. All members of the percussion ensemble can also sit together, in which case the *gakogui* and axatse players sit to the right and left of the drummers.

DANCE MOVEMENTS AND CHOREOGRAPHY. The *agbadza* dance requires no special dance training. The dance is learned mainly through participation in traditional events. Once the music starts, seated dancers will sing and accompany the music with handclapping or stick clappers.

In twos, threes or at most fours, men and women will leave their seats and perform the dance in the circular arena or outside — especially during funerals and other larger social gatherings. There is no specific choreography for an *agbadza* performance. It is

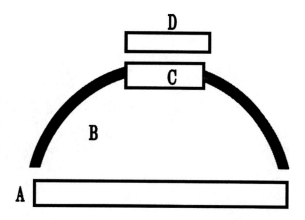

FIGURE 3.2: *Agbadza* performance arena A. Key: A: audience; B: dancers; C: drummers; D: elders.

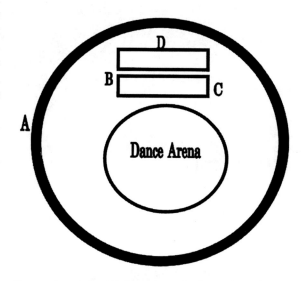

FIGURE 3.4: Aŋlɔ Afiaɖenyigba *Agbadza* male and female dancers.

regarded as a free dance during which dancers are allowed to recreate the basic dance movements.

The dance occurs mainly during the *banyinyi*, *aυɔlunyanya*, *vutsɔtsɔ* and *adzo* phases. There are three main components of the dance: *adasasa*, preparatory movement; *dzimeŋeŋe*, main dance movement; and *ɣekɔkɔ*, round-off dance.

Adasasa. In this preparatory movement, the dancers, in anticipation for the *sogo*'s (lead drum) signal, move their feet side-to-side (left to right and right to left), with their arms slightly curved in front and moving front and back simultaneously. Dancers look at each other gracefully, with beautiful smiles as they await the signal, which usually corresponds with one phrase or rhythmic cycle of the *gakogui* pattern or timeline.

The lead drummer's signal takes the dancers to *dzimeŋeŋe*, the main movement. Duration

Figure 3.5: Aŋlɔ Afiaɖenyigba *Agbadza* male and female dancers.

of *adasasa* performance varies from dancer to dancer but most often guided by how long the master drummer waits before executing the signal.

Dzimeŋeŋe. The main dance movement involves strong chest contractions and releases uniquely peculiar to southern Eʋe traditions. The body is slightly tilted forward with knees bent. Dancers dance across the arena, towards or from the direction of the drummers.

Unlike in the *adasasa*, the dancers themselves determine the duration of this movement. Space availability may sometimes restrict the forward movement in *dzimeŋeŋe*. Stamina is most often the deciding factor in determining the duration of this movement.

Xekɔkɔ. The round-off movement, *ɣekɔkɔ*, has three components. It usually starts with the dancers suddenly looking at each other or, when three are involved, the dancer in the middle stretches both arms to touch the other two to signal the end.

The second stage involves an abbreviated form of *adasasa*, which leads to the literal meaning and symbolism of *ɣekɔkɔ*, "throwing away the dance." In this final section, dancers move their bodies left and right and finally throw their arms forward to signify the end of the dance.

The rule of thumb is for dancers to start and end their left and right movements with the beginning stroke of the *gakogui* timeline pattern.

Figure 3.6: Aŋlɔ Afiaɖenyigba *Agbadza* male dancers in performance (2008).

Costumes and Other Visual Art Forms

Costumes used in *agbadza* are the ordinary *awu* and *avɔ* cloths for women, and *atsaka*, special knee-high dancing shorts typical of the Eʋe with a cloth around the waist, for the men. It is very important to note that men may sometimes go to the performance with no cloth. They can easily secure cloths from women who may want to dance with them.

4. *Atibladekame* Women's Funeral Dance-Drumming Ceremony

Historical Background and Development

"Atibladekame," an Eʋe philosophical thought meaning "United we stand; divided we fall," has become the name for six distinct women's dance-drumming groups at Afeteƒe, Dafɔnyame, Kpɔdoave, Fiagbedu-Afegame, Adidokpi and Agbikpɔnu—all *to* (wards/divisions) in Dzodze, in the Volta region of Ghana. These groups will come together to sing choral laments, dirges, recite eulogies and dance at funerals for loved ones and relatives.

Prior to the establishment of this composite group, women would gather, usually at dawn, to sing dirges when a member of the community had died. Songs performed were compositions of renowned composers of the old funeral dance-drumming music *atsigo, akpalu* or *agoha*, which was almost extinct at the time, and others, such as *agbadza* and *atrikpui*.

There was no central organization for these performances until the early 1950s, when the late Madam Catherine Afiwor Young, alias Daavi, consulted with some prominent women in the various wards to reorganize the old funeral dance-drumming music. The origin and revival of these groups could be traced individually to the musical talents that existed in the various divisions at the time.

Afeteƒe Atsigo, the first to be reorganized under the leadership of Daavi, was inaugurated in 1960 with an official three-day celebration. After this noble success with the *Afeteƒe* group, Daavi continued with her consultations with the other ward leaders, which resulted in the reorganization of the dance-drumming in all other wards of Dzodze. Each group tried to have an identity and so gave different names to their groups, but in theory, all the groups were performing the same music and dance.

Figure 4.1 Catherine Afiwɔ Younge, alias Daavi, in 1960. The founder of *Atibladekame* in Dzodze.

Figure 4.2 Aɟeteɟe Atigo executives in 1974.

Daavi went further to bring all these groups under one umbrella with a central governing council, which she headed in the mid–1960s until the early 1990s. This was the beginning of *Atiblaɖekame*. Before discussing this composite group, it is helpful to look at a brief historical background of each ward group.

Aɟeteɟe Atsigo

Togbui Dey, a warrior and composer, fled with his children from Ŋɔtsie during the great migration of the Eʋes from Ŋɔtsie in the early 14th century. He first moved to *Kevi* in present-day Togo with his people and finally settled in *Dzodze* in Ghana. Many of his followers perished during the journey and so he would compose choral laments, which were used during the funerals. These songs, together with eulogies, were performed in the evenings.

Frequent deaths among his people caused Dey to institute an official celebration during funerals. Instead of just the funeral songs, drumming and dance was added. They would perform *atsigo,* which stands for "hollow wood," to console themselves. The advent of Christianity and other social factors caused the near extinction of this dance-drumming celebration.

The 1950s and 60s saw the revival of atsigo through the efforts of Madam Catherine Younge. The first executives included Madam Afasi Avinu, Somaenya Ƒodi, Alobusode Gbagba, Sodon-shie Agbleke and Cate Young — all of blessed memory. The group is presently led by an executive council comprised of Madam Bertha Ahiable, president; Madam Awunyeseɖe Dzila, secretary; and Madam Alodzeseɖe Denyo, treasurer.

Dafɔnyami Anyanui

A farmer by trade, Ahiagbede Dzishinu was one of the noted composers of dirges and choral laments for the women and other dance-drumming groups in *Dafɔnyami* of *Dzodze*. Most of his songs were mournful and were used to console bereaved families.

Dzishinu's songs were referred to as *Anyanui,* the good message, which was the name that would be given to the reorganized dance-drumming. With the urge from Madam Younge and *Afetefe Atsigo*'s example, two elders from *Dafɔnyami,* Mr. Amanyo and Avinu, encouraged the women to revive *anyanui* songs. So started the anyanui celebration as women's funeral dance music in the early 1960s. The first executives included: Madam Anna Ahiabenu, Setɔva Kpeli, Sevamaɖe Nɔdzro, Adzovɔ Kemeh, and Ashie Amanyo as patron.

Anyanui has become a very popular dance-drumming type among the people of *Dafɔnyami,* and it is always performed when an elderly woman dies. Current executives include: Amewuseɖe Nɔshie, Korsiwɔ Bayikpa, Paulina Adzie, Womanɔ Tɔsu, Sotɔnyo Able and Doga Amanyo, as patron.

Kpɔɖoave Akpalu

History has it that around the 1920s one Madam Sodaede Agortimevor of Kpɔɖoave, who was once married at *Anyako* in the Anlɔ district of Ghana, lost her brother, Miheseɖe Agɔtimevɔ, under strange circumstances. During the funeral celebrations, mourners came from *Anyako* to *Dzodze* with the *Akpalu* funeral dance-drumming group to console her.

Sodaede got so interested in dance-drumming that she and her sister Somaenya Agɔtimevɔ vowed to bring *Akpalu* funeral dance-drumming to Kpɔɖoave. They invited a lead singer of *Akpalu* by the name Mr. Amemawu to come and teach them the songs at *Dzodze.*

Amemawu succeeded in teaching them several songs which they perfected and sang at funerals. With the addition of drumming and dance, *Akpalu* became the most popular women's funeral dance-drumming at *Kpɔɖoave.*

Fiagbedu Agbikpɔnu Nyanu (Nyawuame)

Eʋe culture has a special place for songs. Songs are used to run commentary on life so that in time of crises, sicknesses and death, the people will call on singers to perform for them. Composers would be looking for topical issues and other themes for their compositions.

Mr. Hodor of Agbikpɔnu of Fiagbedu in Dzodze was one of the best composers who lived in this ward of Dzodze. His songs were mostly inspired by death and pain, and so he composed consolatory and mournful songs for his people. His lyrics were so touching that people sang the songs at funerals and at places where people might need consolation.

These songs were described as *nyawuame,* "overwhelmed with several thoughts," the name that would be given to funeral dance-drumming music of the area in the 1960s. *Nyawuame* was revived through the ingenuity of the following female singers of the community: Ayiɖenshie Gonyi, Soxɔmade Alakpa, Aʋaya Dɔdunu and Sodonshie Akpagana.

Fiagbedu Aɖidokpui Ɖegbato

Sometime in the 1900s, Davor Ludzu, a young boy living at Aɖidokpui of Fiagbedu in Dzodze, was heard composing songs to the dismay of his elders. His songs were very slow and in free rhythm, which made them sound mournful. His parents and other elders at the time were surprised at the deep philosophical content of his compositions and exclaimed, "Ɖegbato," which means, "something strange is happening."

Elders Kpotsi Ludzu and Daku Davor gave Davor moral encouragement and support. His songs became "must-hears" at any funeral to console mourners. Female lead singers who sang and led the songs during the rebirth in the 1960s included Dzikunshie Gbikpo, Sonyamedɔ Dorgbetɔ, Amentɔnshie Tame, Sodahoe Tame, Setsamaɖe Alornyo and Dodoaye Tɔkpo.

Singing of *degbato* songs became popular over the years and was adopted to suit the Atibladekame experience. Present-day leaders include Sonyekode Amegavi Atike, Amewusode Ahiadɔme, Sonyamade Gbeve Alɔnyesede, Ɖeadovu, Sefayide Gbedema and Dzatugbui Xedagbui.

Fiagbedu Afegame Dekoenu (Dekɔlenyanu)

"Our great grandfathers and mothers were born musicians with innate abilities for composing songs," recounted Somabe Dzila, one of the lead singers of the present group, in a July 2007 interview. After their migration from Ŋɔtsie, disputes pertaining to land acquisition and marital problems were resolved through traditional arbitration courts.

Once the problems or cases were resolved, one of the elders would stand up and conclude the proceedings by announcing, "*Ɖe kɔ le nya ma nu*," "Let's leave and forget that matter," meaning the case is therefore closed. A composer present would then be asked at the spur of the moment to compose a song to celebrate the occasion or "to cool down" the parties involved.

Some of these songs might lead to the ridicule or praise of those involved in the dispute. These compositions gradually evolved into *halo* (Avorgebdor 1994) and choral laments and dirges.

This evolution or recontextualization of the "arbitration songs" into funeral and *halo* songs dated as far back as the 1850s. Some of the early composers and lead singers at the time were: Ahiadzro Dagbale, Agbedɔ Atieku, Vidreku Dzata, Adzogble Ahiamale, Ahɔzo Ahiamale, Gamado Afɔtrɔ, Ahiable Afɔtrɔ, Aloewonude Agutɔ, Hutɔnshi Agutɔ, Somabe Ahiavɔ, Suikede Ahiavɔ, Alɔmade Agɔbia and Somalade Agɔbia.

The next generation of lead singers who revamped these songs to be performed with drumming and dance and also led this group be part of Atibladekame were: Bohlishie Agbaglo, Somabe Dzila, Alɔnyenshie Adzogble, Sodalor Ɖufe, Sotsamade Ahiafokpɔ, Sodahoe Adome, Somalade Kpɔdzo, with Nɔshie Vidzreku and Senyo Dorgbefu as patrons.

Current executives include: Theresa Dzila, Mana Bedzra, Sonyaede Afɔtude, Kɔsinɔ Hɔnyo, Alɔmade Ablɔmetsi, and Afiwɔ Agbalenyo, with Ese Takpa, Xine Sorokpo, and Koblatse Agbanyo as patrons.

Because of the long social interactions of the people of *Dzodze*, it was very easy to have all these groups sympathize or mourn with one another during funerals and other sad moments. The groups were able to perform together under one umbrella when the *Atibladekame* concept was introduced by Madam Cate Afiwor Younge.

In 1950, using the same instrumentalists, Madam Cate Afiwor Younge of blessed memories started mobilizing these groups in Dzodze, which today has resulted in the largest women's funeral dance-drumming music in Ghana.

The founding members and first executive council include: Akakpovi Ziddah, Nɔshie Vidzreku, Kwamivi Seku, Afashega Avinu, Soalade Akpabli, Sodayide Amable, Somaenya Ɉodi, Kɔsɔnshie Xenyo, Amewusode Ahiagbede, Sonyamade Ahama, Alɔbusode Gbagba and Kole Ahiatsi.

Atibladekame is now popularly called "*Miwɔdeka Lɔlɔnyo Habɔbɔ*," "Let us Unite Love is Good Group." Before any performance, the name of the union is chanted:

Lead: *Miwɔ deka* "Let us unite"
Chorus: *Lɔlɔnyo* "Love is good"
Lead: *Atibladekame* "Trees tied together"
Chorus: *Me nya ŋe na o.* "Cannot be broken"
Lead: *Ho ɖo ɖio* "Are you ready?"
Chorus: *Hoo* "Yes."

Organization of the Dance-Drumming Ceremony

FORM AND STRUCTURE. There are three main phases of the performance:

   i.   *Uulɔlɔ* the procession;
   ii. *Adzotsotso* tribute to the ancestors and gods; and
  iii. *Uutsɔtsɔ* main dance-drumming phase.

Phase One: *Uulɔlɔ.* *Atibladekame* may begin with a short procession. This performance involves only the female participants who will sing and accompany themselves with bells and rattles. *Uulɔlɔ* is not performed on every occasion.

When the group is invited to special functions such as festivals, members will assemble at the house of the president or lead singer and proceed from there to the performance arena. This phase of the performance can also be seen during funerals.

Phase Two: *Adzotsotso.* Once the arena is set, the performers will converge at the center of the dance ring and perform a series of songs in free rhythm, standing with bodies slightly bent forward — especially the lead singer. The songs serve as an invocation to the gods and a remembrance of all the ancestors who have passed, especially those who were once members of the various groups.

The songs may include choral laments, dirges and other mournful songs. Once the lead singer changes to a strict rhythm, the bells, rattles, and drums join the performance.

At this time, the performers will stand erect to usher in a brief *Uutsɔtsɔ* phase, which involves drumming, singing and limited dancing. *Adzotsotso* is always led by the *Afetefe Atsigo* lead singer as a tribute to this group for being the first to be formed.

Figure 4.3: Dzodze *Atibladekame* performing Adzotsotso (2007).

Phase Three: *Uutsɔtsɔ.* Once *adzotsotso* ends, participants will take their seats and wait for *Afetefe Atsigo* to start the *Uutsɔtsɔ* phase, which is the main dance-drumming phase. *Kpɔdoave, Dafɔnyame, Afegāme, Adidokpui* and *Agbikpɔnu* groups follow this performance. There are six stages of the *Uutsɔtsɔ* phase. Each stage is directed or led by the lead singer *hesinɔwo* of the various groups. The *hesinɔwo,* the lead singers, are easily identified by the *sɔshi* they carry during performances.

Each stage begins with a brief performance of songs in free rhythm, which is led by the lead singer of particular group. The unique feature of the *Uutsɔtsɔ* phase is that the same musicians/ drummers accompany all the groups, most of whom are from the *Afetefe* group.

A typical performance will begin about 1:00 P.M. and end around 6:00 P.M. depending most often on the weather. *Uutsɔtsɔ* may be interspersed with rituals for the dead and also announcements about future performances and other issues affecting the welfare of the various groups.

Songs

Songs in *Atibladekame* reflect the experiences, attitudes and history of the Eʋes. The songs serve as commentary on the past, present and future lives of the people. Songs, therefore, include historical, personal experiences, topical issues, death, poverty, and philosophical and reflective themes. The majority of the songs, however, are the sorrowful/mournful type, which often lament the many problems humans face on this earth: poverty, barrenness, sickness, loneliness, and suffering.

Most of the songs performed today by the groups are all derived from the old *atsigo* songs, which were popularized in the early 19th century by the renown Eʋe composer and singer Vinɔkɔ Akpalu of Anyako in the Aŋlɔ district of Ghana (Nayo 1968).

Tonal arrangements in *Atibladekame* songs make use of melodic fragments based on both hemitonic and anhemitonic forms of the pentatonic and sometimes the hexatonic scales as in the *Agbadza* and *Adzogbo* songs. The songs are usually in call and response pattern, litanical, solo and chorus refrain or a mixture of all the above.

Atibladekame songs are conceived and composed in monophony — single-line music. Harmony is generally the result of the women singing with occasional use of fourths, fifths, seconds and thirds in their chorus responses. Unison singing is the norm but the pentatonic forms may make use of intervals of a fourth below or a fifth above the melody at cadential points or as it appeals to the chorus during the performance.

There is no apportioning of parts apart from the lead singer's. Other singers making up the chorus may choose to sing the primary response or sing something else against it provided it is traditionally accepted.

Unrelated tones, or shouts, yells, and grunts may also add another polyphonic texture to the performance.

The Percussion Ensemble

Instruments of the ensemble include:

  i.   The *agbomlɔanyi,* or *atsimeʋu,* as the lead drum, directs all other instruments of the ensemble. It functions as the *sogo* in the *Agbadza* percussion ensemble.
  ii. The *agbobli,* or *sogo,* serves as a response and supporting drum that plays in dialogue with the Agbomlɔanyi. Agbobli is sometimes doubled since one may assume the role of the master/lead drum during the performance.
  iii. The *kpetsi* or *kidi,* also responds and supports the lead drum as the *sogo* does.

FIGURE 4.4: Dzodze *Atibladekame* Percussion Ensemble (2006). Seated from left: *kagan* (covered by the lead singer), *kidi, sogo,* and a second *kidi.* The *axatse* and *gakogui* are not shown. Standing: *atsimeʋu.*

iv.   The *kegeyi,* or *kagan,* another supporting drum, plays a basic ostinato-accompanying pattern.

v.   The *gakogui* plays the timeline, which serves as a reference for all other instrumentalists, dancers and singers. There are about five used in the performance. One plays the main reference pattern and the rest provide additional supporting patterns.

vi.   The *axatse* also supports but mainly emphasizes the *gakogui.* Most of the females during the performance will play the *axatse* as they sing. The female participants are responsible for playing the *gakogui* and *axatse.* The few males seen at the performance play the drums.

Dance Organization

DANCE ARENA. Atibladekame is performed in a circular arena as shown in Figure 4.5.

There is a second dance arena for when the performance is staged for special guests at festivals or special events at which the drummers and dancers face their guests, as in *Agbadza* dance-drumming (Figure 3.2).

DANCE MOVEMENTS AND CHOREOGRAPHY. Very limited dance accompanies *adzotsotso,* the first phase of the performance. Once the lead singer changes her song to a strict rhythm, the bells and rattle begin, followed by the master drum and other supporting drums.

In twos and threes, the women will leave their seats and perform the dance in the circular arena during the *Uutsɔtsɔ phase*. There are three main components of the dance: *adasasa*, preparatory movement; *dzimeŋeŋe*, main dance movement; and *ɣekɔkɔ*, round-off dance — as in *Agbadza*.

There are no major significant differences between the *Agbadza* and *Atibladekame* dance movements. Dancers are more relaxed in executing their movements in *Atibladekame*. The slower tempo of the percussion ensemble makes it possible for the dancers to sing and dance at the same time.

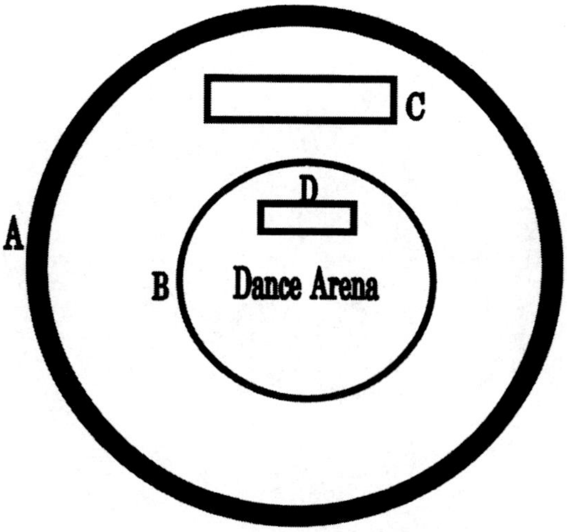

Costumes and Other Visual Art Forms

Figure 4.5: Atibladekame performance arena. A: audience; B: women chorus/dancers; C: drummers; D: lead singers/bell players and executives.

Women use two types of costumes in *Atibladekame*. *Atible*, the original costume that is more extensive, can be seen on very special occasions such as festivals, political rallies or during special rituals when an executive member dies.

The *atible* costume is comprised of a two-yard strip of cloth which is tied under the armpits and wrapped around the body; a second one is wrapped around the waist, and hangs to knee-level. A special pillow is made from extra pieces of cloth, which is tied around the waist under the cloth that hangs to the knee. This serves as an extension of the buttocks. Jewelry usually consists of beads worn on the knee, wrist, and elbows.

A head kerchief wrapped around the head completes the costume. Other appendages carried when *atible* is used

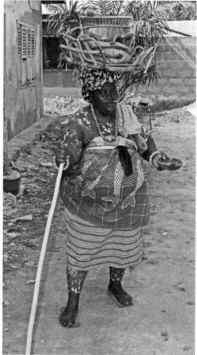

Figure 4.7: Front view of *Atibladekame* female dancer Theresa Dzila with props (2006).

FIGURE 4.6: Female Dancers in *atible* costume showing their backs.

Figure 4.8: Dancers in contemporary *atible* costumes.

Figure 4.9: Hesinɔ Cecilia Kassah of Afetefe *Atsigo* performing with *Sɔshi.*

include the traditional lantern, walking staff, and a collection of antique cooking utensils in a *tsikpo,* an antique traditional basket used in the olden days by women to carry their belongings.

The second type of female costume is the traditional *avɔ,* two two-yard pieces of cloth wrapped around the body from the waist to the ankle with an *awu,* a blouse, to match. This is the contemporary costume that can be seen during funerals. The drummers wrap a two-yard cloth over any knickers.

5. *Atrikpui* Warriors' Dance-Drumming Ceremony

Historical Background and Development

If song texts provide relevant data in the study of African history, then most of the historical data on the musical practices of the Anlɔ Eʋe prior to their present settlements can be derived from songs of the elders, of which *atrikpui* songs form a major part.

Atrikpui is popularly referred to as *kaleʋu* or *ŋutsuʋu*, the musical type of heroes or men of the southern Eʋes of Ghana. Consequently, the music was associated with the warriors who fought and defended the region in time of wars, disputes and crises. As stated clearly in the song below, those who went to war were referred to as heroes:

> Mie ke e gbeadzi, kaleawoe,
> Agbo 'ye la gbae;
> Atrikpuiviwo dogovɔ kaleawoe,
> Agbo 'ye la gba godogodo.
> Atrikpuiviwo dogo egbeadzi,
> Kaleawoe agbo la gbae,
> Nutsufeviwo dogo kaleawoe;
> Agbo 'ye la gba godogodo.

Literally, this song refers to the warriors, "*kaleawoe*," and their strength on the battlefield:

> When we reach the battle field, the Valiants,
> The barricade will be crushed.
> Atrikpui people now in battle,
> The barricade will be crushed in to pieces.
> When Atrikpui people reach the battlefield, the Valiants,
> The barricade will be crushed.
> When men meet in a battle, the Valiants,
> The barricade will be crushed into pieces.

The name *atrikpui*, as oral tradition reveals, evolved from the statement "*ɖeko miakuatri*," or "*negbe ɖeko miaku kpuide*," meaning, "we can only die instantly or die shortly." *Atrikpui*, therefore, referred to the instant death envisaged when the great forefathers of the land went to war. The music and dance performed during and after wars was then called *atrikpui*, and was regarded as one of the oldest *aʋaʋu* (war dances) of the southeastern Eʋes.

Critical analysis of some *atrikpui* song texts provides a probable period of origin, although it is very difficult to trace the exact year when this musical type was started. Fiagbedzi (1977) puts the origin of *atrikpui* and other ancient dances (*amegãxoxoʋuwo*) to be around (1650 to 1886. He supports this argument with the following *atrikpui* song text:

> The warriors in battle dress are locked in combat
> Gunshots reverberate in Anago
> The warriors of Dahomey in battle dress
> Are gone to meet the kings of Dahomey
> The warriors in battle are locked in combat
> Let the Fɔn army take the lead
> For we are advancing, come what may
> We are going to encounter the kings of Dahomey
> [Fiagbedzi 1977].

As will be shown in subsequent pages discussing the costume and other extensions of the body and mode of performance, *atrikpui* could not have started after this alleged war. The song text Fiagbedzi used as a source makes reference to "gunshots"; however, no western or European weapons such as guns were known in the early history of the Eʋe when the music was used for wars.

Principal weapons of war in the those early days were bows and arrows, shields, clubs and "black magic." It can be deduced that *atrikpui* might have started long before the sojourn of the Eʋes in Ŋɔtsie.

Distribution of *atrikpui* covers the entire region of the southern Eʋe territories of West Africa. A similar type, called *agbobli* after the master drum of the ensemble, is also performed by the Aves of Ghana.

In the olden days *atrikpui* was performed before and after wars to celebrate defeat or victory. There were specific songs for every occasion relating to the mood of the people.

The music is performed today at burial and funeral rites of very important elders of the community, including chiefs and very old people. It is also performed in *Anlɔga* when a male dies suddenly by violent means where much blood is shed. This is known as *dzogbeku* or *amekuʋumeku*.

At yearly traditional festivals *atrikpui* features with other ancient dances as a prelude to celebration. Annual rites for Eʋe state deities, *fetatɔtrɔ*, such as *Nyigbla, Hugbato, and Gbe*, may also be incorporated into the performance of *atrikpui*.

Organization of the Dance-Drumming Ceremony

FORM AND STRUCTURE. Under normal performance situations, *atrikpui* has three basic phases: *asafosetsotso, aʋolunyanya* and *vutsɔtsɔ*, which are interspersed with *haflɔflɔ* or *hatsiatsia*. To these may be added *atrilɔlɔ*, a processional dance-drumming used during funerals, ceremonies for state gods, and state festivals.

Phase One: *Asafosetsotso*. *Asafosetsotso*, or *adzotsotso*, which starts the performance, involves the participants singing songs in free rhythm. These special songs, referred to as *asafo-hawo*, *kaleseye* (songs of valor), *dzidefohawo* (songs of courage), and *atamkahawo* (songs of oath), are aimed at warming up the participants.

The songs were used in the past to stir the people into action, as they were believed to invoke the spiritual forces. In the past *asafosetsotso* motivated the warriors to fight gallantly, bearing in mind the great oath taken before battle. This ritual song is performed today to recount the preparation for wars in the past.

Thus, before any performance the participants will converge at the center of the dance arena led by the lead singer to perform. The performance is in free rhythm and in call and response form.

Although varieties of style exist among the southeastern Eʋe, themes of the songs remain the same. A special feature of *asafosetsotso* is the cluster of languages used: Eʋe, Akan, and Akwamu — all Ghanaian languages.

Asafosetsotso is performed before *atrilɔlɔ,* the processional dance and at the performance arena before the *uutsɔtsɔ* phase. These performances usually last for about two minutes respectively.

Asafosetsotso is also performed outside *atrikpui* at the courts of chiefs when ceremonial state drums are being played or during burial rites when the coffin is to be carried or lifted into the grave.

Phase Two: *Avɔlunyanya.* The structure of *avɔlunyanya* is the same as in *Agbadza* dance-drumming. This section involves singing and instrumental accompaniment with very limited dancing.

Avɔlunyaya in *atrikpui* is a ritual that remembers the past musicians. This is a sacred opportunity for the performers to commune and invite the spirits of these musicians to the performance. *Avɔlunyaya* may be omitted during performances.

Songs in this phase are carefully selected to reflect the function and mood of the performers. This section is repeated at most two times before the *vutsɔtsɔ* phase.

Phase Three: *Uutsɔtsɔ.* The third phase, *vutsɔtsɔ,* which is the main dance-drumming ceremony, is simply referred to as *atrikpui*. *Uutsɔtsɔ* utilizes *Agbadza* drumming variations with additional support and reinforcement from the *atsimevu, agblovu, atopani* and *tavuga* drums.

This phase may last for two to three hours interspersed with *hatsiatsia* to avoid complete silence during intermissions when drinks are served. *Hatsiatsia,* which is known as *Hafɔflɔ* in *Atrikpui,* involves the singing of very old historical songs in free rhythm or with *gakogui* accompaniment.

Occasional dance or dramatic gestures by anybody moved by a particular song accompany these songs. *Hafɔflɔ* may be performed immediately after the *asafosetsosto* phase when *atrilɔlɔ* begins the whole performance.

Phase Four: *Atrilɔlɔ.* It is in *atrilɔlɔ,* the processional dance-drumming, that most of the original characteristic features of the *atrikpui* can be seen. These characteristic features are discussed under dance movements.

In funeral contexts, *atrilɔlɔ* precedes or ends the performance. The *gakogui* and *agblovu* are the main instruments used to accompany this phase but the whole percussion ensemble joins in when the performers enter the performance arena.

Songs

Atrikpui songs can be classified as historical because they relate to the various facets of the past lives of the Eues. A majority of the songs speak of the wars fought, migration stories, and their peculiar life patterns.

The age of the songs has resulted in words termed "Old Eue," as some are *Fɔn* and *Yoruba.* As these historical songs are passed from generation to generation, younger people may sing them but not necessarily know their meaning. The songs very often use lyrics derived from different, sometimes archaic, forms of existing languages, due to the natural movement of the people.

Atrikpui songs were composed to warm the warriors up during wars, and are therefore very short in phrasing and utilize themes relating to war scenes such as:

> Klāla mee madɔ
> 'Dzo tso ŋutsuviwo
> Klala mee madɔ
> 'Dzo tso ŋutsuviwo
> Klāla mee madɔ.

Which literally means:

> I shall sleep in calico
> War has come upon the sons of men
> I shall sleep in calico
> War has come upon the sons of men
> I shall sleep in calico.

Other songs are full of frequent bragging about achievements or what the warriors can do.

Allusions to the hardships of war and the risks of death are also used in Atrikpui song themes. The warrior knows that death may be impending — he goes to the frontline fully prepared to die with the knowledge that if anything should happen, he will have done his duty.

Reflections on defeat or dire hardship may be found in the songs of *atrikpui*. Such defeats or misfortunes may be embodied in an oath, a pre-war ritual in the form of a covenant which binds warriors during battles. In effect, it is a pledge made to each other that whatever happens, the warriors will take care of each other and fight to the end. It can serve to spur the warriors on, as in the *asafosetsotso* song below:

> Asafose wo aye dwuma
> Osee wo aye dwuma
> Aflimayi so aflimayi so
> Woaye dade woaye dade
> Akɔmyi akrɔfo
> Adenwo klebetsia kunua
> Adenawɔ ade yia akrɔfo
> Ade ase
> Krofuna sem.

Which literally means:

> Warriors, you can work hard
> Yes, you can work hard
> You cannot go to war without a knife
> Only with the knife "cutlass" only
> The knife "cutlass" can take you to victory
> What can you do?
> You have reached the war front
> Nothing can be done.

Other song texts relate to the conveying of the dead, insult, and the prestige of the chief.

Atrikpui songs are generally in simple binary form, A:B, or ternary, A:B:A, with many repetitions. Call and response, solo and chorus, refrain and mixed sectional forms are other features of the songs. The tonal material of the songs includes the use of hemitonic and anhemitonic forms of pentatonic and hexatonic scales.

Atrikpui songs are conceived and composed in monophony. Melodies may begin and end on any pitch of a scale. Melodic contour may correspond to or, in some cases, defer from, the speech contour of words. In practice, the length and boundaries of musical phrases are defined by that of the text.

A speech utterance expressing a complete thought may consist of one or more complete sentences or a single word. Hence, the melody of a song can be based on the elaboration of such phrases.

The principal harmonic device peculiar among the southeastern Eʋe is male and female voices singing in parallel octaves. Harmony, or for that matter polyphony, in *atrikpui* music is the result of performance roles and may arise out of melodic processes and is therefore closely linked with the scales or model types and melodic movements.

The songs are composed as single melodic lines and harmony occurs sporadically as it appeals to the chorus at a particular performance. In general, harmony makes use of intervals of thirds, fourths, fifths, sixths and octaves. Other polyphonic devices include overlapping and crossing of parts, unrelated tones or shouts, and yells and grunts from the chorus.

Both free and strict rhythms are employed in *atrikpui* songs. The lead singer uses free rhythm songs during the *hawuwu* section. Free rhythms are also used during the *asafosetsotso*, *avɔlunyanya*, and *haflɔflɔ* phases. Most songs in the *vutsɔtsɔ* and *atrilɔlɔ* phases are organized in strict or metered rhythm.

The Percussion Ensemble

Instruments and their functions in *Atrikpui* are:

    i.   *agbobli sogo* master/lead drum;
   ii. *kpetsi /kidi* supporting drum;
  iii. *kagan/kegeyi* supporting drum;
  iv. *atopani* played in pairs, supporting drum;
   v. *agblɔvu* talking drum, supporting drum;
  vi. *tavugā / vugā / abuḍu* supporting drum;
 vii. *gakogui / tigo* bell, time cycle; and
viii. *axatse* as a rattle supports the time cycle.

Agblɔvu, *atopani* and *tavuga* are not always used in the *atrikpui* performance. *Agblɔvu* is the only drum used during the early days of *atrikpui*.

Figure 5.2: Dzodze Afetefe *Atrikpui* Group Percussion Ensemble. Seated, from left: *Agbobli, kpetsi, kagan* (*atopani* standing in front), *kagan*; standing in the back row: *gakogui, axatse* and *tavugā*.

Dance Organization

THE DANCE ARENA. The organization of the *Atrikpui* dance is free in conception. Before any performance, the dance arena is arranged in a circular form as shown in Figure 5.3. During staged performances for special guests at festivals or special events such as funerals, a second dance arena is preferred. This occurs when the drummers and dancers have to face their guests, as in *Agbadza* dance-drumming. This arena is shown in Figure 5.4.

DANCE MOVEMENTS, DRAMATIC ENACTMENT AND CHOREOGRAPHY. During the *atrilɔlɔ* processional dance, the participants move like a mob or battalion advancing to the war front. In the lead is an elder of the community or a war veteran representing an ancestral war captain.

This symbolic elder represents the legendary *Tɔgbui Tegli*, who led the Eʋe from *Ŋɔtsie* during their great exodus in the 13th century. Stationed in the middle of the "mob" are the musicians, which would have been typical in former war practices. The procession does not look like a western parade by soldiers, as there is constant overlapping of lines and individuals. Some may also run forward or backwards, enacting war scenes.

The *atrikpui* dance is primarily for the purposes of extolling the glories of past wars and the advantages of peace and unity. It also serves as an opportunity to recount the great deeds of the warriors in the past, and, lastly, to celebrate the pride and dignity of the southeastern Eʋes. These objectives are expressed in the dance movements depicting episodes of war.

Top, FIGURE 5.3: *Atrikpui* performance arena A. A: elders; B: drummers; C: ; D: singers/dancers; D. lead singers; E: audience. *Bottom,* FIGURE 5.4: *Atrikpui* performance arena B. A: elders; B: drummers; C: singers and dancers; D: lead singers; E: audience.

The dance movements involve the unique traditional strong chest contractions and releases, which are uniquely southern Eʋe, as used in *Agbadza*. Apart from that basic movement, movements may communicate other things, such as "take cover," "take your sword," "kill the enemy," or "stop and retreat." All the above movements are free and their use depends on the experiences and mood of the dancer.

The *atrikpui* dance starts with *adoɖeɖe* or *adasasa*. This is the preliminary movement used to warm up the arms and legs while waiting for the master drummer to usher the dancer into action.

The round-off of the dance, *ɣekɔkɔ*, known in *atrikpui* as *adasasa* or *adzadada*, is characterized by *abebubuwo*—proverbial and symbolic actions and gestures.

The principal dance movement peculiar to *atrikpui* is known as *aklitete*. This is a forward and backward step movement with both legs. The right leg steps forward on beat one and backwards on beat two as the left leg does the same on three and four, corresponding with the rhythmic pattern played on the *gakogui*. The movements of the legs therefore divide the pattern of the *gakogui* into four equidistant parts.

Some common *abebubuwo* and their symbolisms include:

    i.   Movement: Dancer dances and stops suddenly, looks up into the sky and then around.
        Meaning: This implies that he has remembered some past event.

    ii.   Movement: Dancer dances, folding his arms on his chest and laughs.
        Meaning: This implies he is among people or he has been born among very important people.

   iii. Movement: Dancer swings both arms then puts them on his chest.
        Meaning: This means his child or relative was once a soldier who went to battle.

   iv. Movement: Dancer throws both legs to the aside and suddenly freezes.
        Meaning: He is not afraid of any person at the battlefield.

    v.   Movement: Dancer removes his hat, bends, and laughs a little before retreating to his seat.
        Meaning: He has lowered himself to all who are present since someone stronger might be around.

   vi. Movement: Dancer turns his face very often around himself.
        Meaning: This indicates that enemies are around but he also has the strength to fight them.

  vii. Movement: Dancer dances with arms folded around his neck and shakes with a very sad facial expression.
        Meaning: This implies many have died during the battle, leaving him alone.

FIGURE 5.5: Dzodze Aƒeteƒe *Atrikpui* dancers in the *Uutsɔtsɔ* phase (2007).

   viii. Movement: A dancer touches the ground with one finger and then touches his fore-head.
        Meaning: He fears only death.
    ix. Movement: Dancer raises a finger.
        Meaning: He refers to God alone as his protector.
     x. Movement: He dances and grunts.
        Meaning: He shows pity for his enemies.
    xi. Movement: The dancer points to the east and west.
        Meaning: When the warriors meet in a battle, it will be a day and night affair.
    xii. Movement: Two dancers perform, shake hands, and grunt in each other's faces.
        Meaning: This indicates that they remember some past misdeed not known to any-body.

All of the above movements and many more are free in expression depending on the experience and mood of the dancer.

Another important feature of the dance is *aladada* by the lead singer. After he has sung through a song cycle in the free rhythm, known as *hawuwu,* he starts the *vutsɔtsɔ* song. When he gets to the end of the song, he sings loudly, jumps high, circles round and lands on one leg at an exact point in time when the whole performance is flung into action. This movement concludes the *hawuwu* section of songs in free rhythm.

Costumes and Other Visual Art Forms

In the early days of Atrikpui, the costume was mainly knickers known as *kamegbi, kamego,* or *kamegodi,* generally referred to as *wokadzia.* These knickers were made from the bark of a logo tree (the same tree used for drum construction) tied around the waist with a twine. The bark, beaten to make it soft and netlike, was then passed under the twine waistband to conceal the private parts.

For a shirt, the performers used a *dabawu,* similar to the present-day northern Ghanaian *batakari,* a smock also made from the bark of the logo tree known as *logobo.* Hats known as *loglo,* made from animal horns, served as camouflage headdresses.

Items carried or attached to the dancer's bodies included implements of war: *kpo,* club; *yi,* cutlass; *hlo* or *akplɔ,* spear; *adekpui,* dagger; and later *tu,* guns— introduced by Europeans. All these were carried in readiness for war. As the years went by, the *logobo* used in *kamego* was replaced with calico, red cloth or any decent textile print depending on the context of the performance.

The *kamego* is retained and used by very old women or young girls up to puberty. The twine waist rope is replaced with a set of beads and the *logobo* by a special red cloth, popularly called *godidze.*

In present-day performances, the men wear *atsaka,* knickers with points behind the knee and a cloth around the waist as in *Adzogbo* and *Agbadza.* Any type of shirt can be used. Women performers wear the usual cloth and blouse.

Figure 5.6: *Afetefe Atrikpui* male dancer Vincent Agbalekpɔ in *loglo* (2007).

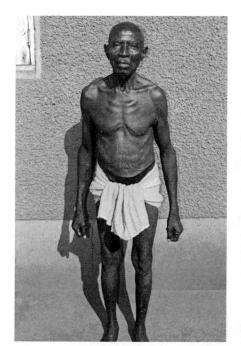

Top left, FIGURE 5.7: Afeteƒe *Atrikpui* male dancer Adegbedzi Kamassah in *kamego* (2007). *Top right*, FIGURE 5.8: Afeteƒe *Atrikpui* male dancer Eko Ahiable in *loglo* and *kamego* (2007). *Bottom*, FIGURE 5.9: Afeteƒe *Atrikpui* female dancers in varied costumes (2007).

When *atrilɔlɔ* is involved, however, an attempt is made to reenact the original *atrikpui* with the old costumes so that the dancers appear to be real warriors. *Kamego, dabawu* or other imitations, in addition to present-day new and old military uniforms, are used in this context.

Masks are used with some dancers painting their faces black and red in contemporary performances. The firing of guns is a common phenomenon in contemporary *atrilɔlɔ*.

6. *Atsiagbekɔ* Warriors' Dance-Drumming Ceremony

Historical Perspective and Development

Atsiagbekɔ is classified among the oldest traditional dance-drumming types of the southeastern Eʋe territories of Ghana. This dance-drumming ceremony spread throughout all of the southern Eʋe populations of West Africa and the *Fɔn*-speaking people of Benin. The people of *Anyako, Dzogadze, Aŋlɔ Afiaɖenyigba, Aŋlɔga, Dzodze, Kedzi,* and *Aflao* perform it in traditional contexts in Ghana.

Legend has it that *atsiagbekɔ* was first performed by monkeys and was adapted by hunter-warriors. In those days, the performance was considered a warriors' or hunters' dance, or *aʋaʋu*. Its presentation was reserved for the warriors when they returned from the battlefield. This history can be seen today in most of the dance movements, which depict scenes of war.

Atsiagbekɔ was called *atamugā,* the great oath, when it was used as a war-time dance-drumming ritual. The name changed to *atsiagbekɔ,* or simply *agbekɔ,* in the absence of wars. So how and when did the monkeys come into the picture?

The Eʋe of old were very close to nature and were known to be great hunters, farmers and warriors. Most of their inventions and creations were at the time derived from the forest and the inventors' process and methodologies were kept secret.

So it was with *atsiagbekɔ* and other dance-drumming types. Only the hunter-warriors know the true story of origin and how monkeys may have been involved. The first performance was credited to the hunter-warriors, men of valor, who used it for their battle rituals around the 1500s (Mamattah 1978).

Unlike in the past when *atsiagbekɔ* was performed after battles so that the warriors could demonstrate their deeds of valor on the battlefield to those at home, it is performed today during funerals of important chiefs, stool festivals, state festivals and by professional and amateur cultural groups for entertainment.

Organization of the Dance-Drumming Ceremony

FORM AND STRUCTURE. There are five main phases of a traditional performance:

i.	*ʋulɔlɔ*	the processional ritual;
ii.	*adzo*	a tribute to the old warriors;
iii.	*ʋutsɔtsɔ*	main dance-drumming phase;
iv.	*hatsiatsia*	joining of songs or song cycle; and
v.	*ʋulɔlɔ*	the recessional ritual.

Phase One: *Uulɔlɔ*. The *vulɔlɔ* phase of the performance begins as a processional ritual from the home of the group's president or the chief of the village to the performance arena. This procession can take the performers throughout the whole village, dramatizing the original ritual done by the warriors to announce their arrival from war.

Through this procession the whole community is informed that the celebration will commence as soon as they arrive at the performance venue. *Uulɔlɔ* may sometimes be performed in the arena as part of the fourth phase, *hatsiatsia*. This performance is called "*slow agbekɔ*" by some academic institutions in Ghana. The *vutsɔtsɔ* in this context (academic classification) is also referred to as "fast agbekɔ."

Phase Two: *Adzo*. *Adzo*, or *adzokpa*, is an introductory ritual performance that pays tribute to the old warriors. It is performed as a remembrance of the warriors who died in battle and to invite their spirits to the celebration.

Adzo is also performed as an invocation to the gods and all the ancestors. The *adzo* ritual thus "opens the gates" for a successful performance, as recounted by dancer Killer Fiebor of Aŋlɔ Afiaɖenyigba.

This phase involves songs performed in free rhythm. The male dancers, starting with the lead dancer, will come forward to announce their names and explain the power behind their names and their bravery as warriors. Different songs will be called with response from the rest of the male dancers.

This exchange continues until the drummers join in to usher in the *vulɔlɔ/atsiawɔwɔ* phase. Female dancers sometimes join the *adzo* with their own songs.

FIGURE 6.1: Dzogadze *Atsiagbekɔ* male dancers in *Adzo* phase (2008).

Phase Three: *Uutsɔtsɔ*. *Uutsɔtsɔ* also referred to as *atsiawɔwɔ*, the main dance-drumming phase, can last for several hours depending on performers' stamina and the weather conditions at the time. The master drummer leads this phase of the performance. All other drummers, cantors and dancers take their signals from him.

Top, FIGURE 6.2: Dzogadze *Atsiagbekɔ* female dancers in *Uutsɔtsɔ* phase (2008). *Bottom*, FIGURE 6.3: Dzogadze *Atsiagbekɔ* male dancers assuming the role of the female dancers in the *Uutsɔtsɔ* phase (2008).

He dictates which *atsia* (stylistic dance routine or dance-drumming sequence) is performed and how many times it is performed. Female dancers who are positioned behind or to the side of the percussion ensemble will accompany the dance-drumming with songs.

Uutsɔtsɔ is interspersed with *adzokpi,* in which dancers dance in pairs or small groups. This is the highlight of the whole performance. Male dancers use this time to show off or to impress the audience with their well-rehearsed dance formations.

Female dancers who are positioned behind or beside the drummers will also take their turn in the performance arena during the *vutsɔtsɔ* and *adzokpi* to perform their dance routines. The male dancers assume the singing role of the females at this time.

Phase Four: *Hatsiatsia.* This phase involves the singing of songs based on philosophical, historical, reflective, topical, and human relationship themes. *Hatsiatsia* creates the opportunity for the dancers and musicians to rest and be ready for the next *vutsɔtsɔ* phase. *Hatsiatsia* may also be performed immediately after the *adzo* phase as an extended warm-up for the dancers.

Two types of songs are performed: i. songs that are accompanied partially by bells, rattles and beating the side of the wooden shell of the master drum, *atsimevu*; and ii. songs that are sung in their entirety in free rhythm with no accompaniment.

The lead dancer, sometimes assisted by the next best dancer in the group, leads the singing. They move forward with symbolic gestures to intone the songs. Though the goal is to provide room for relaxation, dancers may add light movements to emphasize specific points or themes in the songs.

The *hatsiatsia* phase is not included in most traditional performances in Ghana today. Much emphasis is put on the *adzo* phase to make up for this omission.

A second *vutsɔtsɔ* phase follows the *hatsiatsia;* otherwise, a brief *vulɔlɔ,* performed as recessional music and dance, ends the performance.

Songs

Atsiagbekɔ songs constitute an important part of the heritage of Eυe oral literature and are notable for their profound and thoughtful texts. The song texts are mostly a mixture of Eυe, proper Fɔn and corrupted Fɔn languages.

It is very difficult to understand some of the songs sung during performances. Themes largely concern the circumstances of war. Proverbs and other forms of allusive speech are usually used in *agbekɔ* songs. Texts generally relate to:

i.   divinities and gods;
ii.   historical facts;
iii. war circumstances of military conflict and stress, such as courage, loyalty, death, cowardice and sorrow; and
iv. social comment on topical issues.

Three categories of songs are performed in *atsiagbekɔ* performances: *vulɔlɔ, adzo* and *vutsɔtsɔ* songs. The main form used in these songs is mostly call and response. Tonal arrangements make use of the hemitonic and anhemitonic forms of the pentatonic scale. Refer to Part Six for transcriptions and analysis of songs.

The Percussion Ensemble

Instruments in the atsiagbekɔ ensemble and their functions are:

i.   Gakogui: Performs the timeline. May be replaced by *vukɔgo,* "beating the side of Atsimevu."

ii.   Axatse: Supports the timeline
iii. Kagan: Supporting drum
iv.   Totodzi: Supporting drum
v.   Kroboto: Supporting drum
vi.   Kidi: Supporting drum
vii. Atsimeʋu: Master/lead drum

FIGURE 6.4: Dzogadze *Atsiagbekɔ* percussion ensemble. Seated from left, front row: *kroboto, kidi, totodzi* and *kagan*. Standing from left: *atimeʋu*, timekeeper playing the side of the *atimeʋu* and *axatse*. The *gakogui* is not shown in this photograph but usually stands to the right of the *atimeʋu* (2008).

Dance Organization

DANCE ARENA. During the *ʋulɔlɔ* phase, the lead male dancer is followed by the other male dancers and the percussion ensemble, with the female dancers at the rear. The performers assume a military-style formation. Selected women and young apprentice drummers carry all the drums of the ensemble on their heads with the exception of the bell and rattles. This formation is shown on page 75, in Figure 6.5.

As performers enter the performance space, the percussion ensemble moves to the front of the arena, facing towards the center of the space. The male dancers take their position in the center of the space, facing the drummers.

The female dancers then take their position behind or by the side of the drummers with the audience encircling the performance space. The performance space is now set for the rest of the celebration.

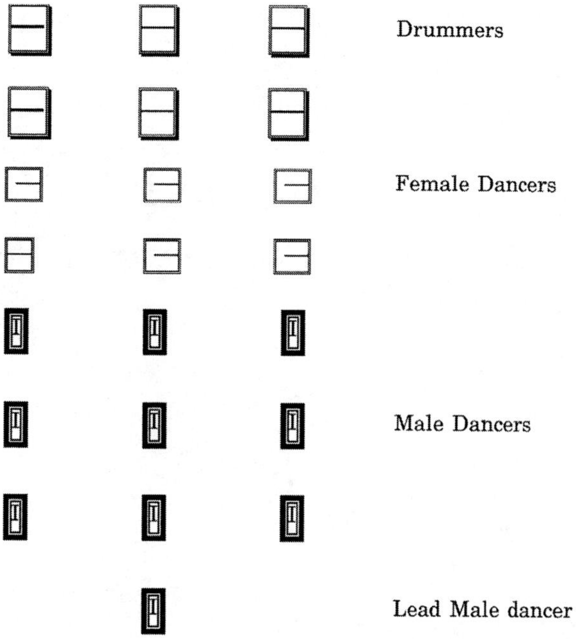

DANCE MOVEMENTS, DRAMATIC ENACTMENTS AND CHOREOGRAPHY. *Atsi-agbekɔ* is a highly stylized dance with specific movements based on Eʋe oral history. One of the outstanding features of the dance is the interaction between the master drummer and the dancers: "Every rhythmic theme played on the master drum has a corresponding sequence of dance movements which is timed to precisely match the drum rhythms" (Lock 1978).

Atsiagbekɔ can best be described as a strict dance. Participation is controlled. It takes quite a long period of rehearsals before a group comes out to perform. The master drum, atsimeʋu, controls the symbolic movements, *atsia*, executed by the dancers. Specific rhythmic patterns demand specific dance movements.

Movements or dance sequences may vary from place to place but there is little variation in Xekɔkɔ, or Xetsotso, the round-off dance, in the communities that perform Atsiagbekɔ.

Drummers

Female Dancers

Male Dancers

Lead Male dancer

FIGURE 6.5: *Atsiagbekɔ Uulɔlɔ* formation

According to Mawere Opoku, *Agbekɔ* dance makes use of real war motifs and stylized war movements. The women in the dance cheer up and counsel the male dancers (warriors) with their circling arm movements and songs.

FIGURE 6.6: Dzogadze *Atsiagbekɔ* Group in *Uulɔlɔ* phase (2008).

FIGURE 6.7: *Atsiagbekɔ* drums being carried in *Uulɔlɔ* phase (2008).

For effective communication, facial expressions must be natural, indicative of the dancers' feelings. Appreciation and admiration are expressed in the carriage of the head and torso, the slant of the body and the facial expression of the dancers (Opoku 1971, 11).

Costumes and Other Visual Art Forms

Varieties of costumes in traditional performances exist from place to place. Generally, the men wear *atsaka*, the special southern Eʋe dancing shorts, with a piece of cloth around the waist and a collarless top.

Female dancers wear a blouse with a double cloth wrapped around the body to knee-level, or *atible*, a cloth that is wrapped across their sternum area and hangs down to

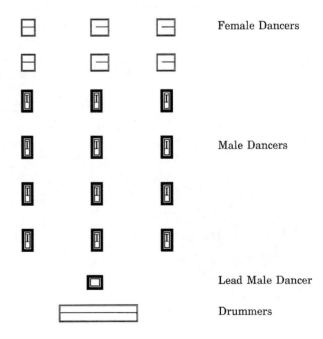

FIGURE 6.8: *Atsiagbekɔ Uutsɔtsɔ* and *Adzo* performance space

Above, FIGURE 6.9: Dzogadze *Atsigbekɔ* female dancers in *atible* costume (2008). *Right*, FIGURE 6.10: Dzogadze *Atsiagbekɔ* male dancer, S.K. Agudzamega with *sɔshi* (2008).

knee-level, stuffed at the buttocks, as in *adzogbo* and *atibladekame*.

Another visual used by male dancers as an extension of the body is the horsetail switch, known as *sɔshi*. In the olden days, actual war implements such as cutlasses, daggers, and guns (introduced by Europeans in the 16th century) were used. These real implements have been replaced with wooden ones.

Male dancers sometimes wear *kuku*, or *Togbenya,* a floppy hat. The lead dancer may carry a pouch symbolizing his status as the best dancer.

7. *Gadzo* Warriors' Dance-Drumming Ceremony

Historical Background and Development

Gadzo is one of the oldest traditional war dance-drumming ceremonies of the Eʋe in Southern Ghana and Togo. It was originally a war dance-drumming ritual performed in Ŋɔtsie after a successful battle.

The name gadzo, adopted from *gaxodzo,* or *gadzodzo,* which means hot iron, signifies the bravery of the Eʋes in Ŋɔtsie. It was this type of bravery and "hotness" on the battlefield that helped the southeastern Eʋe to escape from Ŋɔtsie, then ruled by King Agɔkɔli I, to their present locations in Ghana.

From Ŋɔtsie, *gadzo* spread through several towns in Togo—namely, *Tsiviefe, Yɔfe, Kevi,* and *Nuiefe*—and, finally, to southeastern Ghana. The late Mɔtu Agbovɔ and Bokɔ Agbukpa Wɔɖui are credited for introducing this dance-drumming ritual to Aŋlɔ-Afiaɖenyigba and Dzodze Kpɔɖoave respectively in the early 19th century.

Gadzo is also called *gazo, kini* or *yelu. Yelu* is derived from *helulo,* meaning, "Be ready with your weapons or spiritual powers," an invocation used by the Yeʋe cult during their ritual worship. A phase of *Yeʋe* religious dance-drumming performance, *misego,* is presently performed by the *Aŋlɔ Afiaɖenyigba gadzo* group and others as a tribute to the warriors who fought and died on behalf of the people during their migration from Ŋɔtsie.

Other performing groups in Ghana and Togo perform *adzotsotso* instead of *misego,* but with the same symbolic meaning. During performances, chants such as *"awezo,"* which means "be alert," and *"zobligeɖeme,"* which means, "the opponents are coming," are chanted as a call to arms to depict the original intent of this dance-drumming ritual.

Gadzo is usually performed in an open space with enough shade to protect the participants as in *agbadza* at *ʋɔnu* in the community. *Uɔnu* is a designated assembly ground in all Eʋe communities, used for state assemblies, meetings, and dance-drumming performances.

Gadzo is performed today as recreational dance-drumming at funerals, weddings, political and other social gatherings in the absence of wars.

Organization of the Dance-Drumming Ceremony

FORM AND STRUCTURE. A traditional performance usually has six phases:

i.	*misego*	tribute to the ancestors;
ii.	*ʋulɔlɔ*	the processional ritual;
iii.	*ʋutsɔtsɔ/Atsiawɔwɔ*	main dance-drumming phase;

iv.	*hatsiatsia/dzododo*	joining of songs;
v.	*vutsɔtsɔ/atsiawɔwɔ*	main dance-drumming phase; and
vi.	*vulɔlɔ*	the recessional ritual.

Phase One: *Misego*. *Misego* is performed in this context as *adzotsotso*, a religious ritual in honor of the ancestors who gave their lives during battles, especially those who led the migration of the Eʋes from Ŋɔtsie. *Misego* is exclusively performed by the *Aŋlɔ Afiaɖenyigba gadzo* group.

Most amateur groups, as well as professional national dance companies, in Ghana who stage this performance outside traditional contexts have adopted the *Aŋlɔ Afiaɖenyigba* version. *Misego*, also called *hūsago*, was the dance-drumming used by the southeastern Eʋe of Ghana during their migration from Ŋɔtsie in the Republic of Togo to their present settlements. *Misego*, or *hūsago*, is one of the phases in *Yeʋe* ritual performance.

Yeʋe, the traditional god of *Xebieso*, *Hū* or *Tɔhonɔ*, is a thunder god, the member of a pantheon with historical relations to the Yoruba Shango and Xevioso of Benin. The Yeʋe cult is one of the most "powerful" and most secretive among those that exist in West Africa. The Yeʋe musical repertoire usually involves at least seven, or at most nine, dance forms, such as *tsitrenuha*, *hūsago*, *aʋleʋu*, *adaʋu*, *soʋu*, *afɔtɔe*, *sogbadze*, and *sogbaʋu*.

Misego is performed with the full percussion ensemble in strict rhythm with the dancers in a military-style formation. The dance movements take the dancers forward and backwards, incorporating varied agbadza dance elements.

Other groups, especially those in the hinterland, start their performances with *adzotsotso*. *Adzotsotso*, unlike *misego*, is performed when the dancers converge at the center of the performance arena, standing with their bodies slightly bent forward and singing songs in free rhythm. This introductory phase is performed in other dance-drumming types, such as Atrikpui, Atibladekame and Agbadza.

Phase Two: *Uʋlɔlɔ*. Once *misego* is completed, the performance arena is reset for the *vulɔlɔ* phase. The performers then retreat to change costumes for the procession to the performance arena.

FIGURE 7.1: Aŋlɔ Afiaɖenyigba *Gadzo* Percussion Ensemble and Chorus in *Misego* phase (2007).

FIGURE 7.2: Aŋlɔ Afiaɖenyigba *Gadzo* Dancers in *Misego* phase (2007).

This processional dance-drumming reenacts the return of the warriors after a battle, similar to the *atsiagbekɔ vulɔlɔ* phase. A detailed description of this phase can be found under Atsiagbekɔ. Communities that do not perform the *vulɔlɔ* usually move straight from *adzotsotso* to *vutsɔtsɔ*, the third phase.

Phase Three: *Uutsɔtsɔ.* Henɔ, the lead singer, who in most cases is the lead male dancer as well, leads *vutsɔtsɔ* or *atsiawɔwɔ*, the main dance-drumming phase. Other male and female dancers who form the chorus, *haxiawo*, support the lead singer.

Uutsɔtsɔ starts in free rhythm with only songs, but this section quickly changes into strict rhythm accompanied by the full percussion ensemble. It is in this phase that the male dancers reenact war scenes as in *atrikpui* dance-drumming.

Phase Four: *Hatsiatsia.* Hatsiatsia, or *dzododo*, in gadzo involves the performance of songs based on the history and gallantry of the Eυes. It is during this phase that the percussion ensemble is refreshed to be ready for the next *vutsɔtsɔ* phase which is more dramatic and intense.

Songs, which are led by the male lead singer or dancer, may be performed in free rhythm, accompanied partially by bells, rattles and/or a few drums. Although the intent is to provide an opportunity for the dancers to relax and gather energy for the next *vutsɔtsɔ* phase, dancers may add light movements to emphasize specific points or themes in the songs.

A second performance of *vutsɔtsɔ* follows the *hatsiatsia* phase. This phase may include staged war stories, "dance drama," and *adzokpi*, as in atsiagbekɔ, when dancers perform in smaller groups. A final *vulɔlɔ* phase, performed as a recessional dance-drumming, concludes the performance with songs, hand-clapping, and with or without the rest of the percussion ensemble.

Songs

Songs in *gadzo* are of the *atsiagbekɔ* type. The texts talk about the history, religious beliefs, social life and gallantry of the Eυes. Four types of songs are performed: *adzotsotso* or *misego* songs, *vulɔlɔ* songs, *hatsiatsia* songs and *vutsɔtsɔ* songs.

Songs sung in both *misego* and *adzotsotso* serve as invocations to the spirits of the ancestors

FIGURE 7.4: A scene from a dance drama by the Aŋlɔ Afiaɖenyigba *Gadzo* Group (2008).

and gods and as a remembrance of all the warriors who have passed — especially those who fought battles and led the people on their migration.

Themes of the songs in *misego* in particular are those dedicated to Yeʋe, God, and the migration stories of the Eʋe. *Adzotsotso* songs, however, are those of the Atrikpui type, which relate to the gallantry of and oaths taken by the warriors before battles.

Ʋulɔlɔ and *hatsiatsia* songs are those that recount the history of the Eʋes with particular reference to their sojourn in Ŋɔtsie. A close study of these songs reveals the strength, values, beliefs and other aspects of the sociocultural background of the Eʋe. These songs are therefore more strophic, with solo and chorus refrains, declamations, and chants, and structurally are in simple ternary form.

Ʋutsɔtsɔ songs, on the other hand, are in simple binary form. They may be comprised of one or two simple phrases performed by the *henɔ*, lead singer, and chorus, repeated several times with variations in the text, melody and rhythm by the *henɔ*. These songs provide excitement for the dancers.

The Percussion Ensemble

The *gadzo* percussion ensemble originally included: *agbomlɔanyi* as lead drum, *kidi*, *kagan*, *tigo*, and several *axatse* as supporting instruments. The present instruments of the percussion ensemble include: *gadzoʋuga*, a medium-sized version of the *atsimeʋu* as lead drum; *kpetsi/kidi*; *kagan/kegeyi*; *agbobli/sogo*; *tigo/gakogui*; and *axatse*, which could be doubled. *Agbobli* may be omitted during the *misego* and replaced with a second kagan or all together.

Dance Organization

THE DANCE ARENA. In the context of *misego*, the dancers assume a military-style formation in front of the percussion ensemble. The same formation is used for the staged performance after the *ʋulɔlɔ* phase.

During the *ʋulɔlɔ* phase, as in *atsiagbekɔ*, the lead male dancer, followed by the rest of the

FIGURE 7.6: Aŋlɔ Afiaɖenyigba *Gadzo* Percussion Ensemble in *Misego* phase (2006). Seated, from left: *kagan*, *kagan* and *kidi*. Standing is *gadzovuga* with *gakogui* and *axatse* partially covered; seated at opposite sides.

male and female dancers, leads in the percussion ensemble. The remaining performers serving as chorus are positioned at the rear as shown below.

DANCE MOVEMENTS, DRAMATIC ENACTMENTS AND CHOREOGRAPHY. Dance movements in the *vutsɔtsɔ* phase in gadzo are full of *abebubuwo,* which are proverbial, symbolic actions and gestures. These dance movements, symbolizing episodes in battles, are highlighted during staged performances. Such groups as the Aŋlɔ Afiaɖenyigba *gadzo,* and those that they have influenced, perform this group dance choreography.

A critical study of Eʋe traditional performance culture that is "based on some sorts of attitudes which incorporate its myths, legends, history, bards and arts" (Amoaku 1975, 1), provides the meaning of these dance movements and also prepares the dancers to execute the movements with precision and passion.

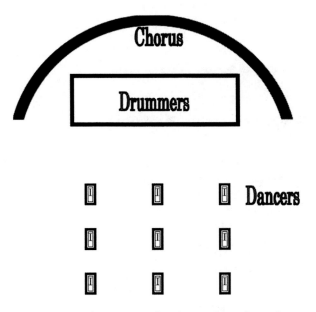

FIGURE 7.7: *Gadzo Misego* and *Atsiawɔwɔ* dance formation

Learning the dance and drumming for the staged group choreographies and performances may take several months. Gifted dancers can easily pick up the dance movements through participation and observation but they also need frequent practice and rehearsals under the direction of the lead singer, dancer and master drummer.

Practices and rehearsals are usually held nocturnally as decided by the group. Apprentice trainee programs are also conducted to induct young dancers and drummers into the groups.

The basic dance movement in *vutsɔtsɔ* involve the agile movements of the body, arms and legs. At times, the legs move consonantly with the arms—i.e., the legs and arms move backwards and forwards with much agility. Varieties of *Agbadza* dance movements are also exhibited.

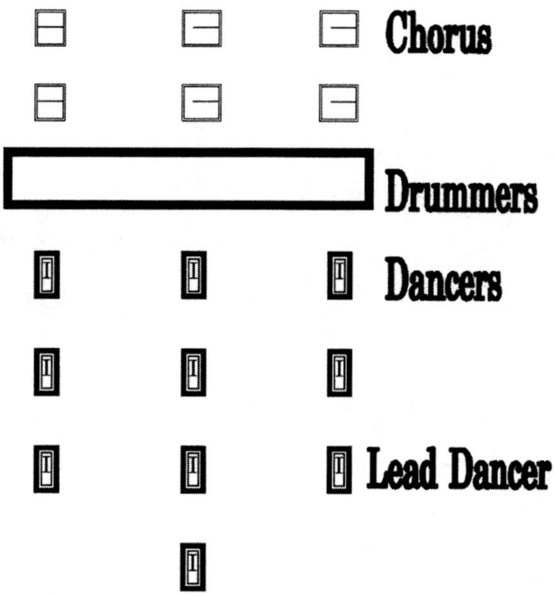

FIGURE 7.8: *Gadzo Uulɔlɔ* formation

Costumes and Other Visual Art Forms

Costumes used in the past were full war regalia with talismans and other props associated with hunting, farming and wars. The dancers also carried daggers, guns and short, sharpened cutlasses.

Contemporary costumes for the dancers include *atsaka*, the special southern Eʋe dancing shorts with a piece of cloth (usually red in color) around the waist held in place by an *agbadza,* a war girdle, to hold their daggers. All performers also wear a collarless top or shirt.

Some groups are replacing sharpened daggers and cutlasses with wooden ones or batons. Groups that perform *gadzo* for recreation and funeral prefer *sɔshi*, horsetails or switches, to the wooden daggers.

Females in the performance usually wear a blouse with a double cloth wrapped around the body to knee-level or *atible*, a cloth that is wrapped across the sternum area, hangs down to knee-level, and is stuffed at the buttocks, as used in *atsiagbekɔ.*

8. *Gahʋ* Recreational Dance-Drumming Ceremony

Historical Background and Development

Gahu emanated from the rich cultural practices associated with marriages, presentation of new babies to the community and puberty rites of the *Yoruba* of Nigeria in the early 19th century. Originally, it was performed by the Eʋes in Badagri in southeastern Nigeria and the Xɔgbonu of Benin, and was brought to Ghana in the early 1950s.

The Nigerian origin of the ceremony can be seen today in the rich Yoruba costumes worn by dancers, and in the lyrics of some of the songs, which are in corrupted versions of the Yoruba and Fɔn languages of Nigeria and Benin, respectively. Gahu was, and is still today, a recreational dance-drumming for the southeastern Eʋe in Ghana and Togo to demonstrate or "show off" their wealth and social standing.

In Ghana specifically, this dance-drumming is performed at *Avete, Xetɔlogo, Akatsi* in the *Avenɔ* traditional area, and *Anyako, Keta, Tadzeʋu, Devego, Penyi* and *Dzodze,* all in the *Aŋlɔ* traditional area. Unfortunately, due to the lack of rich Yoruba costumes, youth interest, and dedicated trainers, *Gahu* is fast becoming extinct. Work by professional, amateur and educational dance companies, however, is helping to reverse this trend.

The words *ga*, meaning money, wealth, or greatness, and *hū* or *Uu*, meaning drum or dance-drumming type, combine, describing this performance as a "money dance-drumming" or money dance ceremony. *Gahu* is now performed in traditional context during festivals, political events, weddings and funerals—when a member dies or is bereaved.

Organization of the Dance-Drumming Ceremony

FORM AND STRUCTURE. Gahu is performed in four main phases: *hatsiatsia, atsiawɔwɔ, ayoɖeɖe* and *ʋutsɔtsɔ.* The sequence or order of these phases may vary depending on the context of performance.

Phase One: *Ayoɖeɖe. Gahu,* like other southeastern Eʋe dance-drumming types, starts with a ritual ceremony with greetings and prayers to the ancestors. Known as *ayoɖeɖe*, or simply *ayoo* in this context, this performance begins after the performance arena is set.

Ayoo can be identified mainly by its songs rather than its categorization as a distinct phase of the performance. *Ayoo*'s placement in the performance varies by location and context. Since the songs are to welcome and greet the audience or spectators, whose role is vital for a successful performance, many groups will delay this phase of the performance until they arrive.

Ayoo songs are mostly performed in free rhythm with occasional accompaniment by bells and rattles while the dancers, who serve as the main chorus, walk in a circle and sometimes stop to salute the audience with specific gestures. *Hatsiatsia* usually starts most traditional performances as a way to announce to the community that the performers are ready to begin the performance. See Figure 8.1 on page C-5 of color insert.

Phase Two: *Hatsiatsia*. *Hatsiatsia*, song cycle, or joining of songs phase, serves as a rehearsal or review of songs that will be used in *ʋutsɔtsɔ*, the main phase of the performance, in addition to alerting the public of the beginning of the whole performance. The songs in this context are of the *ʋufoha*, dance-drumming type, and provide sustenance for the dance and dancers in the *ʋutsɔtsɔ* phase.

The *hatsiatsia* phase may be performed after the *ʋutsɔtsɔ* phase. In that case, the songs are directed to the public instead of the dancers. The songs address and relate to topical issues that emanate from society.

The songs are very lyrical and strophic. In both instances, the dancers/chorus move anticlockwise in a circle, accompanied by bells and rattles. A signal from a whistle blown by the lead cantor ends this phase of the performance.

Phase Three: *Atsiawɔwɔ*. The *atsiawɔwɔ*, or *adzo*, phase of the performance includes several brief dance-drumming types adopted from the Eʋe dance-drumming repertoire, such as *Adzro*, *Agbadza*, *Akpalu*, and *Kinka*. This phase serves as a warm-up and preparation for the *ʋutsɔtsɔ* phase.

Each dance-drumming selection is started with an unaccompanied, free-rhythm, introductory song solo in which the cantor establishes all of the textual, melodic, rhythmic and structural aspects of the song. The chorus/dancers then join with full percussion accompaniment with specific dance movements.

Only members of the group with prior knowledge of the choreography are allowed to participate in this phase of the performance. Inexperienced dancers are also excused from this phase of the performance.

Phase Four: *Uutsɔtsɔ*. *Uutsɔtsɔ*, the main dance-drumming phase, which follows, may last for several hours. Dancers, as in the *hatsiatsia* phase, perform in a circular, anticlockwise direction.

Vigorous dance movements (emphasized by the *gboba*, the lead drum), an increase in the volume of singing, and the percussion ensemble with audience participation are highlights of this phase. It is in this phase that the essence of the *Gahu* dance-drumming is exhibited.

Another feature of this phase is that the dance becomes more vigorous, brisk and faster when the *gboba* plays a signal, which prepares the dancers to end the singing and focus on the dance. Songs in this phase are very unique because they mirror the dance movements. The dancers act out the main themes of the songs with specific dance gestures. Only instrumentalists and elders sit during the entire performance.

Songs

Themes of *Gahu* songs relate to historical, philosophical, topical and human issues. Some of the themes illustrate proverbs, greetings, love, courtship, death, praise, ridicule and gratitude. As observed in *atrikpui*, *Gahu* songs use a liturgical language comprised of fragments of French, Yoruba, Fɔn, Hausa and Eʋe.

Gahu songs are generally in simple binary and ternary forms. Call and response, solo and chorus refrain are the main forms used in the songs. Hemitonic and anhemitonic forms of tritonic, tetratonic, pentatonic, hexatonic and heptatonic diatonic scales are used in the songs. These tonal arrangements are attributed to the vast spread of *gahu* and its influence from several cultures in West Africa.

Polyphony is conceived melodically as parts performing different roles. The overlapping and crossing of parts develop into layers of harmonic structures. Sporadic occurrence of thirds, fourths, fifths, sixths, and octaves between different voices results in multi-part singing.

The Percussion Ensemble

Instruments of the contemporary *Gahu* percussion ensemble are: *atoke, gakogui, axatse, kagan, kidi, agbobli, gboba* and *atsimeʋu*. The *atoke*, or *toke*, performs the timeline, a cyclic rhythmic framework that guides the rest of the ensemble and the dancers.

The *gakogui* sometimes functions in place of the *toke*. It may be used to embellish the *toke* when the two are used in performance. Several *axatse* and a *kagan* perform supporting ostinato patterns to the *atoke* and *gakogui*.

The *kidi* and *agbobli,* as response drums, play in dialogue with the *gboba*, the master drum. The *agbobli* assumes the function of the *gboba* when the *latter* takes a rest for a brief period when vigorous dancing is not going on.

The *atsimeʋu* is now being used in Gahu because of its role during the *atsiawɔwɔ* phase. It is the lead drum in this phase and can also be used in the *ʋutsɔtsɔ* section of the performance by some groups.

The sound and rhythmic patterns and variations on the *gboba* makes *Gahu* what it is, so this instrument will be emphasized in the main dance section.

Dance Organization

THE DANCE ARENA. *Gahu* is performed in a circular arena. The instrumentalists sit on a bench at the rear, and in front of them sit elders and executives, with the cantors standing. The

FIGURE 8.2: Tadzeʋu *Gahu* Percussion Ensemble. Seated from left, front row: *agbobli, kidi, kagan, gakogui* and three *axatse* players. Standing, from left: *gboba* and *atimeʋu*, partially covered in this photograph (2007).

dancers, who form the core of the chorus, form a big circle in front, moving anti-clockwise. During the performance, the cantors can also move both clockwise and anticlockwise when intoning songs, traveling in and out of the dancers' circle.

DANCE MOVEMENTS, DRAMATIC ENACTMENTS AND CHOREOGRAPHY. *Gahu* is a sophisticated, stylistic, waist and "shake-your-bottom" dance that requires special long training sessions. The dance movements are specially choreographed so that no audience member can just join in without prior rehearsal with the group.

Mawere Opoku, a renowned Ghanaian choreographer and founder of the Ghana Dance Ensemble, describes the *Gahu* dance as a blend of the pelvic shift style of the Yoruba and a softer and lighter version of the southern Eʋe torso contraction. He further states that inflections, gaiety and abandonment form the expressive keynotes in the dance (Opoku 1971, 14).

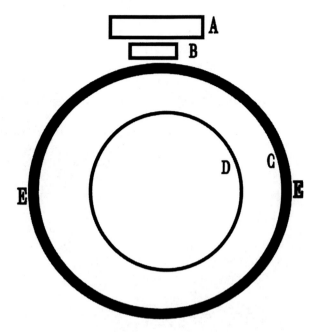

FIGURE 8.3: *Gahu* performance Arena. A: percussion ensemble; B: elders/executives; C: chorus/dancers; D: cantors; E: audience.

The dance itself provides opportunity for individual expression and improvisation. It is flexible and light-hearted. The movements in the dance itself are characterized by a two-count forward movement by the left foot, and then by the right. At an exact point in time, the hip moves with the legs.

The shoulder also twists to the right and left accordingly, with the dancer holding his arms

FIGURE 8.4: Tadzeʋu *Gahu* Group dancers at the start of a performance (2007).

curved and stretched forward. A good dancer is judged not only by responding accurately to the rhythms of the instruments, but also by his or her facial expressions.

Although during festivals and other social occasions involving the whole community everybody is permitted to join in the *ʋutsɔtsɔ* phase, the *atsiawɔwɔ* phase is still reserved for the group.

Costumes and Other Visual Art Forms

Costumes in *Gahu* are a variety of the rich Yoruba of Nigeria *agbaɖa* and *buba*, worn by

men and women for wedding ceremonies. Both *agbaɖa* and *buba* have several components made up of expensive jewelry, necklaces, beads, dresses made from silk materials, headgear, and earrings. Extensions of the body can be seen in the use of very expensive dark spectacles or sunglasses, and handkerchiefs with shoes or sandals to match.

The main Gahu female dress has several layers adopted from the Yoruba women's wedding outfit, *buba*. Traditionally, the Yoruba *buba* has four components: *buba*, blouse; *iro*, wrapper; *gele*, headgear; and *ipele*, shawl. In Gahu, the *iro* is doubled and worn up to below knee-level under *aʋlaya*, a type of skirt made up of several layers of cloth (with different designs) as in *Adzogbo*.

The *ipele* is worn around the waist to secure the *aʋlaya* in place instead of the shoulder.

The men's' *agbaɖa*, also known as *boubou* or *bubu*, is made up of three dresses or layers: *sokoto,*

Left: FIGURE 8.5: Tadzeʋu *Gahu* female dancer in full costume. *Below:* FIGURE 8.6: Tadzeʋu *Gahu* female dancers in costume (2007).

FIGURE 8.7: Tadzeʋu *Gahu* male dancers in costume (2007).

trousers that narrow towards the ankles; *dashiki*, a long-sleeved shirt; and *agbaḍa*, a wide-open gown with a cap to match.

Both *agbaḍa* and *buba* in Gahu were originally made from silk, but due to financial constraints, kente and other cotton textile materials are now being used. *Agbaḍa* is also being replaced with *batakari*, a smock-like tunic usually worn over any pair of long pants in Ghana.

Part Two.
Dance-Drumming of the
Central and Northern Eves

"*Lack of knowing who you are, identifying your strengths and weaknesses, makes you a slave.*"
— Eve Proverb

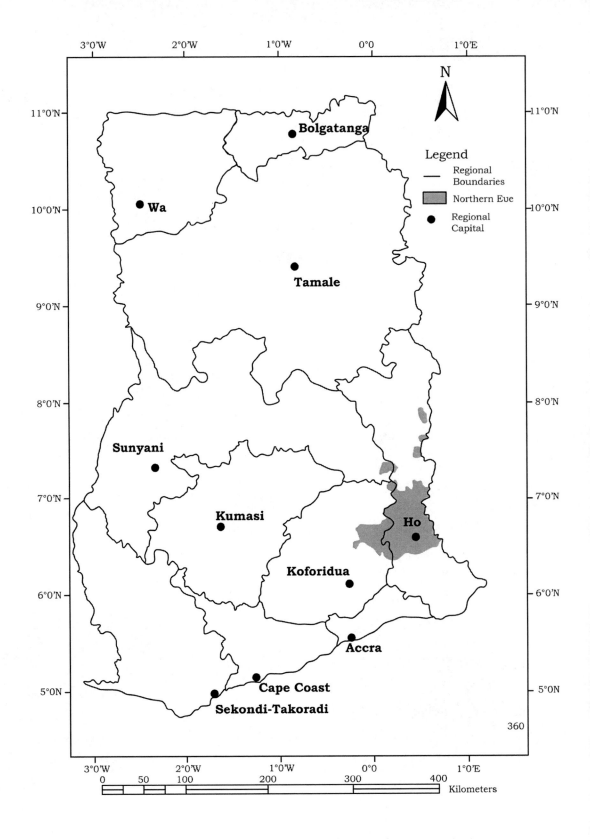

FIGURE 9.1: Map of Ghana Showing Central and Northern Eʋe Territories

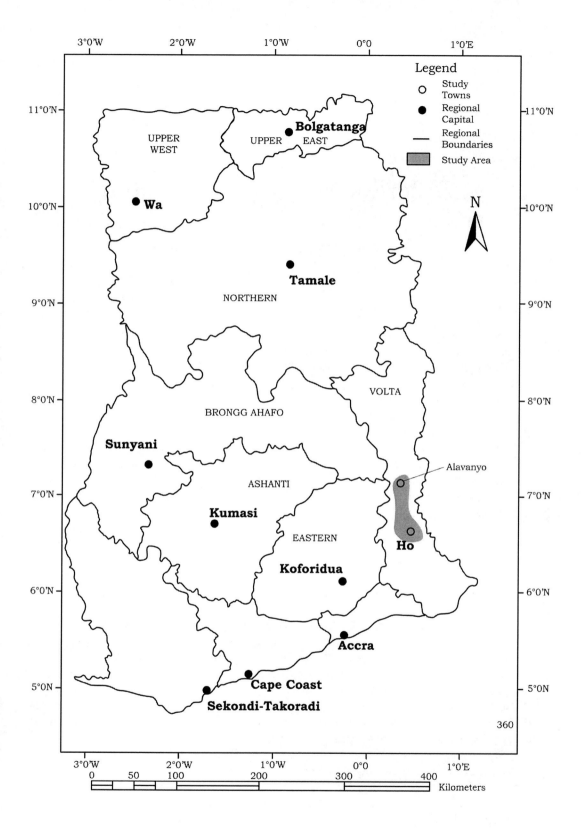

FIGURE 9.2: Map of Ghana Showing Research Area

9. Historical, Geographical, Cultural and Social Background of the Central and Northern Eʋes of Ghana

The People and the Land

The central and northern Eʋes, conveniently designated as Eʋemeawo or Eʋedomeawo—the Eʋes from the Dip Valley, are part of the major Eʋe block that migrated from Ŋɔtsie to their present settlement early in the 14th century. Present northern Eʋeland is bounded in the south by the southeastern Eʋe territories; in the north by the Buem and Krachi traditional and political administrative districts—all in the Volta region; in the east by the Republic of Togo; and in the west by the Volta River and parts of the eastern region of Ghana.

The northern Eʋe territory is divided into two major geographical blocks: central uplands and the plains. The uplands are part of the Togo-Akwapim mountain ranges that cut across most of Togo and Ghana and are comprised of ranges such as: Abutia-Taviefe-Dodome, Peki-Avatime, Kpoeta-Agɔme-Dayi-Akpɔsɔ, and other scattered mountains at Logba, Leklebi, Santrokofi, Akpafu and Buem. The highest point in Ghana, Afajato Mountain, is located in the Kpoeta-Agɔme-Dayi-Akpɔsɔ range.

The plains are mostly the areas between the various mountain ranges. These areas comprise the southern, central and northern plains. The southern plain is made up of savanna vegetation with scattered baobab trees. The central plain also enjoys savanna vegetation with scattered semi-deciduous forests and the northern plains provide the conditions for evergreen forests.

The Eʋemeawo occupy the central and northern Eʋe territories of the Volta region in Ghana and Togo. In Ghana, they are located in the Ho, Peki, Kpando, Hohoe and Awudome traditional establishments, and are comprised of the following people: Asogliawo, Pekiawo, Awudomeawo, Danyiawo, Agome Kpalimeawo, Kpedzeawo, Kpandoawo, Alavanyoawo, Gbiawo, Dzoloawo, Anfoegawo, Leklebiawo, Veawo, Logbawo, Adakluawo, Abutiawo and Vakpoawo. For administrative convenience, the Eʋemeawo are grouped into the Adaklu-Anyigbe, South-Dayi Ho, Kpando, Hohoe and Jasikan political districts.

Dialects overlap and dialectical variations exist galore with confusion reaching perfection in the Fiafiagbe areas. These Fiafiagbe areas are essentially pockets of non–Eʋes who have their own distinct languages but now utilize a great deal of Eʋe vocabulary.

The Eʋes in general call these people Fiafialawo, the people who speak a strange language, indicating that they are non-indigenous ethnic groups. Some of these Fiafialawo live in the Avatime, Tafi, Logba, Likpe, Bowli, Akpafu and Santrokofi traditional areas.

Pockets of Akan-speaking people also reside further north among the Eʋedomeawo, such as the Buems, Krachis, and Nkonyas, as well as others found in Kadjebi, Jasikan, Papase, Wora-

94

wora and Apesokubi. Despite the conflicting dialects spoken, the Volta River has united the Evemeawo into a single ethnic unit and brought the area into a geographical entity that is not homogenous, but does have similar customs, beliefs and habits.

Historical Background

The Evedomeawo share a history with their southeastern Eve counterparts beginning during the period before their settlement in Ŋɔtsie until their migration. Once the Eves left Ŋɔtsie, the Evedomeawo of today traveled in small or extended family groups and totemic clans which were led by famed hunters and farmers towards the Volta River in the north. They would occasionally stop to establish temporary villages, camps and farms wherever they found rivers and arable land. The search for and the desire to protect these fertile lands for their livelihood resulted in many intertribal wars. The fittest retained the land and the defeated moved on to find new locations. This was the settlement history of the majority of the Evedomeawo.

The Fiafialawo, however, migrated from other regions of Ghana in the early 18th century to their present settlements. Those Fiafialawo found in the Avatime area, for example, came from among the Ahanta and those in Santrokofi from among the Nzema in Wenchi from the western region of Ghana.

The Fiafiagbewo, unique languages spoken by the Avatime people — Siyase, and Seleh, spoken by the Santrokofi, are a mixture of Eve and Ahanta and Eve and Nzema respectively. Pockets of Akan-speaking people found among the Evedomeawo of today in the Buem, Jasikan and Krachi districts came in the early 18th century from the Brong Ahafo and eastern regions of Ghana through the Afram Plains when the Volta River displaced them.

The Evedomeawo were also involved in several wars with the Asantes of the present-day Ashanti region of Ghana. In particular, in the war between the Asogliawo of Ho and the Asantes on June 26, 1869, "the Asantes saw the greatest humiliation and lost most of their valiant men in the hands of Hoawo under Howusu of Dome on behalf of the Fiaga of Asɔgli state" (Fianu 1986, 26). Many of their artifacts, including musical instruments, were also captured in the process.

Social and Cultural Profile

POLITICAL AUTHORITY. Political systems among the Evedomeawo are similar to those in the southeastern Eve settlements as well as other West African groups such as the Ga, Adangbes and Yorubas, who share a common migratory history.

The chief is the center of political activity among the northern Eves. The basis of social organization is the clan and membership passes through the father. Inheritance is through the male line. Clan heads select chiefs. Succession to chiefship is vested in the family through stool elders, *zikpuitɔwo* or *zikpuimegawo,* and is patrilineal.

Festivals among the Evedomeawo, though varied, have roots in the harvest festivals celebrated by all Eves in Ŋɔtsie. The main crops were yam and wheat, which were harvested annually, and the harvest season opened with a great yam festival, *Teduza.*

This festival is celebrated during the lunar month of September. After the migration to Ghana, this festival came to be celebrated separately under different contexts in addition to new festivals, which related to specific episodes and problems encountered during their migrations. Some of these festivals are: i. *Sasadu,* celebrated by the people of Alavanyo, Sovie, Saviefe and Akrofu; ii. *Danyibakaka-Kpando*; and iii. *Gligbaza-Ho, Lukusi-Ve* areas, *Agadevi-Have, Duawokpeza-Vakpo* and seven sister towns.

ECONOMIC ACTIVITIES. Subsistence farming of yams, maize, cocoa, vegetables and timber are the main economic activities of the people. Inland fishing is practiced by settlements along the many rivers including the Volta River, the longest and largest in Ghana. Modern commerce, petty trade, and small business are common among the people.

RELIGION. Religious practices among the Eʋedomeawo include the worship of numerous deities and cults through which the people reach the Supreme Being, *Mawuga*. Eʋedomeawo believe in the existence of ancestral spirits and therefore reserve worship for them. Worship of their gods includes pouring libation and worship of ancestral stools, *zikpuiza*, or *kpukpowawa*.

The introduction of Christian religions, the Catholic and Basel missionaries and their churches to the Eʋedomeawo in the early 19th century, and the introduction of other church groups in the 20th century, have provided other avenues for worship. Both the indigenous and Christian religions continue to shape the moral and social behaviors of the people.

PERSPECTIVES AND MUSICAL CONCEPTS. Eʋedomeawo hold the same perspectives about the performing arts—especially music and dance—as do the southeastern Eʋes discussed in Part One of the book. As a result of several encounters with the Akans, Guans and other ethnic groups however, the Eʋedomeawo have adopted many elements of their musical style.

Various forms of the heptatonic scale are preferred over the pentatonic scale. The traditional performance norm is to keep the normal pitch of the seventh degree of the scale in the heptatonic scale when ascending but flatten it when descending in a song or any melodic organization. Harmony or multi-part singing or organization of melodies results in intervals of thirds, sixths, and octaves.

The various socio-cultural activities governing life events, starting with the outdooring (naming ceremony) of newborns—*vihehedego*, through puberty rites—*gbɔto*, to funeral celebrations and other religious activities, are all music and dance events. Music and dance are an integral part of these activities, and are intended to entertain during events in which the whole community takes part.

Religious music for the numerous deities and cults is simply called *trɔvu* or *dzovu*. Occupational music and dance is mainly for the hunters and warriors, who are called *adevu* and *akpi*, respectively. Activities for life cycle events include puberty songs, *gbɔtohawo*, which are performed mostly by women; children's play songs, *fefehawo*; and choral laments, *avihawo*, also a female performance.

Although the majority of musical types such as *tuidzi, akpese, gbolo, agbeyeye, totoeme, zigi, asiko, pramproʋu,* and *egbanegba*, center around social occasions, there are specific music and dance types for political institutions. Political music and dance are specific traditions associated with chieftaincy. These musical activities referred to as "court music" are connected with the installation of chiefs, destoolment, state assemblies, state processions, state funerals and durbars.

Vocal music at the courts of chiefs includes female praise songs (*osaye*) and male songs (*ampoti*) or war declamations. Specific instruments are also reserved for political musical activities such as *atumpani*, talking drum; *laklevu*, leopard drum; *ladzo*, horn; *ekpo* or *kpodoga*, single bell; and *gakpevi*, double bell.

Instruments favored in most traditional musical types and those used discussed in this section are: *gakpevi, mba, dawuro, kretsiwa, mba, akoge, ladzo, akaye, ʋuvi, asiʋui, tamali, krokoto* and *ʋuga*.

With the exception of the *tamalin*, all drums used by the Eʋedomeawo are carved. This process is known as *ʋukpakpa*. *Ʋukpakpa* involves the same process that is used in *ʋutoto* by the southeastern Eʋe.

INSTRUMENTS. **Gakpevi.** The *gakpevi*, also known as the *gagbleve*, is described as the double bell. It is adopted from the southern Eʋe people and is a recent addition to percussion ensembles—especially contemporary recreational groups. It is also made from a solid metal scrap.

The instrument is made of two bells (small and big) joined together so that the smaller bell rests on the big bell. Sound is produced by either striking on the small or big bell with a straight, one-foot stick. Refer to Part One, Chapter 1 for more notes and a playing technique for this instrument.

Mba. Wooden clappers made from bamboo strips. These are played in pairs as rhythmic instruments to emphasize bell and rattle patterns and also to accompany songs and other dance-drumming types. In *adevu*, hunters' music, for example, the *mba* is used instead of bells.

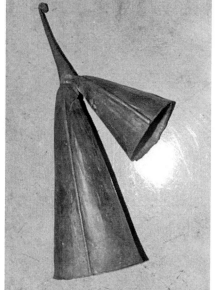

FIGURE 9.3: *Gakpevi*

Left, FIGURE 9.4: *Mba*

Kretsiwa. The *kretsiwa*, also known as *akoge*, is described as a finger bell or castanet. It is made from a solid piece of metal. The instrument has two parts. The main body is egg-shaped with an opening at one end. The middle finger passes through this opening

FIGURE 9.6: *Kretsiwa*

Left, FIGURE 9.5: *Mba* technique as illustrated by members of the Alavanyo *Adevu* Group (2007).

to support the body of the instrument. The second part of the instrument is a metal ring worn on the thumb. Sound is produced by striking the ring against the body. Two or three of these instruments may be used in an ensemble. Players of these instruments usually perform while standing. See Figure 9.7 on page C-6 of color insert.

Gakogoe. The *gakogoe* is similar to the *atoke*, a boat-shaped or slit bell used by the southeastern Eʋe. This is a self-sounding bell constructed from iron metal materials. Striking the top outer body of the bell held loosely in the left palm with a piece of straight iron or a six-inch nail held in the right hand generates sound. The *gakogoe* keeps the timeline in most dance-drumming performances. When two are combined, they are tuned to different pitches. See Figure 9.9 on page C-6 and Figure 9.10 on page C-7 of color insert.

Lādzo. The *lādzo*, or *eko*, the horn from a buffalo or variety of big game or animals, is technically regarded and used as a side-blown wind instrument reserved solely for the chief. The *lādzo* is played as a solo "talking wind instrument" to praise chiefs or in pairs in dance-drumming ensembles at the court.

In *Adevu* dance-drumming however, the *lādzo* is used as an idiophone, providing rhythmic phrases that serve as guides to the whole performance. Sound is generated by striking the side outer body of the horn held

FIGURE 9.8: Varieties of *gakokoe*

FIGURE 9.11: Varieties of *ladzo*

loosely in the left hand with a piece of straight stick, or *mba*, held in the right hand. A pair is used in this context.

Akaye. The *akaye* is classified as a shaken, non-melodic idiophone. It is made of beads or seeds placed in a hollowed gourd. It emphasizes the rhythmic pattern played by the *gakokoe* in most dance-drumming types. Sound is produced on the *akaye* by holding the neck with one hand and throwing, rolling or shaking it in the air or striking the body against the second cupped palm. The *akaye* is used solely by women in all northern Eʋe musical events.

Uʋvi and ***Asiʋui.*** These are single-headed drums with bottle necks at the base. They are

Left, FIGURE 9.12: *Ladzo* techniques as illustrated by members of the Alavanyo *Adevu* Group (2007).

Above, FIGURE 9.13: *Akaye. Right*, FIGURE 9.14: *Akaye* techniques as illustrated by members of the Alavanyo *Gbolo* Group (2007).

played in sitting position with the drums slightly tilted forward and held between the knees. The *vuvi* and *asivui* may be carved in the same size. You can differentiate the two by tuning the *vuvi* a little higher in pitch. The *asivui* leads most percussion ensembles while the *vuvi* serves as the main supporting drum. The hand or palm tech-

Above left, FIGURE 9.15: *Uuvi. Right*, FIGURE 9.16: *Uuvi* techniques as illustrated by a member of the Alavanyo *Gbolo* Group (2007).

nique is used on these drums. A special Asivui used exclusively in *Adevu* is called *ade-asivui*. This drum is covered with raffia which represents the spirit of the hunters and ancestors who have died.

Above, FIGURE 9.17: *Asivui. Right*, FIGURE 9.18: *Asivui* technique as illustrated by Gbolo Kwasi of the Alavanyo *Gbolo* Group (2007).

Above, FIGURE 9.19: *Ade-Asivui. Right*, FIGURE 9.20: *Ade-Asivui* technique as illustrated by Donkor Tumbua of the Alavanyo *Adevui* Group (2007).

Top, FIGURE 9.21: Front view of the *tamalin*. *Bottom*, FIGURE 9.22: Back of the *tamalin*. *Left*, FIGURE 9.23: *Tamalin* technique as illustrated by a member of the Ghana Dance Ensemble.

Krokoto. The *krokoto*, also known as the *ʋukpo*, is used both as a signal and speech drum. This instrument is reserved exclusively for the chief, and the hunters' and warriors' associations.

The *krokoto* serves as a speech surrogate in the chief's palace. It announces the arrival of chiefs at functions and plays messages related to the cultural values of the people. The *krokoto*, like the *agblɔʋu* among the southeastern Eʋes, used to be one of the main drums used during wars to transmit messages.

No northern Eʋe chief will travel today to any official duties without the accompaniment of the *krokoto*. A *krokoto* is used if requested by the chief to summon the people for any collective action or community work.

When used for the chief, the player has to perform standing. Sound is generated on the drum by the player hanging it on the left side of the body with a sling attached and hitting the center of the membrane with two curved sticks.

When played seated by the hunters and warriors during their dance musical events, the drum is tilted forward, away from the drummer. Open tones or bounce-strokes are realized by bouncing the sticks alternately at the center of the membrane. Pressing the sticks at the center of the membrane generates closed tones or press strokes. Curved sticks are also used in this context.

Uʋgā. The *ʋugā*, also called the *havana*, is the master or lead drum for the Bɔbɔɔbɔ percussion ensemble. It is a single-headed drum played upright between the legs. The lifting of the drum

Above, FIGURE 9.24: *Krokoto*. *Left*, FIGURE 9.25: *Krokoto* technique as illustrated by John Apinti of the Ala-vanyo *Adevu* Group (2007).

Above, FIGURE 9.26: *Uuga*. *Right* FIGURE 9.27: *Uuga* technique as illustrated by Theophilus Akpa of the Ho Agbenya *Bɔbɔɔbɔ* Group (2007).

with the thighs provides a spectacular visual effect during a performance but, most importantly, produces the desired bass tone.

Two or more *vugã* can be used in a performance but only one leads. Techniques used on this drum include the open bounce technique, the smack or slap technique, the bass or deep sound technique and the dead tone technique.

10. *Adevu* Hunters' Dance-Drumming Ceremony

Historical Background and Development

Adevu, a dance-drumming ceremony for *adelawo*, hunters, originated among the Eʋes during their settlement in Ŋɔtsie. There were only two main occupations available for the men at the time: farming and hunting. Since Ŋɔtsie was in the hinterland, fishing was undertaken by the very few men along the rivers.

Hunting was by far the most revered occupation and because of this the best hunters were highly decorated and respected. Hunters would therefore travel long distances for the best game so as to be accorded the title of *ademega*, the chief or headhunter. The *ademega* title would only be bestowed on a hunter who was able to hunt one of the following animals: lion, leopard, buffalo, elephant, tiger or hyena.

To become a hunter involves initiation rituals. These were performed by the *ademega* in order to forestall mishaps or death by wild animals. This initiation took seven days during which the *adekplɔvi*, apprentice hunter, was officially handed the tools/weapons he would use for hunting. His meals during this seclusion would be the meat from the heart, jaw and kidneys of any of the wild animals mentioned earlier.

The parts of the animal selected for the meals symbolized bravery, strength and endurance. The final ritual, which was observed on the seventh day, involved the preparation of the animal's head. The new hunter would be dressed in full hunting regalia and made to sit on the head to demonstrate his prowess and total superiority over all animals of the forest. This initiation ritual is presently performed as a purification rite for a hunter who kills any wild animal.

Special dance-drumming would be performed for the new hunter to demonstrate his hunting skills through miming the hunting experiences or symbolic characteristic movements of wild animals. This was *Adevu*, a dance-drumming ritual for hunters. The hunters also performed *Adevu* during their sojourn in Ŋɔtsie, before and after hunting expeditions.

When the Eʋes migrated to Ghana, the Eʋemeawo who moved hinterland were mostly hunters and farmers and, as result, kept the *Adevu* dance-drumming ceremony. It is performed to celebrate the beginning of the major hunting season, the successful killing of wild game and funerals for hunters.

Other occasions for performance include festivals, funerals of chiefs, and traditional religious worship for various state gods. *Adevu* can also be seen when a new chief is being outdoored or at a gathering of chiefs or individuals who have performed feasts of bravery.

The hunters were and continue to be the warriors of the Eʋedomeao; hence, any performance of *Adevu* also pays tribute to all the ancestors who shed their blood for the people. *Akpi*, a warriors' dance-drumming ceremony, is included in the performance for this purpose.

Adevu is well established in the Alavanyo Uudidi, Alavanyo Dzogbedze, Kpando, Peki, Ho, Tsito, Sokode, Abutia and Aḍaklu communities in Ghana.

Organization of the Dance-Drumming Ceremony

FORM AND STRUCTURE. There are four distinct stages or phases of the *Adevu* performance: *adezɔlizɔzɔ*, the procession; *adekaka*, dramatization of a hunting expedition; *adevu*, the hunters' main dance-drumming; and *akpi*, the warriors' dance-drumming.

Phase One: *Adezɔlizɔzɔ*. *Adezɔlizɔzɔ*, the processional dance-drumming ritual, symbolizes the journey of the hunters to and from a hunting expedition. This procession is led by *ademega*, the chief hunter, who is followed by the carrier of *adegba*, the hunters' god, and a shrine representing the spirits of the hunters, warriors and ancestors who have died. Contained in this shrine are game trophies such as the heads, horns and jaws of wild animals killed.

Accompanying the *adegba* is the carrier of *adetre*—a calabash filled with *wɔtsi*, a mixture of water and roasted corn flour. *Wɔtsi* is regarded as the food of all the ancestral spirits and is also used for libation. The percussion ensemble and the rest of the group complete the procession.

Once the group arrives at the performance's arena, *adegba* is situated in front of the percussion ensemble. The soul of the shrine, the person who carried the *adegba* to the arena now sits to its left or right, the position he will keep during the rest of the celebration. The arena is purified with *wɔtsi*, which is followed by a brief dance-drumming to end this phase of the ceremony.

Above, FIGURE 10.1: *Adetre* with *wɔtsi. Right,* FIGURE 10.2: *Adegba*

Phase Two: *Adekaka*. *Adekaka*, the dramatization of a hunting expedition, is the second phase of the performance. This involves a reenactment of a hunting expedition, which is led by the *ademega*, assisted by the *adekplɔvi*. There is a celebration dance by the two actors to complete this phase of the ceremony. *Adekaka* is performed as a civic lesson to educate the young and aspiring hunters.

Phase Three: *Adevu*. *Adevu*, the main hunters' dance, then commences. Several hunters and their wives will take turns dancing. This phase may be repeated three or four times depending on the occasion. *Abrase*, which is *gbemefofo* in *Adevu*, starts every phase of the *Adevu* performance.

FIGURE 10.3: Alavanyo Uudidi *Adevu* dancer in *Adevu* phase (2007).

Phase Four: *Akpi*. *Akpi*, the warriors' dance, is performed at the climax of the celebration. The purpose of this phase is to remember and pay tribute to the past warriors and hunters. Another *Adevu* is then performed to end the performance.

Songs

The Eʋedomeawo hunter believes and operates in two worlds: the invincible or spiritual and physical worlds. The invincible world includes the domain of the gods, ancestors and other forces that provide spiritual support for the people, while the physical world includes the home environment as well as the forest and all its inhabitants.

Adevu songs are composed to reflect the relationship between the hunter and both worlds. Songs remind the hunters of bravery and also stimulate them into warlike actions and demonstrations. Songs remind them of what happens during acts of combat or hunters' encounters with wild animals in the forest.

Themes of songs focusing on the physical world in particular make reference to the power and strength of hunters over animals, successful games, episodes encountered on hunting expeditions and weapons used in their daily activities. Songs referencing the spiritual world focus on protection from the gods and ancestors.

Hunters also believe that the spiritual forces dictate dance movements and are responsible for a successful game and performance. *Adevu* songs use both the Eve and other Ghanaian languages such as varieties of Akan. This situation makes it difficult to understand the meaning of some of the songs.

The main structural organization of the songs is based on call and response. During performances the lead singer creates variations on the call, which are based on melodies and texts of songs. Use of vocable or nonsense syllables is also very common. Ending phrases of songs are usually sustained or prolonged, especially during *abrase* performances using vocables.

Ampoti, songs of exhilaration usually performed by the warriors, are also used — especially during the *akpi* phase in *Adevu*. Both *abrase* and *ampoti* are performed in a recitative or declamatory style.

Tonality in *Adevu* songs is derived mostly from varieties of the pentatonic scale. Tritonic and tetratonic scales are also used. Melodic phrases or entire melodies are limited to three to five pitches. Although all songs are composed in monophony, there are instances of sporadic use of parallel thirds, fourths, fifths, and octaves, resulting in harmony and multi-part singing. Overlapping of the cantor and chorus, use of yells, grunts, shouts are other harmonic devices incorporated into *Adevu* songs.

The Percussion Ensemble

Instruments used in the *Adevu* percussion ensemble include the following: *ade-asivui*, *krokoto, vuvi, ladzo* and *mba*. These instruments are decribed in Chapter 9.

Role of instruments in the ensemble:

    i.   *Lādzo* #1: Plays the timeline. This pattern guides the whole ensemble. It provides entry cues for the rest of the ensemble.

    ii.   *Lādzo* #2: This instrument emphasizes the pattern of the timeline.

    iii.   *Mba* #1 and #2: Support or double the timeline.

    iv.   *Uuvi:* Supporting drum.

    v.   *Ade-Asivui:* This is a supporting drum but has the opportunity to improvise during the performance. *Ade-Asivui* plays a minor lead function in the ensemble.

    vi.   *Krokoto:* Lead or master drum. This drum may start and end a performance with *ade-asivui*. It serves as the conductor of the ensemble.

Dance Organization

DANCE ARENA. The dance arena in *Adevu* follows a simple formation. In every performance, the drummers in the percussion ensemble are first seated. Positioned behind them forming a cluster are other instrumentalists and the rest of the group. In front of the drummers are *adegba* and *adetre*. Audience or spectators then form a circle around the performers. The formation of the performers is shown in the picture below.

DANCE MOVEMENTS AND CHOREOGRAPHY. *Adevu* dance movements are free in conception and are executed solo (only one person dances at a time). Dancers take turns performing movements, which imitate certain forest animals and/or episodes encountered during hunting expeditions.

There is a dance ritual the dancer performs before beginning a routine. Tradition requires the dancer to pay homage to the drummers, chiefs or important dignitaries and audience by taking a quick bow or by touching the ground in front of them. The drummers will not play their best if a dancer does not go through this pre-dance ritual.

Above, FIGURE 10.4: Alavanyo *Adevu* Percussion Ensemble. Seated from left, front row: *krokoto, ade-asivui, vuvi*. Standing from left: *mba, mba, lādzo* and *lādzo* (2007). *Below*, FIGURE 10.5: Alavanyo Uudidi *Adevu* Group (2007).

Appendages such as the *kpo*, club; the *yi*, cutlass; the *hlo* or *akplɔ*, spear; the *adekpui*, dagger; and the *tu*, hunting gun; and others carried in the *adekotoku*, hunting pouch: the *xa*, a broom; knife; the *sɔshie, sebe* or *badua,* animal tail, are used by the dancer as props and extensions of the body.

The basic dance movement focuses on the feet. This involves short and brisk syncopated alternating movement of the feet forwards and backwards. The dancer may also step in and out or cross their legs in front.

The symbolic and artistic use of the arms, facial expressions and gestures, in consort with proper feet movement by an expert dancer, produces a theatrical spectacle of cultural mime. The *krokoto* player is at his best during these dance routines.

FIGURE 10.6: Alavanyo Uudidi female dancer in action (2007).

Costume and Other Visual Art Forms

The are three basic components of the hunter's costume: an *adewu,* hunter's dress, with a *loglo,* hat, *agbadza*, war girdle, and other appendages carried or attached to dance bodies such as: *kpo,* club; *yi,* cutlass; *hlo* or *akplɔ,* spear; *adekpui,* dagger; and *tu,* hunting gun — introduced by the Germans but now locally manufactured.

Adewu, the main dress, is made from the bark of *gboloba* or *logo azagu,* a species of the cedar tree, which is used in drum-making. *Batakari,* woven or tailored

FIGURE 10.7: *Loglo*

Left, FIGURE 10.8: Alavanyo Uudidi Ademegā Ata Nyawuto in *loglo* (2007). *Above*, FIGURE 10.9: *Adeko-toku*

Left, FIGURE 10.10: Alavanyo Uudidi Ademegā Ata Nyawuto wearing *adekotoku* (2007). *Top*, FIGURE 10.11: *Agbadza. Bottom*, FIGURE 10.12: Alavanyo Uudidi Ademegā Ata Nyawuto in *agbadza* (2007).

smock from calico which is dyed in red, green
or black, is also used for the performance.
Adewu is worn over any dark knickers.

Ademega and his assistant also carry *adekotoku,* a pouch containing a broom, knife, *sɔshie,
sebe* or *badua,* animal tail, whistle and other
protective herbs (traditional first aid materials).
The performers also wear amulets or charms and
strips of red cloth as protective gear. The color
red symbolizes blood and the spirits of all forest
animals.

FIGURE 10.13: Alavanyo Uudidi Ademegā Ata
Nyawuto in full costume (2007).

11. *Bɔbɔɔbɔ* Recreational Dance-Drumming Ceremony

Historical Background and Development

The joy upon achieving independence in Ghana was expressed in various ways by the entire populace of the country. The new life envisaged resulted in the emergence of several new musical types. These new musical creations, basically relating to the "freedom" that would be enjoyed through independence, have roots in the popular Ghanaian highlife. *Bɔbɔɔbɔ* is one of the creations of the independence in Ghana.

Bɔbɔɔbɔ is the most popular recreational dance-drumming of the Eʋedomeawo. *Bɔbɔɔbɔ*, also known as *Agbeyeye* (New Life) and *Akpese* (Music of Joy), emerged from a village called Kpando in the Volta region of Ghana during the independence struggle in the country between 1947 and 1957. This recreational dance-drumming was derived from an older secular dance called *Konkoma*, due to the ingenuity of the late Francis Nuatrɔ, popularly called F. C.

Because of F. C.'s special love for and interest in music — especially singing, he decided to join the then Kpando *Konkoma* Band after his retirement from position of sergeant in the Ghana Police Service. *Konkoma* was the only main recreational dance-drumming in Kpando before the dawn of *Bɔbɔɔbɔ*.

F. C. wasted no time in experimenting with new ideas such as expansion of the percussion ensemble to include new instruments, the nature of the dance and, especially, the use of more topical, philosophical and human themes in his songs.

These new developments resulted in a deviation from the old *Konkoma* mode of performance in Kpando. This unique new style of performance style caused the change of the name of the group to Kpando *Bɔbɔɔbɔ* Band.

F. C.'s popularity grew within a short time, resulting in jealousy and leadership problems in the Kpando *Bɔbɔɔbɔ* Band. The early 1950s gave birth to the formation of F. C.'s own *Bɔbɔɔbɔ* band. Many Eʋedomeawo attribute the leadership crisis in the old Kpando *Bɔbɔɔbɔ* Band as the main reason Bɔbɔɔbɔ is widely performed in Ghana today.

Although *Bɔbɔɔbɔ* recreational dance-drumming was initially confined to a few towns and villages in central and northern Eʋeland, it has now spread to all Eʋe-speaking territories in Ghana and Togo. Bɔbɔɔbɔ can also be seen in some non–Eʋe-speaking communities, including those in the big cities. All *Bɔbɔɔbɔ* bands in Ghana today are based on the foundation laid by F. C.'s *Bɔbɔɔbɔ* band of Kpando.

The history of *Bɔbɔɔbɔ* cannot be complete without discussing the role F. C. played in its initial development. By the late 1950s, F. C.'s unique artistic presentation of *Bɔbɔɔbɔ* was recognized throughout the Volta region and the country as a whole.

Dr. Kwame Nkrumah, the first president of Ghana, personally loved Bɔbɔɔbɔ and made sure that F. C.'s band was part and parcel of the C. P. P. (Convention People's Party), his party in the Volta region, as *Kpanlongo* recreational dance-drumming was in the greater Accra region. F. C.'s band was known as *Osagyefo's Own Bɔbɔɔbɔ* from 1957 until 1966 when Nkrumah was removed from power.

The overthrow of Dr. Kwame Nkrumah nearly brought the performance of *Bɔbɔɔbɔ* to an abrupt end, but F. C., being a great politician and gifted musician, tactfully reorganized the band and performed more at funerals and other social occasions rather than at political functions. *Bɔbɔɔbɔ* has since become the most popular entertainment music and dance among the central and northern Ewes of Ghana and Togo.

Christianity, western art music and the British system of formal education have also greatly influenced the development of *Bɔbɔɔbɔ* since the 1970s, which is evident in new dance formations, instruments, costumes, themes of songs and musical elements of style.

Organization of the Dance-Drumming Ceremony

FORM AND STRUCTURE. *Bɔbɔɔbɔ* is generally seen today at all social community events, particularly funerals and festivals. Although *Bɔbɔɔbɔ* bands are well established groups, it is sometimes difficult to distinguish between audience and performers at very large and festive occasions.

When the band is hired to perform at special functions, participation is restricted to only members who perform in their costumes. However, during some festivals and funerals, everybody can participate in the performance.

There are four distinct stages or phases of *Bɔbɔɔbɔ* performance: *azɔlizɔzɔ*, the procession; *ahomu*, preparation of the voice; *vuofofo*, the main dance-drumming; and *azɔlizɔzɔ*, the recessional performance.

Phase One: *Azɔlizɔzɔ*. All *Bɔbɔɔbɔ* performances start with a short procession by the band to the dance ring, funeral or festival grounds. *Azɔlizɔzɔ*, the processional dance-drumming, usually begins from the home of the leader or the location where the group rehearses.

Traditionally, in any processional performance or dance, Evedomeawo move as a mob or in clusters of small groups. In *Bɔbɔɔbɔ* however, the performers—especially the dancers—form two lines and march as school children or in a military style. Some groups describe this first phase of the performance as "march past." The dancers form a semicircle or a circle around the drummers once they arrive at the dance arena.

Phase Two: *Ahomu*. A special performance singing technique used by the Evedomeawo in most of their traditional musical activities is *gbemefofo*, clearing of the voice. *Gbemefofo* in *Bɔbɔɔbɔ* is referred to as *ahomu*.

Once the drummers are seated and all performers are in place, songs are performed in free rhythm or are accompanied by only bells and rattles. *Bɔbɔɔbɔ* is organized in duple rhythmic structure — usually in 2/4 signature. *Ahomu*, however, may be performed in compound time — usually in 6/8 time.

Dancers walk with the music or move in free style when they perform *ahomu* around the drummers. There are no specific dance movements during the *ahomu* performance. The purpose of this phase is to prepare the voices or clear the performers' throats for *vufofo*, the main dance-drumming phase, or to warm up the performers.

Phase Three: *Vufofo*. *Vufofo*, the main dance-drumming phase, begins with the lead cantor accompanied by the bells. The signal to commence or usher in the dancers is given by the master drum —*vugã* or, the hourglass drum — when the circle is completely formed.

The essence of *Bɔbɔɔbɔ* is exhibited during this phase. Choice of songs reflects the context

FIGURE 11.1: Ho Agbenya *Bɔbɔɔbɔ* performing *azɔlizɔzɔ* (2009).

FIGURE 11.2: Ho Agbenya *Bɔbɔɔbɔ* performing *ahomu* (2009).

FIGURE 11.3: Ho Agbenya *Bɔbɔɔbɔ* performing *vufofo* (2009).

of performance. At a funeral, for example, the tempo of drumming may be considerably slow as compared to happy occasions when the performance moves at a faster tempo.

The *vufofo* phase may be repeated two or three times depending on the duration or time allowed for the performance. Another procession or recessional dance-drumming may sometimes end the performance. The end of the performance is also signaled by any of the two drums mentioned earlier.

Songs

Folk songs from sub–Saharan Africa reflect daily occurrences in the lives of the people. As observed by Nketia (1974), an African song should be treated not only as a form of speech utterance but as a medium that recounts the experiences of the people. *Bɔbɔɔbɔ* songs can be understood and interpreted if the lyrics are treated as such.

The repertoire of songs of any Bɔbɔɔbɔ band is very wide. The changes in style and form depend on the mood and context of performance. Tempo is the main distinguishing factor among the various styles. The choice of songs during a particular performance is also guided by the function taking place.

Prior to the introduction of European ideas on *Bɔbɔɔbɔ* performance, themes of songs were more philosophical, reflective on life and death in general. Generally, songs relate to every aspect of community life.

Religious and funeral themes are by far the most common themes used in *Bɔbɔɔbɔ* songs. Other themes may relate to: human issues, praise and ridicule, topical issues, death and afterlife, history, and the social and cultural beliefs of the people.

It can be said that the dance mirrors the song in any performance, as the dance gestures dramatize the song text. A change in song results in a change in dance movements on many occasions.

Melodic lines usually follow the word contour and rhythm of speech patterns. Harmony is realized when the chorus sings in unison with the use of sporadic or consequent thirds, fifths, sixths, octaves, or a combination of all these techniques.

Bɔbɔɔbɔ songs are performed in call and response and solo and chorus form. One soloist is the ideal but sometimes two or more may introduce a song before the chorus enters.

Western art music has greatly altered many aspects of *Bɔbɔɔbɔ* performance. Christian hymns and songs composed with biblical texts have replaced the traditional compositions.

Traditional singing styles and forms—especially the call and response, have been replaced by Christian hymnody. Tonal arrangements in *Bɔbɔɔbɔ* songs which are are based on the heptatonic (7-tone) scale, lend themselves to the use of Western hymnal-style harmonic arrangements. Attempts are made to sing songs in perfect diatonic harmony.

Although these new trends greatly affected some of the traditional performance practices, and many songs relating to the culture of the people and singing styles were lost, *Bɔbɔɔbɔ* in contempoarary times has contributed greatly to the advancement of the Christian churches among the Eʋedomeawo.

Christian services have become more lively as church choirs now perform their hymns and other anthems accompanied by *Bɔbɔɔbɔ* percussion ensemble and dance. Most church services, especially during the offertory or collection phase of the Catholic Mass are now more like a recreational dance-drumming celebration.

The Percussion Ensemble

Instruments of the *Bɔbɔɔbɔ* ensemble have undergone several modifications. Initial instruments used were the *kretsiwa*, finger bell; the *ʋuvi*, small drum; the *asiʋui*, hand drum; the *pati*, tom tom; the *ʋuga*, master drum, and bugle. Contemporary *Bɔbɔɔbɔ* ensembles are comprised of the following instruments: the *kretsiwa*, finger bell (2 may be used); one *tigo*, double bell or one *atoke*, slit bell; one *akaye*, rattle; an *ʋuvi* and *asiʋui*, small supporting drums; a *pati*, concert tom may be used in the absence of *ɖonno*; a *ɖonno*, hourglass drum; an *ʋugā/havana*, master drum (2 or 3 may be used); and *biglo*, a bugle/trumpet.

Contrasting rhythmic patterns played on the *kretsiwas* are very essential in any performance. Apart from the master drums, no other instrumentalists are required to improvise during a performance. If more than one master drum is played, only one can lead the performance. The bugle/trumpet is used to accentuate specific points in the dance.

Role of instruments in the ensemble include:

i. *Kretsiwa #1:* Plays the timeline. This pattern guides the whole ensemble. It provides entry cues to the rest of the ensemble.
ii. *Kretsiwa #2 and 3:* These instruments emphasize the pattern of the timeline.
iii. *Tigo:* Supports or plays the timeline.
iv. *Akaye:* Supports the timeline.
v. *Ɖonɖo:* Supporting drum, but may start or end a performance.
vi. *Uuvi:* Supporting drum.
vii. *Asiʋui:* Supporting drum. This instrument plays an interlocking pattern with the *ʋuvi*.
viii. *ʋugā:* Master drum. This drum may start and end a performance. It serves as the conductor of the ensemble

Dance Organization

DANCE ARENA. The dance ring can vary depending on the function of the performance. In a communal performance like a funeral or festival when participation is not restricted, the instrumentalists will be positioned in the middle and surrounded by dancers who move around in a circular direction. This formation is shown in Figure 11.5.

FIGURE 11.4: Ho Agbenya *Bɔbɔɔbɔ* Percussion Ensemble. Seated from left, front row: *vuvi, asivui,* small *vuga,* medium *vuga* and master *vuga.* Standing from left: *akaye, kretsiwa* and *tigo* (2009).

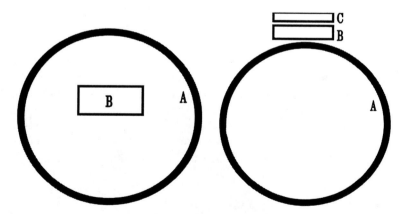

Left, FIGURE 11.5: Traditional spatial arrangement for *Bɔbɔɔbɔ* performance. Key: A: chorus and dancers; B. drummers. *Right,* FIGURE 11.6: Theatrical arrangement for *Bɔbɔɔbɔ* performance. Key: A: dancers; B: drummers; C. chorus.

In a theatrical arrangement where only members of the band are allowed to perform, the dancers will dance in front of the instrumentalists and a small chorus standing at the rear. This arrangement is shown in above.

DANCE MOVEMENTS AND CHOREOGRAPHY. Music that is integrated with the dance emphasizes and develops rhythms that can be articulated in bodily movement. The rhythmic structure
of music mostly influences the patterns of dance movements.

In Bɔbɔɔbɔ music, the organization of rhythms both linearly and multi-linearly, resulting
in regular or irregular accents and cross rhythms, well-placed, guide the dance. Linearly, the
rhythms to be articulated with bodily movement are organized in strict time and are grouped
into patterns or phrases, imparting a feeling of regularity.

Basic dance steps, therefore, relate to the timeline. Multi-linearly, all the different percussion
instruments play varied patterns which reinforce the basic pulses. The dancer will take cues
from the rhythmic framework to articulate the dance movements.

A close correlation between music and dance in Bɔbɔɔbɔ is also illustrated when specific
songs direct specific dance steps. Depending on the context of performance, music and dance
can be used to express artistic, cultural, psychological, communicative, economic, and political
behaviors, and poetic expression.

Depending on the context of performance, Bɔbɔɔbɔ can include memorial drama during
festivals. Dancers may enact episodes showing social relations, beliefs, and values.

Symbolic gestures by dancers during funerals may relate to sorrow. Social drama can be
seen at festivals or other social occasions in order to reflect topical issues. Symbolic gestures
may also dramatize joy and happiness.

Movement is an essential and integral part of sub–Saharan musical events. It serves as an
avenue for creative response and aesthetic appreciation exhibited during any musical performance. The main factor that generates movement is rhythm. Organization of rhythm in any
instrumental or vocal music is seen as movement in the whole music. The dance, therefore, is
an outward manifestation of rhythm in African dances.

African dances serve as a form of reaction to music and medium for communication. The
dance is "a language, a mode of expression, which addresses itself to the mind, through the
heart, using related, relevant, and significant movements which have their basic counter-parts
in our everyday activities, to express special and real life experiences in rhythmic sequences to
musical and poetic stimuli" (Opoku 1968, 11).

Bɔbɔɔbɔ is organized as a circular dance into which the dancers come from a short procession. This dance requires great flexibility and fluidity of movement, and is therefore performed
by women who, by African standards, are more flexible than men.

The specific dance movements and gestures are symbolic. The basic step of the ritornello
dance movement, known as the "cutting move," symbolizes a clearing of the pathway towards
a happy future devoid of oppression. In this basic movement, the leg placement of the dancer
divides the timeline into four, or multiples if the music is going very fast. The right leg moves
forward on the strong beat and the left follows on the second. This is repeated for the third and
fourth beats. Other gestures which are illustrated in this activity relate to social, religious, and
human issues of life. Refer to Chapter 32 of Part Seven for dance descriptions.

Costume and Other Visual Art Forms

Selection of costumes in African dances depend on the type of music being performed, the
nature of dance, and the requirement of dramatic enactment. Costumes in Bɔbɔɔbɔ can also be
seen as bodily extensions or appendages. The white handkerchief seen in Bɔbɔɔbɔ is an extension
of the personality of the dramatic personae.

Costumes used in Bɔbɔɔbɔ vary from band to band. Two are very common in contemporary
times: i. The women will wear a designed T-shirt, usually with the band's logo worn over a cloth

FIGURE 11.7: Costumes of *Bɔbɔɔbɔ* dance: Type One. Ho Agbenya *Bɔbɔɔbɔ* Group (2009).

FIGURE 11.8: Costumes of *Bɔbɔɔbɔ* dance: Type Two. Ho Agbenya *Bɔbɔɔbɔ* Group (2009).

tied to the waist line. The men will wear the same T-shirt over any pair of knickers or trousers; ii. The most common costume is an *awu*, which is a type of blouse worn over matching cloth.

This is the traditional dress of all Eʋe women. The men will wear a shirt made from the same cloth over any pair of knickers or trousers, as in the first type. All women dancers in *Bɔbɔɔbɔ* carry a pair of white handkerchiefs as appendages to symbolize joy, victory, and freedom. The spirit of *Bɔbɔɔbɔ* is evidenced in the stylistic waving of the white handkerchiefs.

12. *Egbanegba* Recreational Dance-Drumming Ceremony

Historical Background and Development

Like older northern Eʋe musical types, the origin of *Egbanegba* is shrouded in mystery. There are many stories relating to its origin, but two stand out the most. One story has it that *Egbanegba* was brought from Ŋɔtsie during the migration of the Eʋe by the Kpandoawo, under the name *Gabaɖa*. Another story states that it was created by the people of Alavanyo Uudidi and Kpando during the late 19th century, long after their migration.

Chiefs and master drummers confirmed this second story when I visited the area several times during my research. According to Gbolo Kwasi, the master drummer, composer and lead singer of the contemporary Alavanyo Uudidi *Egbanegba* group, *Egbanegba* started as *Gabaɖa*, a courtship or love dance-drumming in Alavanyo Uudidi during the 1930s.

In those days, families would gather after evening meals to listen to stories or engage in proverbial quizzes. It was during one of these evening entertainments that Komla Gbolo, Gbolo Kwasi's uncle, a wood carver and master drummer, suggested that instead of just the stories, they should compose topical songs and also add some drums to make the story sections more enjoyable and last the whole evening. The natives readily applauded this idea.

Komla carved two small drums, which he called *asiʋui*. He also composed songs, which were used. Story sessions became recreational dance-drumming events, which attracted more women. As the performances went further and further into the night, women became targets for sexual harassment. The performances became occasions for men to seduce or court women. There was still no specific name for this dance-drumming during its initial stages.

Soon, the storytelling sessions were replaced by dance-drumming performances. Men became involved in sexual gratification from the performances and were looking for charms—especially love charms—to seduce the women — even the married ones. This was the beginning of using the name *Gabaɖa*, to refer to the dance-drumming.

Komla's idea of family-friendly entertainment soon took a spiritual or ritual dimension. It became known as *dzoʋu*, a ritual dance-drumming celebration. Men with stronger spiritual powers might end up sleeping with three different women on a particular night.

The story goes that the chief of the area became so disgusted by the events that he placed a ban on this music and dance. However, there was much opposition from the citizens of Alavanyo Uudidi, and there was a riot to combat the chief's order. The police were called in to maintain peace and order. Komla Gbolo and other leaders of the group were arrested and consequently imprisoned in Accra. His wife, Biasa Yevumetse from Agɔxoe, was also arrested, assaulted and later tied to a tree.

On Komla's release from prison in 1933, he left Uudidi and founded a village called Ðedelameta Metu, a few miles away from Alavanyo Uudidi. He continued carving and playing this music and dance, which he now called *Egbanegba*, until his untimely death in 1963.

His eldest son, Kwasi Gbolo, who was with him during his lifetime, learned the arts of carving and composing songs and has kept the music alive until now. Despite several sanctions imposed on Komla, *Egbanegba* flourished and has spread to several towns and villages—especially in the Kpando traditional area and specifically in Anfoe and Deme.

It is generally accepted by the northern Eʋes that *Egbanegba* was developed in the Kpando traditional area in the first decade of the 20th century. Alavanyo remains the cradle of this dance-drumming.

Egbanegba is performed today for recreation, at funerals, festivals, national celebrations, and visits of state dignitaries. *Egbanegba* bands can be seen in most Eʋedome settlements in the Volta region of Ghana. Membership in such groups depends on an individual's musical and dance ability and interest.

Organization of the Dance-Drumming Ceremony

FORM AND STRUCTURE. *Egbanegba* is performed in five stages: *gbemefofo*, preparation of the voice; *egbanegba*, main dance-drumming; *adzomadɔloe*, lovers' performance; *dzeɖoɖo*, the conversation; and *egbanegba*, main dance-drumming. Some of these phases may be repeated during the performance.

Phase One: *Gbemefofo*. The *egbanegba* performance starts with a solo vocal warm-up performance to clear or prepare the voice. *Gbemefofo*, a unique vocal performance style, starts almost every dance-drumming among the Eʋedomeawo.

This phase is known as *abrase* in Uudidi, and *asabra, sabrabɔbɔ* or *akrodoedodo* in other Eʋedome areas during Egbanegba performances. This introductory performance is in declamatory style. The singing exists at the confluence of speech rhythm and lyricism.

The text in the *abrase* performance relates to the song that follows later to begin the second phase, *Egbanegba* (Dor 1986, 32). The bells and rattles may accompany *abrase*.

Phase Two: *Egbanegba*. Egbanegba, the main dance-drumming phase, begins with the bells and rattles in strict rhythm. After a brief *abrase* led by the cantor, the chorus and the rest of the percussion ensemble join in the performance.

The performance arena is now open for the dancers. This phase may be repeated before the next phase. Songs in this phase are more reflective and philosophical.

Phase Three: *Adzomadɔloe*. *Adzomadɔloe*, meaning, "Lovers cannot sleep when it is performed," represents the lovers' dance-drumming phase, a revisit to the courtship intent of the original *Gabaɖa* performance. Through hand and arm movements, gestures, and facial expressions, dancers tease the audience.

In the past, these symbolic movements would be directed towards the opposite sex. Individual stylistic movements are referred to as *atiɖeke, kedome* and *viviese*, individual dance or self-expression. Dancers in this phase try to show acceptance, rejection, and sadness through their movements. Songs during this phase focus on human tragedies, lost love and death.

Phase Four: *Dzeɖoɖo*. Dzeɖoɖo, or *nkɔmɔ*, the next phase of the performance, expresses friendship and happiness. *Dzeɖoɖo*, which means a conversation between lovers, shows the climax of the performance. Most of the songs focus on love.

The dance movements are very suggestive, gay and enticing. This phase invites many dancers to the arena since the performance may end after this phase. Another *Egbanegba* is usually performed to end the whole celebration.

Songs

Themes of *Egbanegba* songs may center on love and intimacy, consolation for broken relationships, death, and morals. Human attitudes and topical and historical facts are not left out of the songs.

The form of the songs is mostly call and response. Polyphony develops when the main cantor or other soloists alternate with the chorus, resulting in overlapping or crossing of parts. Harmony can be heard in the use of parallel and sporadic thirds and sixths. Three-part harmonies are also common.

Pentatonic, hexatonic and heptatonic scales are mostly used in *Egbanegba* songs. The flattened seventh degree of the heptatonic scale is frequently used when descending and it resolves to the submediant. There is shifting of tonality in most *Egbanegba* songs.

The Percussion Ensemble

Instruments of the *Egbanegba* percussion ensemble include: two *gakogoe, akaye, vuvi, asivui* and *tamalee*. These instruments are decribed in Chapter 9.

Role of instruments in the ensemble:

    i.   *Gakogoe* #1: Plays the timeline. This pattern guides the whole ensemble. It provides entry cues for the rest of the ensemble.

    ii.   *Gakogoe* #2: This instrument emphasizes the pattern of the timeline.

    iii.   *Akaye:* Doubles the Gakogoe #2 pattern. *Akaye* is usually played by the females. This was not part of the original ensemble. It was adapted from *Gbolo* dance-drumming by women.

FIGURE 12.1: Alavanyo Uudidi *Egbanegba* Percussion Ensemble. Seated from left, front row: *tamalee, asivui* and *vuvi*. Standing from left: *akaye, akaye, gakogoe, gakogoe* and *akaye* (2008).

iv.   *Uuvi:* Plays supporting ostinato patterns.

vi.   *Tamalee:* This is a supporting drum that plays the same pattern as *Akaye* and *Gakogoe* #2.

vii. *Asivui:* Lead or master drum. This drum may start and end a performance. It serves as the conductor of the ensemble

Dance Organization

DANCE ARENA. The chorus and other instrumentalists are arranged in a cluster behind the drummers who are seated and facing the spectators. Those standing may overlap the sides of the drummers to create a semicircle or horseshoe formation during the entire performance.

DANCE MOVEMENTS AND CHOREOGRAPHY. *Egbanegba* is performed as a solo or by twos or threes at most during all the phases with the exception of *dzeḍoḍo*. The dance movement in *Egbanegba* involves intricate and fast staccato footwork. Usually, the right leg leads. The dancer

FIGURE 12.2: Alavanyo Uudidi *Egbanegba* Group, ready for a performance (2008).

FIGURE 12.3: Alavanyo Uudidi *Egbanegba* dancers in action (2008).

steps with the right foot and then immediately with the left, continuously in a shuffling fashion. This movement was adapted from *Gbolo,* the only recreational dance-drumming in Alavanyo Uudidi at the time.

The body is slightly tilted forward with the arms swinging side to side. White or blue handkerchiefs are used to extend the arm movements. During the *adzomadɔaloe* and *dzeḍoḍo,* the same footwork is used but the body is tilted more towards the ground. The movements are bold during these phases.

Costume and Other Visual Art Forms

Costumes worn by women include *dzimewu,* a blouse, worn over *alivoe,* a two-yard piece of cloth around the waist, with *taku,* a head kerchief, and earrings. The women dancers also use handkerchiefs and *akaye* as extensions of the arms.

Men in *Egbanegba* use a colorful shirt over long pants or put on a big cloth over the shoulders peculiar to all Eʋes of Ghana.

FIGURE 12.4: Alavanyo Uudidi *Egbanegba* dancers in costumes (2008).

13. *Gbolo* Recreational Dance-Drumming Ceremony

Historical Background and Development

Gbolo is principally a women's recreational dance-drumming performance among the Gbiawo, Pekiawo and Akpiniawo of Peki, Hohoe and Kpando traditional areas in the Volta region of Ghana. Major towns and cities presently performing *Gbolo* include: Blengo, Wudome, Dzogbati, Afeviwofe, Avetile, Tsame and Dzake of Peki, Hohoe, Bla, Uegbe, Kpeme, Atabu, Kledzo and Kpoeta of Hohoe and Alavanyo Uudidi and Alavanyo Deme of Kpando.

Oral tradition and works by Mamatah (1979), Obianim (1957), and P. Wiegrabe, state that *Gbolo* is one of the oldest musical types performed by the Euedomeawo of Ghana. History, as told by Da Cruz, has it that *Gbolo* was created in old Dahomey, now Benin, by then–King Tegbousson (1732–1775), together with other musical types such as *Dogbo, Agbadza, Hanhye*, and *Gokwe*. *Gbolo* was one of the performances that followed the morning celebrations of *Dogbo* and *Hanhye* from about 10 A.M. to mid-day at the king's court (Nketia 2005, 261; Cruz 1954, xii).

The Eues performed *Gbolo* and *Agbadza* when they lived with their neighbors the Fɔns in Benin, and they continued these performances when they moved to Ŋɔtsie. *Gbolo* was brought by the Gbiawo and Pekiawo, who lived under one stool name, *Gbi*, in Ŋɔtsie during their further migration to Ghana.

The name *Gbolo*, meaning the "loved one," was misinterpreted by many and was categorized as a dance-drumming for *ashaiwɔ*, harlots or prostitutes, during the advent of Christianity — even though most of the songs and symbolic dance movements relate to death, sorrow, pain and other topical issues. It was discouraged and banned by early Christian missionaries, especially the Catholics and Evangelicals, but it survived. In those days, enrollment in school or becoming a member of a church simply meant you could not participate in any *Gbolo* performance.

Gbolo is best described as a recreational dance-drumming used mainly for funeral celebrations for members, relatives of members who have passed, or when the band is invited for such celebrations. Ironically, due to the efforts of many traditional artists in Peki Avetile and Alavanyo Uudidi, to mention just a few, *Gbolo* has found its way into Christian churches and other social events such as festivals and marriage ceremonies. *Gbolo* songs and percussion ensembles are also influencing new African sacred songs used in Christian worship.

Organization of the Dance-Drumming Ceremony

FORM AND STRUCTURE. Gbolo is performed in two phases: *gbemefofo*, the preparation of the voice; and *gbolo akaye,* the main dance-drumming stage.

Phase One: *Gbemefofo*. *Gbemefofo,* which begins almost every dance-drumming among the Evedomeawo, in this context serves as a warm-up for performers to clear the throat (*gbemekɔkɔ*) and prepare the voice (*gbemedradradɔ*) before the main dance-drumming phase. Songs led by the cantor are in declamatory style. They use a speech rhythm and are full of lyricism.

Bells in free or strict rhythm and rattles in free rhythm accompany the songs.

Phase Two: *Gbolo Akaye*. *Gbolo Akaye,* the main dance-drumming phase, may begin with the bells, which are later joined by the rattles or the lead cantor, bells and rattles. Once the tempo is established, *vuvi,* the only supporting drum, enters. *Asivui,* the lead drum, then enters to invite the dancers. The phase may be repeated several times. An abridged version of *gbemefofo* usually begins each of these *Gbolo Akaye* repetitions. An entire *gbemefofo* may be incorporated into the dance-drumming phase. In this instance, the rattles and bells play in strict rhythm while the songs are in free rhythm.

Songs

Since *Gbolo* is featured mostly at funerals, themes dealing with death are given prominence. Songs show the cruelty of death, recount the deeds of the deceased, the relationship between the living and the dead and other sorrowful themes.

Other themes relate to topical issues, antisocial practices, advice to the youth, the environment or abode, poverty, riches, and historical facts relating to the bravery and achievements of ancestors.

Gbolo songs are performed in call and response form, a type of antiphony where the cantor alternates and sometimes overlaps with the chorus. Repetition is another structural form used, as the songs are short—usually not more than four phrases long. The lead cantor is given the opportunity to create variations based on the melody and text.

The heptatonic and, in some cases, the hexatonic and pentatonic scales, are used in construction of melodies. The shifting of tonal centers is very common when the flattened seventh is used. As observed in *Egbanegba,* the final note of phrases or songs is extended by use of syllables or mnemonics such as *aa, oo, ee,* or words such as *ayee, ayoo,* etc.

Songs are composed and conceived as monophony but are scarcely performed in their entirety in unison. Use of parallel thirds, fifths and occasional sixths, form the basis of polyphony. A whole song may be performed using these parallel intervals among the voices conceived as independent melodies. Unlike in western harmony, the voices are constructed horizontally, each adding a unique melody to the one established by the cantor.

Overlapping and crossing of the cantor and chorus also result in multi-part singing.

The Percussion Ensemble

The *Gbolo* percussion ensemble has undergone several changes, but three instruments remain and are used by all groups: the *akaye, vuvi* and *asivui.* Other instruments used include: the *akoge,* castanet; *gagbleve,* double bell; *adondo,* hourglass-shaped drum; and *gakogoe.*

Role of instruments in the ensemble:

   i. *Akaye: Akaye* is usually played by the females. This was the main and only instrument of the original ensemble used exclusively by the women. *Akaye* performs the basic beat which serves as the metronome and guide to the whole ensemble.

  ii. *Gakogoe #1* and *Akoge:* Play the timeline. This pattern guides the whole ensemble. It provides entry cues to the rest of the ensemble.

iii. *Gakogoe #2* and *Gableve*: Either of these instruments may support the timeline or emphasize the *akaye* pattern.

iv. *Uuvi*: Plays supporting ostinato patterns.

v. *Aḍonḍo*: Serves as supporting drum but occasionally plays variations. The *aḍonḍo* is not used by the majority of the groups.

vi. *Asivui*: Lead or master drum. This drum may start and end a performance. It serves as the conductor of the ensemble. It may also be called *vuga* in this context.

See Figure 13.2 on page C-7 of the color insert.

Dance Organization

DANCE ARENA. The performance arena forms a semicircle. With the exception of the *#uvi* and *asivui* players, the rest of the percussion ensemble, other male participants, chorus, and dancers perform standing. The female dancers with *akaye* flank the instrumentalists on both sides, with the audience surrounding the entire group.

FIGURE 13.1: Alavanyo *Egbanegba* Percussion Ensemble without *akaye*. Seated from left, *asivui* and *vuvi*. Standing, from left: two *gakogoe* players (2008).

FIGURE 13.3: Alavanyo *Gbolo* Group, ready for a performance (2008).

Dance Movements and Choreography. *Gbolo* performance is free in conception as the dance ring is open to everybody — those in the band and the audience. Dowoeh describes the dance sequence and presentation in *Gbolo* as:

> In Gbolo band, female chorus who flank the instrumentalists both on the left and right, hold rattles in their hands. They lean slightly forward and move to the music. As they move, they hit the rattles at the left palms, which are cupped. The left arm is kept close to the body with the elbow bent while the right arm also with a bent elbow holds the rattles. The right arm gets close to the body as the rattle hits the left hand and strikes away from the body as the rattle goes off the left hand. The female chorus' feet remain virtually "in place" though there is movement. Any slight movement is a movement of a stylized performance mannerism that a dance proper [Dowoeh 1980, 29].

The main dance sequence is graceful and full of symbolic and philosophical movements and gestures. The legs and arms move alternately in consonance with the rhythmic movements of the waist and buttocks. The dancer's steps are usually in rhythm with the *gakogoe* or *akoge*.

The movement starts with the dancer leaving her rattle in front of the drummers, bowing to them and to any other important personality before resuming her dance. Apart from evening rehearsals dedicated mostly to songs, no special training is required for the dance.

The dance body is bent forward and leans on to the leg that is in motion. The arms also move simultaneously with the legs. Symbolic gestures incorporated in the dance are varied. Some are:

i.   When one dances and claps both hands at the back, it means, "I have lost my parents and I am now lonely."

ii. When one dances with both palms facing the ground, turns them gradually and later on raises the fingers to the sky, it means, "We are the Gbolo group and no one can ever deter us from the performance" (Dowoeh 1980, 31).

Costume and Other Visual Art Forms

The original costume used for *Gbolo* is known as *atifu*. This is similar to *atible* of the southern Eves, which is used for *Atibladekame, Adzogbo* and *Atsiagbeko* female dancers, as described on page 59. Very young or old members of the group presently use *atifu* on special occasions.

In the absence of *atifu*, the most

Figure 13.4: Alavanyo *Gbolo* female costumes (2008).

FIGURE 13.5: *Gbolo* male dancers of Ghana Dance Ensemble, Legon, in cloth (2008).

common costume used by women includes *dzimewu,* a blouse worn over *alivoe,* a two-yard piece of cloth around the waist, with *taku,* a head kerchief, beads and earrings. A second cloth may be worn on top of the blouse.

Men in *Gbolo* use a colorful shirt over long pants or put on a big cloth over the shoulders. No sandals are worn during the *Gbolo* performance.

Part Three.
Dance-Drumming of the Gas

"The animal that knows how to hide in the forest lives longer." —
Ga Proverb by Ephraim Kotey Nikoi

Orthography of Ga

(a)	sounds like a in father	(aa)	sounds like ar in far
(e)	sounds like a in take	(ee)	sounds like ay in lay
(ɛ)	sounds like e in bet	(ɛɛ)	sounds like air in fair
(i)	sounds like ea in read	(ii)	sounds like ee in fee
(o)	sounds like o in pole	(oo)	sounds like oo in fool
(ɔ)	sounds like o in pot	(ɔɔ)	sounds like o in or
(u)	sounds like oo in good	(uu)	sounds like wo in two
(ts)	sounds like ch in church	(tsw)	sounds like ch in chair
(sh)	sounds like sh in she	(shw)	sounds like ur in sure
(gw)	sounds like ua in guava	(hw)	sounds like wh in what
(gb)	sounds like kp but heavier	(kw)	sounds like q in quad

(kp) position the velum as fork, the lips as for p, and then release the two, closing simultaneously.

| (ny) | sounds like n in canyon | (ŋ) | sounds like ng in sing |

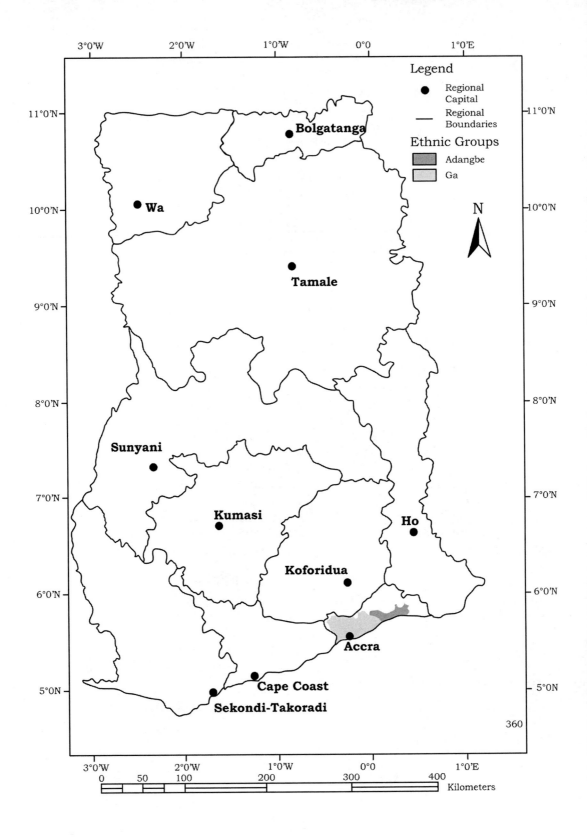

FIGURE 14.1: Map of Ghana showing Ga-Dangme territories

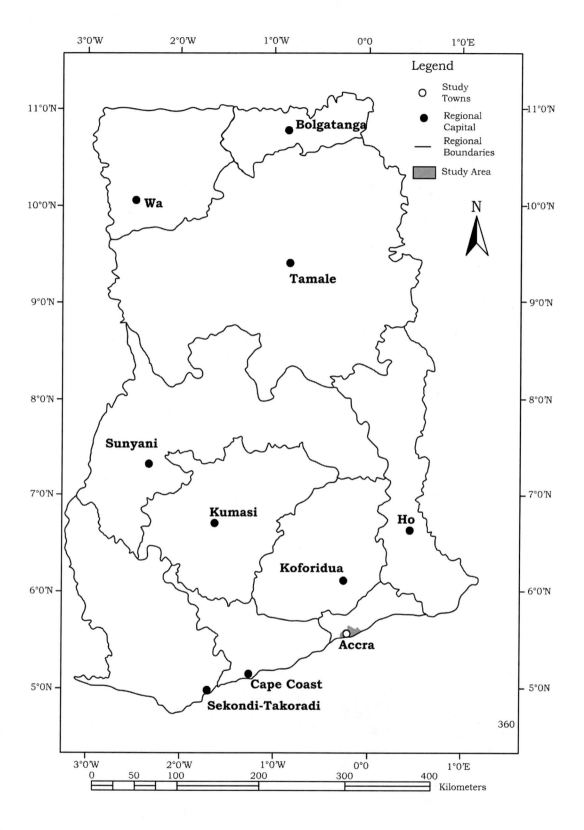

FIGURE 14.2: Map of Ghana showing research area

14. Historical, Geographical, Cultural, and Social Background of the Gas of Ghana

The Land and the People

Ga is the name for the inhabitants and settlements around parts of southeastern Ghana. The Tsenmu lagoon near Tema bounds this area in the east; in the west it is bounded by the Sakumɔ River; in the south by the Atlantic Ocean; and in the north by the Akwapim Mountains.

Ga, however, is generally applied to Gamei/Gas, the people and land from the Lanŋma in the east, to the Volta. This coastal ethnic group inhabits a stretch of land that extends about 70 kilometers (28 miles) along the coast. The seven towns forming the Ga traditional area are: Osu, La, Nungua, Tema, Teshie, and Gamashi, comprising Jamestown and Usher Town.

For almost four centuries, the Ga heartland consisted of a series of coastal towns, each with independent coastal and inland villages. The capital city of Ghana, Accra, and other major towns, Osu, La, Teshie, Nungua and Tema, are welded into a loose confederation under the Ga *maŋtsɛ-nukpa, Ga-maŋtsɛ,* " Ga paramount chief."

Due to the political administrative structure in Ghana, Ga is now part of the Greater Accra Regional Administration. This region is made up of the Accra Metropolitan Area, Tema Municipal Area, Ga East, Ga West, Dangme West and Dangme districts under district chief executives appointed by the central government.

As a result of these new boundaries and demarcations, the Ga settlements are now combined with other ethnic groups, such as the Akan, Dangme, and Eʋe, to form the Greater Accra Region. The Gas, however, form the majority sub-ethnic grouping, accounting for about 19 percent of the region's population.

Traditional rulers still continue to perform their functions and duties in the new administrative structures, assisting the district assemblies and coordinating councils by focusing on matters regarding the interpretation, protection, and observance of traditional customs and the resolution of land issues.

Ga also represents the language of the people. This language is part of the western Kwa linguistic language clusters, which include Akan, Eʋe, Dangme and Guan, which share a common historical origin. Dangme is the language most closely related to Ga in terms of structure and other linguistic features, since both ethnic groups have been living together for centuries.

Traits of the various Akan languages such as Twi, Fante and Akwapim, can also be heard in Ga. Historical interaction with the Eʋes from the Volta region has also resulted in similar terms, names and words used in daily conversations such as: *tokota,* sandal; *tu,* gun; papa, fan; *samfee* (spelled *safui* in Eʋe), key; and *maŋtsesi* (spelled matsesi in Eʋe), matches.

Various rainfall patterns, wet and dry seasons and topographical features give rise to varieties of vegetation. The vegetation is a mixture of savannah shrubs and coconut groves in the coastal areas, with palm, shea butter, baobab and other semi-deciduous forest trees inland. This situation significantly guides the economic activities of the people.

The coastal areas favor fishing and salt mining while those inland engage in the farming of crops such as cassava (yucca, yuca, yucca root, yuca root, manioc, mandioca), maize (corn), and vegetables. The climatic year is divided into six seasons for effective utilization of the weather for their economic activities. These seasons include:

i.   *Maawε:* Cold season from early August to the first half of September.
ii. *Gbo:* Rainy season from September to December.
iii. *Aharabata:* Harmattan cold season. Dry northeast trade winds from the edge of the Sahara Desert cause humidity to drop on the coastal area. January to early February.
iv. *Otso Kilikili:*Hot season with dry winds and minor rains.
     Late February to April.
v.   *Agbeona:* Rainy season from May to July.
vi. *Alemele:*Cold and dry season with little sunshine. Starts late August with climax in November (Henderson-Quartey 2002, 20).

Other names of weather patterns that guide farming activities include:

i.   *Oflɔ:* The name of the flower that grows in the hinterland. Farmers look for the appearance of the flower to plant yams and maize in February.
ii. *Otsokriki:* A very sunny month. The weather is very, very warm and suitable for fishing or outdoor activities— usually in March.
iii. *Abεibe:* April, when butterflies and moths are in abundance. They are found around fruit-bearing trees, especially mango trees (mango season).
iv. *Agbieεnaa:* The month of May, when the rains begin. This is the end of the Ga year.
v.   *Maawε:* The name of a cool breeze that is experienced during this time. It is believed to be responsible for the multiplication of diseases and consequently death, of the elderly. This happens usually in July.
vi. *Manyawale:* The name of the rain that showers intermittently, ideal for planting yams or other root crops in August (Allotey 2005, 23).

As in most parts of Ghana, the preparation of the land and farming starts before the rainy season. Fishing in the surrounding lakes and lagoons is an all-year economic activity, but sea fishing is at its height in the rainy season.

Likewise, the harvesting of crops and hunting happens mostly in the hot and dry seasons. Although by tradition the Gas are mostly fishermen and farmers, modern commerce and white-collar jobs have taken over as major economic activities.

Historical Background

There were no tangible or reliable documentary sources on Ga history before the 1600s. Most of the history can be found in folktales, songs, legends, myths, poems and other traditional oral sources.

Before their present settlements in Ghana, the Ga, together with the Eʋe, Dangme, Krobo and Akwamus, once lived in Nigeria, Benin and Togo (Fianu 1986).

According to Azu (1926, 1927, 1928) and Reindorf (1950) it was from Togo during the chaos in Ŋɔtsie under King Agɔkɔli that the Ga, Dangme, Krobo and Eʋe dispersed further east in various splinter groups. The Ga traveled in three major groups: Ga Mashi, Ga Wo and Ga *Boni*, but in small family units.

These family units later converged under the three major group affiliations to claim settlements in Accra, Tema, La, and Osu, with Ga Mashi as their main coastal settlement. The Dangme also went through the plains of Accra near Kpong—called Tagologo before present settlements were established.

Even though there were conflicting historical accounts about the history of the Ga prior to the 1600s, there is significant evidence to support their presence among other ethnic groups in the ancient Sudanic empires of Mali Ghana and Songhai in the 11th and 12th centuries and Chad in Central Africa (Henderson-Quartey 2002).

A strong historical link through trade between the Gas and the Portuguese was also established before the 16th century (Henderson-Quartey 2002, 77), and that Gas were in Ghana before the arrival of Europeans in 1471 cannot be disputed.

Coastal Accra began to assume its cosmopolitan character after the Gas defeated the Akwamus in a battle around the 1730s as representatives of diverse ethnic groups who had traveled there to participate in overseas trade with the Europeans. Ga settlements began to play a significant role in the commercial life of Accra, which has since been the major center of economic activity in Ghana.

Social and Cultural Profile

POLITICAL AUTHORITY. The most important social unit of Ga society is *we*, "the family." *Webii* "members" join by birth and, less frequently, by adoption. This is the founding father's or the clan head's house where all descendants regard as their spiritual home or *Adeboo shia*, "house of origin."

Gas also claim that their society was initially theocratic and that secular authority associated with chieftaincy was introduced later. Their rulers were the *wulɔmɔ* (*wulɔmei*, pl.), priests, assisted by *mankralo* and *mantsɛ*, king.

Inheritance and traditional Ga traditional government is patriarchal and the *wulɔmɔ* is the ruler high priest. The Gas consider the nomenclature, paraphernalia, rituals and many symbolic articles associated with chieftaincy such as umbrellas, gold ornaments and kente cloth, to be based on the Akan model.

Several Fante Akan terms constitute the appellations associated with Ga political offices. Akan drums and music are played at Ga political ceremonies; the *asafo* military structures have been borrowed from the Fante.

External influences on Ga culture are not only from the Akan. The Dangmes—their eastern neighbors who speak a closely related dialect—as discussed earlier, have greatly affected Ga cultural life.

As suggested by Nketia (1958b), "although the Ga do not accept the view that they are an 'off-shoot' of the Dangme," as documented by N. A. A Azu (1926, 1927, 1928), "they do not deny their close cultural and linguistic affirmatives with them as evident in their musical and religious practices."

The music of the *Me* deity in Ga society, as well as certain aspects of traditional political institutions and customs, reflects these historical ties and contacts with the Dangmes. Despite the many influences on Ga culture, the Dangmes remain their closest neighbors.

There is a movement in Ghana to unite these two ethnic groups and their customs, especially their festival—hence the new ethnic and language classification in Ghana, Ga-Dangme. The new coastal line of Ga-Dangme starting from Kokrobite in the west to Ada in the east is almost 225 kilometers (122 miles) long.

RELIGION. The Gas believe in the unity of the universe. They believe in a close relationship between the physical and the spiritual world, the natural and the world of humans and, above all, one *Nyɔŋmɔ*, Supreme Being, who is the creator of the universe.

Nyɔŋmɔ is believed to be invincible and the everlasting father who controls and directs all human endeavors and also is the head of all the deities through which humans interact with the spiritual world. The *jemawɔji*, deities, through which the Gas commune with *Nyɔŋmɔ*, are harbored in special places in the communities such as the rivers, lakes, trees, hills, *aklabatsa* (groves), *gbatsu* (shrines), and animals.

Nature of the sky, strong winds, thunder and other strange weather conditions are also attributed to the work of *Nyɔŋmɔ* and his *jemawɔji*, lieutenants, or smaller gods. There are *wulɔmɛi*, traditional priests, who serve as servants of the gods and the interpreters for the people of the will of the gods.

Ancestral worship, cleansing of the various *sɛŋ*, sacred stools, of the rulers, warriors, and worship of state deities create the opportunity for the people to be in harmony with the universe. The state deities include: *Kple, Kpledzo, Kpa* and *Me*— some of whom are of Dangme and Akan origin. The deities whose worshippers use the *Otu* and *Akɔn* types of dance-drumming and songs are *yɛlɛ*, yam-eating gods, of the Fante and Akwapim origins respectively.

The main deity of the Gas is *Kple*. Rituals associated with this deity closely relate to the "social organization of the Gas in which the relationships between households, or the structural relationships are defined by reference to the ordered relationships between household gods" (Nketia 2005, 282), and forces of nature are invoked. Much of the history of the Gas can be derived from *Kple* songs.

The Gas have also adopted Islam and several Christian modes of worship. These include the main orthodox Christian religions such as the Catholic, Methodist, Baptist, AME Zion, Anglican and Presbyterian churches, in addition to various Pentecostal, Charismatic and so-called "Born Again" churches. Christians make up the largest religious group followed by Muslims (Moslems), atheists and those worshiping indigenous or traditional religions, who account for about 2 percent of the populace.

The traditional belief in the unity of the universe and the forces of nature makes it possible for some Christians to participate in traditional rituals, especially during festivals and worship of their state deities and sacred stools.

FIGURE 14.3: Nuumo Wolomo Abordai III, chief priest of Kweikuma Tsoshishie, Jamestown, Accra (2009).

Most Christians who participate in these traditional rituals see this as not conflicting with their religious beliefs and practices.

FESTIVALS. Festivals are very important to the Gas. They provide opportunities for family reunions, remembrance of their ancestors and all those who passed during the year, purification of sacred stools, planning of development projects and resolving disputes.

Apart from the yearly *Hɔmɔwɔ*, hooting at hunger, the main harvest festival, other festivals celebrating episodes in their history, religious beliefs, and occupations are celebrated throughout the year. *Asafotufiam*, celebrated in Ada, and *Ŋmayem*, in the Shai and Osudoku settlements, are festivals that unite the Ga-Dangme of today.

Perspectives and Concepts of Music

CONTEXT AND ORGANIZATION OF MUSICAL ACTIVITIES. Traditional musical activities of the Gas relate principally to political, recreational and religious events. Categories of traditional musical types include popular or recreational types such as *Sɔnte, Oge, Gome, Kpanlongo, Kolomashie,* and *Fume Fume,* in addition to strictly female types such as *Amedzulɔ, Tuumatu, Tsuimli, Suolele* and *Awaa Adzawe.*

Religious musical types are reserved for the ritual worship of the *Kple, Kpledzo, Me, Kpa, Otu, Akɔn,* and *Nana* deities. Occupational performances include *Adaŋ* or *Aklama,* "hunters dance-drumming," and songs performed by fishermen during their expeditions.

An interesting feature of musical practice among the Gas is the adoption of non–Ga concepts, instruments, terms and musical types. Influences from Akan musical practices include musical types such as *Adenkum* and *Adowa,* predominantly female dance-drumming types, *Asafo,* dance-drumming for warrior organizations, and *Obonu,* court dance-drumming and the use of the heptatonic (seven-note) scale.

Several instruments are also borrowed from the Akan, such as the *atumpan,* the principal talking drums of the Akan; *bɔmmaa* or *fɔntɔmfrɔm,* also known as *obonu; donno,* an hourglass-shaped drum; and *ɔperenten,* also known as *oblente,* and *apentemma,* both of which are bottle-shaped drums.

MAKING A MUSICIAN "DRUMMER AND DANCER." The most recognized traditional *miyilɔ* (drummers), dancers, and other performing artists of the Gas, have their training in the numerous shrines and royal palaces of the chiefs. As a result, most of the instruments and secular recreational music and dance-drumming ceremonies evolved from the ingenuity of religious, political, ceremonial music and dance ceremonies and their practitioners.

Tetteh Addy (an expert in religious dance-drumming), the eldest brother of Mustapha Tettey Addy, Yakubu Addy and Obo Addy (all master drummers from Avenor), created the most recent of all Ga recreational musical types, *Fume Fume,* in the late 1970s. Although a recreational dance-drumming ceremony, almost all lyrics of the songs, dance movements and instrumental rhythmic patterns of *Fume Fume* are derived from traditional Ga religious dances such as *Kple, Akɔn, Otu, Nana* and *Tigare.*

One becomes a drummer, dancer or singer by participating in traditional religious and political worship and events, in addition to apprenticing with lead drummers, dancers and singers at the shrines or palaces or by joining amateur and professional bands or drumming and dance ensembles which specialize in specific dance-drumming styles.

Drum-makers or carvers among the Gas are traditionally also musicians. The *miyilɔ* takes care of his own drum. Most drummers encourage their children or closest relatives to continue their trade, hence there are families of singers and drummers among the Gas.

MUSICAL SOUND SOURCES: VOCAL VS. INSTRUMENTAL MUSIC. The voice remains the most used sound source of the Gas in their musical activities. Traits of different languages may be heard in songs because of the long history of interaction with several ethnic groups and with Europeans.

Lala in Ga is the term for categories of songs or song types, function of a song or the act of singing. Types of *lala* include: *haaji lala,* twin ritual songs; *kpɔjiemɔ lala,* songs for outdooring or introducing new born babies to the public; *adesa lala,* songs performed as interludes during storytelling sessions; *adaawe lala,* puberty or maiden songs; and *oshwebɔɔ lala,* introductory singing or preludes to invoke the spirit of the deities to guide a performance and also to warm up or prepare the voices of performers. *Oshwe* is the first phase of every dance-drumming ceremony when *oshwebɔɔ lala* is performed.

Most of the categories of songs mentioned above are performed unaccompanied. Other songs may be accompanied by a *dodompo,* castanet; *maa,* stick clappers; *ŋoŋo,* single bell; *ŋoŋonta,* double bell; *shekeshe,* rattle (with beads woven outside the gourd); shakers; maracas (container rattles); or may be combined with several *mi,* drums. Song types that accompany dance-drumming are found in religious, political and recreational events.

Two varieties of scales, the pentatonic (five-note) scale and heptatonic (seven-note) scale, are used in song creations among the Gas. Religious, political and other sacred songs use mostly varieties of the pentatonic scale. The heptatonic varieties are used mostly in the recreational or Akan-influenced songs. The hexatonic (six-note) scale has also found its way into some of the recreational songs.

Organization of melodies using varieties of these scales result in modal shifts during song performances. A song can start or end on any note of the scale. The position of the tonic may not be the beginning or the last note of the song.

There is a close relationship between musical intonation and speech tones because Ga is a tonal language. This is not always the case — especially when the lead singer recreates songs during performances.

Call and response between the solo and chorus or interaction between male and female voices are the structural forms used in Ga song performances.

In dance-drumming events, the lead singer, who introduces or decides on songs to be performed, assumes the title of *lalatsɛ,* "the father of songs." *Tsɛ,* in Ga, is the head or father of the family. The success of a performance rests on him as well as on the lead drummer. It is also expected of the *lalatsɛ* to effectively and appropriately use texts and melodic variations of songs. *Lalatsɛ* brings the performance to life.

In religious performances such as *Kple, Otu, Akɔn,* and *Nana,* the role of the *lalatsɛ* becomes very critical and significant. Together with the priests or priestesses at a religious ceremony, the purpose of a ritual worship is achieved through effective coordination and performance of songs, for it is believed the songs and prayers provide the bridge to the spiritual world and the ancestors.

Harmony in vocal music using the pentatonic scale/mode is realized by the use of octave duplications, unison, and the overlapping of parts (male and female or solo and chorus). Songs based on heptatonic scales may be sung in unison but break occasionally in two or three parts. Intervals of thirds, fifths and sixths are heard when this situation occurs.

Other sound sources used in music-making among the Gas, in addition to the voice, are varieties of idiophones (bells and rattles)and membranophones (drums). The combination of these instruments, accompanied by singing and dance during religious, political and recreational ceremonies, depends on the requirements of the specific ceremony.

Strictly instrumental traditional performances made up of drums, rattles and bells, and wind instruments, such as horns, can be heard at the shrines and *maŋtsɛwe* (palaces) of the chiefs or during the *Hɔmɔwɔ* festival when, during the *Oshi* dance-drumming, "the special Hɔmɔwɔ dance," the horn is used instead of the *ŋoŋo* (Nketia 1958b, 26).

Some of the instruments favored during dance-drumming ceremonies are: *ŋoŋo, ŋoŋonta, shekeshe, maa, dodompo, gome* (box drum), *obonu, atumpan, donno, mpintintoa,*(gourd drum), *asafo drums, oblente, apentemma* and *atwereshi* (conga-type drum).

Instruments of European origin were introduced to the Ga through trading activities, slavery, Christianity and military duties during the two world wars. These include: trumpets; bugles; trombones; *kyen kyen* (cymbals); *pati* (concert tom), which is an adaptation of the British military field drum used during the Second World War; *tamalin* or *tamalee* (frame drum), which is a reconstruction of the tambourine; shakers; and maracas. The guitar, mandolin and accordion have also found their way into many recreational traditional dance-drumming ensembles.

Instruments used in the recreational dance-drumming ceremonies, *Gome, Kolomashie* and *Kpanlongo*, discussed in this book, include *ŋoŋo, ŋoŋonta, shekeshe, maa, dodompo, gome* (box drum), *Donno, Apentemma* and *Atwereshi, Pati, Tamalin* (frame drum), shakers, and maracas.

The playing technique and description of *ŋoŋonta* are in Part One, Chapter 1 and those of the *tamalin* and *maa* in Part Two, Chapter 9. The description and playing techniques of the *apentemma* are similar to those of the *uuvi* and *asivui* of the central and northern Eʋes, as shown in Part Two, Chapter 9.

Ŋoŋo. *Ŋoŋo* provides the timeline for most Ga percussion ensembles. It is a single non-melodic and clapperless bell made from iron metal pipes of about three inches in diameter by blacksmiths who specialize in building these instruments. There are four stages

FIGURE 14.4: *Ŋono*

involved in making *ŋoŋo*: stage one, cutting the pipe; stage two, flattening the pipe; stage three, making the handle; and stage four, opening.

In stage one, the metal pipe is measured and cut to the desired length. A chisel and hammer are used to cut the pipe on an anvil after heat is applied to the area marked to be cut. In stage two, the cut section of the pipe to be used as the playing area is reheated until red. It is then hammered from time to time with intermittent heating until it becomes flat at one end.

At this point, the second section of the pipe is heated and then hammered to a round shape to complete stage three. The wider end of the flattened metal is reheated for opening with a chisel and hammer. The bell under construction is turned upside down and gradually the wider or bigger end is opened using different sizes of chisels to complete stage four.

FIGURE 14.5: Playing technique on the *Ŋono*, demonstrated by Alphonse Ahumani of the Ghana Dance Ensemble, National Theater of Ghana (2010).

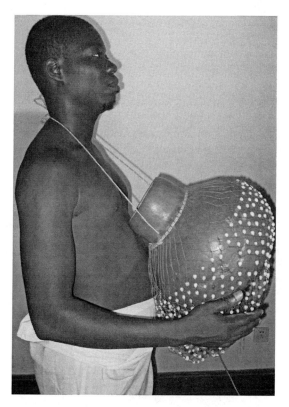

Above, FIGURE 14.6: *Shekeshe*. *Left*, FIGURE 14.7: Playing technique of the *shekeshe*, demonstrated by Alphonse Ahumani of the Ghana Dance Ensemble, National Theater of Ghana (2010).

Wooden rods are also used as the opening becomes bigger. Reheating continues until the desired size is reached.

Maracas. This is a container rattle used in pairs. It is the reconstruction of the Taino

Above, FIGURE 14.8: Maracas. *Right*, FIGURE 14.9: Playing technique on maracas, demonstrated by Alphonse Ahumani of the Ghana Dance Ensemble, National Theater of Ghana (2010).

(Puerto Rican indigenous natives), Cuban, Venezuelan, Guatemalan, maracas that are now used in most Latin and Caribbean percussion ensembles.

The maracas is one of the few instruments brought back by freed slaves and the Gas who participated in the two world wars. The Gas make their instruments from empty milk tins or gourds filled with seeds or beads.

The maracas is a self-sounding, rhythmic or non-melodic idiophone. Sound is produced by shaking and alternating two of the instruments held in both hands. It is used mostly in recreational dance-drumming ensembles instead of the *shekeshe* to support or emphasize the bells.

Dodompo. Dodompo is a finger bell or castanet. It is known as *firikyiwa* or *asem aba* in Akan and *kretsiwa* among the central and northern Eʋe. The *lalatsɛ* mostly uses the *dodompo* during performances as a support to the *ɲoɲo*.

The *dodompo* is also crafted by blacksmiths from a 1.22 × 1.83m (4 × 6 inch) iron rod or bar. The rod is heated and hammered into a flat shape.

The flattened bar or rod is measured and marked into the shape and design. The shape or design is cut out after heating. The cut out shape is again heated and rounded at all ends and made into an oval shape. The oval shape is finally joined at the top to complete the instrument.

The metal ring worn on the thumb to play the *dodompo* is also crafted from a one-inch iron bar. The bar is heated, hammered flat and bent round into a circumference that can fit an average thumb. Refer to Part Two, Chapter 9 for further description and playing technique of this instrument, under *kretsiwa*.

Left, FIGURE 14.10: *Pati. Right,* FIGURE 14.11: Playing technique of the *pati*, demonstrated by Alphonse Ahumani of the Ghana Dance Ensemble, National Theater of Ghana (2010).

Atwereshie. The *atwereshie* or *kpanlongo mi*, a conga-type drum, has become the standard drum for any aspiring percussionist in Ga dance-drumming. Early *atwereshies* were constructed using the *ʋublala* (stave construction) method as with Eʋe drums, described in Chapter 1.

Drummers wanted a new type of drum for their new highlife experiment. They needed a new drum to symbolize the approaching independence from the British so they preferred this new method (borrowed from the southeastern Eʋes) rather than carving from solid wood, which was used for constructing other traditional drums.

Stave construction of *atwereshie*s, however, was short-lived. In the early 1970s, construction reverted back to the carving method as there were not readily available carpenters to make these drums; also, it was a matter of convenience for the drummers to easily make them.

The Gas are at the forefront of hand-drumming in Ghana. No other ethnic group in Ghana is so versatile in using hand-drumming techniques as the Gas. There are five basic sounds or tones available in recreating or manipulating rhythmic patterns using hand-drumming techniques, which are also employed on the *atwereshie*.

A drummer assumes the title of *dadefoɔkye* or *miyilɔkye*, master drummer, if he can produce the five tones correctly—but, most importantly, if he can combine them creatively during performances. These tones are named for their specific tonal qualities and functions in the overall organization of musical sounds in the percussion ensemble:

   i.   *milɛ gbee*   original sound of the drum;
   ii.   *miishi mɔ*   pounding of the drum;
   iii.   *nyɛmɔ*   pressing of the drum;
   iv.   *ayawa*   bragging with the drum; and
   v.   *gbla mii*   tearing up the drum.

Milɛ gbee. This is the voice and the dominant tone used by the drummer. It is best described and recognized as an open tone. To generate this tone, the drummer keeps his fingers close and firm with the palm slightly cupped. With this position of the hand, he strikes the area of the head marked "A" (area closest to the drummer's body) with only four fingers (from the base to the tips of the fingers), excluding the thumb and quickly bouncing off the head.

To produce the correct tone, the base of the fingers must align with the outer edge of the ring of the drumhead. This sound is vocalized as *Pe Pe Pe*, which is used in teaching and learning the tone and other rhythmic patterns.

Miishi mɔ. This is the bass and lowest voice of the drum. It is a very deep-sounding tone—hence the description "pounding the drum hard." The posi-

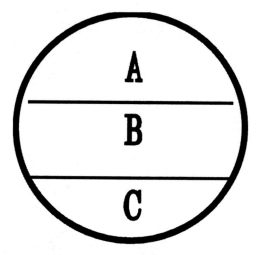

FIGURE 14.12: The *kpanlongo mi* drumhead

tion of the hand before agitating the head is the same as in *milɛ gbee*; however, the whole hand, all fingers included, up to the wrist must strike the drum. The hand covers the areas "A" and "B" of the head shown in Figure 14.12. This tone is vocalized as *Dun Dun Dun*. In a fast tempo, it is vocalized *Du Du Du*.

Nyɛmɔ. This tone is best realized as a closed or muted sound of *milɛ gbee*. The preparation of the hand and the area stroked on the head, "A," is the same as in *milɛ gbee*. The main difference in sound production is that instead of bouncing off, the drummer presses against the head, producing a dead, muted or closed tone. This tone is vocalized as *Pì Pì Pi* at a very low pitch. It is vocalized as *Piti Piti Piti* when played in succession.

Ayawa. This is the most difficult of all the tones. The innovative use of this tone makes you an excellent drummer. The master drummer is recognized by his technical virtuosity and creative uses of this tone, hence its name "bragging or showing off." In hand drum pedagogy, this tone is recognized as an open slap tone.

To generate this sound, the hand, especially the fingers, must be relaxed. The drummer strikes the same area of the head as in *mils gbee* but with the fingers loose and detached from each other. Only the tips of the four fingers to their base touch the head. The fingers may also strike the head at an angle with the forefingers tilting towards the center of the head. Fingers must quickly bounce off the head as in *mils gbee*.

The vocable used for teaching this tone is *Maa Maa Maa* for single notes and long note values, and *Mada Mada Mada* for fast and alternating short note values.

Gbla mii. *Gbla mii* is recognized as a closed slap tone. The position of the hand and striking area are the same as in *ayawa*. Instead of bouncing off the head, the fingers seem to grab onto the head. *Gbla mii* is the soft or muted sound of *ayawa*. This sound is vocalized as *Pa Pa Pa* and *Pata Pata Pata* when *Gbla mii* is performed in succession and in fast tempo.

In the hands of *dadefɔɔkye*, all the areas, including the "C," are utilized in performance. The vocables of these tones are used presently only in teaching aspiring drummers. The functional names *mils gbee, miishi mɔ, nyɛmɔ, ayawa* and *gbla mii*, which are known to the very old drummers, were used in the past for teaching and during performances.

FIGURE 14.13: *Kpanlongo mi.* FIGURE 14.14: *Kpanlongo* technique as demonstrated by Alphonse Ahumani of the Ghana Dance Ensemble, National Theater of Ghana (2010).

Gome. *Gome* was originally a wooden box drum created by Congolese fishermen, which was later adopted by freed slaves and Ga fishermen in Fernando Po in the early 19th century. This is the main instrument and also the name of the dance-drumming known as Gome among the Gas of Ghana.

There are two ways of constructing this drum depending on the type, tools and materials used. The original type uses the peg technique as in Kpanlongo, while the contemporary method uses the four-in-one or single bolt and nut (screw) technique. Both of these approaches result to the same acoustic quality of the drum. The screw type has a longer life span — especially the drumhead and outer shells— and makes the tuning much easier. This is the preferred method used among the Gas of today.

Major components of the *Gome* drum include an outer shell, inner shell, single or four-in-one bolts and nuts, and the drumhead, which is either from a deer or goat skin, held in place by battens.

Construction of the Outer Shell (See Figure 14.15a). Four pieces of wood ten inches in length (AI), are joined to four pieces of wood (AII) to form the outer shell (2.5 feet long) of the drumhead. Once this is completed, the other ends are then dado joined to wood (AIII) (halved lap joint) to complete the outer shell.

Finally, the face of wood AI and wood AII are nailed together to create miter joints and dado joints of AII to AIII. This creates a halved lap joint, which is determined by the width and thickness of both pieces of wood. The halved lap joint is constructed by removing half of the thickness of each piece of wood from the area to be joined to that of the thickness of the finished joint when put together.

Construction of the Inner Shell. The construction of the inner shell is similar to that of the outer shell but sufficiently smaller in size to freely fit into the outer shell to be moved in and out. Pieces of wood (BIII) are butted on both sides to form a cross-shaped piece of wood like wood (AIII), but small enough to hold wood (BII) to form the determined inner shell when it is half-jointed to the four BII woods.

Construction of the Bolts and Nuts. Wood C is bolt-joined about 1.5 inches (3.83 centimeters) away from the inserted inner shell on wood (AII) and its opposite one. Two metal plates are fixed on wood C and wood (BIII). A flat metal plate (OI) is screwed onto the right side of wood (BII) to prevent the bolt from creating a hole and to absorb the pressure during tuning.

The other metal plate of the same size with a bolt is welded at the center of the plate with a hole through both plate (OII) and wood C to plate (OI) to accommodate the pressure when screwed while tuning the drum.

The *Gome* Drumhead (Figure 14.15b). Either the skin of the goat, antelope or deer is used for this purpose. The skin is soaked in water for about 15 to 30 minutes, depending on the thickness of the skin. The skin is then stretched over the drumhead of both the outer and inner shells.

The skin is then pulled and tack-nailed around the four corners of the head about one-inch (2.54 centimeters) below the head. Wood battens (Z) are nailed to hold the skin to protect

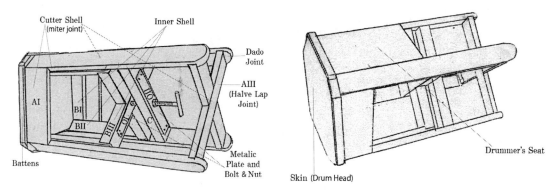

FIGURE 14.15a: Parts of the *gome* drum frame. *Right*, FIGURE 14.15b: Parts of the *gome* drum frame showing the drumhead and drummer's seat.

Above, FIGURE 14.16: Completed *gome* drum. *Right*, FIGURE 14.17: *Gome* technique front view, as demonstrated by Alphonse Ahumani of the Ghana Dance Ensemble, National Theater of Ghana (2010).

the head from damage. The extra skin below the battens is then cut off. The completed drum is then sun-dried before use. The drummer sits at area S to play the drum.

The playing technique on the *gome* is similar to the Cajón, the main Afro-Peruvian musical instrument used mostly in the rumba dance. The drummer uses both the heels and slapping the head with hands to generate sounds (David Amoo 2010).

15. *Gome* Recreational Dance-Drumming Ceremony

Historical Background and Development

Gome is one of the oldest recreational dance-drumming ceremonies of the coastal Gas of Ghana. This musical type was first introduced in Ghana by the coastal fisherman of Accra who learned and brought it from the Congolese fishermen from the Fernando Pó Islands (which became Bioko in 1979) in the Gulf of Guinea, most probably in the early 19th century. Why the origin in the Fernando Pó Islands? What were the Ga fishermen doing in Fernando Pó?

The decline of slavery in most parts of West Africa in the early 19th century and among the Gas in particular around the 1830s, created the need for new economic ventures. The elders, chiefs and middlemen who participated in and made fortunes from the slave trade and whose children and relatives benefited from European formal education became the new elites among the people.

In this group were also the *Mulatofoi*, indigenous Gas-Africans who were children of European men and African women. *Mulatofoi*, the mixed race, and the educated elite became the most important people among the Gas. These elites held the highest offices and the best jobs when the Danes, and later the British, colonized the Gas.

The end of slavery and subsequent lack of well-paying maritime jobs forced skilled workers, including carpenters, blacksmiths and other artisans who were not in the "elite class," to look for jobs elsewhere. Fernando Pó was the preferred destination for most of these skilled workers from West Africa.

There was a major influx of Gas, Dangmes, Eves and Akans to the two major towns, Pico de Santa Isable and San Carlos, which served as major commercial centers for both European and American traders during and long after the abolition of the slave trade in Fernando Pó.

This island nation, then a Spanish province/colony, provided work for the new immigrants on coffee, cocoa, banana, oil palm, tobacco and sugarcane plantations and ports. Before the arrival of this new workforce, there were already slaves who could not be transported to the Americas doing most of the work.

The Gas and some of the coastal Eves and Fantes worked mostly in the fishing and maritime industries. The fishing industry was the most lucrative of all, and it attracted many fishermen and their families to the island. It is still a common practice today for coastal Ga, Fante and Eve fishermen to travel long distances along the West African coast to fish off several islands in the Gulf of Guinea.

As part of relieving boredom and stress, the new arrivals joined their counterparts, the freed slaves, to sing as they carried out their daily chores. Relaxation at home after a hard day's work created other opportunities for them to recount and reenact their experiences at the various work places through dancing, singing and drumming using various improvised percussion instruments.

Improvised instruments included work tools such as hammers, saws, six-inch nails, wooden clappers, empty cans, and wooden boxes which were later covered with animal hide to become *gome*, lending their name to the dance-drumming. The Congolese fishermen led these performances and also constructed the *gome*, box drums, that were used.

Weekends were also occasions for social gatherings at bars, homes and nightclubs where music was performed. Since the workers were from different African ethnic groups, English and corrupted Spanish became the preferred languages used during performances.

I could not find any clear documentation of how *Gome* was performed, the nature of the dance, costumes or types of instruments used in Fernando Pó. The only clues left of its origin in Fernando Pó are the main drums, the *gome* and *tamalin,* the only instruments that survived the journey back to Ghana. Other instruments from the shrines were later added to recreate this new dance-drumming among the Gas.

There is a consensus among the Gas that a returning group of fishermen led by Papa Nii Amoo (who later became the chief priest of Keitsoshishi of Jamestown) first introduced *Gome* in Accra. His nephew, Kwaku Nii Noona, however, popularized this dance-drumming among the Gas in the late 19th century.

Fishermen were the only people who performed *Gome* as a recreational musical type after their expeditions in Accra in its early days. It was reserved for only the old since young people were not permitted at that time to go sea fishing.

The aging of the fishermen and popularity of *Gome* among the Gas during festivals and other social occasions compelled other workers, especially the artisans who were also once in Fernando Pó, to take over the performance.

Age has since ceased to be a requirement for or hindrance to participating in *Gome* dance-drumming ceremonies. It was *Gome* that started the long tradition of youth being actively involved and taking key roles in traditional dance-drumming ceremonies. This new trend resulted in the creation of new recreational types: *Kolomashie, Oge, Konkoma,* Kpanlongo and most recently *Fume Fume,* by the Gas.

All genders and age groups who share the interest and love for *Gome* are encouraged to join, as it has become a celebration of the people's history, depicting their spirit of endurance, struggle and artistic creativity. Because of the dexterity, agile movements and strong rhythmic sense expected of dancers, only those with high musical ability, interest and discipline join *Gome* groups.

As a recreational music celebration, *Gome* is performed on all social occasions, such as funerals, marriage and wedding ceremonies, festivals and visits of members of the central government. *Gome* groups are organized as bands and may only perform upon invitation, which usually attracts a token fee.

Gome is performed today in several Ga towns— especially in the coastal areas of Sukura, Chorkor, Agbogbloshie, Korle Gornno, Chorkor, Teshie, Nungua, Mamprobi, and Akweteman with La Labadi, where it is highly concentrated.

Organization of the Dance-Drumming Ceremony

FORM AND STRUCTURE. *Gome* is mainly performed for entertainment. Participation is restricted to members of the group but the audience may join when invited by dancers during a performance. There are three distinct phases of this recreational dance-drumming ceremony. These are:

i. *nkpai*   pouring of libation;
ii. *oshwe*   warm-up singing; and
iii. *gome*   the main dance-drumming ceremony.

Phase One: Nkpai. With the arena set, the performance starts with a brief pouring of libation by the leader or designated *wulɔmɔ* of the group. This ritual, in the form of a prayer, calls the spirit of *Nyɔŋmɔ,* the *Supreme* Being, the *jemawɔji,* land deities, and the ancestors to be present during the performance. It is a common belief among the Gas that any social gathering invites bad or evil spirits so there is a need to cleanse the dance space and safeguard the safety of the performers by reconnecting with the spirit world.

As indicated earlier, originally most of the lead drummers and singers were from the shrines so importance was attached to prayer before any dance-drumming activity — even recreational events, such as *Gome.* It is rather unfortunate that many of the existing *Gome* groups omit this phase during their performances simply because members, especially the musicians, have no connection with the shrines or have become Christians.

Phase Two: Oshwe. Once the libation is completed, the *lalatsɛ* leads *oshwebɔɔ lala,* warm-up songs, which are aimed at preparing the voices of the participants, motivating the dancers and setting the mood for the main dance phase.

Oshwe (*oshweii* pl.) is performed unaccompanied, with instruments, and in flexible rhythm. This phase also serves as an opportunity to review songs to be used in the main dance phase.

Phase Three: Gome. The main dance phase which follows may last for several hours. There are short breaks during this phase when refreshments are served. Singing may continue during these short breaks without the percussion ensemble. The number of breaks usually depends on the occasion and duration of the performance.

To start this phase, the lead *gome* drummer may play a series of introductory rhythmic patterns as a signal to alert the percussion ensemble and the singers to prepare for the main event. *Maa,* wooden clappers, start the timeline and the rest of the percussion ensemble follows when the *gome's* initial signal in flexible rhythm changes to strict rhythm. The singing resumes after all members of the percussion ensemble start to play.

This initial performance with the percussion ensemble before the dance is known as *choke-cho,* "Let the *maa* go (play)." The purpose is to blend the percussion ensemble and the singing before the dancers take the stage. The *lalatsɛ* sometimes says the word *tsoketso,* which cues in the *maa* players to start this phase of the performance.

The arena is now cleared for the dance to commence. A brief *oshwe* is performed to start all subsequent repeats of this phase and may sometimes be performed to end the entire performance.

Songs

Lyrics in *Gome* relate to human affiliations, social and topical issues, political and historical events and those themes making fun of the colonial masters — especially the British. Unlike *Kpanlongo,* which started as a youth dance-drumming, its song-texts likely to focus on courtship and indecent themes, *Gome* songs do not encourage vulgarity or profanity. The original performers, the "old folks," did not allow songs with such texts and this tradition has been kept until today.

A special feature of *Gome* songs is the use of *pidgin English,* corrupted English. Two such songs are transcribed below:

1. I am a poor man o,
   I am a poor man o,

Nobody I know.
My wife I know.

2. Me don know trouble,
Father sick me no hear,
I get telegram say e die.
Me don know trouble.

Both of these songs relate to issues of poverty, sickness and death. The second song indirectly relates to the pain encountered during the Gas' sojourn in Fernando Pó, from which they could not easily return home in case of sickness or the death of relatives.

Gome songs are usually performed in call and response form between the two lead cantors and chorus. One lead cantor usually starts a song, which is taken over and completed by the second. Trading or splitting of sections of the melody by the cantors is a unique performance practice in *Gome* ceremony. The chorus then joins in by performing the whole song or sections may be shared with the cantors.

Melodies of songs are based on varieties of the pentatonic, hexatonic and heptatonic scales. Harmony is derived by singing in unison, parallel octaves between the female and male voices, and sporadic use of thirds, fifths, and sixths against the melody when the chorus breaks into parts. Occasional intervals of fourths can be heard in very old pentatonic-derived songs.

The Percussion Ensemble

The original drums used in the percussion ensemble were the *gome, tamalin,* and *apentemma*—the last adopted from their religious ensembles. The *maa,* hammer, saw and nails were also used initially, but were later replaced with *ŋoŋo, dodompo* and *shekeshe.*

FIGURE 15.1: Abodzentse *Gome* Group in action (2007).

A typical ensemble today has a *gome* as the lead drum that sets the tempo and controls the whole performance. *Tamalin* and *apentemma* serve as supporting drums. Multiple *maa* played by members of the chorus provide the timeline with support from *dodompo*, which is played by the lead cantor, and *shekeshe*, played by another percussionist to emphasize the *maa* parts. *Ŋoŋo*, when used, doubles the *maa* part.

Other instruments that may be seen today as part of the ensemble are the *atwereshie* and *donno*.

Dance Organization

DANCE ARENA. *Gome* is performed in a loose semicircle formation. The lead drummer sits on his instrument in front with other members of the percussion ensemble and chorus either sitting or standing behind him, facing the audience.

There is enough space created between the audience and performers for the dance to take place. The performance space looks like the diagram at the right.

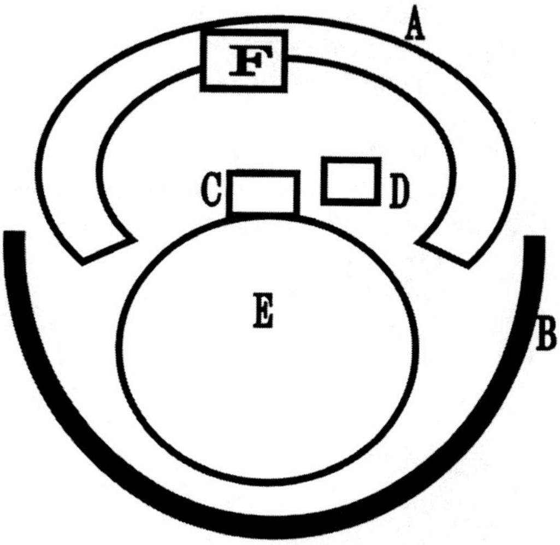

DANCE MOVEMENTS AND CHOREOGRAPHY. *Gome* is classified as a free dance. Dancers are not controlled or directed by any signal from the drummers to execute their movements. Once the mood is set after *tsokɛtso*, the dancers who are part of the chorus enter the arena to express themselves.

The dance is usually performed as a solo. An entry of another soloist/dancer in the dance arena serves as a cue for whoever is dancing at the time to transition from being a soloist to being part of the chorus. The main dance movement by the men is an exaggeration of the way a colonial master walked.

FIGURE 15.2: *Gome* performance space. A: chorus and other instrumentalists; B: audience; C: lead drum/*gome*; D: *apentemma*, seated; E: dance arena; F: lead cantor.

This movement is initiated by standing erect with the arms bent at the elbows, the dancer moving forward by walking in a syncopated fashion. Legs and arms moving in opposition and stepping right-left-right then left-right-left (a 1-2-3 count) accent the third count by switching to the opposite foot. The whole body is stiff and upright, leaning side-to-side and overall movement appears stiff and staccato. The mood and expression is comical as the dancer imitates his impression of a European colonial master.

At certain times, the dancer breaks from the above-mentioned movement and quickly takes his hands to his sternum and then extends them out in front of himself. While executing this movement, the dancer changes the footwork either by placing the right foot (the metatarsal) behind the left heel or the left foot (the metatarsal) behind the right heel. In this position, the dancer pushes down on the metatarsal enough to raise the foot in front.

This movement is executed quickly and is repeated as the dancer moves around the dance arena; this is performed in a quick one-two, one-two count. The dancer freely transitions between these two basic movements and other movements that may fit with the theme of the dance.

Other behavioral patterns of the "masters," such as smoking cigars, pipes and drinking are also depicted in the dance. Military drills and commands: halt, salute, stand at ease, march, run and stop are also incorporated into the dance.

Women dancers show support for the men dancers through graceful movements of the arms and legs. Similar to the men's second movement, the dancer places the right foot (the metatarsal) approximately three inches behind the left heel. At times she alternates by putting the left foot (the metatarsal) approximately three inches behind the right heel. In this position, the dancer pushes down on the metatarsal enough to raise the foot in front. This movement is executed quickly and is repeated as the dancer moves around the dance arena; this is performed in a quick one-two, one-two count as with the men's movement. The woman's upper body, however, is more graceful than the man's, as she leans side-to-side with her hands and arms extended in front. Her foot movement also appears less choppy than the man's, and her hip movement (a swaying, shifting or tilting of the hips) is initiated by her quick foot movement.

The dance becomes a theatrical experience, a creative dance drama involving several dancers/actors, when topical issues such as fishing expeditions, romance, courtship, husband and wife quarrels, and other daily episodes are mimed or acted out through the dance.

A special feature of the creative dance drama is the miming of various occupations and economic ventures of the Gas: carpentry, fishing, blacksmithing, farming, weaving, masonry and other artisan crafts. The tools and equipment of these occupations further enhance the dance movements.

Carpentry is the predominant occupation mimed during festive occasions. Women dancers become props for the carpenters wood or bench to be carved during these displays.

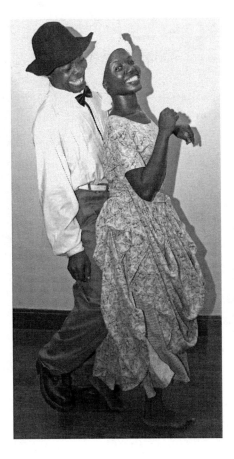

Left, FIGURE 15.3: Members of the Ghana Dance Ensemble, National Theater. *Gome* dancers in performance (2010). *Above*, FIGURE 15.4: Members of the Ghana Dance Ensemble, National Theater. *Gome* dancers in performance (2010).

Costume and Other Visual Art Forms

Costumes bring the *Gome* performance to life. As a tribute, honor, remembrance and respect to the elders who created this dance-drumming ceremony, the participants in this event put on some of the old dresses used by the Gas— especially those worn during colonial times.

The "masters" and the African elites wear long/short pants, long sleeve shirts with bow and long ties, suspenders with walking sticks or canes, and work clothes representing the various artisans.

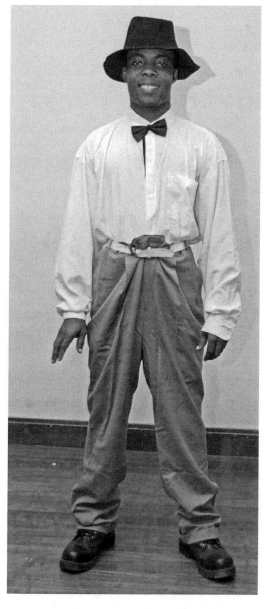 

Left, FIGURE 15.5a: *Gome* male costume demonstration by a member of the Ghana Dance Ensemble, National Theater of Ghana (2010). *Right*, FIGURE 15.5b: *Gome* male costume demonstration by a member of the Ghana Dance Ensemble, National Theater of Ghana (2010).

Women participants wear the usual blouse and cloth wrapped around the body from the waist to the ankle with headgear or a scarf to match. This is the traditional women's dress for most parts of Ghana.

Other women participants in the ceremony wear the old ladies' costume *atofo*, which is comprised of a two-yard strip of cloth which is tied under the armpit and wrapped around the body; a second is wrapped around the waist and hangs to knee-level as in *Atibladekame* and *Adzogbo*.

Left, FIGURE 15.6a: *Gome* female costume. *Atofo* demonstration by a member of the Ghana Dance Ensemble, National Theater of Ghana (2010). *Right*, FIGURE 15.6b: *Gome* female costume. Demonstration by a member of the Ghana Dance Ensemble, National Theater of Ghana (2010).

The buttocks are extended by padding them with extra pieces of cloth, which are tied around the waist under the cloth that hangs to the knee. Colorful beads adorn the neck, ankles and wrists of all the women.

16. *Kolomashie* Recreational Dance-Drumming Ceremony

Historical Background and Development

Kolomashie originated among the Ga-Dangmes as processional dance-drumming before Ghana won its independence from the British in 1957. Ga settlements were small villages and towns scattered along the coast and the hinterland when the Europeans arrived in the late 15th century.

Festivals, especially funerals, were occasions for clans, villages and other family units of the three major groups, Ga Mashi, Ga Wo and Ga Boni, to come together to reconnect with their common heritage at the time. Music and dance formed a major part of these celebrations.

Bereaved families would usually invite other families from far and near to join in the funerary rites. Before final internment, the body of the deceased would be transported to his or her *adebɔɔ shia* for a final visit. There were no wooden coffins or hearses to transport the dead to their ancestral homes and then to the cemetery. Processional drumming, singing and dance became the main vehicle for these activities.

Procession of drummers and singers from one corner of the village to another meant that either the community was being alerted and invited to an impending funeral or the departed was being transported to his/her *adebɔɔ shia* or the cemetery.

The fishermen along Jamestown took this processional dance-drumming to a different level. Drumming groups or bands were formed. These groups were hired to perform during funeral processions. There was no specific name then. It was known only as funeral processional music.

The arrival of Europeans had a tremendous influence on coastal Ga-Dangmes, especially on their funeral processions and musical practices. The introduction of western musical instruments such as the guitar, accordion, mandolin and brass instruments, the teaching of those who were enlisted in the colonial armies, the ending of slavery, and the First World War opened up new mediums for musical creativity.

The influx of freed slaves from Brazil and the indigenous African elites used western instruments to distinguish their westernized "high living" from the locals. Instead of the traditional instruments that were used for funeral processions, western instruments were incorporated.

The context of performance also changed dramatically. Instead of being solely a funeral processional performance, this became the newest recreational dance-drumming, performed when people would party, sing, and dance. At the end of the show, people would process through the streets—especially during the annual *Hɔmɔwɔ* harvest festival and other festive occasions.

This was the dawn of the reconstituted funeral dance-drumming called *Kolomashie* around the 1920s and 1930s. The name was derived from two words: *kolo* and *emashie*. *Kolo* literally means, "an old phenomenon or practice." *Kolo* is also used as a nickname for the colonial masters, an abbreviation of the word "colonials," spelled with a "k" instead of "c." *Emashie*, or *mashie*, means, "It exists, is alive or present." The new name therefore alluded to the fact that the funeral music still existed or the influence and power of the colonial masters was still present even after slavery.

In a further attempt to copy western forms of entertainment and dance band music, popular western styles such as blues, waltz and La Congo, "Congolese pop," were recreated and performed in addition to highlife, which was the "main piece."

Highlife was used as a generic name for various types of new urban entertainment music in vogue at the time, notably *Konkoma*, *Kolomashie* and *Ashiko*. These new styles incorporated western instruments (mandolin, accordion, guitar, brass) and western melodic and harmonic structures.

The highlife phase was the climax of the performance, which usually continued on to the streets. This is the only phase performed today.

This new approach to the performance emerged in Accra (where most freed slaves from Brazil and the indigenous African elites lived). It later spread to other Ga-Dangme towns like La, Osu, Teshie, Nungua and Prampram.

An increase in the number of freed slaves, African elites, and institutions of urban life such as hotels, bars, and dance halls where the westernized and their "masters" would be entertained, increased the appetite for diverse musical styles in the 1940s and early 1950s in Accra.

Brass bands, dance bands, guitar bands and concert bands were formed to satisfy these growing urban needs. As result of this new trend, *Kolomashie* has since been performed for its original traditional function and intent as a processional dance-drumming ceremony among the Gas.

Kolomashie, no doubt, is one of the precursors of and foundation for highlife, the standard Ghanaian popular music today. It remains, since Ghana's independence, the first choice of music by politicians during political campaigns and rallies when processions and parades are involved in Ga constituencies.

Participation in *Kolomashie* is open to all, but because of the running and fast tempo of the music, only those with stamina and in good health take part. No formal training is required but those handling the instruments form themselves into bands and therefore require long rehearsals.

Kolomashie is also called *Jama* by some of the coastal youth who perform it at sporting events (soccer games), political rallies, on floats and other social functions. The name *Jama* is said to be derived from jamming, or jam session, an influence of the Jamaican reggae movement. There are no boundaries or strict rules regarding audience participation. Participants get loose and join the fun when they hear *Kolomashie*.

Organization of the Dance-Drumming Ceremony

FORM AND STRUCTURE. During the early stages of *Kolomashie*, the performance was organized in five phases: highlife, blues, waltz, La Congo and highlife. Presently, the performance has only two phases: *oshwe* and *kolomashie*.

Phase One: **Oshwe**. *Oshwe*, as discussed in the section on *Gome*, is a typical traditional performance of a series of songs that precede most Ga dance-drumming ceremonies. In this context, it is known as *Kolomashie oshwe*, "warm-up song phase," before the main dance-drumming.

Since parading the streets or procession is the main feature of *Kolomashie*, *oshwe* is performed without the dance or traveling around. The songs are performed unaccompanied and in flexible rhythm. After a series of songs the instruments join.

Phase Two: *Kolomashie*. In the 1940s and early 1950s when *Kolomashie* was a stage performance, the event would start with the *lalatsɛ* who served as the conductor of the orchestra. He would accompany himself with *dodompo* while introducing the first song after the *oshwe* phase. The chorus would later join with other instruments.

Some bands or "orchestras" relied on the *lalatsɛ*, conductor, to signal the whole ensemble into action. He would sometimes be seen conducting the performance.

Currently, this phase begins with *ŋoŋo, dodompo* and *shekeshe*, after *oshwe*. This initial performance of the bells and rattles establishes the tempo and the rhythmic framework for the performance.

Once the desired rhythmic foundation is established, the bass drum, *pati, tamalin* and other instruments join in. *Lalatsɛ* then follows with response from the chorus. The movement of the musicians signals the beginning of the dance or procession.

FIGURE 16.1: Emashie *Kolomashie* in action (2006).

Songs

Songs in *Kolomashie* serve as avenues for reflection, communication and creative verbal expression. Song themes may relate to various issues of life, day-to-day occurrences and topical issues. Human affiliations, ridicule of foreigners, enemies and politicians, praise of historical figures and recounting of the history of the Gas— especially during colonial rule — are also common.

Kolomashie songs are treated as part of the musical activity. Songs are selected to suit the particular event. In the context of funerals, songs relating to the lineage of families and relatives of the deceased are heard.

Christian hymns or biblical texts have also found their way into the *Kolomashie* song repertoire. Words like halleluiah, amen, Jesus, *Onyame* (the Akan name for God), and Israel, are frequently used since the majority of the Gas who now perform *Kolomashie* are Christians. Some of the earliest songs include slave plantation songs, protest songs and Negro spirituals.

Elements of style in *Kolomashie* songs are similar to those in *Gome*. Organization of tonal arrangements, harmonic devices and forms are the same but unlike in *Gome*, the cantor does not sing the whole song through before the chorus enters. One or two cantors lead the songs in both *Kolomashie* and *Gome*.

The Percussion Ensemble

Instruments of the percussion ensemble include: *ŋoŋo, dodompo, kyen kyen, shakers* (maracas) or container rattles, three *tamalin* (different sizes and pitches), two *pati* (treble and alto drums), and the bass drum, which is scarcely now used.

Trumpet, trombone and accordion may also be added to the ensemble. These melodic instruments do not actually play melodies but create more excitement for dancing with bugle calls or fanfares during the breaks from singing. Dancing reaches its climax during these sections of the performance as in *Bɔbɔɔbɔ* dance-drumming of the northern and central Eʋe of Ghana.

As in *Gome, ŋoŋo* plays the timeline with support from *dodompo, kyen kyen, shakers* and *shekeshe*. In the absence of the bass drum, the bass *tamalin* leads the ensemble and together with the *lalatsɛ* co-directs the whole performance.

FIGURE 16.2: Part of Emashie *Kolomashie* Percussion Ensemble. From left: *tamalin*, two *patis* and shekeshe.

Dance Organization

DANCE ARENA. There are two performance spaces for a stage performance and procession as shown in the diagrams below.

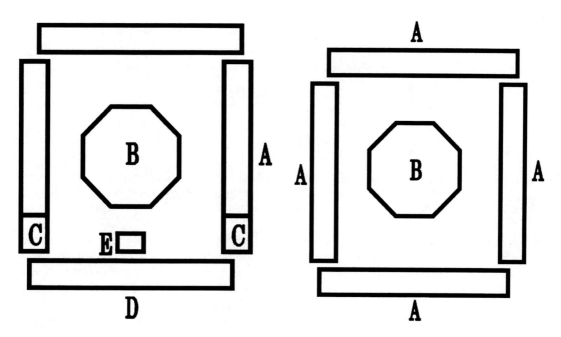

Left, FIGURE 16.3: Stage performance space. A: chorus; B: dance arena; C: idiophones; D: drums and brass; E: *lalatsɛ*. *Right*, FIGURE 16.4: Processional performance space. A: chorus/dancers; B: musicians; drums, brass, *lalatsɛ*, etc.

During parades or processions, the formation becomes a cluster or a mob scene similar to street carnivals in New Orleans, Toronto, New York, Brazil, Trinidad and other Latin/Caribbean countries. Musicians lead these processions. Dancers, chorus and other participants move back and forth, walking, running amidst dancing, singing and merry-making around the musicians.

DANCE MOVEMENTS AND CHOREOGRAPHY. *Kolomashie* is open to all. It is a free-style dance with no special training and as such, there is no rigid or special dance movement required. Dancers move according to the rhythmic patterns of the percussion ensemble and songs. The dance is performed solo so there is always room for self-expression.

Costume and Other Visual Art Forms

There is no specific costume for *Kolomashie*. In the olden days when *Kolomashie* was staged, men would wear a white or dark pair of short or long pants with multi-colored shirts to match. White canvas shoes without socks were preferred. Presently, any tightly-fitting short/long pants, shirts, black shoes or sneakers are worn. Sandals are not recommended because of the nature of the dance.

Female participants dress in any smart-looking dress. A nice long skirt to the knee and blouse are the norm during performances. Extensive jewelry is not recommended.

17. *Kpanlongo* Recreational Dance-Drumming Ceremony

Historical Background and Development

Circumstances surrounding the origin of *Kpanlongo* among the Gas are similar to those of the central and northern Eʋe *Bɔbɔɔbɔ* recreational dance-drumming. The struggle for independence in Ghana from 1947 to 1957 provided the climate for the youth across Ghana to create new music for political rallies.

Whilst *Konkoma* and *Tudzi* groups flourished among the central and northern Eʋes, *Ashiko* and *Konkoma* were popular among the Gas. In an attempt to create new types of entertainment music to purposely suit and celebrate the new life envisaged after freedom from British rule, many traditional Ga musicians started experimenting with new ideas by borrowing from existing dance-drumming ceremonies.

Other reasons for the need to create new recreational dance-drumming ceremonies were the result of *Kolomashie* changing its function back to being a solely processional musical activity, *Gome* being restricted to artisans, and, sadly, *Ashiko*, *Konkoma* and *Oge* (other recreational dance-drumming ceremonies among the Gas) losing their patronage because of the popularity of *Kolomashie* and *Gome*.

Kolomashie and *Gome* were very popular, restricted their membership, and, most importantly, could not satisfy the urgent needs of the youth of the independence movement. The youth needed something unique and new.

They needed another fast dance-drumming similar to *Kolomashie* as performed in the 1920s and 1930s without the procession. So began experiments by various Ga musicians in the 1950s in the wake of Ghana's independence to come up with a new recreational dance-drumming.

Kpanlongo emerged as the new dance-drumming ceremony solely for and by the youth. Hence it was called the "The Dance of the Youth," (Acquah 1987, 36). It was an offshoot of *Gome*, *Ashiko*, *Kolomashie*, *Oge*, *Konkoma* and other highlife styles.

As a result of this evolution, *Kpanlongo* retained most of the characteristic features (elements of style such as tonal organization, rhythmic concepts and structures, harmonic devices and forms) and instruments of these earlier recreational dance-drumming ceremonies.

Kpanlongo became a movement. Many names were used to describe this new highlife, such as *Kpalogo*, *Kpanlongo*, *Kpanlogo*, *Lolo*, and *Lolo Mashie* (the last two referring to love or the existence of love and the romantic nature of the dance movements). Many varieties of *Kpanlongo* also emerged as many musicians created their own styles.

The same situation continued with new additional instruments and modes of performance into the 1990s, but the basic dance movements, rhythmic patterns of the core instruments (*tama-*

lin, ŋoŋo, apentemma) and lead drum variations remain the same. These rhythmic patterns are shown in Part Six under a description of the percussion ensemble.

The exact origin, name and terms associated with most dance-drumming ceremonies in Ghana are shrouded in mystery and so it is for *Kpanlongo*. According to John Collins, however, one Otoo Lincoln was the originator and the first to use the name *Kpanlongo*. He derived the name from a folktale his grandfather told him in 1956 involving three sisters, Kpanlongo, Mma Mma, and Alogodza (Collins, 1992, 43).

Collins further alleged that it was around 1962 that Lincoln created this new dance-drumming with his friends Okulay Foes and Ayitey Sugar (drummers) and that it was in 1965 that Kpanlongo was officially launched and recognized by the Ghanaian government (Collins 1992, 44).

I do not want to doubt Collins' claims regarding the origin of *Kpanlongo*, but in the same interview, Lincoln stated that during the 1950s there were others who performed *Oge* (introduced by Liberian Kru seamen), which he described as slow *Kpanlogo*. It is worth noting that *Oge* is performed both in slow and fast tempo.

I found during my research that a group of Liberian fishermen staying at Kru Town in James Town at the time instead brought a musical type called *Waka*, not *Oge*. The Gas did not embrace *Waka*, so it quickly disappeared when the Liberians left soon after Ghana attained her independence.

Long before they left, the Liberians were also performing their version of *Kpanlongo*, which many confused with *Waka*, as the beginning of the Ga *Kpanlongo*. The instrumentation Lincoln described for *Oge*, "one drum, clips and saw and nail to scrape it" (1992, 44) pointed rather to some of the instruments used in *Gome*.

Maybe Lincoln was the first to use the name *Kpanlongo* to describe his group's new experimentation in the 1960s, but my research could not identify him or any other individuals as solely responsible for creating this new dance-drumming.

The idea that *Kpanlongo* was created around 1962 also requires further scrutiny. *Kpanlongo* was very much alive and featured during the independence celebrations on March 6, 1957. The main drum in the *Kpanlongo* percussion ensemble, *atwereshi*, a conga-type drum, could be seen being carried during the celebrations when Osagyefo Dr. Kwame Nkrumah (first president of Ghana), gave his midnight speech at the Old Polo Grounds in Accra (now Kwame Nkrumah Mausoleum).

Tamalin was an essential drum of the *Kpanlongo* percussion ensemble from the beginning, but a photograph of Lincoln's group in 1962 used by Collins to support his argument (1992, 45) did not include this instrument. Was *atumpan* ever a part of the *Kpanlongo* ensemble as shown in the same photo or was that the beginning of the lead drummer playing two drums? It is hard to tell in the photo but the dance posture of Lincoln, the *ŋoŋo,* and the *apentemma* are all traits seen in *Kpanlongo* from the 1960s on.

Kpanlongo dance-drumming became very popular after Ghana's independence. It quickly spread to other parts of the country through political and sporting events. Highlife and dance bands also created their own commercial varieties for radio/television and those who attended parties, clubs and bars.

Some of the dance bands played the traditional varieties of dance-drumming, but others created fusions with *Kpanlongo* and *Gome*. Notable groups in the 1970s and 1980s included Wulɔmei, Suku, Dzadzeloi, Blema Bii, Adzɔ, B Soyaya Extra O, and K.K.'s No.2 (Ofei 1992).

Kpanlongo soon became the political entertainment dance-drumming for the C.P.P. (Convention Peoples Party, Nkrumah's political party) in Accra, as *Bɔbɔɔbɔ* was in Kpando in the 1960s. The late president, Dr. Kwame Nkrumah, who greatly loved this music, funded most of the *Kpanlongo* bands at the time.

Although there were those who alleged that it was not accepted by the elders from the start because most of the song texts were mainly profane and dance movements too romantic and not decent for elders to see, my research work in La, Osu, Accra and Korle Gorno, the homes of *Kpanlongo*, revealed that the musical type was rather embraced and well patronized by both young and old from the very beginning.

The issue of indecent texts and dance movements was resolved quickly through negative audience reactions during performances. Groups would choose their songs and dance movements depending on the context of performances.

Kpanlongo since has been performed during festivals, state holidays and other special occasions. It is also performed during the visit of state dignitaries. Despite the many varieties, one can still see a performance of the 1960s version during funerals in La.

Kpanlongo is by far the most popular recreational dance-drumming ceremony of the Gas. Bands, which are very organized as mixed groups, can be found in every Ga town. Various amateur and professional groups have also incorporated *Kpanlongo* into their repertoire. Audience participation is encouraged when *Kpanlongo* is performed.

Organization of the Dance-Drumming Ceremony

FORM AND STRUCTURE. There are two main phases of *Kpanlongo: oshwe* and *kpanlongo*.

Phase One: *Oshwe*. A performance of *Kpanlongo* in the late 1950s and early 1960s or presently during funerals in La, will commence with *nkpai*, pouring of libation. Few bands still perform this ritual outside funeral contexts. In the absence of *nkpai*, *Kpanlongo* dance-drumming ceremony starts with a series of songs in free rhythm led by the *lalatsɛ* as in *Gome* and *Kolomashie*.

In this context, the songs are aimed at invoking the spirits of the traditional gods of the land and ancestors who used to be members of the band. *Oshebɔɔ lala*, as it is called, also serves as a warm-up for the participants.

Phase Two: *Kpanlongo*. Once *oshwe* is completed, the *lalatsɛ* calls the *ŋoŋo* to start its pattern (the timeline that will guide the whole performance), and the chorus to clap: "*Atswade, atswade*," "Let us clap let us clap." One or two songs may be performed with just the clapping and *ŋoŋo* to establish the desired tempo for the performance.

Lalatsɛ then starts another song which ushers in the rest of the percussion ensemble and the chorus with the master drummer on *atwereshi* dictating the tempo and mood for the performance. The arena is now open for the dance to begin. The duration of this phase of the performance depends on the occasion.

Songs

The majority of *Kpanlongo* songs relate to events of Ghana's independence struggle, African unity, pan–Africanism and other political issues. Themes based on human emotions such as love and hatred are also common. Topical themes dealing with contemporary issues create the opportunity for spectators to be informed about events in the community.

Tonal arrangements in *Kpanlongo* are the same as in *Gome* and *Kolomashie*. Two or three other singers may assist *lalatsɛ*, also known as *lala woolɔ*, "caller of songs." Call and response forms the structural foundation of *Kpanlongo* song performance.

The Percussion Ensemble

The original instruments of the *Kpanlongo* percussion ensemble which are still in use at La during funerals are: *ŋoŋo*, *ŋoŋonta*, *dodompo*, two *tamalins*, *bongo drums*, two *atwereshie* (master drums played by one person), bugle or trumpet (optional), and harmonica (optional).

Instruments and their functions preferred by most bands include:

i. *Ŋoŋo*: Performs the timeline.
ii. *Ŋoŋonta*: May replace the *ŋoŋo*. In this case only the bigger bell is played.
iii. *Dodompo*: Supports the *ŋoŋo*.
iv. *Shekeshe*: Supports the *ŋoŋo* and *ŋoŋonta*.
v. *Tamalin* (two sizes): Serve as supporting drums.
vi. *Atswereshie "Kpanlongo Mi"*: Three or four, which are tuned to different pitches, may be used. In an ensemble of three drums and drummers, the highest and lowest pitches are used as supporting drums with the third as master drum. When two drummers are available, the master drummer plays the lowest two drums with the third serving as supporting drum. When four drums are used, the highest and lowest pitches serve as supporting drums with the master drum using the remaining two.
vii. Bugle or trumpet (optional) may be used for excitement when the *Lalatsɛ* takes a break.

See Figure 17.1 on page C-8 of the color insert.

Dance Organization

DANCE ARENA. See diagram at right.

DANCE MOVEMENTS AND CHOREOGRA-PHY. Although dance movements in *Kpanlongo* are free in conception and dancers react to the percussion ensemble in their own stylistic ways, there are three basic movements which form the core dance vocabulary. Every dancer is expected to know these movements and recreate them during performances.

Usually, two dancers (male and female) perform at a time, facing each other. During festivals, the dance arena is open to anybody moved by the ensemble. The three basic movements are: i. introductory or processional movement; ii. the main *Kpanlongo* dance movement; and iii. show-off movement.

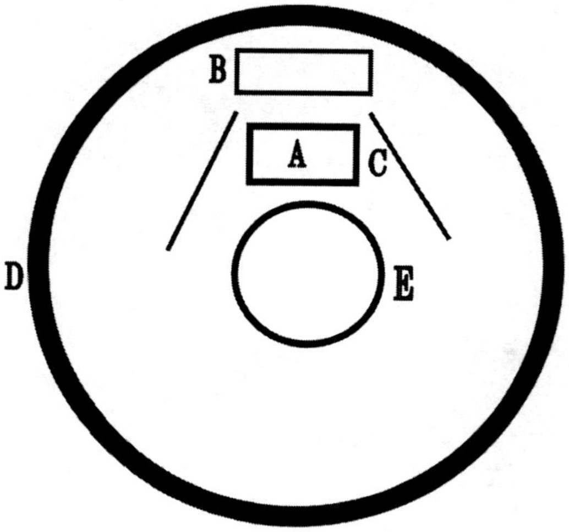

FIGURE 17.2: A: *atwereshies* (seated); B. other members of the percussion ensemble (standing); C: chorus/dancers; D: audience; E: dance space.

Introductory or Processional Movement. This introductory movement enables the dancer to travel in and around the dance arena. To start this movement, the dancer assumes a beginning posture: legs bent, torso leaning forward and upper back slightly arched.

From this position the dancer cups his hands around an imaginary ball in front of the sternum, left hand over the right with palms facing each other. The movement is initiated by the right side of the hip lifting with the right shoulder dropping in the direction of the right hip (to the side) at the same time.

As the dancer steps down with the right foot, the left shoulder drops and the left side of the hip rises. The feet step alternating right-left-right on four count, with the hands rolling the imaginary ball. On the fourth count, the dancer prepares to repeat the movement on the opposite side by lifting the left side of the hip up, dropping the left shoulder down and positioning the left hand on top (and right hand on the bottom) of the imaginary ball.

The Main *Kpanlongo* Dance Movement. This movement is described as the basic or main

Above, FIGURE 17.3: Different front views of the *Kpanlongo* processional movement as demonstrated by Zelma Badu-Younge. *Below*, FIGURE 17.4: Side view of the *Kpanlongo* processional movement as demonstrated by Zelma Badu-Younge.

movement in the *Kpanlongo* dance vocabulary. With the body positioned in the beginning posture as in the introductory movement, the dancer reaches or extends the right hand out diagonally to the side (as if handing someone something, palm up), the left hand is faced palm down in front of the sternum at the same time, the right heel is extended to the side on the same diagonal. This is count one or step one of the movement.

To transition this movement to the opposite side, the dancer twists his or her hips twice (like a washing machine), with the left side of the hip initiating the move by pulling back (counts two and three). On count three the dancer pulls the right foot into position next to the left. As the hips twist, the elbows shift back and forth: The right elbow shifts back to front and left elbow shifts front to back. Count four is a pause. The same positions, movements and counts are repeated on the opposite side leading with the opposite hands, heel and hip.

FIGURE 17.5: *Kpanlongo* main movement as demonstrated by Zelma Badu-Younge.

Show-off Movement. This movement is reserved for female dancers to show off their beauty. The dancer positioned in the beginning posture, as in the previous movements, takes a stance as if she is pulling the cord of a stand-up lawn mower.

FIGURE 17.6: *Kpanlongo* show-off movement starting from right to left as demonstrated by Zelma Badu-Younge.

FIGURE 17.7: *Kpanlongo* show-off movement starting from the back view to the front as demonstrated by Zelma Badu-Younge.

With the left foot stationary, the dancer slides the right foot forward while the left side of the hip shifts to the left, and the left leg slightly straightens. At the same time, the right elbow extends to the right side in opposition to the hip. This is count one.

On count two, the dancer then bends the left leg and slightly straightens the right. The movements on counts three and four are repeats of one and two. The dancer repeats these sequences of movements until he or she sketches an imaginary circle around her body (on the ground) with the right foot.

Costumes and Other Visual Art Forms

There are no specific costumes for a *Kpanlongo* performance. As in *Kolomashie,* any decent attire is allowed. Bands may decide to use similar knickers/pants with short- or long-sleeved shirts for the males and skirts just below the knee and blouse for the female participants.

FIGURE 17.8: Emashie *Kpanlongo* Group in action (2010).

FIGURE 1.10: *Agblɔʋu* technique as illustrated by Prosper Kɔku Dokli of the Aŋlɔ Afiaɖenyigba *Gadzo* Group (2006).

FIGURE 1.16: *Atopani*, unlike other Eʋe instruments, are reserved for political events.

FIGURE 1.31: *Tavugā/Uugā/Abuɖu* technique as illustrated by Isaac Kassah Ahiamaɖia (left), and assistant, of the Dzodze Aƒeteƒe *Atrikpui* Group (2009).

Figure 2.2: Aflao Mawulikplimi *Adzogbo* libation. Performed by their patron, Kofi Yibɔ (2006).

FIGURE 2.1l: Aflao Mawulikplimi *Adzogbo* lead male dancer with *sɔshi* (2006). See Chapter 2 for details on the components of this costume.

FIGURE 3.1: Aŋlɔ-Afiaɖenyigba *Agbadza* Percussion Ensemble. Instruments from left, front row: *kagan*, *sogo* and *kidi*; back row from left: three *axatse* players and *gakogui* (2006).

FIGURE 8.1: Tadzeʋu *Gahu* performing *Ayooɖeɖe* (2007).

FIGURE 9.7: *Kretsiwa* technique as illustrated by Bright Quarshie of the Ho Agbenya *Bɔbɔɔbɔ* Group (2007).

FIGURE 9.9: *Gakokoe* techniques as illustrated by a member of the Alavanyo *Gbolo* Group.

FIGURE 9.10: *Gakokoe* techniques as illustrated by a member of the Alavanyo *Gbolo* Group.

FIGURE 13.2: Elavanyo *Egbanegba* Percussion Ensemble. Seated from left: two *akaye*, *asivui* and *Uuvi*. Standing from left: two *gakogoe* and *akaye* players (2008).

FIGURE 17.1: Ghana Dance Ensemble, National Theater of Ghana, *Kpanlongo* Percussion Ensemble (2010).

FIGURE 18.6: *Kwadum* playing technique as demonstrated by a member of the Ghana Dance Ensemble, University of Ghana, Legon (2009).

FIGURE 19.1: Members of the National Dance Company of Ghana, University of Ghana, Legon, performing *Adowa* (2009).

FIGURE 20.4: Members of the National Dance Company of Ghana, University of Ghana, Legon. Asaadua male dancers in action (2009).

FIGURE 22.1: *Kete* Percussion Ensemble of the National Dance Company of Ghana, University of Ghana, Legon. Standing from left to right: *donno, kete dawuro, ntorowa,* and supporting *dawuro*. Sitting from left to right: *aburukuwa, kwadum, apentemma,* and *aburukuwa* (2009).

FIGURE 23.10: Playing technique on the *saɣyelim* as demonstrated by a Kpegu *Jɛra* drummer (2009).

FIGURE 25.1: Jakpahi Dang Maligu *Bla* Percussion Ensemble (2009).

FIGURE 25.11: Jakpahi Dang Maligu *Bla* dancers in full costume (2009).

FIGURE 26.9: Kpegu *Jɛra* lead dancer in full costume (2009).

C-14

FIGURE 27.1: Abdul Rahaman Mohammed, director of the Tamale Youth Home Cultural Group, in full *Takai* costume (2009).

FIGURE 30.1: Traditional *Kente* and printed textile cloths worn by members of the Ghana Dance Ensemble, University of Ghana, Legon (2009).

FIGURE A.1: Aflao Mauwulikplimi *Adzogbo* Group (2006).

FIGURE A.4: Dzodze Aɸetefe *Atrikpui* Group (2006).

FIGURE A.18: *Kete* royal dance-drumming ceremony as performed by the National Dance Company of Ghana, University of Ghana, Legon (2009).

Part Four.
Dance-Drumming of the Akans

"Knowledge is more valuable than wealth."— Akan Proverb

Orthography of Ashanti Twi

(a)	sounds like a in gas	(e)	sounds like a in gate
(e)	sounds like i in sit	(ɛ)	sounds like e in bet
(i)	sounds like i in sit	(o)	sounds like o in coal
(o)	sounds like u in put	(ɔ)	sounds like o in hot
(u)	sounds like oo in book	(gy)	sounds like gy in gym
(hy)	sounds like sh in shell	(hw)	sounds like wh in what
(kw)	sounds like qu in quack	(ky)	sounds like ch in church
(nw)	sounds like nu in enumerate	(ny)	sounds like ny in canyon
(nw)	sounds like nu in nuance	(dw)	sounds like j in John
(tw)	sounds like ch in chew	(g)	sounds only like g in goat

(b, d, f, h, k, l, n, p, r, s, t, w and y are pronounced as in English.)

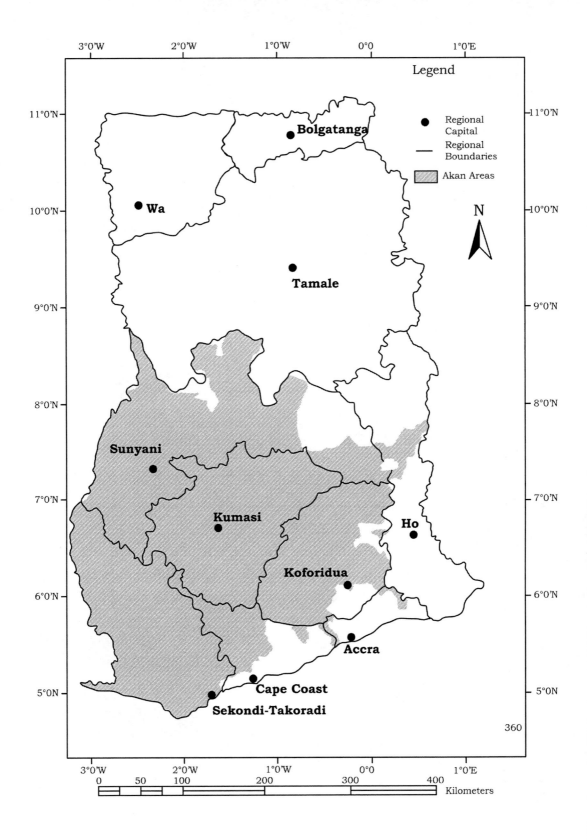

FIGURE 18.1: Map of Ghana showing Akan territories

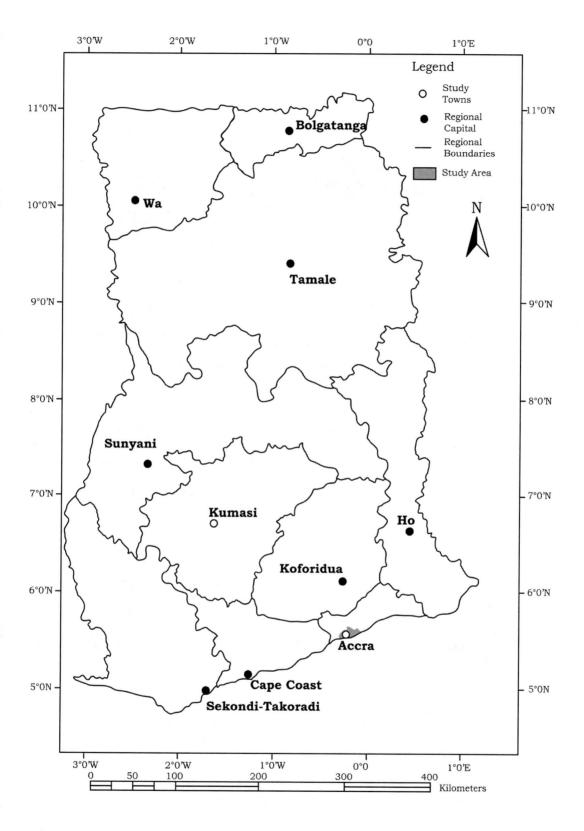

FIGURE 18.2: Map of Ghana showing research area

18. Historical, Geographical, Cultural, and Social Background of the Akans of Ghana

The Land and the People

The Akans occupy a very large area in the middle belt of Ghana, located mostly in the Ashanti, Brong-Ahafo, western, central, and eastern parts of the Volta region. The major Akan groups in these regions include Bono, Kwahu, Wassa, Ahanta, Denkyira, Nzema, Sefwi, Adanse, Asante, Akwamu, Akyem, Akuapem, Dɔma, Assin, Gwira and Fante.

These groups share similar political, social, religious and other cultural institutions and practices due to their common history. The Akans also speak variants of the language known as Akan. Twi and Fante are the most dominant and closely related variants. There are also various dialects of Twi spoken in the eastern region, such as Akwapem Twi. The Akan variants spoken in the western region, such as Nzema and Ahanta, differ significantly from the Ashanti Twi and Fante.

The economic activities of the Akans vary from area to area. These activities, which are determined by the contrasting ecology, rainfall patterns and vegetation, are also guided by the lunar months as shown in Twi on the following page.

i.	*Ɔpɛpɔn:*	January	Dry and cold season
ii.	*Ogyefuo:*	February	Preparation of the land for major farming activities
iii.	*Ɔbɛnem:*	March	Season for planting major crops, e.g. maize
iv.	*Oforisuo:*	April	Season to plant yams; short rainy season
v.	*Ɔkɔtɔnimaa:*	May	Crab fishing in the lakes and rivers
vi.	*Ayɛwohomumɔ:*	June	Heavy rainy season
vii.	*Kitawonsa:*	July	Pre-harvest season
viii.	*Ɔsanaa:*	August	Harvest season; food is stored and preserved (Sanaa)
ix.	*Fanokwa/Ɛbɔ:*	September	Foggy season
x.	*Ahinime/Ɔbese:*	October	Another short rainy season
xi.	*Obubuo:*	November	Harvesting of yams
xii.	*Ɔpɛnimaa:*	December	Minor dry season; preparation starts for farming (Nkansa-Kyeremateng 1999).

Guided by this lunar calendar, the coastal Fantes depend mainly on fishing as their commercial economic venture. Further inland, economic activities center on farming. Cultivation of cocoa and other crops and mineral mining, especially gold and diamond, abound in these areas. Timber production is another lucrative commercial activity.

Modern commerce is quite pronounced in the big cities. Another lucrative economic activity among the Akans is weaving. The Asantes are well recognized for their *kente* and *adinkra* industries.

Historical Background

There are varied stories about the history of the Akans. Some scholars traced the various Akan groups of Ghana to as far as the Far East and the ancient Sudanic empires. Adu Boahen, a Ghanaian historian, believes that the Akan culture evolved here in Ghana in the basin of the Pra and Offin Rivers, and that the matrilineal clan groups typical of the Akans also definitely started in these areas.

Most Akans themselves generally believe they migrated from the present Côte D'Ivoire (Ivory Coast) in several small groups to their present habitations in Ghana.

Mamattah (1978), however, painted quite a different history of the Akans. He alleged that the different Akans were grouped together with the Eves, Gas, Dangmes, and Yorubas as slaves in bondage. The deliverance by Musa, or, Moshe, Moses, caused the various groups to migrate to several parts of Sub-Saharan Africa.

The Akans, together with many present West African ethnic groups, were believed to have traveled south to establish the Sudanic empires of Ghana, Mali and Songhai around A.D. 300 to A.D. 400. The fall of the Ghana Empire in A.D. 1235 caused the Akans to move further south. Together with its closest allies the Eves, Gas, Dangbes, Yorubas and Ibos, the Akans settled on the banks of the River Niger in present-day Nigeria.

In search of peace, freedom, self-identity and more farmland of their own, the Akans were the first to migrate in smaller groups towards the west. The Fantes settled along the coast and other groups, such as the Akwamus and Asantes, went further inland (Mamattah, 1978, p. 44). Akan culture was well established before the first Europeans set foot in Ghana in the early 14th century.

Social and Cultural Profile

POLITICAL AUTHORITY. Political systems in Akan communities revolve around the chief.

Chieftaincy is based generally on the lineage system. Descent, and therefore chiefship, is traced through the matrilineal heritage. There are eight matrilineal clans or groups, which are derived from *abusua,* the family unit comprised of the man, his wife or wives, children and the extended families of the wife.

Succession to property as well as to any political position is handed down in the matrilineal line. Extended families of the *abusua,* the matrilineal heritage, play a key role in educating the Akan child. This is derived from an old Akan proverb, *Abofra sɛ ne se nanso ɔwɔ abusua,* meaning, "The child resembles the father but it belongs to the family."

There are rigid administration and observance of rules and regulations regarding marriage, inheritance and lineage by *abusua panin,* heads of families; *mpaninfoɔ,* elders; or *asafohene,* military commanders of the various *asafo* organizations who, by their positions, are counselors to the chiefs.

Some of the *abusuas* are *aduana, agona, asakyiri, aseneɛ, ayoko, bretuo* and *ekoɔna.* In addition to the *abusua,* there are also the *kra* or *ntoro*—the patrilineal affiliations of an individual relating mostly to institutions reserved for men, such as the *asafo,* warrior organizations; *abɔfoɔ,* the hunters' association; and ritual specialists. Akans by birth are protected both by the *abusua* for their livelihood and by *kra* for their security and safety (Buah 1988, 8).

The chiefs are the overall rulers over the entire clans and occupy very important positions in Akan political life. Before colonization and up until the 1900s, Akan chiefs were military heads who commanded the armies to battles, assisted by their elders. In addition to this role, they were the administrators and religious heads as well. Present-day practice sees them as administrators and custodians of the land. Arbitration courts instituted by chiefs and elders settle conflicts and other private or public disputes when they arise.

The effectiveness of Akan chiefs in discharging their duties rests squarely with the council of elders and other specialized attendants at the palaces.

i.	*Mankrado*	Director of administration and legislation.
ii.	*Ɔkyeame*	Linguist; the official spokesman for the chief.
iii.	*Gyasehene*	Coordinator of events and guests.
iv.	*Ɔkra*	Chief's soul-bearer; a royal prince who personifies the chief's purity and sacredness of the throne.
v.	*Ɔsɛn*	Court crier; maintains order at meetings.
vi.	*Aprahofoɔ*	Protects the chief from evil spirits.
vii.	*Ɔbrafoɔ*	Executioner, carries out death sentences or sacrifices to the deities as directed by the chief.
viii.	*Werɛmpefoɔ*	Bodyguards, custodians of the chief's property including the sacred stools.
ix.	*Dabehene*	Bed chamber attendant; makes the royal bed, decides which clothes the chief wears on a particular occasion, and also settles disputes in the royal family.
x.	*Soodohene*	Royal cook.
xi.	*Sanaahene*	Director of finance; handles all the finances of the palace, etc.

Other attendants include the *akyerɛmadefoɔ,* drummers; *kwadwomfoɔ,* minstrels; *asokwafoɔ,* horn blowers; *sumankwafoɔ,* herbalists; *banmufo,* keepers of the royal mausoleum; and *atumtofo,* gun bearers (Nkansa-Kyeremateng 1999, 76–84).

The role of the *ɔbaa* or *ɔhemmaa,* queen mother, is by far the most essential to the effective governance by the chief. *Ɔbaa,* apart from having the final say when choosing, installing and impeaching a chief, remains the principal advisor to the chief.

RELIGION. All Akans of Ghana have accepted *Nyame* as the name of the universal God, the one supreme deity without beginning or end. This God is regarded as being so great that worship of him is never done directly. There are attributes of the supreme God, which are invoked through several mediums serving as vehicles for communicating or affirming the values of the Akan society.

The various attributes of the Supreme Being determine the various objects worshipped through which the almighty God is personified. These include:

i.	*Onyame*	The Moon god: Mother goddess who is believed to have given birth to all men and hence is responsible for death.
ii.	*Ɔdomankoma*	The Sky god: The Father god who made the world with His hands as a craftsman. He is boundless.
iii.	*Onyankopɔn*	The Sun god: The personified male aspect of the moon, the only great god of the universe.
iv.	*Ɔmaɔmee*	The god who grants our wishes and satisfaction.
v.	*Toturobonso*	The god of thunder who provides rain.
vi.	*Bɔrebɔre*	The god of creation; the supporter of life.
vii.	*Twereampɔn*	The god who supports mankind in all endeavors.

These attributes of God are viewed as vehicles for communicating or affirming the values and beliefs of the Akan society. Several lesser deities, spirits, cults and totems are worshipped through which prayers are offered to the Supreme Being.

These lesser spirits are believed to be harbored in trees, rivers, rocks, and other objects under the supervision of *Asase Yaa,* Mother Earth or the Earth Spirit, which supports life.

In addition, Akans believe in the work of good and bad spirits who operate through ghosts, *nsamanfoɔ/nananom* (ancestors which are worshipped through sacred stools), *suman* (special charms or amulets prepared by specific cults for protection), *nkonyaa* (magic), *bayie* (witchcraft), *mmotia* (dwarfs), and *sasabonsam* (the great devil of the earth).

These traditional beliefs and their repercussions for the daily life cause most people to participate in rituals for deities that are administered by *ɔkɔmfoɔ,* traditional priests and priestesses. The advent of foreign religions such as Christianity has also added new forms of worship in Akan areas of Ghana.

FESTIVALS. Festivals among the Akans include ritual, ceremonial, artistic and recreational activities, which take place in different locations according to defined schedules. The major festival of the Akans is the *Adae,* which is for remembering ancestors and for renewing the spiritual and political bonds that allow for the continued participation of the dead in the affairs of the living.

A set of rituals which are focused on the ancestors and other ceremonial activities that surround the chief as the link between the living and the dead, dominate the events of the *Adae.*

Other festivals relate to gods of a given locality, concerns with nature as a revered force, agricultural products, harvest or devotion to the ancestors. These festivals include: *Apafram-Akwamu, Kurufie-Ejura, Odwira-Kibi, Akim Abuakwa, Akropong, Akwapim, Aburi, Apɔ-Wenchi, Ohum-Akwapim towns, Aboakyer-Efutu (Winneba), Bakatue-Elmina, Okyir-Anomabu* and *Munufie-Nkoranza,* etc.

Perspectives and Concepts of Musical Activities

Nketia, a renowned Ghanaian ethnomusicologist, has written extensively about the musical traditions of the Akans. In addition, the following will provide an overview of Akan musical traditions as they apply to dance-drumming activities.

CONTEXT AND ORGANIZATION OF DANCE-DRUMMING CEREMONIES. Various dance-drumming types are reserved for religious rites, recreation, and economic and political activities among the Akans. Bands are formed in communities to cater for the various types of musical activities.

Apart from ordinary citizens singing a variety of songs as they undergo their daily chores, major economic dance-drumming activities revolve around *abɔfoɔ* and *asafo,* hunters' and warrior's organizations, respectively.

Abɔfoɔ dance-drumming ceremonies are organized to celebrate the initiation of a new headhunter, when a hunter kills an extraordinarily large animal such as a tiger or elephant, the death of a fellow *abɔfoɔ* (master hunter) or *abɔmmɔfoɔ* (apprentice hunter), or during festivals when various musical groups come out to display their arts. A unique feature of the hunters' dance-drumming ceremony is the dramatization of their hunting expeditions.

Warrior dance-drumming activities are associated with *asafo,* groups that are closely associated with courts of chiefs. Members of these groups are mainly the soldiers who defended the communities in the past and in the absence of wars today are visible members of the chief's entourage at festivals and other ritual events.

Officers who organize *asafo* groups and their dance-drumming activities include: *asafo-hene/asafoakyɛ,* leader commander; *asafo supi,* public relations officer; *asafo bataan,* the counselor; *asafo kɔmfoɔ,* the high priest; *frankaatufoɔ,* flag bearer who directs parades; *asafo kyerɛma,* master drummer of the group; and *nnawutabɔfoɔ,* double bell player (Nketia 1963b, 105–106. *Asafo* dance-drumming groups are visible during festivals, royal funerals and funerals of fellow members.

Religious dance-drumming ceremonies among the Akans center around the worship of numerous deities, cults, totems, spirits and the ancestors. Musical instruments or drums, *twene,* are reserved and kept in shrines for specific rituals. Each ritual worship or cult has its own set of instruments.

The instruments of the shrines may be the same type of instruments used in either political or recreational events but because they have been concentrated and can only be used for particular ritual worship, they are regarded as sacred.

Recreational or dance-drumming groups for entertainment are by far the most celebrated in Akan communities. Popular bands or musical groups for such occasions are well patronized and can be seen at various events, the funeral being the most attended. For effective organization of each band, there are traditionally accepted offices each group adheres to. These offices are not limited to but should have at least the following:

i.	*agɔrohene*	male leader of the king of the band;
ii.	*agorɔhemmaa*	female leader of the queen of the band;
iii.	*abaa kutafoɔ*	disciplinarian at a performance;
iv.	*ɔhyɛ nsa*	serves drinks/public relation officer;
v.	*agorɔhemma*	lead female singer;
vi.	*ngyesoɔ*	female chorus;
vii.	*ɔkyerema panin*	master drummer;
viii.	*ɔkyerema ba*	supporting drummer; and
ix.	*dawurofoɔ*	bell players.

Most of these popular groups are not widely distributed. They are very unique because they specialize in specific dance-drumming types. Membership is open to all who have the interest and talent, is unrestricted to any context of performance, and membership length depends on how well they perform or are patronized by their local communities.

As a result of this trend, there are many Akan popular or recreational dance-drumming types that were once very popular, such as *Asɔnkɔ, Awaa, Sanga, Ntan, Ɔmpɛ, Tɛtea, Asiko, Ankadam* and *Osekye,* but are now extinct.

At the courts of chiefs, special drums and dance-drumming types are reserved solely for the enjoyment, entertainment and observance of official ceremonies and rituals. It is only at the royal palaces that all the three modes of drumming — signal, speech and dance — can be experienced.

The principal "talking drum" used in the speech mode is the *atumpan,* which plays *ayan,* verbal texts and messages. Signal drums are used to send messages, invite the elders to meetings, and summon those who commit crimes to arbitration or to inform the community of impending communal work or calamity.

Drums used for this purpose include: *nkrawiri, mpɛbi, dua korɔ, susu biribi, kantamanto, mmidie, adedenkuraa, prɛmpɛ, kwasafokɔko* and *tutuiɛ,* etc. There are also special dance-drumming ensembles reserved solely for the courts, which include: *Apirede, Kete, Fɔntɔmfrɔm* and *Mpintin.*

Instruments used for political events are treated as those for religious events. They are kept as part of the stool regalia and are regarded as sacred.

MUSICAL SOUND SOURCES. The voice remains the most used sound source among the Akans. There are also a variety of drums, bells, wind and string instruments that are used in dance-drumming events.

Wind instruments, which include *ntahera,* trumpets; *mmɛnson,* horns; *odurugya,* end-blown flute made from cane; and *atɛntɛbɛn,* bamboo flutes, are used exclusively in ensembles for chiefs. The development of the latter by Dr. Ephraim Amu, the grandfather of Ghanaian new classical art music, has increased its usage in educational institutions and by contemporary music ensembles. *Seperewa,* the Akan harp, is the only recognized string instrument.

Other instruments that are used in dance-drumming types which are discussed in this part of the book include: *apentemmaa, petia, atumpan, tamalee, dawuro, adawura, firikyiwa, nnawuta ntorowa, sikyi, kwadum, aburukuwa,* and *donno.*

Some of these instruments are similar but may come in different names, sizes and decorations as used among the Eʋe, Ga and Dagbamba ethnic groups. Those that have been discussed in previous portions of the book are listed below:

Atumpan	*Atopani* (Eʋe) Part One: Fig. 1:16 and Fig. 1.17.
Tamalee	*Tamalin* (Eʋe) Part Two: Fig. 11:21, Fig. 11:22 11:23.
Dawuro	*Ŋoŋo* (Ga) Part Three: Fig. 18:10.
Adawura	*Atoke* (Eʋe) Part One: Fig. 1:5 and Fig. 1:6.
Firikyiwa	*Kretsiwa* (Eʋe) *Dodompo* (Ga) Part Two: Fig. 11:6.
Nnawuta	*Gakogui, Tigo* and *Gakpevi* (Eʋe) Part One: Fig. 1:3.
Ntorowa	*Akaye* (Eʋe) Part Two: Fig. 18:10.
Apentemma	*Asiʋui* (Eʋe) Part Two: Fig. 11:16 and Fig. 11:17.
Sikyi	*Uuga* (Eʋe) Part Two: Fig. 11:26.
Kpanlongo	*Mi* (Ga) Part Three: Fig. 18:24.

DESCRIPTION OF OTHER INSTRUMENTS. Petia. *Petia* is the smallest drum of the Adowa percussion ensemble. It is an open, semi-cylindrical drum played upright as an *aburukuwa.* It is difficult sometimes to differentiate between *petia* and *aburukuwa* when the latter is not covered for use in *Kete.* Generation of sounds and other techniques used on *petia* are the same as with the *aburukuwa.*

Kwadum. *Kwadum* is the lead drum of the *Kete* percussion ensemble. This is an open cylindrical drum played upright with two *nkonta,* drumsticks, which are curved. Similar sticks are used on the Atumpan drum. The drummer sits and positions the drum, which is tilted forward, away from the body, between the legs.

Three basic tones are generated on this drum. The open/bounced tone and muted or stopped tone are the same as on the *kidi* of the southeastern Eʋe. The third tone is realized by stopping/muting the head with one stick and hitting it with the other as in the open or bounce stroke. See Figure 18.6 on page C-9 of color insert.

Aburukuwa. The *aburukuwa* is one of the high-pitched supporting drums of the Akan percussion ensembles. Sometimes referred to as *akukuadwo,* it functions as both a "talking drum" and a signal drum. *Aburukuwa* is a single-headed open drum carved from the *tweneduro* or *tweneboa* tree, as are most of the Akan drums.

The process of construction is the same as illustrated with Eʋe carved drums in Chapter 1. *Aburukuwa* is played with the drummer seated and the drum held upright between the legs. Two straight sticks of about ten inches (25.4 centimeters) are used to generate open and closed/stopped tones on this drum, as on the *kidi* drum of the southeastern Eʋe.

Donno. The *donno* is a double-headed, hourglass-shaped drum also known as a *ḍondo.* It was adopted from the Dagbama ethnic group of Northern Ghana. The *ḍondo* is used as both a lead and supporting drum in various dance-drumming ensembles. A donno may also be used for "talking" in the speech mode during these performances.

Sound is generated on this instrument by holding it under the armpit and hitting the head with a curved stick. Squeezing and releasing the tension of the head, held in place by

Left, Figure 18.3: *Petia*, a supporting drum in *Adowa* (2009). *Right*, Figure 18.4: *Petia* playing technique as demonstrated by a member of the Ghana Dance Ensemble, University of Ghana, Legon (2009).

Above, Figure 18.5: *Kwadum*, the *Kete* lead drum (2009). *Right*, Figure 18.7: *Aburukuwa*, the *Kete* supporting drum (2009).

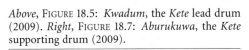

Above, FIGURE 18.8: *Aburukuwa* playing technique as demonstrated by a member of the Ghana dance Ensemble, University of Ghana, Legon (2009). *Right, top*, FIGURE 18.9: *Donno* playing technique as demonstrated by a member of the Ghana Dance Ensemble, University of Ghana, Legon (2009). *Right, bottom*, FIGURE 18.10: *Apentemma* playing technique as demonstrated by a member of the Ghana Dance Ensemble, University of Ghana, Legon (2009).

Top, left, Figure 18.11: *Kete Apentemma* playing technique as demonstrated by a member of the Ghana Dance Ensemble, University of Ghana, Legon (2009). *Top, right*, Figure 18.12: *Adawura* playing technique as demonstrated by members of the Ghana Dance Ensemble, University of Ghana, Legon (2009). *Above*, Figure 18.13: *Ntorowa* playing technique as demonstrated by a member of the Ghana Dance Ensemble, University of Ghana, Legon (2009). *Left*, Figure 18.14: *Atumpan* playing technique as demonstrated by a member of the Ghana Dance Ensemble, University of Ghana, Legon (2009).

several leather thongs, produces three different sounds: low, middle and high.

The *donno* player can also effectively produce these three tones without hitting the drum on each occasion. He can, for example, play a low tone and immediately squeeze the thongs to glide to a higher tone or squeeze and play a higher tone and release to glide to a low tone.

FIGURE 18.15: *Sikyi* playing technique as demonstrated by a member of the Ghana Dance Ensemble, University of Ghana, Legon (2009).

19. *Adowa* Funeral Dance-Drumming Ceremony

Historical Background and Development

Adowa is by far the most widespread and frequently performed social dance-drumming of the Akan-speaking people, especially the Asantes/Ashantis of Ghana. This classic dance-drumming is featured mostly at funerals because of its unique historical origin.

Legend has it that *Adowa* started with the observance of a funeral celebration by chimpanzees during which an antelope was sacrificed to appease the spirit of the dead.

The story is that during a hunting expedition, one *abɔfoɔ*, a hunter, sighted some chimpanzees drumming and dancing in the forest. When he went closer to see this performance, he was surprised to realize that the chimpanzees were celebrating the death of one of their own. He recounted that the animals were playing on dried wooden logs with straight sticks to accompany their dance and laments.

From his hideout, this hunter suddenly saw an antelope, which was being chased by another hunter, run into the midst of the chimpanzees' celebration. To his dismay, the antelope did not feel threatened by the chimpanzees as it joined the celebration with its own dance movements and gestures.

The chimpanzees, however, saw the appearance of the antelope as a good omen from their ancestors. Even when they drew nearer the antelope, it continued to jump up and down, already behaving as "an animal ready to be sacrificed."

The chimpanzees killed the antelope with little resistance. Its blood was poured on the dead colleague as a parting ritual before its final internment in a nearby forest.

The hunter, upon his return from the hunting expedition, recounted this experience to the queen mother and other hunters who were members of the *asafo* (warrior organization).

In order not to forget this remarkable experience, young *asafo* warriors were enlisted to learn the movements of the antelope. They would reenact the whole experience through a dance drama at funerals and other social events.

The queen mother at the time got so interested in these all-male performances that she directed women groups to learn some of the dance movements to be incorporated in their funeral laments and dances. Women groups became better at executing these dance movements and eventually took the whole celebration from the men. Thus, chimpanzee and antelope encounters became institutionalized with drumming, dance and singing to be known as *Adowa* among the Asantes.

The symbolic movements associated with the dance are believed to be from the gestures and movements made by the antelope during this ceremony, hence the name *Adowa*, which means antelope, given to this dance-drumming.

I have also heard another story about the origin of *Adowa.* This story tells us that there was once a queen mother in Asante called Aberewa Tutuwa. She suddenly fell ill and when the *abosom,* a deity, was consulted, it was requested that a live antelope be sacrificed to the gods before she could be healed.

It was alleged that the *asafo,* warriors and hunters, were promptly dispatched to the forest by the king to look for the antelope to be sacrificed. On their return, the hunters observed in amazement the strange jumping and other movements made by the antelope as they awaited the ritual sacrifice.

The story continued that after the queen mother was cured, the hunters, in jubilation, performed some of the movements of the antelope accompanied by their *asafo* drums. This gave birth to the *Adowa* dance-drumming. Both of these stories, though varied, confirmed some basic information about the origin of *Adowa:*

    i.   the *asafo* warrior organizations and hunters started this dance-drumming;

    ii.   the name of the dance-drumming was derived from the sacrifice of an antelope;

    iii.   the dance movements were derived from the initial ones made by the antelope; and

    iv.   *Adowa* started among the Asante and later spread to other Akan communities.

Adowa is best described today in Akan musical traditions as a women's dance-drumming because women dominate the performance. The few men that are members of any group handle the musical instruments.

Adowa is presently performed in the Ashanti, Brong-Ahafo, eastern and central regions of Ghana. National and regional dance companies, educational institutions and amateur cultural groups also teach and perform *Adowa* all over Ghana.

Akapoma is another name for *Adowa* in certain Akan communities. In Brong-Ahafo and among the Akyems/Akims who live mostly in the eastern region of Ghana in particular, it is called *Abaadam.* Only stick clappers are used as percussion to accompany the dance in these types.

In coastal Akan areas, especially among the Fantes of Winneba, *Adowa* is known as *Adzewa.* This is performed only by women using different size gourd rattles. Legend has it that a Guan woman warrior called Awo Osimpam, who led a group of Effutus to settle in Winneba, started this performance as thanksgiving and praise to their god, Penche Otu.

Adzewa is lighter in character and may only incorporate a single *apentemma* drum. A similar type of *Adzewa* is called *Mpreh* among the Asantes.

Apart from funerals, yearly state festivals, durbars of chiefs, visits of important dignitaries, or other social events may incorporate the performance of *Adowa* dance-drumming. As a result, *Adowa* groups are organized as popular bands in several Akan communities. Membership is open to all except the royal bands where membership is restricted. Only members of the royal families are allowed to join.

A female leader, *adowahemmaa,* directs each *Adowa* group. Other leaders or members of the group who perform special functions include the following:

    i.   *agorɔhemmaa*   lead female singer;

    ii.   *ngyesoɔ*   female chorus;

    iii.   *ɔkyerema Panin*   master drummer;

    iv.   *ɔkyerema ba*   supporting drummer;

    v.   *dawurofoɔ*   bell players; and

    vi.   *donnofoɔ*   hourglass drummers.

Organization of the Dance-Drumming Ceremony

FORM AND STRUCTURE. There are three main phases in *Adowa* dance-drumming: *anyanee, atene,* and *ahuri.*

Anyanee. Anyanee in *Adowa* is regarded as *aho* in most Akan dance-drumming performances. This phase is best described as the awakening or warming-up of the stage for the main dance-drumming ceremony.

The phase involves the singing of songs in free or speech rhythm with no instrumental accompaniment. Songs can be sung solo by the lead singer(s) or by the lead singer(s) and chorus.

These songs may start as *abeɛ,* a recitative, by the lead singer(s) with *krumuu,* chorus response, or *aho,* choral chants, where selected songs are performed in simple call and response form.

During *aho,* the melody is divided between the lead singer(s) and chorus. Some of the *aho* songs may be used in other phases of the performance.

Whenever dignitaries, elders, and chiefs are present at a performance, the *atumpan,* the lead drum of the ensemble, signals the end of *anyanee* by playing *ayan,* drum messages.

Ayan rhythmic patterns played on the *atumpan* may be associated with texts that relate to proverbs, praise appellations of chiefs, greetings, invocation of ancestral spirits, panegyrics or eulogies, and refer to death and burial in general (Nketia 1963b, 32–50).

At the end of an *ayan* performance, the *atumpan* calls the whole ensemble through the *adawura* to be ready for the performance: *"Adawura Kofi Brempon, ma wo humene so,"* which means "Adawura Kofi the great, be ready." The *adawura* starts the timeline to usher in *atene,* the next phase, after a brief introduction of *adawura's* rhythmic pattern by the *atumpan.*

Atene. Atene brings in the entire percussion ensemble performing with the chorus. This phase prepares the stage for the dance to begin. The *ɔkyerema panim* on the *atumpan* sets the required tempo before allowing the dancers in the performance space. Once the required mood is set, *ahuri,* the climax of the performance, begins.

Ahuri. Ahuri is best described as the main phase of the *Adowa* dance-drumming ceremony. It is during this phase that all the elements involved in *Adowa,* such as drumming, singing and dramatic enactments, can be seen.

An important feature of *ahuri* is the nature of the pieces (rhythmic patterns) played. Rhythmic patterns performed on the *atumpan,* with responses from the two main supporting drums, *petia* and *apentemma,* can be recognized by their texts.

These texts relate to historical events, the nature of the dance movements, chiefs, wars, religious rites, life-cycle events and proverbs. Some of the pieces include: *Adowatine, Sesre bedi, Abubru din dum, Adampa, Otwue bedi mprem, Asokore Manpong, Tekyiman, Yɛ keka no kwa, Akantem, Adowa kete* (also known as *Apɛntɛ*) and *Akapuma.*

All the three phases of *Adowa* may be repeated during a performance. During breaks or interludes when drummers are being refreshed, the female participants may perform *mpere,* songs accompanied by only handclapping. These songs are usually funeral dirges or choral laments.

See Figure 19.1 on page C-10 of the color insert.

Songs

Adowa songs relate to several issues concerning Akan cultural history. The Akans, especially the Asantes, pay serious attention to the dead and so compose most of their *Adowa* songs to celebrate funerals. Themes of *Adowa* funeral songs may include:

i. Historical facts: usually those about their past ancestors, chiefs, and elders. References may be made to the deceased generally or the bereaved lineage.
ii. Themes reflecting on death and the life hereafter may also generally be included.

Other songs may touch on topical issues, cultural and social beliefs and practices, and the praise and ridicule of people. Social themes such as love, marriage, unity and accepted morals or codes of behavior are also common (Nketia 1973a, 89–91).

Adowa songs are usually performed in cantor and chorus form. Two or more soloists may introduce a song before the chorus joins in, although one soloist is the norm.

Melodies usually follow the word contour and rhythm of speech patterns. Melodies make frequent use of intervals between triadic sequences such as D', B, and G or C', A, and F (all in descending order) in a diatonic scale (Nketia 1973a, 90).

These intervallic sequences and direction of most melodies usually result in the interval of a third frequently heard in songs. Harmony or multi-part singing as result is based on unison, sporadic use of thirds, sixths, and their triads, or the combination of the above three forms.

The Percussion Ensemble

The original percussion ensemble used when men only performed *Adowa* were mostly instruments of the *asafo* dance-drumming percussion ensemble. These instruments included *dawuro, agyegyewa, ɔperenten, apentemma, ntorowa,* and a pair of *asafotwene* as lead drums.

A pair of *atumpan* (*ntumpan*, pl.) later replaced the *asafotwene* as lead drums, and *donno*, in addition to *petia*, were added to replace the *agyegyewa* and *ɔperenten*.

A standard *Adowa* traditional percussion ensemble now has the following instruments:

i. *adawura*   boat or slit bell, plays the timeline;
ii. *ntorowa (torowa)*   container rattle, supports the *adawura*;

FIGURE 19.2: *Adowa* Percussion Ensemble, National Dance Company of Ghana, University of Ghana, Legon (2009). Standing from left to right: *adawura, adawura, donno, atumpan,* and *donno*. Seated from left to right: *petia* and *apentemma*.

iii.	*petia*	supporting drum, plays in dialogue with the *atumpan*;
iv.	*apentemma*	a second supporting drum, plays in dialogue with the *atumpan*;
v.	*donno*	supporting drum, this may be doubled;
vi.	*atumpan*	lead or master drum played in pairs, directs the ensemble; and
vii.	*firikyiwa*	finger bell, may be used by one of the lead female singers.

Rhythmic patterns played by the *adawura* and *ntrowa* are not varied during performances. The *petia* and *apentemma* usually play corresponding rhythmic patterns as dictated by the *atumpan*. *Dondo* players sometimes play variations on their patterns or may be heard communicating through texts to the dancers and audience.

Dance Organization

DANCE ARENA. The performance space is arranged in a semicircular shape as in most Akan dance-drumming ceremonies. As shown in Figure 19.3, the female chorus forms around the *atumpan* drummer.

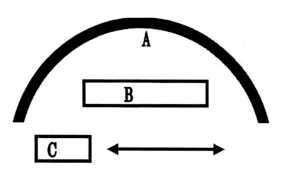

FIGURE 19.3: *Adowa* performance space. Key: A: female chorus and other instrumentalists; B: *atumpan, petia* and *apentemma* drummers; C: *adowa-hemmaa*, female lead singer.

Petia and *apentemma* players, the only drummers who sit during the performance, are positioned closely to the left of the *atumpan* or one on each side. Other instrumentalists stand behind or to the sides of the *atumpan* drummer.

The lead female singer positions herself to the right of the *atumpan* at the start of the performance but moves from left to right in front of the percussion ensemble, facing the chorus, especially when starting a new song. Supporters of the group or audience, depending on the situation, normally form a circle around the band.

DANCE MOVEMENTS AND CHOREOGRAPHY. According to Opoku, "The *Adowa* dance is subtle of movement, sophistication, poise and a highly developed sense of timing and hand and arm techniques are essential to the dance." The *Adowa* dancer affects aloofness throughout the dance and all expressions and movements must reflect spontaneity (Opoku 1971, 5).

The *Adowa* dance involves graceful movements of the diminutive antelope after which it is named. Although the dancer has the space to execute creative and symbolic movements during a performance, there are specific dance rituals she/he has to go through. These include a specific entry into the dance space, acknowledgement of the elders, cutting the dance space, and final signal to exit the dance space.

The dancer enters the arena with humility and respect. She/he goes to the master drummer and by gesture asks permission to be allowed to dance. This simple ritual motivates and encourages the drummers to perform their best.

Omitting this simple dance routine by the dancer may be construed as disregard, disrespect and insult to the musicians. Some drummers will stop playing immediately or intentionally disrupt the entire performance in reaction.

Once the drummers have been recognized, the dancer goes or moves to the direction of the elders and other members of the audience to again seek their permission to dance.

A good dancer then travels across the dance space by cutting or creating a space where she/he will be dancing. It is important that the dance space be wide enough to enable the dancer to communicate effectively with the audience.

Creating a small dance space shows that the dancer is unskilled and very afraid or shy to engage the audience. After a successful dance, the dancer(s) must signal their exit from the dance space. This allows for another dancer to enter the arena or for the musicians to change their pieces.

The basic steps or leg movements in *Adowa* dance "divide the timeline into two or multiples of two; when just two divisions are used for a start, the right foot moves forward on the strong beat of the pattern, followed by the left foot on the next beat, that is, the initial beat of the second half of the pattern. The feet may divide the line into four equal steps" (Nketia 1974, 213).

The legs are usually positioned straightforward as in normal walking. The next step of the basic movement is to stretch or move the right leg to the far right on every strong beat or attack point of the timeline.

In addition, the dancer adds the movement of the upper torso, which involves shifting the body right and left. This movement divides each leg action into two equal halves. A tilt to the right raises the left shoulder and vise versa.

As in *Kete* royal dance-drumming, *Adowa* dance movements and gestures are proverbial and symbolic. Movements depict many social and topical issues in the cultural lives of the Akan. There is social control on the use of some of these movements. Some common symbolic movements are:

    i.   A dancer facing the drummers with the left palm supporting the right elbow joint, with the right lower arm raised high, means, "I promise you, the drummers, a drink."

    ii.   The palms supporting a tilted head or chin denote grief.

    iii.   A dancer who shakes his head from side to side registers his disapproval.

    iv.   Biting a right thumb or a right forefinger indicates a sign of pain and forgetfulness.

FIGURE 19.4: *Adowa* dance symbolism as demonstrated by members of the Ghana Dance Ensemble, University of Ghana, Legon. Biting a right thumb or a right forefinger indicates a sign of pain and forgetfulness (2009).

    v.   Both palms pressed against the stomach means, "I am suffering from stomach pain." It signifies both physical and or psychological pain.

    vi.   Hooked forefingers in front of the body means, "I am in love with you," or, "We are one."

    vii.   When a dancer points the right hand or both hands skywards, he is saying, "I look to God" (E. A. Doudu 1980, 7–9).

FIGURE 19.5: *Adowa* dance symbolism as demonstrated by members of the Ghana Dance Ensemble, University of Ghana, Legon. The palms supporting a tilted head or chin are a sign of grief (2009).

FIGURE 19.6: *Adowa* dance symbolism as demonstrated by members of the Ghana Dance Ensemble, University of Ghana, Legon. The back of the palms placed against the back of the waist means, "I am overwhelmed with problems" (2009).

FIGURE 19.7: *Adowa* dance symbolism as demonstrated by members of the Ghana Dance Ensemble, University of Ghana, Legon. One or two fingers pointing to the eyes means, "Do you see the pain that I see?" (2009).

Costume and Other Visual Art Forms

Female participants in *Adowa* use two different costumes. The first is *baasankye*, which consists of two pieces of cloth. One piece is tied around the body from chest to knee-level. A second piece of cloth is worn so that one end of the cloth is thrown over the left shoulder, leaving the longer end of the cloth hanging behind the dancer.

A special hairstyle reserved for the queen mothers in the form of *dansinkran*, the moon, named for its roundness, completes this costume. The hair may be dyed black or may be covered with a black net. Elderly female members of the group prefer this costume.

The second female costume is made up of a piece of cloth, preferably *kente*, which is also tied around the body from

FIGURE 19.8: Members of the Ghana Dance Ensemble, University of Ghana, Legon. Male *Adowa* dancers in mourning cloths (2009).

Left, Figure 19.9: Mercy Ayettey, lead *Adowa* female dancer of the Ghana Dance Ensemble, University of Ghana, Legon, in *baasankye* costume (2009). *Right*, Figure 19.10: *Adowa* female costume type two, also used in *Kete*, as demonstrated by Vincentia Ahadzigah of the Ghana Dance Ensemble, University of Ghana, Legon (2009).

chest to knee-level. Another piece is then folded into a smaller width and tied around the midriff. A greater part of the upper torso is exposed and decorated with precious beads, gold ornaments and clay designs with this style.

Ornaments are worn around the head, shoulders, elbows and just below the knee. This costume is also used in *Kete* dance-drumming. A white handkerchief is carried by dancers using both costumes as a special appendage to extend the arms or to wipe their sweat.

The color or type of cloth depends on the context of performance. During funerals or rituals, *adinkra*, or black, red or darker clothes, are preferred. Festivals and other joyous events attract bright or white clothes. The male costume is any *ntama*, a traditional cloth draped over the left shoulder.

Before the advent of western textile materials, the Asantes in particular used locally-made fabrics or a type of tie-dye in performing *Adowa*. The "common" people used *kyenkyen* and the rich, including the royalty, preferred *nsaa,* which was of a higher quality and durability.

20. *Asaadua* Recreational Dance-Drumming Ceremony

Historical Background and Development

The independence struggle in Ghana between 1947 and 1957 provided the atmosphere for many traditional musicians to create new recreational dance-drumming types, or to adapt old ones to suit the new national consciousness of freedom from British colonial rule.

The young males of Ashanti created *Asaadua*, as a result, in the late 1950s. The youth wanted something light, fun and youthful. They yearned for a dance-drumming that they could use in processions and political rallies, as *Kolomashie* had been used among the Gas of Accra.

Although the likely date and place of origin of *Asaadua* is not certain, like other popular recreational dance-drumming types, it evolved from the ingenuity of veteran traditional musicians around this time in Akan history.

No one individual is recognized as the creator of *Asaadua*. It emerged from experiments by several traditional drummers and composers who were rooted in earlier musical types such as *Asɔnkɔ, Osoode, Bɔsoe* and others, which were becoming extinct by the late 1950s.

Asaadua was created for sheer enjoyment and pleasure. The name of this new creation, *Asaadua*, which means sweet berry tree, might have been chosen because of the gay and pleasant nature of the dance (Nketia 1973a, 66). The *asaa* tree is commonly found in the forest region of Ghana.

Though initially a males' performance, it is now for both males and females with the females doing most of the singing and dance. Although *Asaadua* became a very popular type of recreational dance-drumming among the Akan-speaking people of Ghana and was performed at many social gatherings such as parties, festivals and funerals, it was already almost extinct and was soon replaced with *Akosua Tuntum* (another recreational dance-drumming which was recreated from *Asaadua*) around the 1970s.

Very few communities in the Ashanti and Brong-Ahafo regions still perform *Asaadua*. As a dance-drumming type, *Asaadua* groups are well organized and membership is open to any young male or female who has a love for and interest in it.

The two national dance companies of Ghana, which are located in the National Theatre and the University of Ghana–Legon, should be credited for keeping *Asaadua* alive. *Asaadua* is presently performed for recreation on any social occasion that requires merry-making.

Organization of the Dance-Drumming Ceremony

FORM AND STRUCTURE. There are two main phases of *Asaadua*: *aho* and *asaadua*. With the dance space set for a performance, participants perform *aho* as a prelude to the main dance-drumming event.

Aho, in this context, is mainly made up of songs sung in speech rhythm and may take the form of *ose*, a type of jubilation chant performed by *asafo* companies during war times or festivals to accompany the chief to the durbar ground; *nsui*, mournful wails or cries by women during funerary rites; *abeɛ*, as in *Adowa*; or songs in simple call and response structure to set the stage for the main dance-drumming.

The sound of the *adawura*, slit bell, in metered rhythm ushers in *asaadua*, which is the next main phase of this ceremony. Once the *adawura* establishes the tempo, other instruments of the percussion ensemble such as *nnawuta, firikyiwa, towora, tamalee* and *donno* join in.

The dance space is now open for anybody ready to dance when the singing starts. There is no restriction, other than availability of space, on who steps in to dance.

This phase may be repeated depending on the occasion. During parades or processions, only *aho* is performed at a standstill position. The dance becomes the procession.

Songs

Themes of *Asaadua* songs relate to human relations and topical issues. There are verbal commentaries relating to the dexterity of dancers. Individual members of the society may also be praised, criticized, ridiculed or insulted in some of the songs.

Human affiliations, feelings of loneliness, joy, sadness and sorrow are not excluded from the songs. God as a protector and judge is also not left out (Nketia 1973a, 66).

Tonal organization of *Asaadua* songs is based on the heptatonic scale. The form of the songs is basically call and response with greater variations in the solo section. Harmony is derived by singing in unison and/or sporadic use of additional melodies, usually in intervals of thirds and sixths against the main melody.

The Percussion Ensemble

Instruments of the *Asaadua* percussion ensemble and their various roles include:

i.	*adawura*	slit bell, performs the timeline;
ii.	*nnawuta*	double bell, supports the *adawura*;
iii.	*firikyiwa*	finger bell, supports the *adawura*;
iv.	*torowa*	container rattle, doubles the *firikyiwa*;
v.	*donno*	hourglass drum, supporting drum, may be doubled; and
vi.	*tamalee*	frame drum, three varied sizes may be used: small, medium and large.

An important consideration affecting the choice of instruments in *Asaadua* is that it must be possible that they can be carried and played at the same time by the instrumentalists.

Dance Organization

DANCE ARENA. The performance space in *Asaadua* is arranged as in *Adowa*. As shown in Figure 20.2 (see page 191), the drummers and other instrumentalists take their positions in front or among the rest of the group who are mostly the female and male singers and dancers. The lead singers may either stand to the sides of the instrumentalists or position themselves among the chorus.

During a performance, the lead singers may move back and forth or to the left and right, facing the rest of the group, or move towards the directions of the spectators.

Audience participation is very essential in *Asaadua*; therefore, spectators observing an

FIGURE 20.1: *Asaadua* Percussion Ensemble, National Dance Company of Ghana, University of Ghana, Legon. Standing left to right: *nnawuta, ntorowa, adawura, tamalee, tamalee* and *ntorowa* (2009).

Asaadua performance may either join in the dancing or singing. Spectators usually form a circle around the *Asaadua* band.

When *Asaadua* is performed in a procession or parade, as is usually the case during festivals to accompany the chiefs, the entire band forms a cluster around the instrumentalists. Dancers, chorus and other participants move back and forth in concert with the percussion ensemble. It is in the processional presentation of *Asaadua* that most of the *Asafo* features are exhibited.

DANCE MOVEMENTS AND CHOREOGRAPHY. According to Nketia, "the manner of *Asaadua* dance movements follows the general pattern of feet and hand movements characteristic of Akan dancing: the stride articulating the motor divisions of the periodic pulse, the shuffle, weighting of the body on the left and the forward swing of the arms as they revolve around each" (Nketia 1973a, 66).

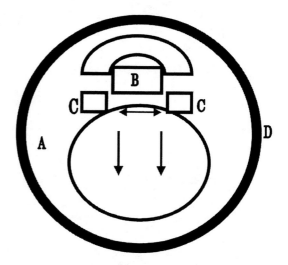

FIGURE 20.2: *Asaadua* performance space. A: female/male chorus and dancers; B: percussion ensemble; C: lead singers; D: audience.

Side to side movement of the upper torso of the body, similar to the *Adowa* and *Kete* dances, results in using the entire body to articulate the rhythmic patterns of various instruments of the percussion ensemble. The body *becomes* the percussion ensemble in *Asaadua* dance-drumming. As in *Adowa* dance, freedom of expression is allowed and encouraged.

Since it is a mass dance, dancers are encouraged to relate to each other. It is not out of the

FIGURE 20.3: Members of the National Dance Company of Ghana, University of Ghana, Legon, *Asaadua* Group (2009).

ordinary in Akan traditional practice to see two males dancing and relating to each other in terms of movement choices, facial expressions and other symbolic gestures in *Asaadua* performance. Female and male dancers interacting together is, however, the cultural norm.

There is no specific dance choreography involved in *Asaadua* performance. Dancers are therefore given the opportunity to recreate the basic movements or create their own during performances.

Costume and Other Visual Art Forms

There is no specific costume reserved for *Asaadua* performance. Choices of costumes are decisions left to individual members of the various groups but the nature and context of the events determines the choice of costumes. Mourning clothes are preferred during funerals, while during special festivals, durbars of chiefs or visits by state dignitaries, participants may be seen in *Adowa* or *Kete* costumes.

See Figure 20.4 on page C-10 of the color insert.

21. *Sikyi* Recreational Dance-Drumming Ceremony

Historical Background and Development

Sikyi, Osikyi, Siti and *Sekyi* are all names associated with an Akan recreational dance-drumming which was very popular in the 1920s. Although the exact date or circumstances leading to the creation of *Sikyi* are not certain, the dance chorography and songs suggest that it was originally associated with flirtation, courtship, and marriage ceremonies.

Historical accounts and views held among the Fantes in Winneba and some Ashantis about the probable origin of *Sikyi* tend to support its features as performed today.

The story among the Fantes reveals that when young girls were of age, past puberty, in most cases mature enough for marriage and to be sent on errands without adult supervision, they would then be allowed by their mothers to fetch water from the riverside on their own.

Knowing quite well that the girls would only be covering their private parts with leaves or pieces of cloth held in place by beads around the waist (the traditional dress for girls at the time) and exposing most parts of their bodies, young men would ambush them and try to expose their private parts by removing the covers.

This is the way the boys indirectly showed interest in the girls, a suggestion for marriage. Whether the boys succeeded in exposing the girls' private parts or not, the girls would run home to report the encounter to their parents.

The significance of this encounter on the part of the girl's parents is that it communicates that their daughter has caught the eye of a lover, a prospective husband. This experience with young men would sometimes speed up the *bragorɔ*, puberty rite, for the girls involved. *Bragorɔ* is a prerequisite for any Akan girl before marriage, especially in the villages.

The young men, on the other hand, would also report the encounter with the girls to their parents who would also immediately start their background investigations of the girl and her family leading to the arrangement of their marriage.

It was during the celebration of the marriage that the new couple and others already married would dance to dramatize how the young men courted the girls. It was a reenactment of their courtship. The dance-drumming was then called *Sekyi*, which literally means "beads" (Mereku 2000, 5.

Among the Ashantis, the story about the origin suggests a possible beginning during the era of the barter system of trade in Africa. Since the Ashantis were very far from the coast, they would wait for goods to come from the coastal areas for exchange.

It was during these waiting periods that the young men and women would perform *Sikyi* to entertain themselves and also to welcome others to the marketplace. These performances depicted "playful flirtation of lads and lasses" (Opoku 1968, 12).

Although the story among some of the Ashantis did not clearly state the circumstances leading to *Sikyi*'s creation, the story provides a historical period when it was probably invented by the Akans. The story among the Fantes clearly showed the probable history of its origin, development and name, *Sekyi*, now known as *Sikyi*.

The Fante and Ashanti stories, however, confirmed the current nature of *Sikyi* dance-drumming. *Sikyi* is presently a very creative recreational and entertainment dance-drumming among the Akans of Ghana.

Sikyi groups are organized as mixed popular bands. Membership is open to all who have an interest in and love for this dance-drumming. Groups are engaged to perform at funerals, weddings, naming ceremonies, festivals and other social gatherings.

Although *Sikyi* started in the 1920s, it wasn't until around Ghana's independence in 1957 that it became known outside Akan areas. *Sikyi* was then performed in the vein of *Kpanlongo* of the Gas of Accra and *Bɔbɔɔbɔ* of the central and northern Eʋes of the Volta region of Ghana. It was a celebration of the youth at social gatherings to express themselves in courtship.

Sikyi, Kpanlongo and *Bɔbɔɔbɔ are* some of the main recreational dance-drumming types that influenced the development of the popular Ghanaian highlife.

Organization of the Dance-Drumming Ceremony

FORM AND STRUCTURE. There are three main phases in *Sikyi* performance. These are *aho, agorɔ,* and *sikyi. Aho* has been discussed fully under the sections on *Asaadua* and *Adowa*. During *aho,* the concept of *Anyanee* is invoked. Inspirational songs are performed in speech rhythm to prepare the stage.

Agorɔ, as *Atene* in *Adowa,* sets the stage for the percussion ensemble and chorus to perform together. Once the desired tempo and mood is established between the lead singer(s) and lead drummer, the dancing begins.

The third and main phase of this performance is named after the whole dance-drumming ceremony, *sikyi.* Dramatic enactments are performed in the form of a dance-drama with a specific courtship storyline. The story usually ends with the females accepting the males' marriage proposal.

In line with Akan recreational dance-drumming features, this phase can be described as *ahuri,* which signifies the climax of the performance, involving singing, dancing, and drumming. The three phases may be repeated during a performance.

Songs

The majority of *Sikyi* song texts focus on issues relating to love, female and male relationships, marriage, divorce, beauty, cleanliness, and other social issues. The meanings of these songs are easy to discern by anybody who understands the language.

There are, however, songs which, although talking about the same themes mentioned earlier, are not easily understood. These songs may be proverbial, full of poetic images and allusions. Such songs most often are meant to "entertain, inform, praise, insult, exhort, warn or inspire the audiences" (Nketia 1973a, 195).

As in *Adowa* and *Asaadua, Sikyi* songs are usually performed in cantor and chorus form. Several soloists may take their turns to introduce songs before the chorus joins in.

Soloists may alter melodic phrases, which usually follow the word contour and rhythm of speech patterns, when they take turns to introduce or elaborate on new songs. Alterations may be due to stylistic preferences or creativity by soloists.

As observed by Nketia (1994) about generative processes in *Seperewa* music, "Once the text and tune of a song are established, variations within their framework, including substitutions of related tones, junctural alterations, lexical and phrase substitutions, become a part of its performance practice" (145).

Harmony in *Sikyi* songs, as in most Akan singing practices, is based on several voices singing in unison, which then break into two or three parts performing sporadic thirds and sixths against the melody.

The Percussion Ensemble

Instruments of the percussion ensemble and their functions include:

i.	*sikyi*	lead drum, directs the ensemble;
ii.	*apentemma*	first supporting drum, plays in dialogue with the lead drum;
iii.	*agyegyewa/adedemma*	second supporting drum, may also play in dialogue with the lead drum. *Petia* is presently used instead of either *agyegyewa* or *adedemma*;
iv.	*tamalee*	third supporting drum, two may be used;
v.	*donno*	fourth supporting drum, may also be doubled;
vi.	*adawura*	plays the timeline;
vii.	*firikyiwa*	supports the timeline, played by one of the lead singers; and
viii.	*ntorowa*	supports the timeline.

FIGURE 21.1: *Sikyi* Percussion Ensemble of the National Dance Company of Ghana, University of Ghana, Legon. Standing from left to right: *adawura, tamalee, donno, tamalee, ntorowa,* and *tamalee.* Sitting from left to right: *petia, sikyi* and *apentemma* (2009).

Dance Organization

DANCE ARENA. The performance space of *Sikyi* is arranged as in *Adowa*. As shown in Figure 21.1, the drummers on *sikyi, adedemma* and *apentemma* drums are seated right in front. Other instrumentalists take their positions among the rest of the group, which is made up of mostly the female and male singers and dancers.

Lead singers position themselves among the chorus at opposite ends; unlike in *Adowa* and *Asaadua,* they do not travel around the dance space during a performance.

Spectators form a circle around the *Sikyi* band. Their participation is restricted in most cases as the performers follow a well-rehearsed choreography during their performances.

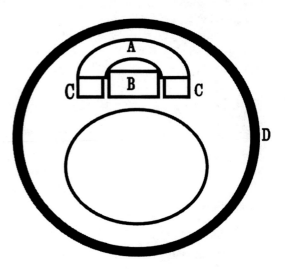

FIGURE 21.2: *Sikyi* performance space. A: female/male chorus, dancers, other instrumentalists; B: *sikyi, apentemma* and *adedemma* drummers; C: lead singers; D: audience.

DANCE MOVEMENTS AND CHOREOGRAPHY. Opoku describes *Sikyi* dance as light-hearted in nature. The movements accordingly are flirtatious, involving "strutting, bobbing up and down, a display of theatrical elegance" (1968, 12). There is, however, a basic dance movement which dancers use to travel around the dance space while performing their dramatic enactments.

This movement may be performed using two handkerchiefs, one placed in each hand, or without the handkerchiefs at all. Performed on a three-count phrase with the *adawura's* timeline pattern, the right hand traces a narrow oval-shaped circle. Accenting count one with the right hand, the dancer subtly circles forward away from the body. The left hand simultaneously moves back towards the body. The dancer completes the circle using the remaining two counts.

The hand movements are performed with the whole body tilted on a diagonal. The upper torso and arms are leaning forward with the arms raised above the head level, positioned in a soft diamond shape (placed diagonally in line with the forehead).

The dancer contracts and releases the upper body (including the hips) using the same three-count phrase previously described. As the right hand strikes forward on count one, the body contracts, and as the dancer completes the hand gestures during the second and third count, the body releases its contraction.

Complementing the above-mentioned movements, the legs are placed in parallel and in a plié (or bent) position. As the hand cuts forward, both feet are flat on the ground. As the dancer completes the movement of the upper body, he or she accents both the second and third counts of the rhythmic phrase with his or her feet, slightly lifting the right foot from the ground and then touching back down on the ground with the metatarsal on count two.

As the right foot is touching down (right heel is positioned off the ground), the left foot slightly raises on that same count (two) and returns down on the ground (with a flat foot) on count three. The dancer turns his or her body to the left diagonal when this leg movement is performed. This movement is repeated using the opposite foot and opposite direction (or opposite diagonal) (Zelma Badu-Younge 2010).

Apart from the basic movement described above, other movements highlight the essence

FIGURE 21.3: Members of the National Dance Company of Ghana, University of Ghana, Legon. *Sikyi* Group at a performance (2009).

of this dance-drumming. These are symbolic movements and gestures that tell the story of the drama. Some may show rejection, jealousy, deceit, disgrace, flattery, happiness, envy, affection, reconciliation, riches, and the acceptance of marriage proposals, etc.

Costume and Other Visual Art Forms

There is no special costume required for *Sikyi*, as in *Asaadua*. Women use *kaba*, the traditional Ghanaian dress for women, which is made up of a blouse worn over a two-yard piece of cloth around the waist with a head kerchief, beads and earrings. A second cloth may be worn on top of the blouse.

The type of fabric used depends on the wealth of the individual. They may range from local or foreign textiles to the local kente cloth. Two white or colorful scarves or handkerchiefs are used as extensions of the arms.

As in *Asaadua*, the men use *ntama*, a big cloth worn loosely over the left shoulder. A pair of knickers is worn under the cloth. No sandals are worn during the performance as in most recreational dance-drumming ceremonies of the Akan.

22. *Kete* Royal Dance-Drumming Ceremony

Historical Background and Development

Kete dance-drumming is commonly found in the royal courts of traditional Akan chiefs, specifically at the courts of chiefs whose status entitles them to be carried in a palanquin.

There are no documentary sources regarding the origin of *Kete* royal dance-drumming. My views on *Kete* in this chapter are based on stories gathered throughout my several years of interviews and interactions with traditional drummers, chiefs, elders and other cultural experts.

Like other dance-drumming types performed in Ghana and elsewhere in Africa, the origin of *Kete* is shrouded in mystery. Three stories/legends provide a probable origin of this dance-drumming ceremony.

The first story alleges that *Kete* was originally performed by *mmoatia*, super human creatures or dwarfs and was first discovered by *abɔfoɔ*, hunters, during their expeditions. To honor the hunters for this invention or discovery, a phase of the dance-drumming ceremony known as *abɔfoɔ* was named after them.

A second legend has it that *Kete* was adopted from the Gyamans of Brong-Ahafo descent during one of their wars during the reign of Opoku Ware I (c 1720–1750). After the death of Nana Osei Tutu, the new Asantehene, Opoku Ware, his grandnephew, continued the expansion regime of the Asante kingdom by waging wars against Sefwi and Akwapim in the south and Techiman and Gyaman in the north.

The war with Gyamans, however, proved to be difficult because of their warrior king, Kofi Adinkra. When the Asantes finally defeated Kofi Adinkra and his battalion, he was captured, beheaded and all his regalia, including the *Kete* orchestra, were taken.

In jubilation, the *Kete*, with all the musicians and the head of Kofi Adinkra, were paraded throughout the streets of Gyaman and Kumasi and finally brought to the royal palace of the Asantehene. *Kete* since has been used to mark and celebrate serious crises. Another phase of the *Kete* ceremony was named to commemorate the defeat the Asantes inflicted on the Gyamans. The phase is simply called *Adinkra*.

A third story has it that *Kete* originated among the Asantes during the reign of Nana Osei Tutu (c 1697–1731) right after the Asante forces fought and defeated the Denkyira under their king, Ntim Gyakari, in the battle of Feyiase between 1699 and 1701.

History has it that after this battle the Asantes continued their conquest of all the neighboring states that had assisted the Denkyiras, especially the Akyems, in their unsuccessful war against the Asantes. It was during this battle with the Akyems that the Asantes took over all their stool regalia including the *Kete* instruments, which they later used to create this royal performance.

Though varied, the above stories show that from its beginning *Kete* was a very serious royal dance-drumming reserved for serious occasions. It was regarded a war dance-drumming. Even though there is not one clear story or legend about the origin of *Kete*, it is clear that it has been part of Akan royal heritage since the 1700s.

Kete is performed presently on state occasions such as durbars, enstoolment of chiefs, the swearing of the oath of allegiance of sub-chiefs, state funerals, and traditional festivals such as the *Adae, Odwira, Ohum, Ahobaa, Kunkum, Kurufie*, etc.

Specifically, *Kete* plays a very vital role during the installation and subsequent outdooring of new Akan chiefs. On such occasions, *Kete* holds the entire celebration to drumming and dancing before the arrival of the new sub-chief and his entourage. New sub-chiefs will perform the *abɔfoɔ* or *apɛntɛ* phases of the dance-drumming before being introduced to the *Asantehene*, the supreme chief of the Asantes, who is also regarded as the king of all the Akans, or the Ɔman-hene, the territorial or paramount chief.

Apart from the strictly royal occasions described above, *Kete* can be performed at any function which requires the presence of the chief outside the palace. Though reserved mainly for chiefs, a queen mother may also request its performance during her installation. In funeral situations, however, *Kete* may be performed to honor elders or heads of traditional associations or bands with permission from the chief.

In the confines of royal palaces, membership in *Kete* ensembles are reserved for men who are members of the royal families, and those who perform and participate in the rituals and other ceremonies in the palace.

Due to the fact that many traditional events take place outside the palaces, and because of the increase in professional and amateur groups promoting *Kete* for educational purposes, female dancers are now seen performing this dance — even within the royal palaces. Visits of government officials may also call for the performance of this dance-drumming.

Organization of the Dance-Drumming Ceremony

FORM AND STRUCTURE. Initially, about eight phases of the dance-drumming were created. These initial phases were known by the general name for the type of drumming and dancing, context, function, general character, name commemorating an event, or the participants involved.

These initial phases as performed in Manpong and Kumasi and documented by Nketia (1963b, 129), include *yetu mpɔ, mpɛ-asɛm, apɛntɛ, abɔfoɔ, adaban* or *tɔprɛ, akatape* or *dabrɛbua, adinkra,* and *adampa* or *adɔsowa twene*. These phases may be performed as separate titles or may be combined.

Since *Kete* was initially associated with war and other episodes marking the history of the Akans, new phases or pieces are currently being created — especially among the Akyems and Akwapims — reflecting their own experiences.

Some may argue that these new phases, as performed outside the Asante area — especially in the eastern, western and central regions of Ghana — are not the traditional phases, but I will argue that if the third historical account is any indication of history, then these new emerging phases might have some cultural significance among all Akans and should be embraced. Some of these new phases include: *adamuabua, akuadum, kwekwenisuo, frimpong manso, wɔfa ata, ɔhene kɔ adwuma* and *akɔkono bɛtɛɛ,* etc.

The sequence and context of performing these phases may vary depending on the specific cultural event or those involved. Some of these are:

    i.   *Yɛretu mpɔ,* which literally means "we are digging gold," is performed during processions. Akan chiefs are usually dressed in gold ornaments to show their wealth and power and their status in the society; the phase or piece is performed to accompany them to state functions.

ii. The *abɔfoɔ*, "hunters," phase or piece is performed for the chief as an acknowledgement of his attributes as a hunter. These special qualities include: bravery, fearlessness, being a courageous leader, intelligence, and, above all, being a spiritual person.

iii. *Adinkra*, as indicated in one of the stories regarding the origin of *Kete*, is performed to mock the Gyamans who the Asantes defeated and also to invoke the bravado and strength of the Akans and their chiefs.

iv. *Tɔpre*, or *adaban*, is used during funerals when the chief is mourning and has to move to perform *trane*, the ceremonial shooting ritual. The symbolic dance which involves "circling" is performed to accompany this ritual by the chief or dancer, and is related to the second name of this phase, *Adaban* (Nketia 1963b).

v.   *Frimpong manso* was a recent creation by the Amammerlso Agofomma in honor of Alexander Ata Yaw Keremanteng, the founder of the former Ghana National Cultural Center in Kumasi, now the Centre for National Culture. This phase was inspired by Asɔkɔre Manpong, an earlier piece also played in *Adowa*.

vi. *Wɔfa ata*, also known as *kyɛnkyɛnhene*, is the most recent creation by Amammerɛso Agofomma in honor of the founder of the youth wing of the group. This is derived from *adamuabua*, which is performed in slow tempo.

vii. *Srɛsrɛ bi di* is performed to accompany a chief to a durbar, funeral or any festive event. It is performed at a slow pace dictated by the chief's majestic walking. The chief may stop to dance before continuing his walk. When that happens, the drummers change to *akatape*, which is performed at a faster tempo.

viii. *Kwekwenisuo, ɔhene kɔ adwuma, akɔkono bɛtɛɛ* and the rest of the pieces/phases are often used in other royal functions for processions and dance.

There are three basic components of *Kete* dance-drumming:

i.   the percussion ensemble music;
ii. *atɛntɛbɛn*, bamboo flutes, and *odurugya*, end-blown flutes made from cane, performing interludes; and
iii. vocalization of the flute melodies.

Both the flute and vocal parts are presently omitted in most ensembles, with the exception of the Asantehenes' special royal ensemble.

It was not possible to observe any performance with all the three components, which is why my analysis of the music of this dance-drumming is limited to the percussion ensemble. Nketia has documented a detailed description of the flutes and vocal parts (1963b, 128).

The Percussion Ensemble

Instruments in the *Kete* ensemble include:

i.	*kwadum*	master or lead drum, directs the ensemble;
ii.	*aburukuwa/akukuadwo*	first supporting drum, plays in dialogue with the *kwadum*;
iii.	*apentemma*	second supporting drum, plays in dialogue with the *kwadum*;
iv.	*donno*	supporting drum, two may be used;
v.	*kete dawuro*	slit bell, performs the timeline; and
vi.	*ntorowa*	supports the *kete dawuro*.

Instruments may be doubled except the *kwadum*, master drum. A unique feature of *Kete* drums is that they are covered in red and black striped cloth. The black stripes symbolize or remind the people of their chiefs who have passed, while the red is in honor of all those who have shed blood and died in defense of Akan heritage.

When the performance space is set, the percussion ensemble begins with the *kwadum* calling all of the instrumentalists to be ready with a brief rhythmic phrase. This pattern is sometimes interpreted as specifically asking the *dawuro* to be ready for his signal to begin.

The *kwadum* then starts with the basic pattern of the *dawuro*, which is immediately followed by the rest of the ensemble performing their patterns depending on the phase being performed. Rhythmic patterns played by the various instruments vary and change according to the phases being performed. The *dawuro* part is the key to an effective performance.

Once the tempo is established, the dancers take turns in the arena, with the *kwadum* having the room to manipulate his variations.

See Figure 22.1 on page C-11 of the color insert.

Dance Organization

DANCE ARENA. The performance space of *Kete* is arranged as in *Adowa*. As shown in Figure 22.2, the drummers on the *kwadum, aburukuwa* and *apentemma* drums are seated right in front. Other instrumentalists and dancers take their positions behind these drummers.

Spectators form a circle around the *Kete* ensemble. The dancers usually dance towards the chief or other dignitaries.

DANCE MOVEMENTS AND CHOREOGRA-PHY. *Kete* dance is usually performed solo. Self-expression and individual creativity is required in executing the dance movements. The dancer is required to organize his or her movements and gestures to the dictates of the *kwadum*.

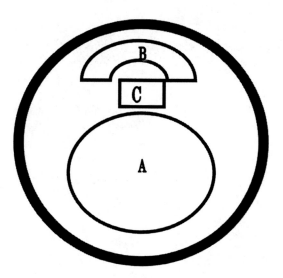

FIGURE 22.2: *Kete* performance space. A: dance space; B: other instrumentalists and dancers, *kwadum, apentemma* and *aburukua* drummers.

As in most Akan dances, *Kete* movements are avenues for communication. The movements and gestures are symbolic and must be used appropriately. Some of these movements are used in other royal dances such as *Fɔntɔmfrɔm*:

i. When a dancer runs and dances into an elder's arms, it means "You are my support, I depend on you."
ii. Biting a right thumb or right forefinger indicates a sign of the pain of forgetfulness.
iii. A dancer who stops dancing and stands akimbo says, "Come what may."
iv. An accented stamping of the feet on the ground means, "I will trample my enemies."
v. The fingers stretched against the back of the neck with the palm facing downward means, "I will kill you" (Duodu 1994, 143).

Some movements and gestures are solely reserved for the chief or very important personalities, e.g., a dancer's forefinger pointing to the sky, to the ground and then to the chest means, "Except God and Mother Earth." Only the chief may use this movement, especially during the *trane* ceremony or other dance situations.

In the eyes of the untrained, *Kete* and *Adowa* basic movements as described in Chapter 19

FIGURE 22.3: *Kete* male costume, *danta*, as demonstrated by Julius Yao Quansah of the National Dance Company of Ghana, University of Ghana, Legon (2009).

can be seen as the same. Similar foot placements and hand movements might be used but the main difference is the height the dancer assumes.

Adowa movements are usually executed more upright than those in *Kete*. Because the dancer is performing for or in front of the chief, there is need to show humility. Most of the movements are done with the body more tilted or bent forward.

Costume and Other Visual Art Forms

In the royal courts, the dancers use no sandals or handkerchiefs. Only the chief can dance with sandals. Instrumentalists are therefore permitted to seize any such items seen used.

Men dancers in the *Kete* performance traditionally put on *danta*, as shown in Figure 22.3, or put on the usual *ntama*, like the instrumentalists, which in this case must be tied around the waist unlike other occasions when the cloth is worn over the left shoulder.

Wearing the cloth around the waist instead of the shoulders is a way of showing respect to the chiefs. Women dancers, if there are any, wear the two *Adowa* costumes shown in figures 19.9 and 19.10.

Part Five.
Dance-Drumming
of the Dagbamba

"My secret is with you; don't take it across the river."— Dagbamba Proverb

Orthography of Dagbaŋli

(a)	sounds like a in hat	(e)	sounds like i in lit
(i)	sounds like ea in meat	(o)	sounds like u in put
(u)	sounds like o in two	(ɔ)	sounds like o in pot
(ɛ)	sounds like e in bet	(ɣ)	a fricative g
(ŋ)	sounds like ng in sing	(ʒ)	sounds like j in French
(gb)	implosive	(kp)	implosive
(ny)	implosive	(Ŋm)	implosive
(ch)	sounds as ch in chain	(sh)	sounds like sh in shilling

The following consonants are pronounced as in English: b, d, f, g, h, j, l, m, n, p, r, s, t, w, y, and z.

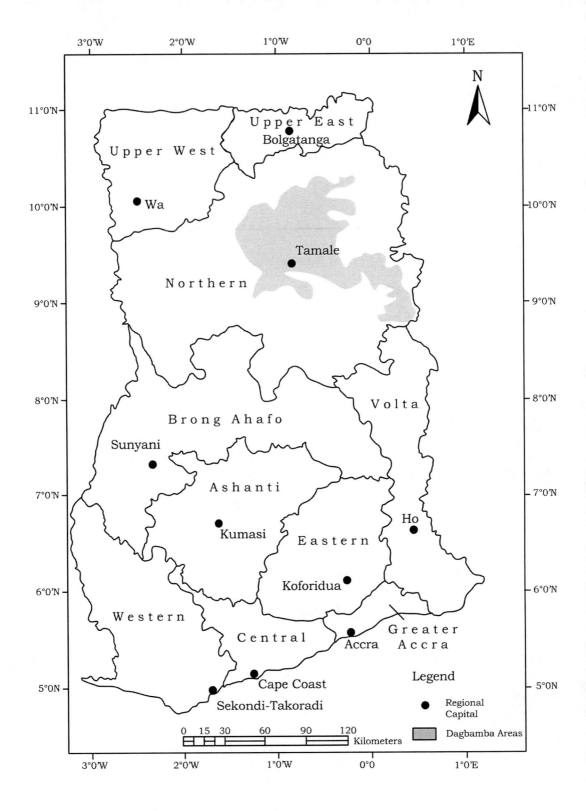

FIGURE 23.1: Map of Ghana showing Dagbamba territories

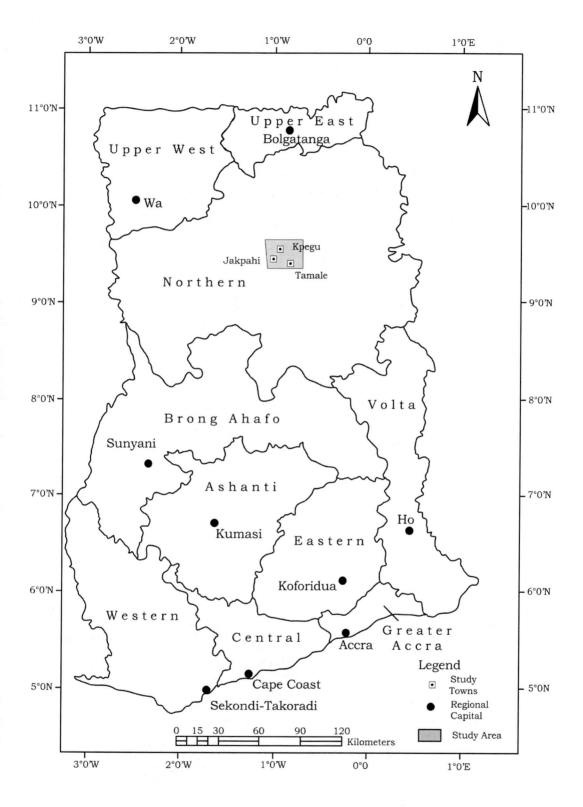

FIGURE 23.2: Map of Ghana showing research area

23. Historical, Geographical, Cultural, and Social Background of the Dagbamba of Ghana

The Land and the People

In the heart of the Voltaian basin lies the land of the Dagbamba, the largest ethnic group in the Northern Region of Ghana. The Northern Region is by far the largest in Ghana in terms of landmass, but is fourth behind Ashanti, Greater Accra and the eastern regions in population.

The Northern Region is divided into 20 municipal and district assemblies which are administered by chief executives. The Regional Coordinating Council, representatives of the chiefs, the district assemblies and heads of decentralized ministries, assist the regional minister who operates from Tamale, the capital, in carrying out policies of the ruling central government.

Dagbamba belong to the Mole-Dagbɔŋ (Mossi-Dagomba), one of the major ethnic groups in the Northern Region. All the major ethnic groups owe their allegiance to their various chiefs. The *ya naa*, with his seat at Yendi (Yeni or Naya), rules over the Dagbamba as the supreme chief.

The Dagbɔŋ area is very extensive, spreading over the whole of the northeastern quarter of Ghana, from the White Volta in the west to River Oti in the east, where Konkomba settlements gradually supersede Dagbamba settlements.

As a result of a single rainfall season between May and October with a long dry season from November to April, the vegetation of Dagbamba settlements and most parts of northern Ghana is mainly grassland with scattered savannah woodlands.

The major economic activities of the people include hunting, with subsistence farming of rice, maize and yam. Other drought-resistant trees, such as guava, acacia, mango, baobab, *tanga* (shea), and *doo* (dawadawa) are cultivated but are scarcely used for domestic purposes. They are regarded as sacred.

Most Dagbamba villages have traditional rulers or tree-chiefs to protect these special species of trees. Notable ones include: *tamainaa*, chief for the shea butter tree; *gondanaa*, kapok tree; *tunaa*, baobab; and *dɔhin-naa*, dawadawa tree.

Another significant cultural value among the Dagbamba, due to the limited rainfall, has caused the preservation and institution of sacred groves. Almost every Dagbɔŋ village has one or more sacred groves which are treated like important forest reserves, sources for medicinal plants and shrines for the people to commune with their land gods under the leadership of *tendamba (tindamba)*, earth or land priests.

Animal husbandry also holds a significant place for the Dagbambas who rear cattle, goats, sheep and poultry. Men do most of the clearing of the land and planting of cash crops and women do the cultivation of garden crops but may sometimes assist in the sowing and harvesting of cash crops.

Dagbaŋli, the language of the Dagbamba, is the most widely spoken in northern Ghana. There are two dialects of *Dagbaŋli.* The eastern dialect is spoken by settlements around Yendi and the western dialect by those around Tamale.

Dagbaŋli, which belongs to the *Gur* language cluster of West African languages, like most Ghanaian languages, is tonal. Accented syllables use higher tones, as questions seem to end on lower tones. A unique feature of *Dagbaŋli* is the eliding of vowels and slurring of consonants.

Traditional or first names are very important to the Dagbamba. Names are given to children in honor of their ancestors, traditional gods or shrines with the help of diviners. Names are given to children mostly according to the day of the week they are born. These are:

Days of the Week		Boy's Name	Girl's Name
Sunday	*Alahari*	Abubakari	Lahari
Monday	*Atani*	Mahama	Tani
Tuesday	*Atalaata*	Isahaku	Talaata
Wednesday	*Alariba*	Yahaya	Lariba
Thursday	*Alaamisi*	Alaasani	Laamihi
Friday	*Alizimma*	Adam	Zimma
Saturday	*Asibiri*	Abudulai	Sibiri

FIGURE 23.3: Birthday names of the Dagbamba

Historical Background

Oral tradition suggests that the present land of the Dagbamba was once occupied by smaller settler communities until around the early 12th century when the area was invaded by migrant Mande warriors, possibly from the old Malian Empire, led by the great commander Tohajie, known as the Red Hunter because of his light skin.

Many early legends also suggest that the same invaders who founded the Kisra states in Nigeria migrated from the vicinity of Lake Chad. On entering Northern Ghana, these migrants first settled at Pusiga, near Bawku, in the present-day Upper East Region of Ghana, and through their consolidation efforts and conquests led by Bawa (Gbewa), the grandson of Tohajie, they formed a new kingdom, Mamprugu (Mamprusi).

Due to political upheavals and several disputes mainly about the succession of power in the new kingdom, Mamprusi, descendants of Bawa dispersed in three groups to establish new kingdoms. To the south, the area below the Gambaga scarp was made into a new kingdom, Dagbɔŋ, by the Dagbamba led by Sitibo, one of Bawa's sons.

Before they established settlements in the 13th century, the Dagbamba had several wars with the Gonja in the west, the Konkomba in the east, and the Ashanti in the south.

Through all these struggles for survival and interactions with many external cultures, the Dagbamba have developed a very strong traditional cultural heritage with traits from Hausa and later from Islam, which they finally accepted in the 17th century. Dagbamba, like other major ethnic groups, were settled in Ghana before the arrival of the Portuguese in 1471.

Social and Cultural Profile

POLITICAL AUTHORITY. The traditional supreme head of the Dagbamba is the *ya naa,* who lives in Yendi. He is assisted by three divisional chiefs and several sub-chiefs who are custodians of the land.

Men rule in Dagbɔŋ. Women are not accorded the same status, mainly because of their perceived lack of strength. Inheritance is through the patrilineal system.

The family unit is organized according to households made up of a man, his wife or wives, and his children, with two or three brothers and their families living in enclosed round houses. Traditional households may also be built according to occupation or religious affiliation, especially in the villages.

RELIGION. Religion is at the root of Dagbɔŋ culture. It permeates all traditional worship and all social or cultural activities have some form of ritual attached.

Various rituals performed during festivals, marriages, funerals and other occasions are meant to express the people's dedication and belief in a supreme power, which they call *Naawuni* (God), who delegates powers through numerous spirits. While traditional authority rests with the chiefs, ritual activities are guided by land or earth priests, *tindambaa*.

Dagbɔŋ is divided into ritual areas for effective observance of the ritual calendar of various communities. Each area may be distinguished by reference to the animal taboo adhered to. For example, the animal in charge of Yendi is *gbuɣunli*, lion, which is also a symbol of kingship. More than one animal may be worshipped in some ritual areas.

Buga, sacred shrines (groves of trees, tall baobab and mud mounds), are located in every ritual "parish" under the care of the *tindamba*. Although settlements may have their own gods, the Dagbamba recognize *Pabo* and *Yanderi* (*Yaneli*) as the two most powerful that function throughout Dagbɔŋ.

Other deities worshipped include *Sapani*, the thunder god who operates during the night, and *tiyanima,* ancestral spirits that are worshipped through heads of families. *Baga,* the soothsayer or diviner, also exists to reveal to every family which sacrifices are to be made for the wellbeing of households.

So was the state of traditional religious practices and beliefs before Islam and Christian religions were introduced to Dagbɔŋ.

Islam is presently the dominant religion followed by the various traditional forms of worship in addition to Christianity, with Roman Catholics being the majority.

Despite this trend, because of the belief in the sacredness of the land, even Moslems and Christians still participate in some of the traditional rituals, especially during festivals.

FESTIVALS. Festivals among the Dagbamba are in two categories. There are the Islamic-derived festivals such as the *Damba,* an annual festival commemorating the birth and naming of the Prophet Mohammed, which is also celebrated as a new year festival; *Eid-ul-Fitr,* which marks the end of *Ramadam*; and *Eid-ul-Adhai,* the Feast of Sacrifice.

The second category of festivals are not Islamic in nature. These are festivals such as *Bugum,* or Fire Festival, which is celebrated to reactivate the spiritual powers of the people; *Kpini,* guinea fowl festival; and other harvest festivals.

Organization of Dance-Drumming Activities

CONTEXT OF MUSICAL EVENTS. Dance-drumming or musical activities of the Dagbamba are very extensive and mostly unknown. There are at least 17 distinct dance-drumming types performed in Dagbɔŋ as part of the political, recreational and religious events.

Most of the cultural activities, however, do not include dance-drumming ceremonies—especially funeral celebrations in communities where Islamic doctrine is rigidly observed. There are however, occasions when even Muslims participate freely without fear of intimidation, such as annual festivals and rituals for the land deities.

THE MAKING OF A MUSICIAN. Musicians, especially drummers (*luŋsi* players), fiddlers (*gonje* players) and praise singers are well respected among the Dagbamba because of their role in preserving the history of the people. These individuals are regarded as verbal artists, historians, genealogists and, above all, entertainers. Because of the setup of traditional households, it is easy to come across families of drummers, fiddlers and praise singers in Dagbɔŋ.

Becoming a musician is therefore a family tradition. One becomes a drummer, a praise singer or fiddler because one's father, uncle, or a close relative is one. Continuing the family tradition is paramount and is highly encouraged.

Learning to become a recognized performer in Dagbɔŋ involves several years of indirect and direct formal training in the household and apprenticeship with master musicians.

Participation in village performing groups has opened the doors for those not born into musical families to learn these art forms. In addition, because of programs instituted by the central government through the Education Service and the National Commission on Culture, all levels of education starting from elementary are now teaching these traditional art forms.

MUSICAL SOUND SOURCES. Dagbamba encourages both vocal and instrumental musical activities. The voice remains the most widely used for music-making and is the only genre in which women fully participate. Dagbɔŋ culture does not allow women to play drums or other instruments, even in their own dance-drumming events such as *Tɔra*.

Singing is taken seriously because of the value attached to song texts. The Dagbamba use songs to teach cultural behaviors, values, and accepted norms of the society.

Advice, caution, warnings, infidelity, good parenting, praise, ingratitude and other human issues are channeled through songs. Songs may teach or highlight the needs of the Dagbɔŋ society. Historical, philosophical and praise themes are the most common.

Traditionally, songs are performed in responsorial form with the lead soloist leading and the chorus singing the refrain. Songs may be performed in speech or metered rhythm. A lead singer may begin a song in speech rhythm and the chorus joins in strict rhythm accompanied by drums.

Melodies make use of three to seven-tone scales. Heterophony is the preferred texture in singing. Harmony is mainly the result of voices singing in unison, octave duplications and sporadic use of intervals of seconds, thirds, fourths, fifths, sixths, and sevenths, depending on the scale.

Instruments favored in most traditional dance-drumming ensembles include varieties of single and double-headed cylindrical laced drums such as *guŋgoŋ* and *daligu;* gourd drums, *bindili* and *batani;* and the hourglass drum, *luŋa.* String instruments include the *gonje,* one stringed fiddle; and the *bieɣu, moɣlo* and *kuntunji,* three-stringed pluck lutes. Wind instruments include the *kalamboo,* cane flute; and the *yua,* notched flute. There are also self-sounding idiophones such as the *feinŋa,* castanet; the *saɣyalli,* container rattle played in pairs; and the *dawule,* double bell.

Following are photographs of some of the instruments used in dance-drumming ensembles. See Figure 23.10 on page C-11 of the color insert.

Guŋgoŋ. The *guŋgoŋ* (*guŋgoŋna,* pl.) functions as the foundation for most Dagbamba dance-drumming percussion ensembles. It is a

FIGURE 23.4: *Guŋgoŋ,* one of the lead drums in most Dagbamba ensembles.

Above, FIGURE 23.5: Playing technique on the *guŋgoŋ* in *Bla* dance-drumming, as demonstrated by the Jakpahi Dang Maligu *Bla* Drummers (2009). *Left*, FIGURE 23.6: Playing technique on the *guuŋgoŋ* in *Baamaaya* dance-drumming, as demonstrated by the Tamale Youth Cultural lead drummer (2009). *Below*, FIGURE 23.7: Playing technique on the *guŋgoŋ* in *Jɛra* and *Tɔra* dance-drumming, as demonstrated by the Kpegu *Jɛra* drummers (2009).

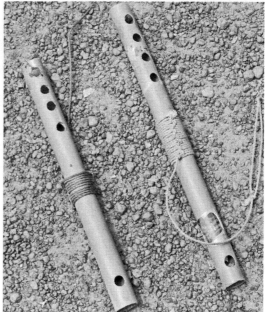

Top, left, FIGURE 23.8: Playing technique on the Dagbamba *luŋa* as demonstrated by the Kpegu Jɛra lead drummer. Refer to Chapter 18 under "*Donno*" for a full description of this instrument (2009). *Top, right*, FIGURE 23.9: *Saɣyelim*, basket container rattles. *Above*, FIGURE 23.11: *Kalamboo*, side-blown flutes. *Left*, FIGURE 23.12: Playing technique on the *kalamboo* as demonstrated by a Jakpahi Dang Maligu *Bla* flute player (2009).

cylindrical two-headed drum carved out of a local species of the cedar tree.

After the wood is carved and dried, fur is removed from a goat skin which is used to cover both ends held in place by *gabga*, rings made from bush twine. *Gbaŋda*, leather strips made from either the goat or antelope skins, are used to connect both heads.

Top, left, FIGURE 23.13: *Yua,* notched flute. *Top, right,* FIGURE 23.14: Playing technique on *yua* as demonstrated by a Kpegu *Jɛra* flute player (2009). *Bottom, left,* FIGURE 23.15: *Fienŋa,* which is used in *Jɛra* dance-drumming. Refer to Chapter 9 under "*kretsiwa*" for a full description of this instrument (2009). *Bottom, right,* FIGURE 23.16: Fienŋa, which is used in *Bla* dance-drumming. Refer to Chapter 9 under "*kretsiwa*" for a full description of this instrument (2009).

Gbaŋzie, pieces of leather, are attached to the *Gbanda* for tuning purposes. When pulled, *gbanzie* tighten the drum to the appropriate pitch level for a performance and are then loosened after playing. Two leather strings are tied across the upper half of the drumheads to produce the snare effect peculiar to the *guŋgoŋ.*

To generate sound on a *guŋgoŋ,* a curved stick, *guŋgoŋ-doli,* is used. Either one or two sticks are used in performance depending on the type of dance-drumming ceremony. There are four basic tones generated by a *guŋgoŋ:* i. the open or the natural voice of the drum is made by hitting and bouncing the stick at the center of the head; ii. stopping or muting at the same area produces a closed tone; and iii. hitting the head with the stick or relaxed hands above the snare string generates the third and fourth tones, respectively.

24. *Baamaaya* Recreational Dance-Drumming Ceremony

Historical Background and Development

Baamaaya is the most popular recreational dance-drumming among the inhabitants of Dagbɔŋ of northern Ghana. The history of this classic dance underscores the philosophy and culture of the Dagbamba and their attitude towards women.

For centuries, women in Dagbɔŋ culture were treated as lesser human beings. This attitude has not changed much at all—even after years of social and cultural reforms in this part of Ghana. This fact is reflected in the number of Dagbana girls enrolled in public schools in Ghana today as compared to boys.

Oral tradition has it that *Baamaaya* was first performed as a religious ceremony to appease the land gods, the *tingbana* of Dagbɔŋ. History has it that somewhere around the early 18th century, soon after the Dagbamba's conversion to Islam, a great famine occurred in Dagbɔŋ due to a severe drought. Many of the inhabitants were dying from hunger. Hunters would go days without any successful hunt. The situation was grim and desperate actions needed to be taken.

The belief in traditional religious practices, oracles and ancestral worship before the introduction of Islam had to be given a second thought and priority in this time of trial and hardship. The *sabooniba*, the rainmakers, performed several sacrifices and rituals but all their actions proved futile.

Further consultation of the oracles revealed that the major issue or reason for their situation was the way women were being treated in society: Unless the men of Dagbɔŋ started to treat women with respect, the gods would continue to punish the entire land. It was not going to be easy for the men to give up their authority and rights over women all of a sudden but they were ready to try anything for the sake of their children and households.

So the story goes that the men were asked by the oracles to dress like women and dance in front of their wives and go through the villages as a public humiliation and atonement for generations of maltreatment of women.

There was yet another hurdle for the men to cross before undertaking their task. Their wives were not going to loan them their clothes for the dance (most of the women did not have clothes in the first place) so they were forced to make their own dresses from corn husks, which became the main *Baamaaya nema*, costumes/clothes and were worn on their *shee*, waists.

Other aspects of women's clothing would also be improvised. Representing the women's long hair was *wɔliɣa*, a hat made from a black monkey's fur; earrings from seeds; *napɔŋkpuɣuligu*, ankle beads, were replaced with metal jingles; *biha*, fake breasts, were created by stuffing their shirts with extra cloth; and *kafiena*, a fan used in the kitchen and also to fan the chiefs, became an extension of the arm.

213

Completing the costume is a towel for wiping sweat and a short horsetail. This whisk is like a personal god, *Sabli*, a protective talisman from evil spirits. With these items, the men took on all the attributes of the women.

With their costumes ready, the men danced nonstop through the streets for three days, accompanied by their drums. The goal was to create a great deal of sound as they paraded the streets, with women and children looking on with laughter.

It took a lot of energy to move all the costumes, especially the *shee* on the waist. The men had to eat a large amount of food before being able to perform the intricate waist movements which started at the feet and knees. The preferred meal was *tubankpiili*. This is one of the all-protein traditional dishes of the Dagbamba, consisting of beans and "groundnuts" (peanuts). The original name for the dance-drumming during those early days was *tubankpiili* (named after the beans and groundnuts dish), which literally means, "Unless you are satisfied you cannot take part in the dance."

The gods were touched by the subdued men of Dagbɔŋ. Three days of prayers and performances yielded continued heavy rainfall for days.

The men continued to perform this dance-drumming throughout the rains, planting new crops until it was time for the harvest. When the valleys, the farms and the land came back to life with green pastures, rivers and cold weather, the elders remarked, "*Baa maaya,*" which means, "The valley is cold" or "The river is wet again." *Tubankpiili* was then renamed *Baamaaya* as a celebration of gratitude to the gods.

Baamaaya was derived from two Dagbaŋli words: *baa*, valley and *maaya,* coolness, which literally mean, "because the rain has come." Men were no longer ashamed of their new way of dressing or, in particular, the new dance movements. They embraced *Baamaaya,* refined the costumes, added more phases to make it the most revered recreational dance-drumming of the Dagbamba.

The dance-drumming has since been performed as a thanksgiving to the gods for accepting their prayers. Performance in the past was done mostly in the rainy season by young men. Islam nearly brought an end to *Baamaaya* because of its rigid doctrine and Friday prayers but with support from all the ruling *Ya-Naas,* it continued to grow.

Unlike in the past when it was performed mainly in the rainy season, *Baamaaya* is now seen during funerals, festivals, and other national celebrations. Childbirth, weddings and other social events may also attract *Bamaaya* groups.

Baamaaya groups are organized as popular dance-drumming ensembles. Women are now allowed to dance. Tamale, the regional capital of the Northern Region of Ghana and surrounding villages, remains the cradle of *Baamaaya.*

Organization of the Dance-Drumming Ceremony

FORM AND STRUCTURE. From a processional dance-drumming that started slowly and changed to fast tempo, *Baamaaya* has developed into a ceremony with at least nine distinct phases: *baamaaya sochendi, baamaaya valiŋa, sikolo, nyaɣboli, kondoliya, dakolikutooko, abalimbee, baaŋa* and *baamaaya valiŋa.* Each of the phases has unique set of dance routines, movements and choreography.

Phase One: **Baamaaya Sochendi.** *Baamaaya* begins with a slow procession from the *shilmalibu shee,* a special dressing room located in the group leader's house, to the dance performance space. Most of the singing is done during this phase of the ceremony because the dancers who are led by the drummers, unlike in *Jɛra,* do not sing as they put on their costumes.

Baamaaya sochendi is performed to remind the dancers of the wet valley. They are cautioned to walk slowly and carefully else they fall. The dance steps are being supported by the rhythmic patterns of the two main drums: *guŋgoŋ* and *luŋa*. The *luŋa* cautions, *Chendi tokul baŋ chendi,* "Walk slowly," and *guŋgoŋ* responds, *Baa maa maaya*, "The valley is wet."

This processional phase is performed in single file. Once the performers reach the arena, the dancers form a circle around the drummers to begin the next phase. The percussion ensemble is not stationary. The instrumentalists may move around and will stop to play around any dancer who dances exceptionally throughout the ceremony.

Phase Two: *Baamaaya Valiŋa*. A signal from the *luŋa* moves the ceremony to its fast dance-drumming phase. This is also the main phase of *Baamaaya*. The ability of the dancer to initiate his waist movements from below the knee sometimes marvels the novice. This phase also encourages the dancers to make the movements their own. Recreating any basic movement is the key to becoming a recognized *Baamaaya* dancer in Dagbⱥ culture.

Phase Three: *Sikolo*. *Sikolo* is one of the proverbs and philosophies of Dagbⱥ culture. You do not open your home to strangers. Always be on guard for your enemies. Be cautious of people who will pretend to be your friend but turn out to be harmful or not supportive when you are in need.

This phase reminds the Dagbamba of their painful past. Nobody was there to help or support them during their crises. They took care of their own problems. You will not be given the key to anybody's home/door if you are not a relative or trusted friend.

Phase Four: *Nyaɣboli*. There is a common proverb in almost all of Ghana, popularly stated in Akan, *Sankɔfa*, meaning, "Always return to your roots." There is need to review the past to make the future better.

Among the Dagbamba, this philosophy is recognized as a moral lesson to teach history and reflections on life. Life is not a race. Patience is required to succeed. Always have the urge to move forward but take needed time to review your strategies for another better leap forward.

During this phase, the dancers take a jump forward and a short step backwards. They will take a brief pause and then leap forward again. These movements are symbolic of this philosophy of life.

Phase Five: *Kondoliya*. *Kondoliya*, or *kanton*, pays special tribute to water as the sustenance of life. *Kondoliya*, meaning, "There lies water," reminds the Dagbamba of the value of water.

Water is treated with respect among the Mamprusis, their close neighbors, as is evident in a proverb which says, "You do not throw bad water away if you do not have good water." Always use water with care because you do not know when the next rains will fall.

Phase Six: *Dakolikutooko*. There is always room for comic relief during *Baamaaya* performances. Instead of women, dancers— usually men — will mock fellow bachelors in society. Dagbⱥ culture places much value on manhood.

A man is regarded as responsible and strong when he has a home with wive(s) and children. The most important duty of a man is to look after his household by providing food and all the necessities of life.

Dakolikutooko, therefore, is created to laugh at bachelors who do not farm because of their laziness. The man without a wife sees no need for a farm.

Phase Seven: *Abalimbee*. The beauty of *Baamaaya* is shown in this phase from the dancers' perspective. The dancers take the opportunity to show that they are really enjoying themselves. *Abalimbee* leads to a break for refreshments.

Phase Eight: *Baaŋa*. There is a song cycle period during every dance-drumming ceremony among the Dagbamba. During *baaŋa* in this context, led by the lead singer, songs reflecting their cultural history as a people are performed. Praise songs are also performed to honor the chiefs, special guests and patrons who are present at the performance.

Phase Nine: *Baamaaya: Valiŋa*. When all the performers are refreshed and final announcements are made depending on the event, there is a final performance of *baamaaya valiŋa* as a processional dance-drumming. This fast dance-drumming is used as a recession back to the dressing room.

Songs

Themes of *Baamaaya* songs relate to many issues in the lives of the Dagbamba. Generally, themes dwell on historical, topical, religious, social and cultural issues and the beliefs of the people.

Singing during a performance is usually difficult except when the dancers are in procession to and from the dance arena. There is, however, a praise singer who praises the dancers as they move around the dance arena.

Songs in *Baamaaya* are mostly in call and response form. Singing involves the use of a very clear but high-pitched, tensed, and nasal voice. Melodic arrangements make use of mostly tritonic, tetratonic and pentatonic combinations.

Ululation is a special feature in *Baamaaya* music and is employed by the women when congratulating the men dancers. Apart from the above, women can be seen appreciating the dancers by singing "praise shouts."

The Percussion Ensemble

Instruments and their functions in the ensemble include:

i.	*Guŋgɔŋ*	Double-headed cylindrical drum; serves as the lead drum; a second *guŋgɔŋ* may be used to support the main lead drum.

FIGURE 24.1: Members of the Tamale Youth Home *Baamaaya* Percussion Ensemble in action. Left to right, standing: *guŋgɔŋ, luŋa, kalamboo, saɣyelim*; kneeling: *guŋgɔŋ* (2009).

ii.	*Luŋa*	Hourglass-shaped drum, comments on the performance, performs messages and praises to invited guests, patrons, elders and other dignitaries; starts all phases of the ceremony, but the *guŋgɔŋa* establish the rhythmic patterns for all the various phases to guide the dancers.
iii.	*Saȥyeli (saȥyelim or saȥyalli)*	A pair of container basket rattles support the drums.
iv.	*Kalamboo*	Side-blown cane flute; originally carved from the blackberry tree or made from a stalk of guinea corn; PVC pipes are being used today.

Dance Organization

DANCE ARENA. Apart from the processional and *baaŋa,* all the other phases are performed in a circle.

FIGURE 24.2: Tamale Youth Home *Baamaaya* Group in action (2009).

DANCE MOVEMENTS AND CHOREOGRAPHY. There are specific movements and gestures for each phase of the dance-drumming. The beauty of the dance-drumming, however, is seen in the main dance movement.

Baamaaya's main movement, which starts from the *baamaaya valiŋa* phase, has quick syncopated footwork with hips rotating or twisting below a still or strongly anchored torso. The dance travels in a circle formation and the dancers rotate around the drummers.

On a three-beat count, the dancer steps down on beat one with the right foot. The first step can be subtle where the foot barely rises from the ground (before being placed down), or more obvious with a higher lift. This depends on the dancer and his personal interpretation and expression. When the right foot lands on the ground, the left foot rises—the distance between the dancer's foot and the ground in this case is generally higher than the first (right) foot.

On beat two, the left foot hits the ground and the right foot lifts up. The phrase is completed on beat three when the right foot returns to the ground as the left foot remains still.

When the left foot rises (on beat one) the left leg slightly (which is bent) turns outward (or at times turns inward) by a rotation in the hip joint. This action initiates the twisting or rotation of the hip. This movement, if done correctly, makes the *mukuru/agbatoro* (the skirt) rapidly swing left to right and right to left. This action resembles the motion of an agitator on a washing machine or the internal mechanisms of a wristwatch.

As the legs move, the arms may fluctuate between bound or free movements and can be placed in a 90-degree angle, straight or somewhere in between, accenting the movements of the rest of the body. The hand, while holding a fan, a horsetail, or two horsetails, may pronate, supinate (initiating from the forearm), clench into a fist or shift in all different directions to manipulate the above-mentioned paraphernalia and accents of the body's motion.

Completing this main movement while all the extremities and hips are moving rapidly, the torso is relaxed and still; however, dancers may choose to accent certain movements with their shoulders and other parts of the torso at will (Zelma Badu-Younge 2010).

Costume and Other Visual Art Forms

The *Baamaaya* costume includes several components. Most of these components have developed as the dance-drumming has changed context over the years. Present costume includes:

i.	*yebsa*	special sewn ruffles worn around the waist on a ladies skirt;
ii.	*mukuru*	"*agbatoro*" ladies skirt worn under the *mokuro*;
iii.	*zupuliga*	head turban, hat or *bɔbga*, headscarf;
iv.	*chaɣla*	secondary rattles worn around the ankles to emphasize dance movements;
v.	*tikpara*	earrings;
vi.	*darna*	spectacles (dark) optional;
vii.	*boduwa*	towel/handkerchief put around the neck to clean any sweat;
viii.	*kafiena*	fan; and
ix.	*bodisi*	brassiere worn under a lady's blouse.

COMPONENTS OF BAAMAAYA COSTUME.

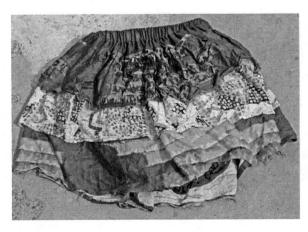

Above, FIGURE 24.3a: *Mukuru agbatoro,* skirt (2009). *Right,* FIGURE 24.3b: Tamale Youth Home *Baamaaya* lead dancer in *mukuru agbatoro* (2009).

Above, FIGURE 24.4a: *Bodisi*. *Right*, FIGURE 24.4b: Tamale Youth Home *Baamaaya* lead dancer in *bodisi* (2009).

Above, FIGURE 24.5a: Blouse. *Right*, FIGURE 24.5b: Tamale Youth Home *Baamaaya* lead dancer in a blouse (2009).

Above, FIGURE 24.6a: *Chaɣla*, secondary ankle rattles. *Right*, FIGURE 24.6b: Tamale Youth Home *Baamaaya* lead dancer putting on a *chaɣla* (2009).

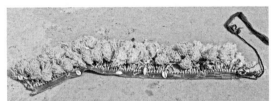

Above, FIGURE 24.7a: *Mukuru yebsa* (2009). *Left*, FIGURE 24.7b: Tamale Youth Home *Baamaaya* lead dancer in *yebsa* (2009).

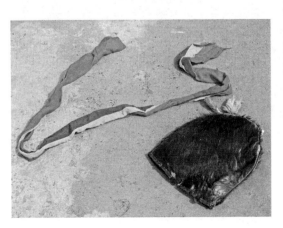

Left, FIGURE 24.8a: *Zupuliga*, hat. *Above*, FIGURE 24.8b: Tamale Youth Home *Baamaaya* lead dancer putting on *zupuliga* (2009).

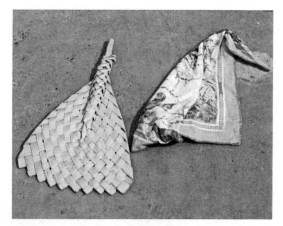

FIGURE 24.9: *Kafiena* and *boduwa*, fan and scarf.

FIGURE 24.10: Tamale Youth Home *Baamaaya* lead dancer in full *Baamaaya* costume (2009).

25. *Bla* Religious
Dance-Drumming Ceremony

Historical Background and Development

Bla is one of the oldest ritual funeral dance-drumming ceremonies among the Dagbamba. The history and development of *Bla* is very essential to understanding some of the values, beliefs, and attitudes toward the role of women in Dagbɔŋ society.

The history of *Bla*, as told by the elders of Jakpahi — one of the few *tiŋsi* (towns) still performing this special dance-drumming ceremony — reveals that, some hundred years ago, a hunter whose name they could not remember went hunting and came across dwarfs mourning their dead, singing and dancing around the corpse. This hunter allegedly stood there for a while to observe this display and, upon his return, narrated his encounter to his household.

The hunter's children were intrigued by the story and begged their father to teach them some of the movements that the dwarfs were doing. The children were soon taught these movements, which they performed with the accompaniment of cans, pots and empty bottles.

The chiefs and elders of the village liked the recreation of the dwarfs' performance so they encouraged other children in the village to join in the performance.

Not long after, someone in the village died and at the recommendation of the hunter the children were allowed to reenact the dwarfs' ceremony by performing around the grave of the deceased. They believed this performance would console the bereaved family and chase the evil spirit that caused the death away from the village.

This first presentation was so successful that the adults in the village decided to learn the movements themselves and were soon performing it as part of their rituals at pre- and post-burial ceremonies. They would roll their waists around and around amid singing, accompanied by their drums, *luŋa* and *guŋgɔŋ*. The rolling of the waist became the name of the dance-drumming, which is derived from the Dagbaŋli phrase, *bil maŋa*, which literally means, "to roll around." *Bil maŋa* was later changed to simply *Bla* or *Bila* as the name for this dance-drumming ceremony.

Bla as an adult performance for funerals started in Yendi, the traditional capital of the Dagbamba and the seat of *ya naa*, the supreme chief, and was soon adopted by other towns — notably Zavelugu and Jakpahi. The last phase of the ceremony, *yaawum*, was created as a tribute to the children who first performed this dance-drumming.

Although *Bla* is mainly performed to honor the dead, chase away evil spirits associated with death, and to console bereaved families, it can be seen at other social occasions such as naming ceremonies, weddings, festivals and visits by government officials.

The Jakpahi Dan Maligu group, which I was privileged to work with, was only recently discovered by the Center for National Culture in Tamale in 1992. The group has since been featured in several regional and national celebrations.

Organization of the Dance-Drumming Ceremony

Form and Structure. *Bla* started mainly with one phase. As time went on, several phases were added. A typical performance during funerals has at least seven phases, some of which may be repeated: *bla, bilje, yila, sagali, zem, damba* and *yaawum*. Only one phase, *bla*, is performed at non-funeral events.

Phase One: *Bla*. The main dance-drumming phase, *bla*, is used as a processional ceremony to begin the performance. On a given occasion, the performers—especially the dancers, converge at the house of their patron/leader to dress up in their costumes.

They will sing as they dress up in the *shilimaalibu shee,* a special dressing room. The procession begins with less vigorous dancing and singing until they reach the performance venue/funeral grounds where they form a circle around the drummers and perform vigorously.

This initial performance is meant to announce the arrival of the group and also to entertain the audience. A brief pause leads into the second movement, *bilje.*

Phase Two: *Bilje*. At the funeral, the first performance after the procession is in honor of the dead. This is performed around the grave to drive away evil spirits believed to be responsible for the death of the individual. This phase leads to another *bla* in honor of the deceased family.

Phase Three: *Yila*. No traditional dance-drumming ceremony is complete without a period of praise singing among the Dagbamba. When performers, especially the drummers, are being refreshed, the dancers perform song interludes or tell stories.

Yila, sometimes referred to as *baaŋa* in other dance-drumming ceremonies, provides an opportunity for members of the community to pay special tribute to the dead and offer condolences. These stories and songs, regarded as essential components of the dance-drumming ceremony, are led by lead singers of the performing group.

Phase Four: *Sagali*. Immediately following the short break is another performance to honor the dead. *Sagali* is performed to allow the spirit of the dead to rest in peace. This is a joyous moment, which leads into another *bla* during which offerings are given. Money is thrown on the grave, drinks are offered to the performers and there is a sense that the celebration is coming to its climax.

Phase Five: *Zɛm*. A special tribute is paid to the warriors, who in Dagbɔŋ culture are also hunters, for discovering this dance-drumming in the first place.

Phase Six: Damba. Festivals are very important among the Dagbamba. They serve as occasions for family reunions amid merry-making. So, even during a funeral, there is a conscious effort made to allow the spirit of the dead an opportunity to participate in the joyous celebration for the last time.

Damba, originally an exclusive Islamic festival observed to honor the birth and naming of the Prophet Mohammed, has become one of the important festivals celebrated by the Dagbamba to celebrate their cultural heritage.

During the *damba* phase of this ceremony, audience participation is encouraged. *Damba*, in this context, refers to the festival and the dance movements.

Phase Seven: *Yaawum*. The concluding phase of this dance-drumming ceremony is *yaawum*, which is dedicated to the grandchildren. Most of the dance movements in *Bla* are similar in all phases, with the exception of *zɛm* and *damba*. The cultural symbolism and significance of the phases are more important to the Dagbamba than are the specific dance movements.

Songs

Themes of *Bla* songs are based on the history and the experiences of the Dagbamba. Songs may relate to topical issues and human relations such as love, gossip, hate, adultery, jealousy, etc.

Proverbial songs are also very common. At the funeral, songs may comment on or mock death as an evil spirit, or may honor the dead or praise important members of the community.

Bla songs, like most Dagbamba dance-drumming songs, are performed in simple call and response form with the lead singers being given the opportunity to recreate the texts and the rhythmic and melodic patterns.

Ornamentation of tones is highly encouraged and required from the lead singer as a form of embellishing the melody. As in *Baamaaya*, melodic arrangements make use of mostly tritonic, tetratonic and pentatonic combinations.

Homophony is non-existent. Most of the songs are performed in unison, with octave duplications between the male and female voices. Female participants (who do not dance but perform praise shouts and ululation to motivate the dancers) provide an additional layer of texture to the melody.

The Percussion Ensemble

Instruments and their functions in Bla performance include:

i.	*Bla Guŋgɔŋ nyaŋ*	Double-headed cylindrical drum; serves as the lead drum.
ii.	*Bla Guŋgɔŋ laa*	Double-headed cylindrical drum; supports the lead drum; two may be used as supporting drums.
iii.	*Luŋa*	Hourglass-shaped drum, comments on the performance, performs messages and praises to the bereaved family, elders and other dignitaries; plays the main supporting role for the two *guŋgɔŋ* (na, pl.).
iv.	*Kalamboo*	Side-blown cane flute; originally carved from the blackberry tree or made from a stalk of guinea corn; PVC pipes are being used today.
v.	*Fienŋa (Feiŋsi, pl.)*	Castanet used by all dancers to accentuate their dance movements.

See Figure 25.1 on page C-12 of the color insert.

Dance Organization

DANCE ARENA. Apart from the first phase, the processional dance-drumming ceremony, which is done in a line and led by the percussion ensemble, the rest of the phases are performed in a circle. The dancers form a circle around the drummers.

The *guŋgɔŋna* are positioned at the center and are stationary. The *luŋa* and *kalamboo* players may travel clockwise with the dancers or sometimes play besides the *guŋgɔŋna* players.

DANCE MOVEMENTS AND CHOREOGRAPHY. This is a dance where the main movement focuses on the hips shifting from a wave-like undulating movement to a quick twist or wiggle. The dance travels in a circle formation and the dancers rotate around the drummers.

In a two-beat phrase, the right (or left) foot steps forward on beat one and returns to its original position on beat two. This step is repeated with the opposite foot.

This movement can be varied by the dancer repeatedly stepping one foot forward while the second foot drags forward behind it; or, the dancer can step forward alternating feet, as when a pedestrian walks.

As the foot lifts to step forward, the hip releases backwards. When the foot lands on the ground the hip moves forward to its original position. This creates a wave-like undulating feel to the main movement. Spontaneously, the dancer will wiggle, twitch, shimmy, rotate or release

FIGURE 25.2: Jakpahi Dang Maligu *Bla* dancers in a procession (2009).

FIGURE 25.3: Jakpahi Dang Maligu *Bla* Group in a performance (2009).

vwith an accent (move back and forth in an articulated fashion) with his hips between the foot movements.

The arms move freely from a loose bent position (at a 90-degree angle) to an elongated position to the side of or slightly behind the torso as the hands are freely moving or holding onto one metal castanet.

The torso moves as an extension or continuation of the hip movement — in a wave-like undulating, twitching or shimmy-like fashion.

The main dance movement is enhanced by the *chinchina,* several clothes tied around the waist (Zelma Badu-Younge 2010).

Costume and Other Visual Art Forms

There are several components and layers of the *Bla* costume worn by dancers. It takes almost one hour to dress up for a performance. The dancer starts by wearing a *krugu* or *kurugu,* a large, long, baggy pair of pants. On top of that is *chinchina,* a six-yard cloth tied on the waist with other lengths of cloth hanging from it, which acts as a belt.

The next components, a lady's blouse, *bodisi,* brassier and *bɔbga,* headscarf, have unique historical significance. Among the Dagbamba women are regarded as inferior to men. They are seen as not having the strength of men to be involved in rigorous activities such as dancing *Bla* and other so-called male dances. However, it happened that at funerals there was a need to represent both genders since the original celebration, as performed by the dwarfs and the children, involved both sexes. Another reason was that women have a very important role at funerals so they could not be left out in any funeral celebration.

In an attempt to satisfy these requirements, the men agreed to dress like women before they could perform this dance. Unlike in *Baamaaya,* women gave their clothes to the men to use. The roles of women have changed in recent years and so selected women who are seen to have the same strength and stamina as men are now being allowed to perform.

Completing this elaborate costume for dancers are *kani,* an armband that is supposed to be a *sabli* (talisman) to protect the dancers from evil spirits, and *sariga,* a shawl worn around the neck. Lipstick, earrings and other female makeup are also used.

Drummers and other instrumentalists are not required to perform in any specific attire; however, the traditional *binɲmaa* or *batakari* (smock) over any decent pants is encouraged.

COMPONENTS OF BLA COSTUME. See Figure 25.11 on page C-12 of the color insert.

Above, FIGURE 25.4a: *Kurugu. Right,* FIGURE 25.4b: Jakpahi Dang Maligu *Bla* dancer in *kurugu* (2009).

Above, FIGURE 25.5a: *Bodisi. Right*, FIGURE 25.5b: Jakpahi Dang Maligu *Bla* dancer in *bodisi* (2009).

Above, FIGURE 25.6a: Lady's blouse. *Left*, FIGURE 25.6b: Jakpahi Dang Maligu *Bla* dancer in a blouse (2009).

Left, FIGURE 25.7a: *Chinchina. Right*, FIGURE 25.7b: Jakpahi Dang Maligu *Bla* dancer being assisted with *chinchina* (2009).

Left, FIGURE 25.8a: *Bɔbga. Right*, FIGURE 25.8b: Jakpahi Dang Maligu *Bla* dancer in *bɔbga* (2009).

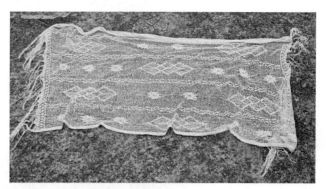

FIGURE 25.9: *Sariga.*

FIGURE 25.10: Jakpahi Dang Maligu *Bla* dancer in full costume (2009).

26. *Jɛra* Religious Dance-Drumming Ceremony

Historical Background and Development

The origin of *Jɛra*, or *Jara*, has a mythical story as do most Dagbɔŋ religious and warrior dance-drumming ceremonies: A hunter discovered it during one of his expeditions.

Legend has it that there was once a famous hunter called Nanjaa who lived in Sakpalua, a Kpariba village, during the early periods of settlements by the Dagbamba, around the 17th and 18th centuries. Nanjaa was noted for his bravery because he only went hunting at night.

During one of his expeditions, he heard strange, distant sounds emanating from the forest. These "drumming and singing" sounds were different from anything he had ever experienced. He knew there were no other villages in the area, so out of curiosity he followed the sound to see what was happening.

The story goes that Nanjaa, out of fear, went with all his protective *sabli,* talismans, to safeguard himself against any evil forces that might try to harm him. He could not believe what he saw. Little dwarfs were entertaining themselves. He hid himself for hours to observe the dwarfs' performances.

For several days, Nanjaa would secretly return to the forest to observe these performances. Gradually, he learned the dance movements, costuming, drumming and some of the songs. Even though he could not understand the language, he was able to memorize some of the melodies.

His next goal was to get closer to see the structure and components of the costume and drums—a risky move, as the dwarfs could see him. Nanjaa had no choice but to steal the drums and set of costumes. He waited one day, and after the dwarfs had finished their performance and put the costumes and drums away, he secretly went for the two drums and a set of costumes.

He brought these items home and finally gathered the whole community and told them about the new dance-drumming he had discovered. As he demonstrated the movements, which involved moving forwards and backwards, the chief of the village exclaimed, *Bo jɛra waa mbogo,* meaning, "What kind of fools dance is this?" And that is the origin of the name of the dance-drumming, *Jɛra,* which means "fool's dance."

Hunters in the village became interested in *Jɛra,* and after days of practice they would perform it exclusively at night during the wake of a deceased elder or hunter in the village. They would also perform it as a ritual dance before and after their expeditions.

As a tribute to Nanjaa for establishing this new dance-drumming in Dagbɔŋ, a song that most groups now use to end their performances was composed in his honor: *Nanjaa zaŋ Jɛra kul na yee* (Nanjaa has brought *Jɛra* home).

From Sakpalua, *Jɛra* spread to other villages in Dagbɔŋ such as Tarikpaa, Sanzie, Kpegu and Bogu, where it is performed for other social events including the installation of chiefs, funerals and festivals. The ritual costumes are still used on these occasions. Unfortunately, Jɛra is not performed any longer in Sakpalua.

The Kpegu Jɛra group is the most active in Dagbɔŋ today. Apart from being taught by drummers and dancers directly from Sakpalua, their two main lead drums, *guŋgoŋ bila* and *guŋgoŋ titali*, were specifically carved and consecrated by the Sakpalua group. The original drums (almost 200 years old) are still being used today.

Participation in *Jɛra* is controlled because of the intricate dance movements. Dancers require long periods of training before they are allowed to perform.

The groups are organized as traditional popular bands. Non-members are not permitted to join in the dance. The audience may show appreciation by singing or applause. Women are allowed to dance *Jɛra* but without the costume.

Since the 1990s, the Centre for National Culture in Tamale and the National Youth Council's Youth Home Cultural group, also based in Tamale, have contributed immensely to educating and spreading *Jɛra* dance-drumming.

Organization of the Dance-Drumming Ceremony

FORM AND STRUCTURE. There are six distinct phases of the *Jɛra* dance-drumming ceremony. Some of these phases may be repeated during a given performance: *jɛra-sochendi, jɛra-tɔra, jɛra-lura, baaŋa, lelba* and *jɛra-sochendi*.

Phase One: Jɛra-Sochendi. On a given day of performance, the dancers and drummers meet at their lead dancer's, or sometimes the head hunter or chief's house, to dress in their costumes. Dancers usually sing as they put on their costumes.

Apart from serving as a warm-up for the dancers, it is also a period to review songs for the performance. Drummers may also join in this preliminary performance in order to tune their drums. All of this happens in seclusion.

Jɛra-sochendi, the processional dance-drumming phase, begins usually with the song, *Kumbaa yoo yee, kumla baa yoo balan kayoma*, meaning, "We are coming to dance." The dancers, led by the drummers, travel slowly in single file to the dance arena.

This phase informs the village or spectators that the group is ready to perform their ritual dance. Upon reaching the dance performance space, the dancers form a circle around the drummers. A signal from the lead dancer ushers in the next phase, *jɛra-tɔra*.

Phase Two: Jɛra-Tɔra. Once the circle is complete, the lead dancer changes his steps to a faster pace as if charging on an enemy or chasing an animal in the forest. This phase is meant to allow the dancers to demonstrate one of the dwarfs' original movements, which involves moving forward very fast and suddenly stopping and then taking a few steps backwards. The music of the percussion ensemble does not change throughout the whole performance.

This phase is best described as a preparation for the main section of the ceremony, *jɛra-lura*, which follows. As the dancers move with arms raised, they are asking permission from the elders and spectators to be allowed to dance. A popular song that accompanies this phase is *Goo yaa yan go yoo, goo yaa yan go, yariga*, meaning, "We are here to ask permission to dance, we are here, we are strong."

Phase Three: Jɛra-Lura. *Jɛra-lura*, the main dance-drumming phase, begins when the lead singer performs in place or with less traveling forward and backwards. The *saɣyelim* (container rattle) player performs in front of the lead dancer to emphasize his movements.

The beauty of *Jɛra* is observed in this phase. The ability of the dancers to play the *fienŋsi* (castanets) and at the same time dance while moving all parts of the body, their faces, the numerous *kani* (arm bands), and other secondary rattles tied to the *napɔŋkpuɣuligu* (ankles) provides quite a spectacle.

Phase Four: *Baaŋa*. As discussed in the section on *Bla*, most dance-drumming ceremonies of the Dagbamba create periods for singing *silma*, praise and historical songs. During this *baaŋa*, as it is known in *Jɛra*, performers are refreshed.

Dancers take the opportunity to readjust their costumes. Songs are accompanied by the *fienŋsi* and sometimes the *luŋa* and *guŋgoŋ*. Phase five, which follows, is a repeat of *jɛra-tɔra* that leads to the climax of the ceremony, *lelba*.

Phase Six: *Lelba*. This phase pays tribute to the main components of the *Jɛra* costume, which is made up of *kpukpuli*, a set of cowries woven on four strands of rope and worn around the waist on top of *laɣmihi*, a bulging bag made of cloth tied around the waist which hangs directly in front of the dancer. Each strand of the cowries represents *bia*, a child.

Kpukpuli, therefore, represents the children in the community. *Laɣmihi* and *kpukpuli* together symbolize the strength and spirituality of each dancer.

Dancers use this phase to show off by constantly raising these items. A dancer is believed to have special spiritual powers when he is able to raise the *laɣmihi* and at the same time command the different strands of the *kpukpuli* to fall individually. *Lelba* leads to the recessional phase, which is a repeat of *jɛra-sochendi*.

Phase Seven: *Jɛra-Sochendi*. After several displays of *lelba*, the lead singer calls the recessional song, *Nanja*, a tribute to the founder of this celebration discussed earlier. This processional phase of the dance-drumming takes the performers back to their dressing room.

Songs

Songs in *Jɛra* are mainly praise songs that are philosophical and proverbial. Themes may also center on crisis in the community in the form of a warning. Songs also pay tribute to hunters for creating this dance-drumming and for sustaining the life of the people by providing meat for the community.

Jɛra songs, like those in *Baamaaya*, *Tɔra* and *Bla*, are performed in call and response. Melodic arrangements include the use of microtonal shakes and glides peculiar to Islamic traditions. Ululation, praise shouts and yodeling are common features in *Jɛra* songs.

The Percussion Ensemble

The basic instruments and their functions in the *Jɛra* percussion ensemble include:

i.	*Guŋgoŋ*	A double-headed cylindrical laced drum. Two are used in a performance. The bigger one with a lower voice, called *guŋgoŋ nyaŋ* or *guŋgoŋ titali*, leads and the smaller one with a higher voice, *guŋgoŋ laa* or *Guŋgoŋ bila*, acts as supporting drum. Straight sticks are used for these drums instead of the regular curved ones.
ii.	*Luŋa*	An hourglass-shaped drum; plays messages; supports the *guŋgoŋna* and comments on the dancers.
iii.	*Saɣyeli (saɣyelim, siyalim or sɣayalli)*	A pair of container basket rattles supports the drums.
iv.	*Fienŋa (si)*	Castanets are used by the dancers to accen-

		tuate their movements. This type of castanet is a miniature version of the Akan *adawura* or Eʋe *atoke*.
v.	*Dawule*	A double bell, may sometimes be used to emphasize the rhythmic patterns of the lead *guŋgoŋ nyaŋ*.
vi.	*Yua*	A wooden notched flute is used to represent the birds in the forest. It may play actual songs or accentuate the dance movements.

FIGURE 26.1: Kpegu *Jɛra* Group Percussion Ensemble in action. From left to right: *saɣyelim, yua, guŋgoŋ titali, luŋa* and *guŋgoŋ bila* (2009).

Dance Organization

DANCE ARENA. Apart from the processional phase, *jɛra-sochendi*, all other phases are performed in a circle. The dancers form a circle around the drummers. Drummers may also travel across the arena. They will go near to any dancer who dances vigorously, especially in the *jɛra-lura* phase.

DANCE MOVEMENTS AND CHOREOGRAPHY. A highly skilled *Jɛra* dancer demonstrates varied qualities

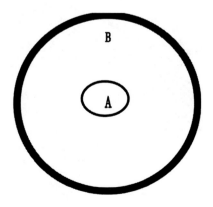

FIGURE 26.2: A: drummers, B: dancers.

of movements. In the main sequence of movements, as they enter the arena, the dancers walk in a fast pace counterclockwise around the drummers, starting with *jɛra-tɔra*.

This quick movement is interrupted by abrupt stops where the dancer bends deeply with his legs and leans his torso forward. The final stop ushers in the *jɛra-lura*, the main dance-movement.

Each dancer either steps forward or back, alternating feet and then repeats the same on a two-beat count. The footwork also includes a repeated tapping action and/or may create a three-beat count starting with the right foot and alternating with the left and finishing by returning to the right. The legs are coordinated with the feet by bending, stretching and rotating in the hip socket.

Footwork includes shuffling, stepping, or rising movements, traveling forward and backward in the circle. The direction of the dancers depends on the whim of the lead or individual dancers.

Depending on the footwork, the hip thrusts forward, raising the *laɣmihi,* strands of cowries, which are attached to the *kpukpuli* up to the chest. The dancer then shimmies the hip in order to drop each individual loop back into place.

On the three-beat count foot phrase, the dancer may continuously thrust the hips forward and relax down, allowing the *laɣmihi* to continuously move up and down as the dancer travels around. The dancer will also rotate the hips around while traveling forward, or shimmy as each foot steps forward and back. He may also just repeatedly tap one foot down, allowing the looped shells to freely swing up and down. At times, the dancer may combine the above-mentioned movements—for example, shimmying while thrusting forward (while walking forward or backwards).

In this main movement, the dancers move their arms through multiple positions. They may place their arms loosely above the head, out to the side, close to the face or chest, near the

FIGURE 26.3: Kpegu *Jɛra* dancers in action (2009).

looped *laɤmihi*, or loosely down near either side of the body with a *fienɲa* (castanet), *zuli* (horse-tail), or *kafini* (a fan), in their hands.

During all of these complicated movements, the torso is held upright and forward on a diagonal (or positioned parallel to the ground) or back on a diagonal, as when the dancer leans back to balance and individually drop the *laɤmihi* loops back into place. You may also see the torso lean side to side in opposition to the hips when they move from side to side (Zelma Badu-Younge 2010).

Costume and Other Visual Art Forms

Dancers in *Jɛra* use very elaborate costumes. As in *Bla*, it takes almost one hour to dress up for a performance. The dancer begins by putting on *kurugu*, long baggy pants. He then covers the lower half of his legs, close to the ankles, with *binchɛra*, a piece of cloth, on top of which he ties *chaɤla* (*cheɤla*), secondary rattles.

Following this, he puts on several layers of arm, wrist and shoulder *gurim* (*guru*), talismans, covering most parts of the upper body. The *laɤmihi*, strands of cowries, are now attached to the *kpukpuli*, the bulging bag that is tied around the waist.

Completing the costume are the *zuɤupilga*, hat; *zuli*, short whiskers (horsetail); and *fienɲa*, castanet. A t-shirt may be worn but it is optional. Young apprentice boys or hunters being trained may be allowed to dance, but with fewer talismans and different props.

COMPONENTS OF JƐRA COSTUME.

Left, FIGURE 26.4a: *Kurugu*. *Right*, FIGURE 26.4b: Kpegu *Jɛra* lead dancer in *kurugu* (2009).

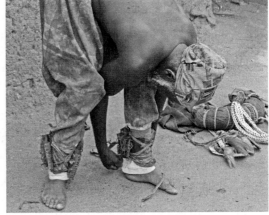

Left, FIGURE 26.5: Kpegu *Jɛra* lead dancer putting on *binchɛra* (2009). *Right*, FIGURE 26.6: Kpegu *Jɛra* lead dancer putting on *chaɣla* (2009).

Left, FIGURE 26.7: Kpegu *Jɛra* lead dancer putting on *gurim* (2009). *Right*, FIGURE 26.8: Kpegu *Jɛra* lead dancer preparing *laɣmihi* and *kpukpuli* (2009).

FIGURE 26.9: Kpegu *Jɛra* lead dancer in full costume (2009). (This figure also appears on page C-13 of the color insert.)

27. *Tɔra* Women's Recreational Dance-Drumming Ceremony

Historical Background and Development

Tɔra is a recreational women's dance-drumming of the Dagbamba of northern Ghana. Although its exact origin is rather obscure, there are three stories that I have encountered that suggest its probable origins.

One story tells us that some Hausa royal immigrant settlers brought *Tɔra* from northern Nigeria in the late 17th century. This was the time in Dagbɔŋ history when Islam was finally accepted after several years of resistance. This period also saw the blend of traditional religious practices and Islam. As a result, Islamic musical practices were interwoven with traditional ones.

A second story alleges that *Tɔra* evolved from *Takai*, a royal dance-drumming for men. The similar patterns and rhythmic features of the percussion ensemble of both ceremonies support this story.

Takai is a royal dance of the Dagbamba, which, according to oral tradition, was performed by the princes in the palaces in the evenings after meals. These performances were later taken outside and performed on market days. The princes would show their wealth in the form of the expensive costumes comprised of *kurugu*, long pants; varieties of smocks, *binɣmaa*, *kpakoto* and *yɛbili* (the most expensive); a *zupilga*, hat; and *muɣuri*, leather boots. See Figure 27.1 on page C-14 of the color insert.

The chief's wives and other females in the palace, not wanting to be left out of the fun, created their own dance movements which they performed alongside the princes any time they would perform *Takai*. This performance came to be called *Tɔra*.

The third story, which provides the most reliable history of the origin, states that, according to oral tradition, there was once a Dagbamba *ya naa* called Naazo-Yenzuo, who had a servant, Naazo Jekunu. The king loved and trusted this servant so much that anything he told the king, the king would believe.

Naazo Jekunu grew arrogant because of his position and relationship with the king, so he started maltreating the king's wives. He made excessive demands of the wives and if any wife disobeyed his orders, she would be reported to the king for punishment. The wives were fed up with Jekunu's betrayal and secretly hatched a plan to remove him from the palace.

It was a serious taboo then, as it is today, for any guard or servant in the palace to engage in any sexual activity with any of the king's wives. The women knew this was the only thing that would make the king upset, so, knowing that one of the wives was pregnant, the women marched to the king and told him that his trusted servant Naazo Jekunu was responsible.

Knowing very well the punishment for such an act is beheading, Jekunu fled the palace and

238

was never seen again. In jubilation, the wives sang, clapped their hands, and danced while hitting their buttocks. Only the wives and other women in the palace knew what had really happened.

The king loved his wives' new creation and he encouraged them to perform this dance during festive occasions. It was then called *Kpari Tɔra* because no drums were used. *Ŋmani*, calabashes, were later used to accompany these performances. Soon, *Tɔra* became a regular feature in the palace for various social occasions.

During one of the performances in the palace the women did not have their *ŋmani*, so they requested the royal drummers who were playing for the *Takai* dancers to accompany them. The impromptu addition of the drums went so well that it has since been a part of the *Tɔra* ceremony.

All these stories share the common theme that *Tɔra* is related to *Takai*. Although the first story did not clearly state the circumstances for its origin in Nigeria, it does support the historical belief among the Dagbamba that they migrated from somewhere in northern Nigeria to their present habitations in Ghana. There is a similar dance performed by Hausa women in Nigeria and also some of the names of the phases are in the Hausa language. The second and third stories are the most reliable and probable accounts about the origin of *Tɔra*.

Tɔra is regarded today as a Dagbamba women's dance-drumming ceremony that is performed all over the Northern Region of Ghana. Specifically, it is performed by the Mamprusis, the Nanumbas and the Dagbamba. The extent of distribution supports the history of the above ethnic groups, who are believed to be descended from the common ancestry of Naa Gbewa, the Red Hunter's grandson.

Although it is a recreational dance-drumming, *Tɔra* can be seen at funerals and other occasions such as marriage and wedding ceremonies, durbars, festivals and visits of state dignitaries. Although it is a women's celebration, men also take part as members of the percussion ensemble. All able-bodied women may join in the performance.

Organization of the Dance-Drumming Ceremony

FORM AND STRUCTURE. From the single original phase only known as *Tɔra*, which involved only singing, clapping and dance, at least 11 new phases have been created. These include: *zamandunia, tɔra, nyaɣboli, ŋundanyuli, damduu, anakuliyela, ŋunmalkpiɛŋ, tɔra yiɣira, ŋunkpelimkpe, bangumaŋa, kookali* and *kondoliya*.

All these phases are distinguishable by their specific dance movements. With the exception of *zamandunia, kondoliya* and most sections of *kookali*, the rest of the phases involve the "hitting of the buttocks" movement to end each dance sequence.

Phase One: *Zamandunia*. On a given performance date, the dancers will converge at the designated *shilmalibu shee*, dressing room, close to the performance arena. From there, they will perform the *zamandunia*, the processional dance, and proceed to the dance arena.

Zamandunia is a Hausa word that means "let us settle together peacefully with love on earth." *Zamandunia* is performed to alert the spectators/audience that the dancers are ready to take the stage.

The dancers come to celebrate joy and happiness and invite all to come and join the celebration. The dancers are also reminded of their role in the community to help build a peaceful coexistence with their neighbors.

Phase Two: *Tɔra*. On arrival at the dance space, the group performs *tɔra* in the original form of *kpari tɔra*. This performance starts with clapping and singing for a while, as they did initially. This performance pays tribute to the wives of the *ya naa*, Nan-Yenzuo, who created this dance-drumming. The singing and clapping period of this phase serves as warm-up for the dancers. After a series of songs, the dance begins.

FIGURE 27.2: Tamale Youth Home *Tɔra* Group performing *Zamandunia*.

Phase Three: *Nyaɣboli*. This phase is adopted from the *Takai* and *Baamaaya* dance-drumming ceremonies. Once upon a time in Dagbɔŋ history, there was a great famine. It is believed that *Tinŋbana*, the land gods, came to the rescue of the people by providing abundant rainfall and a bumper harvest.

As a thanksgiving ritual and celebration to the Gods, *nyaɣboli*, which means "travel the world carefully," was created. Be mindful of your journey in this world. Always take the time to reflect on your past for better success in the future. It was first used in *Baamaaya* and was later adapted by *Takai* and *Tɔra*. The percussion ensemble plays the same music but the dance movements are different in each case. *Nyaɣboli* also signifies wealth in the community.

Phase Four: *Ŋundanyuli*. The Dagbamba's philosophy of life is embedded in several philosophical texts and proverbs. These belief systems and the accepted moral code of behavior are reflected upon during dance-drumming ceremonies.

Ŋundanyuli, "creating a name for oneself," reminds participants to always seek the best for the community in which they live. One wants to be remembered for one's good works. It also literally means that a man who buys yams for a woman takes her "buttocks." You will get a beautiful wife if you behave well in society.

Phase Five: *Damduu*. *Damduu* is another phase used for reflecting on the evils of the society — in particular those individuals who cause problems at home. There are always going to be people who disturb the peace. The dancers during this phase are reminding themselves and the public to be wary of such people among every home. Evildoers are seen as mice — always causing havoc in the house.

Phase Six: *Anakuliyela*. A new creation is *anakuliyela*, "so you are still talking," which mocks those who always want their views heard. There is a Manprusis proverb which says, "A good talk is worth more than a hundred cowries." Talking too much, especially during meetings with others, should be avoided. Do more listening than talking.

Phase Seven: *Ŋunmalkpieŋ*. As indicated earlier, women in Dagbɔŋ culture are regarded by the men as inferior simply because of their perceived lack of strength. They are made to be submissive to whatever the men demanded.

Women cannot stand up to authority so the best way for them to express their frustration is through their songs and dances. *Ŋumalpieŋ*, meaning "only the strongest have the right," reminds women of their role in society. The men, "the strongest species," will always rule in Dagbɔŋ society.

Phase Eight: *Tɔra yiɣira*. This phase is created for the dancers to show their strength and agility.

Phase Nine: *Ŋunkpelimkpe*. *Ŋunkpelimkpe*, "he who remains last always gets the best," is another philosophy of life taught during *Tɔra* performances. There is no need to have haste in life. Patience is a prerequisite for success. This phase also warns the dancers that although patience is needed in life, one should not lag behind. Always go with the crowd or else you'll left behind.

Phase Ten: *Bangumaŋa*. Self-protection is the best recipe for good health and a long life. Women during this phase reflect on the audacity and courage of those women (the wives of the *ya naa*) who took things into their own hands to be free. *Bangumaŋa* is also a praise name for one of the chiefs of Dagbɔŋ.

Phase Eleven: *Kookali*. *Kookali* is another Hausa word to describe yet another phase in *Tɔra* dance-drumming. At this point, the dancers are congratulating themselves for performing well and are ready to end the performance.

Phase: Twelve: *Kondoliya*. Kondoliya, "there lies the water," is another phase adopted from *Baamaaya* to reference the availability of enough water for the people. This is used as a recessional dance which takes performers back to the *shilmalibu shee*. *Kondoliya* may also be performed as a praise dance for a *mangezia*, a female youth leader in the community.

Songs

Singing forms an essential component of the *Tɔra* performance. An excellent performance is judged by the effective organization of its singing. From the beginning of the performance, the dancers, with the lead singer in control of affairs, employ all the techniques of singing found in the northern traditions of Ghana.

Melodic arrangements can be described as full of microtonal shakes and glides. The use of nasal voice qualities and melismatic treatment of texts are common.

The form of songs is principally call and response with a lot of melodic and textual variations by the lead singer. Harmony in *Tɔra* is created by the overlapping of solo and chorus with occasional sporadic homophonic phrase endings of seconds and fourths.

There are also instances of ululations and praise shouts in the performance which contribute to a multi-part performance. Song texts are based on several themes: philosophy, beliefs, historical facts and human relationships.

The Percussion Ensemble

Instruments and their functions in Tɔra performance include:

i. *guŋgɔŋ* double-headed cylindrical drum, serves as the lead drum;
ii. *guŋgɔŋ* double-headed cylindrical drum, supports the lead drum;
iii. *luŋa* hourglass-shaped drum, plays dual roles, starts all the phases but allows the lead *guŋgɔŋ* to dictate the pace of performance, additionally may support the *guŋgɔŋna*; and
iv. *yua* wooden notched flute or *kalamboo*, as in *Bla*, may be added to embellish the songs.

FIGURE 27.3: Tamale Youth Home *Tɔra* Percussion Ensemble performing *Zamandunia* (2009).

Dance Organization

DANCE ARENA. The performance arena may be arranged in two ways: a horseshoe formation by all performers facing the audience, as in Figure 27.4, or an enclosed formation as in
Figure 27.5. In this latter formation, the audience forms around the performers.

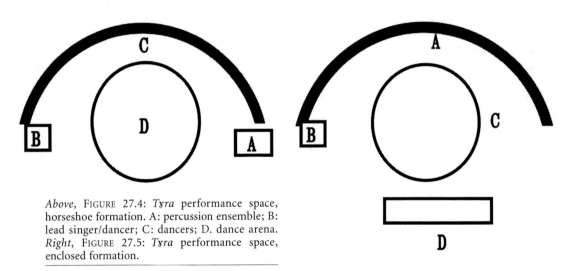

Above, FIGURE 27.4: *Tɤra* performance space,
horseshoe formation. A: percussion ensemble; B:
lead singer/dancer; C: dancers; D. dance arena.
Right, FIGURE 27.5: *Tɤra* performance space,
enclosed formation.

DANCE MOVEMENT AND CHOREOGRAPHY. As in *Baamaaya*, each phase has a specific dance
routine preceding the bump. In the main movement, *Tɔra*, the dancers twirl and spin around
each other, and like magnets, they are drawn together hip-to-hip. The dance starts with a procession into the dance arena and the main movement starts in a line.

As the dancers travel to the performance area with *zamandunia*, they step deliberately,
starting with the right foot and on a bent leg. Each step is emphasized by the foot rising from
the floor led by the heel and moves forward to the next step, led by the knee. As the first foot
is planted on the ground the second foot's heel may rise.

There is also a rocking and/or bouncing quality with each step. This movement continues as the dancers and drummers form one line, a semicircle, or a circle, depending on the formation chosen for the performance.

The dancers then line up shoulder-to-shoulder and shuffle side to side, taking three steps to each side while alternating feet. This is a variation of the processional movement.

With each step, the hip rocks and/or bounces as it shifts side to side in the same direction as the foot's step. The arms sway side to side in a relaxed, bent position and in the same direction as the hips and feet. The hands initiate this swaying movement. The torso leans forward throughout the whole procession.

Tɔra begins when the dancers complete the line and the music of the percussion ensemble stops with the lead dancer leading the others to clap their hands. The lead dancer walks up and down, facing the dancers. After performing a series of songs as part of *kpari tɔra*, the lead singer pays homage to the drummers by kneeling in front of them.

When the lead dancer returns to her original space in the arena, she continues with the opening singing, which is soon joined by the percussion ensemble.

When she is sure that the dancers are warmed up and the percussion ensemble is performing at the right tempo, she starts the dance.

The dancer starts with two quick gallops or a side-to-side skip leading with the right foot. After the second skip or gallop the dancer lands on two feet and then kicks the left heel forward to start the movement in place. As she begins to travel she swings the left foot over or around the right foot (there may be many variations on this movement).

As the left foot swings over or around the right foot, the dancer pivots on that right foot and spins the body in the direction of the left foot. The dancer steps down with the left foot and then unfolds by stepping back with the right foot followed by left. (Note: after the lead dancer starts this movement the whole group eventually joins in with the movement but does not travel.)

The lead dancer then takes an additional quick gallop and lands on two feet to finish the move. She repeats this movement one or two times in place before traveling away from the group, moving perpendicular to the group on the third repeat, and then making a 90 degree angle (moving parallel to the group line) on the fourth repeat.

On her fourth repetition, the second dancer in line to her left moves out. The lead dancer then changes direction (moving back towards her previous position) as the second dancer moves towards her. They both finish their phrase by bumping hips (the bumping takes place after each dancer's last gallop).

The first dancer returns to the line at the back. This pattern is repeated while all the dancers pass through this routine. The full choreography can be repeated until the drummers change to the next phase, which will require a new pattern or movement phrase. The lead dancer usually begins each new dance phrase or phase of the dance-drumming.

During all these traveling movements, the hips initiate the foot or leg spin, creating an arc as it moves in space. One dancer's hip is then used to bump a neighboring dancer's hip, resembling two magnets drawing together.

The arms are loosely held in a 90-degree position or are allowed to freely swing as the body moves—flowing either away from or across the torso. The torso acts as a counterbalance for the hips as they swivel or weave around.

Most strangers who view the dance for the first time quickly give it the name "buttocks dance." This is because of the main dance movements, which involve whirling round and, finally, two dancers "jamming" their buttocks, dictated by the *guŋgoŋna*.

Figure 27.6: Tamale Youth Home *Tɔra* lead dancer in full costume (2009).

Costume and Other Visual Art Forms

Costumes in *Tɔra* are varied. In funeral situations, any traditional women's clothes can be worn, but on festive occasions such as festivals, or visits of state personalities, the performers put on their traditional *chinchini maga*, the local woven cloth.

When young girls perform, their costuming is slightly different from the adults. They will wrap a one-yard piece of cloth around the body, which is tied under the armpit to just below the knee. A second cloth, scarf or shawl is tied around the waist.

Drummers and other instrumentalists may wear any decent attire or the traditional *binŋmaa* over long pants.

PART SIX.
Songs and Percussion Scores

28. Transcriptions and Analysis of Songs

Orthographies have been provided at the beginning of the sections on each cultural area discussed to guide in pronunciation. Most Ghanaian languages, especially those discussed in this book, are tonal. Changes in tonal inflections may sometimes alter the meanings of words and phrases.

To achieve the desired meaning of the songs, a tonal pronunciation system is provided: "1" represents the highest tone, "2" the middle tone and "3" the lowest tone. Intervals between the tonal levels are very relative.

In addition to pronunciation and tonality of language, lyrics of songs in traditional languages, literal and cultural meaning in English, brief analysis of melody, rhythm, form and harmony are provided.

Southeastern Eʋes Songs

ADZOGBO SONGS

• Title: *'Tamkanya ɖewo gblɔe dzro* •

Lyrics in Eʋegbe: *'Tamkanya ɖewo gblɔe dzro,*
Egbekoe miekpe, asi ma le kpɔ̃ o.
'Tamkanya ɖewo gblɔe dzro,
'Gbe koe miekpe lo o 'si ma le kpɔ̃ o.

Lyrics in English: Your oath of threat is in vain,
We have met today; a hand cannot capture a tiger.
Your oath of threat is in vain,
We have met today; a hand cannot capture a tiger.

Cultural Meaning: The original intent of the *Adzogbo* dance-drumming ceremony was to prepare the Eʋe warriors for an impending battle. The warriors believed that after their purification rights and training they were ready and had the strength of a tiger to defeat any enemy. This belief in their strength was not reserved for only the warriors. Eʋes in general don't succumb to any threat in life. They are ready to confront any obstacle or problem that comes their way. This philosophy of regarding an enemy as an inferior fighter guides the Eʋes in life to seek success and victory in all their endeavors.

Form: Solo and chorus, binary form, A: B: Repetitive Form.

Performance Style: The main cantor sings the first section of the first phrase, which is completed by the chorus. The second phrase is performed the same way but with a different melodic response from the chorus.

Scale: Pentatonic (five-note).

Atamkayi
Sword of Oath

Aflao Adzogbo Atsiawɔwɔ Song
Transcription by Paschal Yao Younge
2010

FIGURE 28.1: *Atamkayi*

Melody: Scalic-accent and descent of pitches. Melody follows the tonal inflections of spoken language in most cases. The fourth degree is sometimes altered.

Rhythm: Rhythmic phrases follow the speech rhythm of the spoken text.

Harmony: Use of unison and parallel pitches between the cantor and chorus.

Tonality: *'Tamkanya ɖewo gblɔe dzro*
      1   1 2 31 2   1
     Egbekoe miekpe, asi ma le kpɔ o
     1 33 1   1 31 1 1 3 3

• Title: *Ŋutsuwo La Yi* •

Lyrics in Eʋegbe: *Ŋutsuwo la yi*
                  Adzo tso ŋutsuwo mi la yi
                  E, mi la yi hee
                  Adzo tso ŋutsuwo mi la yi
                  Ŋutsuwo la yi

Lyrics in English: Men shall pass
                  If there is war, men shall pass
                  Yes, we shall pass
                  If there is war, men shall pass
                  Men shall pass

Cultural Meaning: The song is performed during the *kadodo* phase of the dance. Its original

Ŋutsuwo La Yi

Men Shall Pass

Aflao Adzogbo Kadodo Song
Transcription by Paschal Yao Younge
2010

Figure 28.2: Ŋutsuwo La Yi

intent was to remind warriors of their imminent death during battles. The dancers who would soon be fighting were psychologically prepared to face death on the battlefield with ease. Presently, the song is performed as a motivation for the male dancers as they prepare to enter the dance arena.

Form: Solo and chorus, binary form. Repetitive form: A: B:

Performance Style: The main cantor sings the first two lines of the song. The chorus joins from the third line until the end of the song.

Scale: Hexatonic (six-note).

Melody: Melody starts on the dominant and ends on the supertonic, the second degree of the scale. Melody follows the tonal inflections of spoken language in most cases.

Rhythm: Rhythmic phrases follow the speech rhythm of the spoken text.

Harmony: Use of unison and parallel pitches between the cantor and chorus.

Tonality: *Ŋutsuwo la yi*
2 2 1 1 3
Adzo tso ŋutsuwo mi la yi
3 3 3 2 2 1 1 1 3
E, mi la yi hee
1 1 1 3 3
Adzo tso ŋutsuwo mi la yi
3 3 3 2 2 1 1 1 3
Ŋutsuwo la yi
2 2 1 1 3

AGBADZA SONGS

Miʋu Agbo Mayi Kalĕawoe

Open the Gate For Me to Pass Through, Warriors

Agbadza Ʋutsɔtsɔ Song
Transcription by Paschal Yao Younge
2010

FIGURE 28.3: *Miʋu Agbo Mayi Kalĕawoe*

• Title: *Miʋu Agbo Mayi Kalēawoe* •

Lyrics in Eʋegbe: *Miʋu agbo mayi, Kalēawoe*
Dahome nyaflatɔwoe, neʋu agbo mayi
Kalēawoe, neʋu agbo mayi Dahome

Lyrics in English: Open the gate for me to pass through, Warriors
Dahome warriors, open the gate for me to pass through
Warriors, open the gate for me to Dahome
NB: *kalēawoe* and *nyaflatɔwoe* refer to warriors.

Cultural Meaning:The song signifies the begining of the main dance phase of the performance. The main cantor alerts the audience and elders that the dance arena is now open for the dance ritual. This presentation has a unique historical signifance to the Eʋes. It reminds them of their sojourn and oppression under King Agɔkɔli in Ŋɔtsie. The song was composed and used during performances at the time to indirectly petition the king to allow them safe passage to Dahome, from whence they had migrated to Ŋɔtsie.

Form: Solo and chorus, extended binary form. Repetitive form: A: B: A1: B1:

Performance style: This song usually begins the *Uutsɔtsɔ* phase. The main cantor sings the whole song once in free rhythm with no instrumental accompaniment. The second call brings in the response from the chorus with handclapping. This ushers in the percussion ensemble, led by the master drum, *sogo*.

Scale: Pentatonic Scale (five-note).

Melody: Melody follows the tonal inflections of spoken language in most cases.

Rhythm: Rhythmic phrases follow the speech rhythms of the spoken text.

Harmony: i. Use of parallel octaves between female and male voices.
ii. Overlapping of cantor and chorus.
iii. Chorus sings into two parts in intervals of a fourth.

Tonality: *Miʋu agbo mayi, Kalēawoe*
3 3 3 2 2 3 2 2 1
Dahome nyaflatɔ'oe, neʋu agbo mayi
3 3 3   2 2 2   1 3 3 2 2 3
Kalēawoe, neʋu agbo mayi Dahome
2   2 1   1 3 3 2 2 3 3 3 3

• Title: *Saba Ðe Miawo Kɔ Ðe Dzogbedzi* •

Lyrics in Eʋegbe: *Saba ɖe miawo kɔ ɖe Dzogbedzi*
Aya ɖu ge nyea meva
Saba ɖe miawo kɔ ɖe Dzogbedzi
Aya ɖu ge nyea meva
Aya ɖu ge nyea meva
Saba ɖe miawo kɔ ɖe Dzogbedzi
Aya ɖu ge nyea meva

Lyrics in English: War has brought us to the battlefield
I have come to suffer
War has brought us to the battlefield
I have come to suffer
I have come to suffer
War has brought us to the battlefield
I have come to suffer

Cultural Meaning: This song echoes the difficulties associated with wars. The song reminds the warriors of the suffering, pain and destruction that war brings. The song also reminds all humans of the various obstacles, problems and hardships of life. Life is always going to be full of surprises.

Form: Solo and chorus, extended binary form. Repetitive form: A: B: Al: Bl: B2: A :B.

Performance Style: The main cantor sings the first phrase and the chorus answers with the second phrase. The repeat of the first phrase with variation by the cantor is answered by the chorus with two repeats of the second phrase to different melodies. Both cantor and chorus then repeat the initial first and second phrases to end the song.

Scale: Pentatonic (five-note).

Melody: Conjunct melody: scalic-descent of pitches. Melody follows the tonal inflections of spoken language in most cases. There are some deviations.

Saba Ɖe Miawo Kɔ Dzogbedzi
War Has Brought Us to the Battlefield

FIGURE 28.4: *Saba Ɖe Miawo Kɔ Ɖe Dzogbedzi*

Rhythm: Rhythmic phrases follow speech rhythms of the spoken text.
Harmony:　i.　Use of parallel octaves between female and male voices.
　　　　　ii.　Overlapping of cantor and chorus.
　　　　　iii.　Chorus breaks into two parts using intervals of fourths.
Tonality: *Saba ɖe miawo kɔ ɖe Dzogbedzi*
　　　　　1 1　2　1　1　2　1　3　3 2
　　　　　Aya ɖu ge nyea meva
　　　　　2 2　2　1　2　1　1　2

ATIBLAƊEKAME SONGS

Alaga Kpɔ Hɔtɔ, Kliya
The Warrior Has Seen the Enemy, Kliya

Atiblaɖekame: Fiagbedu Afegame Ɖekoenu Uutsɔtsɔ Song
Transcribed by Paschal Yao Younge
2010

FIGURE 28.5: *Alagā Kpɔ Hɔ̄tɔ, Kliya*

• Title: *Alagā Kpɔ Hɔ̃tɔ, Kliya* •

Lyrics in Eʋegbe: *Alagā kpɔ hɔ̃tɔ, kliya*
Alagā kpɔ hɔ̃tɔ, kliya
Alagā kpɔ hɔ̃tɔ, kliya
Alagā kpɔ hɔ̃tɔ, kliya

Lyrics in English: The warrior has seen the enemy, kliya
The warrior has seen the enemy, kliya
The warrior has seen the enemy, kliya
The warrior has seen the enemy, kliya

Cultural Meaning: *Alagā* is the youth wing of the *Yeʋe* cult among the southeastern Eʋes. They only perform when members of the cult violate certain rules such as prostitution, adultery or use profanity against each other. They will dress up in dried plantain leaves, shells, smear their faces with black, red and white colors or wear masks to disguise themselves. *Kliya* represents the sound (it is an onomatopoetic word) that is generated when they dance in their costumes—especially from the dried leaves or other objects attached to their bodies. They move around the community amid wild drumming, singing and dance until the dispute is settled by the elders. Non-members of the cult, usually the youth, follow the *alaga* around harrassing them and sometimes throw stones at them. The *alagās* would chase the youth and sometimes beat them up. In coastal Anlɔ Eʋe towns, an individual may become an *alagā* when he or she is abused by another member or non-member. *Alagā* is also used to describe warriors among the Eʋes. The song as used in the *Atibladekame* context describes the engagement of an enemy by a warrior.

Form: Solo and chorus, ternary form. Repetitive form: A: A1: B: B1: A.

Performance Style: The main cantor sings part of the first phrase and the chorus joins and completes the second phrase with the cantor. This is repeated. The third phrase, which is the second section of the melody, is broken between the cantor and chorus in a call and response form with variations by the cantor. The melody goes back to the first phrase with the chorus without any repetition.

Scale: Hexatonic (six-note).

Melody: Conjunct melody: scalic-ascent and descent of pitches. Melody follows the tonal inflections of spoken language in most cases.

Rhythm: Rhythmic phrases follow speech rhythm of the spoken text.

Harmony: i. Use of unison and parallel pithes between the cantor and chorus.
ii. Chorus breaks into two parts using intervals of thirds.

Tonality: *Alagā kpɔ hɔ̃tɔ, kliya*
3 1 2 2 3 1 3 3

• Title: *Gamadoe Tsɔ Nublablɛ De Asi Na Wò* •

Lyrics in Eʋegbe: *Gamadoe tsɔ nublablɛ de asi na wò*
Uu asi makpɔe ɖa
Gamadoe tsɔ nublablɛ de asi na wò
Uu asi makpɔe ɖa
Kuzunɖe neʋu asi makpɔe ɖa
Kuzunɖe neʋu asi makpɔe ɖa
Gamadoe tsɔ nublablɛ de asi na wò
Uu asi makpɔe ɖa

Lyrics in English: Gamado [name of an elder] has given you a parcel
Open your hand so I can see it
Gamado has given you a parcel

Open your hand so I can see it
Kuzuɖe [name of a young girl], open your hand so I can see it
Kuzuɖe, open your hand so I can see it
Gamado has given you a parcel
Open your hand so I can see it

Cultural Meaning: Under no circumstances should one reveal family secrets to strangers. One should value and protect the customs of one's parents. Children are advised to avoid doing what their elders did not teach. Don't throw away or discard the wisdom and values learnt from your elders.

Form: Solo and chorus, call and response, ternary form. Repetitive form: A: A1: B: B1: A.

Performance Style: The main cantor sings part of the first phrase and the chorus joins and com-

Gamadoe Tsɔ Nublablɛ De Asi Na Wò

Gamadoe Has Given You a Parcel

Atiblaɖekame: Aʃetʃe Atsigo Uutsɔtsɔ Song
Transcription by Paschal Yao Younge
2010

FIGURE 28.6: *Gamadoe Tsɔ Nublablɛ de Asi Na Wò*

pletes the second phrase with the cantor. This is repeated. Both the cantor and chorus with melodic variations sing the third phrase, which is the second section of the melody. Cantor and chorus perform section A without repetitions.

Scale: Penatonic (five-note).

Melody: Melody starts and ends on different pitches. The melody follows the tonal inflections of spoken language in most cases.

Rhythm: Rhythmic phrases follow speech rhythm of the spoken text.

Harmony: i. Use of unison and parallel pitches between the cantor and chorus.
            ii. Chorus breaks into two parts using intervals of thirds.

Tonality: *Gamadoe tsɔ nublablε de asi na wò*
        3   3   1   2   1 1 2 3 3 1 1 3
        Uu asi makpɔe ɖa
        3   3 1 1   1   1
        Kuzunɖe nevu asi makpɔe ɖa
        2   2   1 1 3 3 1 1   1   1

ATRIKPUI SONGS

See page 256 for Figure 28.7 (*Kundovio Tso Ameta Tu Medi O*).

• Title: *Kundovio Tso Ameta Tu Medi O* •

Lyrics in Eʋegbe: *Kundovio tso ameta tu medi o,*
                     Hɔ ne va.
                     Kundovio tso ameta tu medi o,
                     Hɔ ne va.
                     Miede Soɖakɔ keke Dahome, fifia hɔ neva,
                     Miede Soɖakɔ keke Dahome, fifia hɔ neva,
                     Kundovio tso ameta tu medi o,
                     Hɔ ne va.

Lyrics in English: Kundo's Children have beheaded the enemy without a gunshot,
                     Let there be war.
                     Kundo's Children have beheaded the enemy without a gunshot,
                     Let there be war.
                     We went to battle in Dahome
                     Let there be war.
                     We went to battle in Dahome
                     Let there be war.
                     Kundo's children have beheaded the enemy without a gunshot
                     Let there be war.

Cultural Meaning: This song highlights the importance and stature of Kundo as war hero in Eʋe oral history during the sojourn in Dahome, present-day Republic of Benin. Kundo was revered as a great fighter, king, administrator, leader and above all a very religious/spiritual individual. The song alludes to his powers and strength exhibited through his children/warriors. That the warriors were able to fight and defeat their enemies without weapons is a common belief held among the Eʋes of today.

Form: Solo and chorus and ternary form.

Repetitive form: A: a: A1: a2: B:b B1:b1: A3: a.

Performance Style: This is in simple call and response performance style. The lead/main cantor sings sections of the song and the chorus responds.

Kundovio Tso Ameta, Tu Meḍi O

Kundo's Children Have Beheaded the Enemy Without a Gunshot

Atrikpui Song
Transcription by Paschal Yao Younge
2010

FIGURE 28.7: *Kundovio Tso Ameta Tu Meḍi O*

Scale: Pentatonic (five-note).

Melody: Melody follows the tonal inflections of spoken language with some variations.

Rhythm: Rhythmic phrases follow speech rhythms of the spoken text.

Harmony: i. Use of parallel octaves between female and male voices.

ii. Overlapping of cantor and chorus.

iii. Chorus may sing sporadic interval of thirds, fourths, or fifths against the melody.

Tonality: *Kundovio tso ameta tu medi o, Hɔ̃ ne va*

2 1   1   2 1 1 1 1   3   3 3 2   2

Miede Soɖakɔ keke Dahume, fifia hɔ̃ neva

1   3 3   3 3 2 2   3   3 3 1 1   3 2 2

Ga De Seke Gaɖetɔ Meli O
The war is Inevitable

Atripkui Song
Transcription by Paschal Yao Younge
2010

FIGURE 28.8: *Ga De Seke Ga Ɖe Tɔ Meli O*

• Title: *Ga De Seke Gaɖetɔ Meli O* •

Lyrics in Eʋegbe: *Ga de seke gaɖetɔ meli o*

Ga de seke gaɖetɔ meli o

Lyrics in English: The chain/padlock is locked

There is no one to unlock it

Cultural Meaning: Before any impending battle, an oath is taken and purification rites are performed. Once these rituals are completed, all participant warriors are obliged to go to war. The song serves as a reminder to warriors that once a warrior always a warrior. The song is performed presently at the beginning of the *atrilɔlɔ* or *atripkui* phases of the dance ritual.

Form: Binary and repetitive form.

     A: B: A1: B1.

Performance Style: This is a simple call and response performance. The lead/main cantor sings sections of the song and the chorus responds.

Scale: Pentatonic (five-note).

Melody: Melody follows the tonal inflections of spoken language with some variations.

Rhythm: Rhythmic phrases follow speech rhythms of the spoken text.

Harmony: i. Use of parallel octaves between female and male voices.

         ii. Overlapping of cantor and chorus.

        iii. Chorus may sing sporadic intervals of thirds, fourths, or fifths against the melody, similar to *Kundovio tso ameta tu medi* o.

Tonality: *Ga de seke gaḓetɔ meli o*

       3   2 11   3 3 2 2 3 3

ATSIAGBEKƆ SONGS

Kalëawo, Dzogbedzie Nya Le

Warriors, the Action is on the Battlefield

FIGURE 28.9: *Kaleawoe, Dzogbedzie Nya Le*

• Title: *Kalēawo, Dzogbedzie Nya Le* •

Lyrics in Evegbe: *Kalēawo, dzogbedzie nya le*
Kalēawo, dzogbedzie nya le

Lyrics in English: Warriors, the action is on the battlefield
Warriors, the action is on the battlefield

Cultural Meaning: Literally, the text reminds warriors of their duty and expectations on the battlefield. Culturally, the song is a reminder to all men. They are reminded of the proverb, *Afekalē menye kalē o*, which means, "Home bravery is not bravery." True bravey is displayed outside the home, before enemies or on the battlefield, where one faces real challenges. Even though bravery is a highly desired quality for men in the traditional society, it must be displayed within the right context. This song can be used to silence a big brother who is found bullying his younger siblings but is afraid to confront others outside the home.

Form: Solo and chorus, call and response, binary form.

Repetitive form: A: B:.

Performance Style: The main cantor starts the first phrase, which is then completed by the chorus. This second phrase is performed with the same text but with melodic variations. Both phrases are repeated several times.

Scale: Penatonic (five-note).

Melody: Melody follows the tonal inflections of spoken language.

Rhythm: Rhythmic phrases follow speech rhythm of the spoken text.

Harmony: i. Use of unison and duplication of melody by the cantor and chorus; female and male voices.
        ii. Overlapping of cantor and chorus.
       iii. Chorus may break into two parts singing sporadic intervals of thirds and fourths against the melody.

Tonality: *Kalēawo, dzogbedzie nya le*
      2 2   1 3   3   1 3   3

See pages 260 and 261 for Figure 28.10 (*Enyo, Tue Nu Madze*).

• Title: *Enyo, Tue Nu Madze* •

Lyrics in Evegbe: *Enyo, tue nu madze*
Dada be avatu nue madze maga o
Tue nu madze
Dada be avatu nue madze magae
Hɛ nu madze
Bokɔ be avatu nue madze maga o
Tue nu madze
Dada be avatu nue madze magae
Tue nu madze lo
Avatu nue madze lo
Hɔnɖe tso tu ye me dze
Tue nu madze
Dada be avatu nue madze magae
Tue nu madze
Bokɔ be avatu nue madze maga o

Lyrics in English: Yes, I will die by the gun
Mother says I must die with honor by the gun
I will die by the gun

Enyo Tue Nu Madze

Yes, I Will Die By the Gun

Dzodagdze Atsiagbekɔ Hatsiatsia Song
Transcription by Paschal Yao Younge
2010

FIGURE 28.10: *Enyo, Tue Nu Madze* (continues on page 261)

2   Enyo, tue nu madze

Mother says I must die with honor by the gun
I will die by the knife (sword)
The diviner says I must die with honor by the gun
I will die by the gun
Mother says I must die with honor by the gun
I will die by the gun
I will die by a gun at war
Hɔnɖe or Konɖe [was a great F5 war leader] took the gun and I took cover

> I will die by the gun
> Mother says I must die with honor by the gun
> I will die by the gun
> The diviner says I must die with honor by the gun

Cultural Meaning: The song is a reminder to warriors of their impending death on the battlefield. It is an honor to die fighting on behalf of the people. The gun, sword or dagger describes the violent death that awaits the warriors. Hɔn2e symbolizes all the enemies that await the warriors. Even though death is imminent, warriors are advised to take caution on the battlefied. *Dzogbeku menye nukpe o:* Death on the battlefied is not a disgraceful outcome of bravery. Death on the battlefied is always a prestige.

Form: Solo and chorus refrain; call and response, ternary form.

Performance Style: The lead and assistant male dancers and sometimes the lead female dancer direct this and other *hatsiatsia* songs. Section A of the song, measures 1–10, may be performed without the bell accompaniment in free rhythm. Section B and the repeat of Section A, measures 11–36, are accompanied by symbolic movements and gestures to emphasize important themes of the song.

Scale: Pentatonic (five-note).

Melody: Melody follows the tonal inflections of spoken language. Shifting of tonal centers from the tonic to the dominant.

Rhythm: Rhythmic phrases follow the speech rhythm of the spoken text.

Harmony: i. Use of unison and duplication of melody by the cantor and chorus; female and male voices.

       ii. Overlapping of cantor and chorus.

     iii. Chorus or soloists may break into two parts, singing sporadic intervals of fourths against the melody.

Tonality: *Enyo, tue nu madze*
       1   1 1   1   2   3
       Dada be avatu nue madze maga o
       3   1 2 3 3 3 2 2   3 2 2 3
       Hɛ nu madze
       3   1   2 3
       Bokɔ be avatu nue madze maga o
       3 1 233 2 2 2   3 2 2 3
       Tue nu madze lo o
       1   1 2 3   1 3
       Hɔnɖe tso tu ye me dze
       3 1 3 1   1 3   3

GADZO SONGS

See pages 263 and 264 for Figure 28.11 (*Kalēawo, gbɔ mekpea nyi kpe o*).

• Title: *Kalēawo Gbɔ Mekpea Nyi Kpe O* •

Lyrics in Eʋegbe: *Kalēawo gbɔ mekpea nyi kpe o, Kalēawo*
                Kalēawo gbɔ mekpea nyi kpe o, Kalēawo
                Gbɔ mekpea nyi kpe o,
                Kalēawo gbɔ mekpea nyi kpe o, Kalēawo
                Gbɔ mekpea nyi kpe o,
                Kalēawo gbɔ mekpea nyi kpe o, Kalēawo

Kalēawo, Gbɔ̃ Mekpea Nyi Kpe O

Warriors, a Goat Does Not Cough Like a Cow

Anlɔ Afiadenyigba Gadzo Uutsɔtsɔ Song
Transcription by Paschal Yao Younge
2010

FIGURE 28.11: *Kalēawo, Gbɔ̃ Mekpea Nyi Kpe O* (continues on page 264)

2   Kaleawo, Gbɔ Mekpea Nyi Kpe O

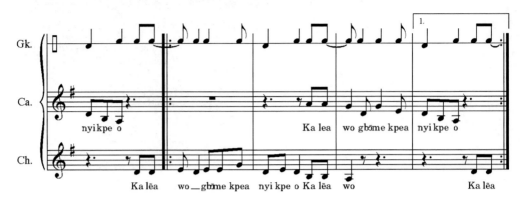

Lyrics in English: Warriors, a goat does not cough like a cow
                   Warriors, a goat does not cough like a cow
                   A goat does not cough like a cow
                   Warriors, a goat does not cough like a cow
                   A goat does not cough like a cow
                   Warriors, a goat does not cough like a cow

Cultural Meaning: Literally, the text admonishes warriors to behave and fight like warriors on the battlefield. Once a warrior always a warrior. There is, however, a deeper philosohpical meaning: One cannot deny his or her ancestry, ethnicity, culture and heritage nor can one plant beans and expect to harvest groundnuts (peanuts). There are several proverbs in Eʋe folklore that emphasize this philosophy: "No matter how a crocodile lives in water, it can never turn into a fish," or "Goodness is always followed by goodness as evil deeds are followed by evil deeds." The main lesson is that one reaps what is planted.

Form: Solo and chorus, call and response, binary form.

Repetitive form: A: A1: B: B1.

Performance Style: The main cantor sings the first phrase twice with melodic variations. The chorus joins and completes the second phrase with the cantor. This section is repeated several times.

Scale: Penatonic (five-note).

Melody: Melody starts and ends on different pitches. Melody follows the tonal inflections of spoken language in most cases. The tonal center of the melody shifts from the Tonic G to the Dominant D starting in measure 8–22.

Nyemanɔ Aŋlɔ Aʋa Nasim O
I Will Not Be at Aŋlɔ to Be Defeated In a Battle

Aŋlɔ Afiaɖʋnyigba Gadzo Uʋlɔlɔ Song
Transcription by Paschal Yao Younge
2010

FIGURE 28.12: *Nyemanɔ Aŋlɔ Aʋa Nasim O* (continues on page 266)

Rhythm: Rhythmic phrases follow speech rhythm of the spoken text.
Harmony: i. Use of unison and duplication of melody by the cantor and chorus.
         ii. The overlapping of cantor and chorus results in an interval of a minor seventh.
Tonality: *Kalēawo gbɔ mekpea nyi kpe o, Kalēawo*
    2   2   1 3 1   1   2   1 3 2 2 1
    Gbɔ mekpea nyi kpe o
    3   1   1 2 1 3

2   Nyemanɔ Aŋlɔ Aʋa Nasim O

• Title: *Nyemanɔ Aŋlɔ Aʋa Nasim O* •

Lyrics in Eʋegbe: *Nyemanɔ Aŋlɔ aʋa nasim o*
                   Ewoewo, Adotriawo, Lashibiawo hee
                   Mizɔ do miakpɔ sotua nu ɖa
                   Sohɔ xɔmi e
                   Nyemanɔ Aŋlɔ aʋa nasim o

Lyrics in English: I will not be at Aŋlɔ to be defeated in a war
                   The warriors of Woe, Adotri and Lashibi
                   Let us move to the battlefield
                   The Thunder God will protect us
                   I will not be at Aŋlɔ to be defeated in a war

Cultural Meaning: The Eʋes have a complex political system ruled by three divisions: civil, military and social chiefs. The military division is controlled by the *aʋadada* (field marshal) and *aʋaklpɔlagāwo/aʋafiawo* (generals, great war leaders), who are designated as the left, central and right wing commanders. The left wing chief/commander is nicknamed *lashibi*, the center *adotri*, and the right wing, *woe*. Unlike the civil and social chiefs and the *aʋadada*, who are designated through patrilineal inheritance, the *aʋaklpɔlagāwo,* the military wing rulers, are determined through valor and other great deads. Throughout their history the Eʋes have depended on the wing generals and their lieutenants to lead all wars. The song is further assuring the entire populace that as they move to any battle, these three wing fighters, with support from the Thunder God "war god," will defeat the enemy.

Form: Solo and chorus, call and response, ternary form. Repetitive form: A: A1: A2: A3: B: B1: B2: B3:A.

Performance Style: The main cantor sings the first phrase, which is repeated with melodic variations by the chorus. This section is again repeated by both cantor and chorus with more melodic variations. The second phrase is sung by both cantor and chorus with repetitions and variations of melody and text. Both cantor and chorus join in to perform the first phrase to end the perfomance with or without melodic variations.

Scale: Penatonic (five-note).

Melody: Melody starts on the tonic D and ends on the dominant A. Melody follows the tonal inflections of spoken language in most cases.

Rhythm: Rhythmic phrases follow speech rhythm of the spoken text.

Harmony: i. Use of unison and duplication of melody by the cantor and chorus.

            ii. Sporadic use of additional tones by the chorus result in P4th, P5th and minor 7th intervals.

Tonality: *Nyemanɔ Aŋlɔ aʋa nasim o*

        2   1 3 2 2 3 3 13   3

        Ewoewo, Adotriawo, Lashibiawo hee

        2   2   1 3 3   1 1 2 2 1 1 3

        Mizɔ do miakpɔ sotua nu ɖa

        3   3 1 1   1 2 1 1   1

        Sohɔ xɔmi e

        3   3 2 1 3

        Nyemanɔ Aŋlɔ aʋa nasim o

        2   1 3 2 2 3 3 13   3

GAHU SONGS

See page 268 for Figure 28.13 (*Efoe, va le ʋua na ma*)

• Title: *Efoe Va Le ʋua Na Maa* •

Lyrics in Eʋegbe: *Efoe va le ʋua na maa*

                Efo Kɔdzoe, va le ʋua na maa

                Na 2o ŋuku ʋugbeawo dzi

                Na nɔ 5o5o ma aleke,

                Efoe va le ʋua na maa

                Efo Kɔdzoe, va le ʋua na maa

Lyrics in English: My brother, come and play the drums for me

                My brother Kɔdzo, come and play the drums for me

                Remember, all the drum texts [patterns]

                And perform them like this,

                My brother, come and play the drums for me

                My brother Kɔdzo, come and play the drums for me

Cultural Meaning: This song reflects on the importance and function of drummers. The song directs the drummers to perform their best during a performance. The song is performed usually during the *ʋutsɔtsɔ* phase of the performance. This song is suitable for all social occasions.

Form: Solo and chorus, repetitive form.

Performance Style: i.   Cantor sings melody alone.

                     ii.   Cantor and Chorus sing melody in unison.

                    iii. The main cantor sings the song through once and chorus repeats. This alternation continues until a new song is introduced.

Efo

My Brother

Gahu Vutsɔtsɔ Song from Dzodze
Transcritpion by Paschal Yao Younge
2010

FIGURE 28.13: *Efoe, Va Le Uua Na Ma*

Scale: i. Hexatonic (six-note).
    ii. Optional use of the flattened seventh degree of the heptatonic scale as shown in measure seven.

Melody: Conjunct melody: Scalic-descent of pitches. Melody follows the tonal inflections of spoken language in most cases.

Rhythm: Rhythmic phrases follow speech rhythms of the spoken text. Dotted rhythm and syncopcation are also used in measures 2, 4, 6, 8, 17, 19, 21, 23 and 25.

Harmony: Use of parallel octaves between female and male voices.

Tonality: *Efo e va le vua na maa*
    2 2 1 3 2 3 2 3
    Efo Kɔdzo e, va le vua na maa
    2 2 3 2 3 3 2 3 2 3

Na ɖo ŋuku vugbeawo dzi
3   2   2   13   1 1   1
Na nɔ fofo ma aleke
3   3   3   3   22   11

Mie Nya Kpɔ Na

You Look Colorful

FIGURE 28.14: *Mienya Kpɔna*

• Title: *Mienya Kpɔna* •

Lyrics in Eʋegbe: *Mienya kpɔna*
Gahuviwo, mienya kpɔna
Dzokotoga le wo si wodona, afɔkpa kpe ɖe enu
Nya ɖe dzɔ le miade dume lo
Mienya kpɔna
Gahuviwo, mienya kpɔna

Lyrics in English: You look colorful
Gahu dancers, you look colorful
You wear very gorgeous and elaborate costumes with shoes/sandals
You look colorful
Gahu dancers, you look colorful

Cultural Meaning: This song reflects on the importance of the elaborate and expensive costumes used in *Gahu* performances. Shoes or sandals are allowed in this performance. The song comments on the visual aesthetics required. Dancers have to look their best during a performance. This song is suitable for all social occasions.

Form: Solo and chorus.

Repetitive form: The main cantor sings the song through to the end once and the chorus repeats. This alternation continues until a new song is introduced.

Performance Style: i.   Cantor sings melody alone.
ii.   Cantor and chorus sing melody in unison.

Scale: Pentatonic (five-note). Both the natural and the sharpened fourth degree of the heptatonic scale are used in the song. Refer to measures 12 and 13 of the transcription.

Melody: Melody follows the tonal inflections of spoken language in most cases. Intervals between pitches are mostly based on major and minor thirds.

Rhythm: Rhythmic phrases follow speech rhythms of the spoken text. Dotted rhythm and syncopcation are also used in measures 2, 7, 13 and 15.

Harmony: Use of parallel octaves between female and male voices.

Tonality: *Mienya kpɔna,   Gahuviwo, mienya kpɔna*
3   2   2   2   3 2 2   2 3   2   2   2

Dzokotoga le wo si wodona, afɔkpa kpe ɖe enu
3 3 3   2 3   2   2 2 2 2   2 2 3   2   2 2 2

Nya ɖe dzɔ le miade dume lo
2   1 3 3   1   2   2 1   1

Mienya kpɔna,   Gahuviwo, mienya kpɔna
3   2   2   2   3 2 2   2 3   2   2   2

Central and Northern Eʋes Songs

ADEʋU SONGS

See page 271 for Figure 28.15 (*Lāwɔda Mezɔ Kple Fe O*)

• Title: *Lāwɔda Mezɔ Kple Fe O* •

Lyrics in Eʋegbe: *Lāwɔda mezɔ kple fe o*
Fe le aku me

Lyrics in English: A ferocious animal never walks with claws extended
The claws are hidden in the paws

Cultural Meaning: Eʋes in general avoid boasting and unwarranted publicity. They are guided by the philosophy that their might and strength should be unleashed only when the appropriate occasion calls for it. You never know what type of weapons your enemies might have so you should be careful when instigating trouble. The text also relates to an everyday approach to life. Always reserve your judgment until the last minute. Be patient and do not rush to conclusions.

Form: Binary, repetitive form and call and response. A: B: A1: B1.

Lãwɔda Mezɔ Kple Fe O

The Ferocious Animal Never Walks on Claws

Alavanyo Adeʋu Song
Transcription by Paschal Yao Younge
2010

FIGURE 28.15: *Lãwɔda Mezɔ Kple Fe O*

Performance Style: This has a simple call and response performance style. The lead/main cantor sings sections of the song and the chorus responds.

Scale: Hexatonic (six-note).

Melody: Melody follows the tonal inflections of spoken language with some variations.

Rhythm: Rhythmic phrases follow speech rhythms of the spoken text.

Harmony: Chorus may sing in unison or in parallel intervals of thirds against the melody.

Tonality: *Lãwɔda mezɔ kple fe o*
    3 3 11 3 1 3 3
    Fe le aku me
    3 3 31 3

See page 272 for Figure 28.16 (*Ɖitsa nakpɔe Ɖa*)

Title: *Ɖitsa Nakpɔe Ɖa*

Lyrics in Eʋegbe : *Ɖitsa nakpɔe ɖa*
                Lã ɖe le nɔvinye

Lyrics in English: Pay him (friend) a visit
                An animal has captured my brother (friend)

Cultural Meaning: Hunters' associations are organized as fraternities. Members look after each

Ɖitsa Nakpɔe Ɖa

Pay Him a Visit

Alavanyo Adevu Song
Transcription by Paschal Yao Younge
2010

FIGURE 28.16: Ɖitsa Nakpɔe Ɖa

other as they would do for their own families. After their hunting expeditions, they are seen either playing games together or taking part in other social activities. The song is a reminder to the hunters to take care of each other, especially during times of sickness.

Form: Binary, repetitive form and call and response. A: A1: B: A2: B1: A3.

Performance Style: This has a simple call and response performance style. The lead/main cantor sings sections of the song with repetitions and the chorus responds with melodic variations.

Scale: Hexatonic (six-note).

Melody: Melody follows the tonal inflections of spoken language with some variations.
Rhythm: Rhythmic phrases follow speech rhythms of the spoken text.
Harmony: Chorus may sing in unison or in parallel intervals of thirds against the melody.
Tonality: *Ɖitsa nakpɔe ɖa*

    3 3 3 1 2

Lā ɖe le nɔvinye

    2 1 121 3

Bɔbɔɔbɔ Songs

Ɖekawɔwɔ Me Ŋusē Le

Unity is Strength

FIGURE 28.17: *Ɖekawɔwɔ Me Ŋusē Le*

• Title: *Ɖekawɔwɔ Me Ŋusē Le* •

Lyrics in Eʋegbe: *Ɖekawɔwɔ me ŋusē le*
                   Miwɔ ɖeka ne dunenyo loo

Miwɔ ɖeka, miwɔ ɖeka
Miwɔ ɖeka ne dunenyo loo

Lyrics in English: Unity is strength
Unite for the good of the land
Unite unite
Unite for the good of the land

Cultural Meaning: Community is at the core of Eʋe culture. Although individual achievements and successes are encouraged, the development, upkeep and success of every community is a collective effort. There are systems and structures put in place to safeguard the collective will of the people for the greater good. Singing is one of the systems that helps to promote and remind the people that they belong to a larger society. The song echoes and emphasizes the Eʋe philosophy, *Tago geɖe, nunya geɖe*, meaning, "Many heads, much knowledge." In other words, it takes a variety of viewpoints and different perspectives to build a just and strong community.

Form: Binary, repetitive form, call and response. A: B: A: B1: C: D: C:D1.

Performance style: This has a simple call and response performance style. The lead/main cantor sings the whole song and the chorus repeats.

Scale: Heptatonic (seven-note).

Melody: Melody follows the tonal inflections of spoken language with some variations.

Rhythm: Rhythmic phrases follow speech rhythms of the spoken text. Frequent use of dotted rhythmic motifs.

Harmony: Chorus may sing in unison, or in parallel or sporadic intervals of thirds and sixths against the melody.

Tonality: *Ɖekawɔwɔ me ŋusē le*
3 1 2 2 2 1 1 3
Miwɔ ɖeka ne dunenyo loo
3 3 31 1 3 1 1 3

See page 275 for Figure 28.18 (*Atsu Kple Asiwo, Mile be na lɔlɔ*)

• Title: *Atsu Kple Asiwo, Mile Be Na Lɔlɔ* •

Lyrics in Eʋegbe: *Atsu kple Asiwo, mile be na lɔlɔ*
Atsu kple Asiwo, mile be na lɔlɔ
Drewɔwɔ ya, menye lɔlɔ ɖe ke o
Dzidzɔkpɔkpɔ yae nye lɔlɔ bliblo

Lyrics in English: Husband and wife, take care of your love
Husband and wife, take care of your love
Quarelling is not part of any loving relationship
Happiness is the fullness of love

Cultural Meaning: The majority of *Bɔbɔɔbɔ* songs relate to human relationships, especially love. Love is believed to be the foundation of human existence and this virtue is taught and perpetuated through songs. Love is seen as a fresh, uncooked egg: if held casually it will fall, and if held too tight, it will break. To avoid problems in any marriage or relationship, couples are advised to avoid deceit, jealousy, hatred, greed, lying and other actions that may result in quarelling. Instead, they should embrace true love and happiness.

Form: Extended binary, repetitive form, call and response. A: B1: C: D:

Performance Style: This is a simple call and response performance style. The lead/main cantor sings the whole song and the chorus repeats in parts.

Scale: Heptatonic (seven-note).

Atsu Kple Asiwo, Mile Be Na Lɔlɔ

Husband and Wife, Take Care of Your Love

Bobɔɔbɔ Song by Ho Agbenya
Transcription by Paschal Yao Younge
2010

FIGURE 28.18: *Atsu Kple Asiwo, Mile Be Na Lɔlɔ*

Melody: Melody follows the tonal inflections of spoken language with some variations.

Rhythm: Rhythmic phrases follow speech rhythms of the spoken text. Frequent use of dotted rhythmic motifs.

Harmony: Chorus may sing in unison, parallel or sporadic intervals of thirds and sixths against the melody.

Tonality: *Atsu kple Asiwo, mile be na lɔlɔ*
        3 1 1   2 2 1   2 1 3 1 3 3

        Drewɔwɔ ya, menye lɔlɔ ɖe ke o
        3 3 3 1 1 1 3 3 3 1 1 3

        Dzidzɔkpɔkpɔ yae nye lɔlɔ bliblo
        3 3 1 1 1 1 3 3 1 2

EGBANEGBA SONGS

See page 277 for Figure 28.19 (*Yesu Kple Petro*)

• Title: *Yesu Kple Petro* •

Lyrics in Eʋegbe: *Gbeɖeka Yesu bia Petro be*
                E, neɖe kua?
                O, nye me ku haɖe o, alɔ me dɔ
                O, nye me ku haɖe o, alɔ me dɔ

Lyrics in English: Jesus once asked Peter,
                Are you dead?
                No, I am not dead, but have fallen asleep
                No, I am not dead, but have fallen asleep

Cultural Meaning: Biblical texts and hymns have found their way into most recreational songs among the Eʋes. This song reflects on the last days of Jesus Christ during his Agony in Gethsemane as recounted in Mathew 26: 36. After the Last Supper, Jesus went to a place called Gethsemane to pray. He took Peter and Zebedee's two sons, James and John, with him. He went a little ahead of them to pray but asked them to be awake with him since he was in great sorrow and distress. On his return, he found Peter and the rest asleep. Jesus asked Peter why he could not stay awake for just an hour with him. Although the scriptures did not state that Jesus asked Peter whether he was dead, the song recognizes the close relationship between the two.

Form: Solo and chorus, repetitive form and extended binary form.

Performance Style: i.   The first section of the song is performed by the cantor.
                    ii.   The second section is performed by the cantor and chorus in call and response form.

Scale: Heptatonic (seven-note).

Melody: Melody follows the tonal inflections of spoken language in most cases. Intervals between pitches are mostly based on major and minor thirds with occasional seconds and fourths.

Rhythm: Rhythmic phrases follow speech rhythms of the spoken text. Dotted rhythm is used in the second section of the song.

Harmony: Use of unison, singing of parallel thirds against the melody by the chorus. Crossing and overlapping of cantor and chorus.

Tonality: *Gbeɖeka Yesu bia Petro be*
        3 3 1 1 2 1 1 2 1

        E, neɖe kua?
        2 3 3 1 3

Yesu Kple Petro

Jesus and Peter

Egbanegba Song from Alavanyo Uudidi Egbanegba Group
Transcription by Paschal Yao Younge
2010

FIGURE 28.19: *Yesu Kple Petro*

O, nye me ku haɖe o, alɔ me dɔ
1 3   1   1 3 1 3 222   1

See page 278 for Figure 29.20 (*Mi Lalam*)

• Title: *Mi Lalam* •

Lyrics in Eʋegbe: *Mi lalam viɖe*
          Mi lalam viɖe

Mi Lalam

Please Wait For Me

Egbanegba Song from Alavanyo Uudidi Egbanegba Group
Transcription by Paschal Yao Younge
2010

FIGURE 28.20: *Mi Lalam*

Mi lalam vide
Matsɔ vɔ deka

Lyrics in English: Please wait for me
Please wait for me
Please wait for me
So I can take one cloth

Cultural Meaning: Costumes are very important in the performance of *Egbanegba*. The original performance required the female dancers to look their best—hence the need to dress appropriately in order to attract the male participants. The song reiterates the appeal from one female dancer to the group to wait for her so she can pick up another cloth before the performance. The original costume for the ladies required two pieces of cloth.

Form: Solo and chorus, repetitive form and extended binary form.

Performance Style: i.   The first section of the song is performed by the cantor.

ii.   The second section is performed by the cantor and chorus in parts.

Scale: Pentatonic (five-note).

Melody: Melody follows the tonal inflections of spoken language in most cases. Intervals between pitches are mostly based on major and minor thirds with occasional seconds and fourths.

Rhythm: Rhythmic phrases follow speech rhythms of the spoken text. Dotted rhythm is used throughout the song.

Harmony: Use of unison, singing of parallel thirds and sixths against the melody by the chorus. Crossing and overlapping of cantor and chorus.

Tonality: *Mi lalam viɖe*
　　　 3   3   1 1
　　　Matsɔ vɔ ɖeka
　　　 3   1   3   3 1

Gbolo Songs

See pages 280 and 281 for Figure 28.21 (*Maɖui Ɖe Hadɔme*)

• Title: *E, Maɖui De Hadɔme* •

Lyrics in Eʋegbe: *E, maɖui ɖe hadɔme*
　　　Afeawo, maɖui ɖe hadɔme
　　　Afeawo, maɖui ɖe hadɔme loo, ayoo
　　　E, metso adegbe gbɔ va ɖa te
　　　E, maɖui ɖe hadɔme
　　　E, metso adegbe gbɔ va ɖa te
　　　E maɖui ɖe hadɔme loo, ayoo
　　　E, maɖui ɖe hadɔme, adegbe gbɔ va ɖa te
　　　E, maɖui ɖe hadɔme
　　　E, maɖui ɖe hadɔme loo, ayoo

Lyrics in English: Yes, I will eat like an ordinary person
　　　People at home, I will eat like an ordinary person
　　　Yes, people at home, I will eat just like you
　　　I have returned from my hunting expedition without much success and had to eat vegetable soup
　　　Yes, I will eat just like you
　　　I have returned from my hunting expedition without much success and had to eat vegetable soup
　　　Yes, I will eat just like you
　　　Yes, I will eat like an ordinary person, returned from a hunting expedition to eat vegetable soup
　　　I will eat just like you
　　　Yes, I will eat just like you

Cultural Meaning: The hunter's meal is always supposed to contain meat. It is a disgrace or mockery for a hunter to prepare a dish without any protein derived from *adela* "meat from

Maɖui Ðe Hadɔme

I Will Eat It As An Ordinary Person

Gbolo Akaye Song from Alavanyo Uudidi Group
Transcription by Paschal Yao Younge
2010

FIGURE 28.21: *Maɖui Ðe Hadɔme* (continued on page 281)

2

Maɖui ɖe hadɔme

his hunt." The song is about a hunter who laments his unsuccesful hunt. However, in the context of *Gbolo*, the song is performed to ridicule unproductive hunters in the community.

Form: Solo and chorus, repetitive form and extended binary form.

Performance Style: i. The first section of the song is performed in free rhythm by cantor and chorus.

ii. Cantor and chorus sing the second section with percussion accompaniment.

Scale: Heptatonic (seven-note).

Melody: Melody follows the tonal inflections of spoken language in most cases. Pitches used in the song revolve around the tonic and the supertonic. The flattened seventh degree usually resolves to the sixth or fifth degree of the scale. Intervals between pitches are mostly based on major and minor thirds with occasional seconds and fourths.

Rhythm: Rhythmic phrases follow speech rhythms of the spoken text.

Harmony: Use of parallel thirds and sixths between cantor and chorus and among the
                  chorus itself. Crossing and overlapping of cantor and chorus.

Tonality: *E, maɖui ɖe hadɔme*
          3   1   2   1   3   3 3
          Afeawo, maɖui ɖe hadɔme
          3 1 1   1   2   1   3   3 3
          Afeawo, maɖui ɖe hadɔme loo, ayoo
          3 1 1   1   2   1   3 3   3 1   3 3
          E, metso adegbe gbɔ va ɖa te
          3   2   1   3 3 1   2   1   3 1

See pages 283 and 284 for Figure 28.22 (*Ameaɖe Ɖunu Me Na Nɔvia*)

• Title: *Ameaɖe Ɖunu Me Na Nɔvia* •

Lyrics in Eʋegbe: *E, mi le kpɔm 'gbea*
                   E, mi le kpɔm 'gbea
                   Ameaɖe ɖunu me na nɔvia
                   Mi le kpɔm 'gbea loo ayoo
                   Ameaɖe ɖunu me na nɔvia
                   Mi le kpɔm 'gbea loo ayoo
                   Ameaɖe ɖunu me na nɔvia
                   Mi le kpɔm 'gbea loo ayoo
                   E, mi le kpɔm 'gbea
                   Ameaɖe ɖunu me na nɔvia
                   E, mi le kpɔm 'gbea
                   Ameaɖe ɖunu me na nɔvia
                   E, mi le kpɔm 'gbea
                   E, mi le kpɔm 'gbea Gbolowoe
                   Mi le kpɔm 'gbea
                   E, mi le kpɔm 'gbea Gbolowoe
                   Mi le kpɔm 'gbea
                   Ameaɖe ɖunu me na nɔvia
                   Mi le kpɔm 'gbea loo ayoo

Lyrics in English: Yes, you have seen it today
                   Yes, you have seen it today
                   A person is eating but refuses to share the meal with a friend
                   Yes, we are seeing this today
                   A person is eating but refuses to share the meal with a friend
                   Yes, we are seeing this today
                   A person is eating but refuses to share the meal with a friend
                   Yes, we are seeing this today
                   Yes, you have seen it today
                   A person is eating but refuses to share the meal with a friend
                   Yes, you have seen it today
                   A person is eating but refuses to share the meal with a friend
                   Yes, you have seen it today
                   A person is eating but refuses to share the meal with a friend
                   Yes, you have seen it today
                   Yes, have you seen it too, *Gbolo* dancers?

Yes, you have seen it today

Yes, have you seen it too, *Gbolo* dancers?

Yes, you have seen it today

A person is eating but refuses to share the meal with a friend

Yes, we are seeing this today

Cultural Meaning: Sharing a meal, whatever the quantity and quality, is one of the ways Eυes

FIGURE 28.22: *Ameaɖe Ɖunu Me Na Novia* (continued on page 284)

2   Ameaɖe ɖunu mena nɔvia

show their hospitality to neighbors and especially to strangers. On arrival at any home, the first thing to be offered to welcome you is water — even before greetings are exchanged. You will be invited to join a family for dinner if by chance on your arrival to the home dinner is being served. This is one of the traditional ways of communal living among the Eʋes. Should anybody fail to adhere to this basic principle of life, he or she is chastised, teased and riduculed through song. This song reflects on the need to share.

Form: Solo and chorus, repetitive form and extended binary form. A: A: B: A1: B: A1: B: A2: B: etc.

Performance Style: i.   The first section of the song is performed in free rhythm by cantor and chorus.

                  ii. Cantor and chorus sing the second section with percussion accompaniment.

Scale: Heptatonic (seven-note).

Melody: Melody follows the tonal inflections of spoken language in most cases. Intervals between pitches are mostly based on major and minor thirds with occasional seconds and fourths.

Rhythm: Rhythmic phrases follow speech rhythms of the spoken text.

Harmony: Use of parallel thirds and sixths and among the chorus itself. Crossing of cantor and chorus.

Tonality: *E, mi le kpɔm 'gbea*
        1   2 2 1   2

        Ameaɖe ɖunu me na nɔvia
        2 2 1 2 1 1 1 3 1

        Mi le kpɔm 'gbea loo ayoo
        2 2 1   2 1 3 3

        E, mi le kpɔm 'gbea Gbolowoe
        1 2 2 1   2   3 3   1

Ga Songs

GOME SONGS

• Title: *Abi Carpenter* •

Lyrics in Pidgin English: *Abi carpenter aa*
                             Knowbody know
                             My wife e know

Lyrics in English: I am a carpenter
                             Knowbody knows
                             Only my wife knows

Cultural Meaning: There exists a unique bond between married couples among the Gas. Third parties are not allowed to interfere with marital problems when they arise. Family affairs are therefore kept private. Most *Gome* songs reflect the conditions during colonialism and the hardships freed slaves faced upon their return to Ghana. The unemployed were not so open with their professions and occupations for fear of being laughed at by those Ghanians (the African elite) who were lucky enough to be working for the colonial masters. Because of the relationship most men have with their wives, only they would know what type of work they did. The song talks about members of the *Gome* ensemble who are mostly carpenters.

Form: Solo and chorus, repetitive form.

Performance Style: This is a simple solo and chorus performance. The lead/main cantor sings the whole song and the chorus repeats in parts.

Scale: Hexatonic (six-note).

Melody: Melody follows the tonal inflections of spoken language with the cantor performing some variations.

Rhythm: Rhythmic phrases follow speech rhythms of the spoken text.

Harmony: Chorus breaks into two parts, with one part singing an interval of a third below the melody.

Tonality: *Abi carpenter*
        2 2 1 1 3

Abi Carpenter

I Am a Carpenter

Gome Song by David Amoo
Transcription by Paschal Yao Younge
2010

FIGURE 28.23: *Abi Carpenter*

Knowbody know
1   1   1 1
My wife e know
2   1 2   1

See page 287 for Figure 28.24 (*Joe Joe*)

• Title: *Joe Joe* •

Lyrics in Pidgin English: *Joe Joe*
Joe dey come oo
Somebody dey fear

Lyrics in English: Mr. Joe Mr. Joe
Mr. Joe is coming
Somebody is in trouble

Cultural Meaning: The fortunate Ghanaians employed by the colonial masters (especially those

Mr. Joe

Gome Song by David Amoo
Transcription by Paschal Yao Younge
2010

FIGURE 28.24: *Joe Joe*

with no formal education) worked under very strict conditions. From the ports and plantations in Pico de Sante Isable and San Carlos in Fernando Pó, and back in Ghana prior to independence, the appearance of a supervisor or manager at a work site meant trouble. The song talks about the constant fear of being humiliated. Mr. Joe is used as code for all the colonial masters.

Form: Solo and chorus, repetitive form.

Performance Style: This is a simple solo and chorus performance. The lead/main cantor sings the whole song and the chorus repeats in parts. There is room for the solo to improvise at any time during the performance.

Scale: Hexatonic (six-note).

Melody: Melody follows the tonal inflections of spoken language with some variations by the cantor.

Rhythm: Rhythmic phrases follow speech rhythms of the spoken text.

Harmony: Chorus breaks into two parts, with one part singing an interval of a third below the melody.

Tonality: *Joe Joe*

      1   2

Joe dey come oo

      1   2 1   3

Somebody dey fear

      1   1 1 2 1 3

Kolomashie Songs

Bonso Oo
The Whale

FIGURE 28.25: *Bonso Oo*

• Title: *Bonso Oo* •

Lyrics in Ga: *Poopo lipopoo oo*
                    Poopo lipo poo
                    Bonso oo
                    Kɛ loo aba ni woye

Lyrics in English: Poopo lipopoo oo [onomatopoeic words representing the roaring "singing" of the whale]
                    The whale
                    Bring us a bumper harvest for consumption

Cultural Meaning: The sea is very sacred to the Gas. There are rituals performed throughout the year to enable the fishermen to have a bumper harvest. The whale is also regarded as one of the gods or the kings of the sea. The fishermen believe that any time the whale roars/sings, it frightens the smaller fishes and forces them to travel nearer the coastline for the fishermen to catch. The song is a tribute and prayer to the whale to continue to assist the fishermen.

Form: Solo and chorus, repetitive form.

Performance Style: This is a simple solo and chorus performance. The lead/main cantor sings a section of the song and the chorus responds in parts.

Scale: Heptonic (seven-note).

Melody: Melody follows the tonal inflections of spoken language with some variations by the cantor. The flattened seventh degree, Bb, is used instead of the natural B.

Rhythm: Rhythmic phrases follow speech rhythms of the spoken text.

Harmony: Chorus breaks into two parts, with one part singing an interval of a third above the melody.

Tonality: *Poopo lipopoo oo*
           2 2 3 2 2   2
           Poopo lipo poo
           2 2 3 2 1
           Bonso oo
           2 3 3
           Kɛ loo aba woye
           2 3 11 2   3

See page 290 for Figure 28.26 (*Te Ole Ake Olele Nmaa Oo*)

• Title: *Te Ole Ake Olele Nmaa Oo* •

Lyrics in Ga: *Te ole ake olele nmaa oo*
                    Te ole ake olele nmaa oo
                    Ni onine bl he
                    Te ole ake olele nmaa oo

Lyrics in English: Don't you know your canoe is full
                    Don't you know your canoe is full
                    You need to pay attention
                    Don't know your canoe is full

Cultural Meaning: Lierally, the song means that fishermen should come home once their canoes are full when fishing—otherwise their boats will sink. The song cautions that greed brings serious and damaging results and so should be avoided.

Form: Solo and chorus, repetitive form.

Performance Style: This is a simple solo and chorus performance. The lead/main cantor sings a section of the song and the chorus responds in parts.

Te Ole Ake Olele Nmaa Oo

Don't You Know Your Canoe is Full

Koloamshie Song by David Amoo
Transcription by Paschal Yao Younge
2010

FIGURE 28.26: *Te Ole Ake Olele Nmaa Oo*

Scale: Hexatonic (six-note).

Melody: Melody follows the tonal inflections of spoken language with some variations by the cantor. The flattened seventh degree, Bb, is used instead of the natural B.

Rhythm: Rhythmic phrases follow speech rhythms of the spoken text.

Harmony: Chorus breaks into two parts, with one part singing an interval of a third above the melody.

Tonality: *Te ole ake olele nmaa oo*
        1 2   2 11 2 2 2 1 2 3
        Te ole ake olele nmaa oo
        1 2   2 11 2 2 2 1 2 3
        Ni onine bɛ he
        1   1 3 2 1 2
        Te ole ake olele nmaa oo
        1 2   2 11 2 2 2 1 2 3

KPANLONGO SONGS

Aadensuo, Awula Ni Yaa He Ee

Aadensuo, the Sister That is Leaving

FIGURE 28.27: *Aadensuo Oo*

• Title: *Aadensuo Oo* •

Lyrics in Ga: *Aadensuo oo*
                    Awula niyaa he ee
                    Owu tsebolo ee
                    Aadensuo oo yaa kɔ mama
                    Ni oya boletoi

Lyrics in English: Aadensuo [name of a girl]
                    Lady that is going
                    Your husband is calling you
                    Aadensuo, take your cloth and go
                    And go and listen to him

Cultural Meaning: This song advises women against leaving their husbands. Once married, both halves of a couple should make it work, for an empty home is worse than having a bad partner. Once divorced you lose the respect of your friends and neighbors.

Form: Solo and chorus, repetitive form.

Performance Style: This is a simple solo and chorus performance. The lead/main cantor sings the whole song and the chorus repeats in unison with occasional part-singing.

Scale: Hexatonic (six-note).

Melody: Melody follows the tonal inflections of spoken language with some variations by the cantor. Uses both the natural F and F # in the melody.

Rhythm: Rhythmic phrases follow speech rhythms of the spoken text.

Harmony: Chorus sings unison and breaks into two parts, singing occassional intervals of thirds below the melody.

Tonality: *Aadensuo oo*
          1   2   1 1
          Awula niyaa he ee
          2 2 1 1 3 2 2
          Owu tsebolo ee
          2   21 3 3   2
          Aadensuo oo yaa kɔ mama
          1   2   11 1   3   3   3
          Ni oya boletoi
          1 3 3 3 3 2

See page 293 for Figure 28.28 (*Oblayoo Niyaa*)

• Title: *Oblayoo Niyaa* •

Lyrics in Ga: *Oblayoo niyaa*
                    Kaadi ohefeo see
                    Ni ofite ohe loo

Lyrics in English: Lady that is going
                    Don't be obsessed with beauty
                    And spoil your beautiful skin

Cultural Meaning: Since *Kpanlongo* started with the youth, most of the songs talk about courtship and the ideal concept of beauty. Ladies are always being reminded of the fact that beauty is more than how one looks. Appearances are sometimes deceitful so ladies should not use cosmetics to change their natural beautiful bodies. Self-admiration or elevation only leads to one's downfall. The song advises all young girls to maintain their natural beautiful bodies.

Oblayoo Ni Yaa
Sister That is Leaving

Kpanlongo Song by David Amoo
Transcription by Paschal Yao Younge
2010

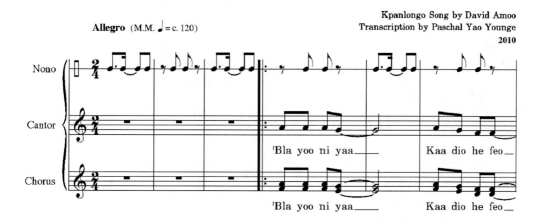

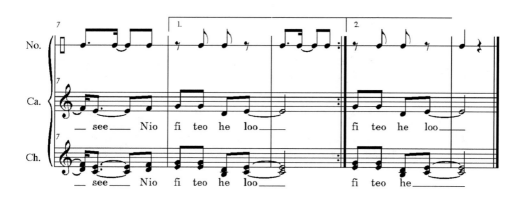

FIGURE 28.28: *Oblayoo Niyaa*

Form: Solo and chorus, repetitive form.

Performance Style: This is a simple solo and chorus performance. The lead/main cantor sings the whole song and the chorus repeats in parts.

Scale: Pentonic (five-note).

Melody: Melody follows the tonal inflections of spoken language with some variations by the cantor.

Rhythm: Rhythmic phrases follow speech rhythms of the spoken text.

Harmony: Chorus joins in two parts, singing intervals of thirds below the melody.

Tonality: *Oblayoo niyaa*
        2   1   3 1   2
        Kaadi ohefeo see
        1   2 11 3 3 3
        Ni ofite ohe loo
        1   21111 3   3

Akan Songs

ADOWA

Yɛ Nya Nni Agorɔ Yiee

We are Making Our Ensemble

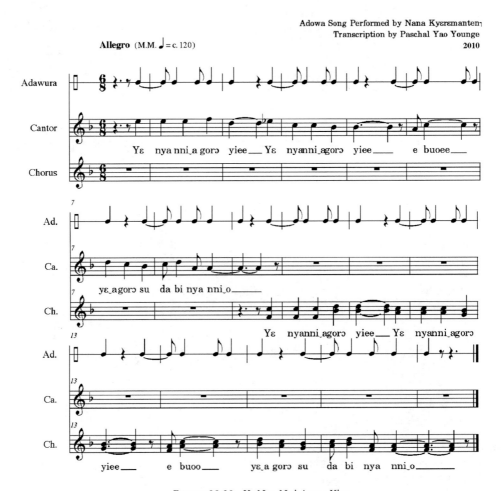

FIGURE 28.29: *Yɛ Nya Nni Agorɔ Yiee*

• Title: *Yɛ Nya Nni Agorɔ Yiee* •

Lyrics in Twi: *Yɛ nya nni agorɔ yiee*
                         Yɛ nya nni agorɔ yiee, e buoee yɛ agorɔ su da bi nya nnio
                         Yɛ nya nni agorɔ yiee
                         Yɛ nya nni agorɔ yiee, e buoee yɛ agorɔ su da bi nya nnio

Lyrics in English: Let us resolve to play/dance with well
                         Let us resolve to play/dance well, you dream and wake up with this play/dance
                         Let us resolve to play/dance with well
                         Let us resolve to play/dance well, you dream and wake up with this play/dance

Cultural Meaning: During Akan dance-drumming ceremonies, dancers encourage one another. Songs are used to stir up enthusiasm and group particiaption. Akans encourage communal activities for the common good of the people. This song encourages the participants to collaborate through play for a perfect performance.

Form: Solo and chorus, repetitive form.

Performance Style: This is a simple solo and chorus performance. The lead/main cantor sings the whole song and the chorus repeats.

Scale: Hexatonic (six-note).

Melody: Melody follows the tonal inflections of spoken language with some variations by the cantor. The seventh degree of the scale alternates between E and Eb.

Rhythm: Rhythmic phrases follow speech rhythms of the spoken text.

Harmony: i. Chorus breaks into two parts, singing intervals of thirds and fifths below the melody.

Tonality: *Yɛ nya nni agorɔ yiee*
     1   3   2 2 2 2 1 2
     Yɛ nya nni agorɔ yiee, e buoee yɛ agorɔ su da bi nya
     1 3 2 2 2 2 1 2 11   1 2 2 2 2 22 1
     nnio
     2 3

See page 296 for Figure 28.30 (*Nana, E Bao*)

• Title: *Nana E Bao* •

Lyrics in Twi: *Nana e bao Nana e ba*
                  Nana e bao Nana e ba
                  Yeee Nana e bao yeee yeee
                  Yei deɛ Nana e bao
                  Na mmo mma yɛ nnye no taa taa

Lyrics in English: The king is coming
                  The king is coming
                  Yes, king is coming, yes yes
                  Yes, king is coming
                  Let's welcome him with his majestic walk

Cultural Meaning: Akan communities respect the authority of chiefs. The presence of chiefs at important ceremonies such as festivals are recognized through songs and poetry. Through songs, dancers praise their chiefs and acknowledge their importance and power. This particular song is performed to herald the entrance or arrival of chiefs at such ceremonies.

Form: Solo and chorus, repetitive form.

Performance Style: This is a simple solo and chorus performance. The lead/main cantor sings the whole song and the chorus repeats.

Scale: Hexatonic (six-note).

Melody: Melody follows the tonal inflections of spoken language with some variations.

Rhythm: Rhythmic phrases follow speech rhythms of the spoken text.

Harmony: Chorus breaks into two parts, singing intervals of thirds below the melody.

Tonality: *Nana e bao Nana e ba*
      2   1 1 2 3 2 11 2
      Nana e bao Nana e ba
      2   1 1 2 3 2 11 2

Nana, Eba O

The King is Coming

Adowa Song Performed by Nana Kyeremanteŋ
Transcription by Paschal Yao Younge
2010

FIGURE 28.30: *Nana E Bao*

Yeee Nana e bao yeee yeee
1   2 1 123 2 1
Yei deɛ Nana e bao
1   12 1123
Na mmo mma yɛ nnye no taa taa
2   1   2 1   2 2 2   1

ASAADUA SONGS

Pɛ Aduro Yɛ, Ababaa Wa ee

Get Yourself Some Medicine, Young Lady

Asaadua Song by Nana Kyeremanten
Transcription by Paschal Yao Younge
2010

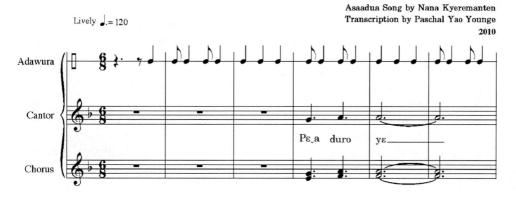

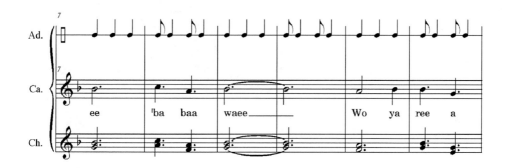

FIGURE 28.31: *Pɛ Aduro Yɛ, Ababaa Wa Ee*

• Title: *Pɛ Aduro Yɛ, Ababaa Wa Ee* •

Lyrics in Twi:
Pɛ aduro yɛ, Ababaa wa ee
Wo ayare akyɛ oo
Pɛaduro yɛ a
Ma obi nware woɛe

Lyrics in English: Get yourself some medicine, young lady
                   You have been for a long time
                   Get yourself some medicine
                   So that someone may marry you

Cultural Meaning: Literally, the song is advising a young woman who is ill to get medical treatment in good time so that she finds a suitable partner. It is, however, satirical. This song was originally performed by an all-male *Asaadua* group. They are telling young women to eschew laziness and other bad habits which they classify as sickness in order to find good husbands.

Form: Solo and chorus, repetitive form.

Performance Style: This is a simple solo and chorus performance. The lead/main cantor sings the whole song and the chorus repeats.

Scale: Hexatonic (six-note).

Melody: Melody follows the tonal inflections of spoken language with some variations.

Rhythm: Rhythmic phrases follow speech rhythms of the spoken text.

Harmony: Chorus may break into two parts singing intervals of thirds with occasional fourths below the melody, or they may perform in unison.

Tonality: *Pɛ aduro yɛ, Ababaa wa ee*
          1 1 2 1 11 1 2   2 2   1
          Wo ayare akyɛ oo
          2   2 2   1 2 2
          Pɛ aduro yɛ a
          1 1 2 1   1 2
          Ma obi nware woɛe
          2   1 2 2 2   1

See page 299 for Figure 28.32 (*Ɔyɛ Adeɛ Yie Nana Safo e*)

• Title: *Ɔyɛ Adeɛ Yie Nana Safo E* •

Lyrics in Twi: *Ɔyɛ adeɛ yie Nana Safo e*
                   Ɔyɛ adeɛ yie yɛma no amo o
                   Ɔyɛ adeɛ yie Nana Safo e
                   Ɔyɛ adeɛ yie, yɛma wo so oo

Lyrics in English: Nana Safo, the repairer
                   The repairer, we congratulate him
                   Nana Safo, the repairer
                   The repairer, we exalt you

Cultural Meaning: Although the song is congratulating a particular chief, Nana Safo, once a ruler of Manpong, it is used today to praise all chiefs or noblemen at ceremonies. A chief or king has several appellations or praise names that speak to his greatness, power, kindness and ability to resolve crisis as a "repairer."

Form: Solo and chorus, repetitive form.

Performance Style: This is a simple solo and chorus performance. The lead/main cantor sings the first half of the song and the chorus joins in with the second half.

Scale: Hexatonic (six-note).

Melody: Melody follows the tonal inflections of spoken language with some variations.

Rhythm: Rhythmic phrases follow speech rhythms of the spoken text.

Harmony: Chorus may break into two or three parts, singing intervals of thirds and sixths below the melody, or they may perform in unison.

Ɔyɛ Adeɛ Yie, Nana Safo E
You Have Done Well, Nana Safo

Asaadua Song by Nana Kyeremanten
Transcription by Paschal Yao Younge
2010

FIGURE 28.32: *Ɔyɛ Adeɛ Yie Nana Safo E*

Tonality: *Ɔyɛ adeɛ yie Nana Safo e*
        2 1 2 12 2 1 1 1 2 1 2
        Ɔyɛ adeɛ yie yɛma no amo o
        2 1 2 12 2 2 2 2 2 21 2
        Ɔyɛ adeɛ yie Nana Safo e
        2 1 2 12 2 1 1 1 2 1 2
        Ɔyɛ adeɛ yie yɛma wo so oo
        2 1 2 12 2 2 2 2 2 1 1

SIKYI SONGS

Ɔmmra oo, Yɛrekɔbɔ Sikyi

Please Come, We Are Going to Perform Sikyi

Sikyi Song by Ghana Dance Ensemble
University of Ghana, Legon
Transcription by Paschal Yao Younge
2010

FIGURE 28.33: *Ɔ Mmra Oo, Ɔmmra*

• Title: *Ɔ Mmra Oo, Ɔ Mmra* •

Lyrics in Twi: *Ɔ mmra oo, Ɔ mmra*
Yɛrekɔbɔ Sikyi Ɔ mmra Edenaa ee
Ɔ mmra oo Edenaa ee, Ɔ mmra oo Edenaa ee
Ɔ mmra Ɔ mmra Edena Ɔ mmra

Lyrics in English: Please come, come
  We are going to perform *Sikyi*, people of Edena
  Please come, people of Edena, please come, people of Edena
  Come, come, Edena, come

Cultural Meaning: This song emphasizes the philosophy and the importance of communal life. The concept of "we" as opposed to "I" is the basis for community survival. Sharing and collaboration is encouraged in every activity in Akan communities. The *Sikyi* group in this context are inviting the people of Edena (a Fante town located in the Central Region) to join in the performance.

Form: Solo and chorus, repetitive form.

Performance Style: This is a simple solo and chorus performance. The lead/main cantor sings the first half of the song and the chorus joins in with the second half.

Scale: Hexatonic (six-note).

Melody: Melody follows the tonal inflections of spoken language with some variations.

Rhythm: Rhythmic phrases follow speech rhythms of the spoken text.

Harmony: Chorus may break into two parts, singing an interval of a third below the melody, or they may perform in unison.

Tonality: *Ɔ mmra oo, Ɔ mmra*
  1 1 1 3 1 1 1
  Yɛrɛkɔbɔ Sikyi Ɔ mmra Edenaa ee
  1   2 1 11 2 1 1 12 2 1 2
  Ɔ mmra oo Edenaa ee, Ɔ mmra oo Edenaa ee
  1 1 1 3 2 2 1 2 1 1 1 3 2 2 1 2
  Ɔ mmra Ɔ mmra Edena Ɔ mmra
  1 1 1 1 1 1 2 2 1 1 1 1

  See page 302 for Figure 28.34 (*Ɔkwantenten Awareɛ*)

• Title: *Ɔkwantenten Awareɛ* •

Lyrics in Twi: *Ɔkwantenten awareɛ, eee menkɔ o*
  Ɔkwantenten awareɛ, eee menkɔ o
  Sɛ menya me kɔ na asɛm bi si m'akyiria mɛyɛ dɛn
  Ɔkwantenten awareɛ, menkɔ o
  O aslm bi si m'akyiria mɛyɛ dɛn mate

Lyrics in English: Marriage is a long journey/road, I will not go [make that journey]
  Marriage is a long journey/road, I will not go [make that journey]
  What if I go and something happens in my absence
  Marriage is a long journey/road, I will not go [make that journey]
  How will I know if something happens in my absence

Cultural Meaning: The song emphasizes the importance of marriage but at the same time reiterates the risks involved. Marriage is a complex and long-standing bond between individuals, and one should marry when one is ready to do so. The song further encourages couples to reflect on the challenges they are bound to face and not to enter into any hasty marriages.

Form: Solo and chorus, repetitive form.

Performance Style: This is a simple solo and chorus performance. The lead/main cantor sings the whole song and the chorus repeats.

Scale: Hexatonic (six-note).

Melody: Melody follows the tonal inflections of spoken language with some variations.

Rhythm: Rhythmic phrases follow speech rhythms of the spoken text.

Ɔkwanten Ten, Awareɛ Eee

Marriage is a Long Journey

Sikyi Song by Nana Kyeremanten
Transcription by Paschal Yao Younge
2010

FIGURE 28.34: *Ɔkwantenten Awareɛ*

Harmony: Chorus may break into two parts, singing an interval of a third below the melody, or they may perform in unison.

Tonality: *Ɔkwantenten awareɛ, eee menkɔ o*
             2 1   1 1   1 2 21 1   2 1   1

Ɔkwantenten awareɛ, eee menkɔ o
             2   1 1   1   1 2 21   1 2   1 1

Sɛ menya me kɔ na asɛm bi si m'akyiria mɛyɛ dɛn
3   3   3 2 1 1 2 1   1 3 2   2 2 3 1 1   2
Ɔkwantenten awareɛ, eee menkɔ o
2   1   1 1 1 2 21   1 2 1   1
O asɛm bi si m'akyiria mɛyɛ dɛn mate
1 1 2 1 1 3 2 2 2 2 3 11 2   1 3

Dagbamba Songs

BAAMAAYA SONGS

Diŋ Vela Nyaɣsa

Good Things Are Sweet

Baamaaya Song by Tamale Youth Bamaaya Group
Transcription by Paschal Yao Younge
2010

FIGURE 28.35: *Diŋ Vela Nyaɣsa, Dahama Kaniyoo*

• Title: *Diŋ Vela Nyaɣsa, Dahama Kaniyoo* •

Lyrics in Dagbaŋli: *Diŋ vela nyaɣsa, dahama kani yoo*
Diŋ vela nyaɣsa, dahama kani
Anduniya nima, Diŋ vela nyaɣsa, dahama kani

Lyrics in English: Good things are sweet, but you lack money
Good things are sweet, but you lack money
People of the world, good things are sweet but you lack money

Cultural Meaning: This song highlights the importance of wealth and good living in Dagbɔŋ culture. Money in this context symbolizes all your wealth. Wealth may be due to the number of cattle you own rather than the size of your bank account. You're respected and loved because of your wealth as is evident in a popular Hausa proverb, "Money is the man; if you have none, no one will love you." The important cultural lesson is that you must work hard to succeed in life. There is no shame in working among the Dagbamba. He who perspires because of work eats well.

Form: Solo and chorus, repetitive form.

Performance style: This is a simple solo and chorus performance. The lead/main cantor sings the whole song and the chorus repeats.

Scale: Pentatonic (five-note).

Melody: Melody follows the tonal inflections of spoken language with some variations.

Rhythm: Rhythmic phrases follow speech rhythms of the spoken text.

Harmony: i. Use of parallel octaves between voices.
ii. Overlapping of cantor and chorus.
iii. Chorus may break into two parts, singing an interval of a third at the end of phrases.

Tonality: *Diŋ vela nyaɣsa, dahama kani yoo*
2   2 2 1   3 2   2   2 2 2   3
Diŋ vela nyaɣsa, dahama kani
2   2 2 1   3 2   2   2 2   2
Anduniya nima, Diŋ vela nyaɣsa, dahama kani
2   2 1 1 1 3   2   2   2   1 3 2   2   2 2   2

See page 305 for Figure 28.36 (*Paɣa yaba yoo yee, paɣa yaba maraaba*)

• Title: *Paɣa Yaba Yoo Yee, Paɣa Ya Maraaba* •

Lyrics in Dagbaŋli: *Paɣa yaba yoo yee, paɣa yaba maraaba*
Paɣa yaba, paɣa yaba, paɣa yaba maraaba
Paɣa yaba ku chaŋ kuluga, Paɣa yaba ŋunni kulmi
Paɣyaba, paɣyaba, paɣayaba maraaba

Lyrics in English: Beautiful girl, beautiful girl, you're welcome.
Beautiful girl, beautiful girl, beautiful girl you're welcome.
Beautiful girl, if you think you're too beautiful to carry water, then go to where you came from.
Beautiful girl, beautiful girl, beautiful girl you're welcome.

Cultural Meaning: This song shows the attitude towards women in Dagbɔŋ culture. Once a woman marries, she is expected to take charge of the household. Cooking and walking for miles to look or fetch water, especially during the long dry season, is one of the duties that makes a responsible and devoted wife. This song warns young females about what to expect when they marry.

Form: Solo and chorus, repetitive form.

Paɣ Yaba Maraba

Beautiful Girl, You're Welcome

FIGURE 28.36: *Paɣa Yaba Yoo Yee, Paɣa Yaba Maraaba*

Performance Style: This is a simple call and response performance. The lead/main cantor sings the first half or section of the song and then the chorus responds with the second half.

Scale: Pentatonic (five-note).

Melody: Melody follows the tonal inflections of spoken language with some variations.

Rhythm: Rhythmic phrases follow speech rhythms of the spoken text.

Harmony: i. Use of parallel octaves between voices.

        ii. Overlapping of cantor and chorus.

Tonality: *Paɣayaba yoo yee, paɣayaba maraaba*
       1 1 1 2 1 2 3 1 1 1 2 1   1 2
       Paɣayaba, paɣayaba, paɣayaba maraaba
       1 1 1 2 1 1 1 2 1 1 1 2 1   1 2
       Paɣayaba ku chaŋ kuluga, Paɣayaba ŋunni kulmi
       1 1 1 2 2   3   2 2 2 1 1 1 2 1 1   2   2
       Paɣayaba, paɣayaba, paɣayaba maraaba
       1 1 1 2 1 1 1 2 1 1 1 2 1   1 2

BLA SONG

See page 307 for Figure 28.37 (*Daani Yee Daanaa Yee, Bombala Daŋmalgu*)

• Title: *Daani Yee Daanaa Yee, Bombala Daŋmalgu* •

Lyrics in Dagbaŋli: *Daani yee daanaa yee, bombala daŋmalgu*
             Daani yee daanaa yee, bombala daŋmalgu
             Guŋgona kumsi kuŋan, saa saɣmmiya daŋmalgu
             Daani yee daanaa yee, bombala daŋmalgu
             Daani yee daanaa yee, bukana nomal daŋ
             Daani yee daanaa yee, bombala daŋmalgu

Lyrics in English: Family members should respond to family calls.
             If you call your family members they will respond.
             Sounds of *guŋgon* "drums" cannot sound like thunder
             If you call your family members they will respond.
             The head of the family must sacrifice a goat before family disputes are settled.
             If you call your family members they will respond.

Cultural Meaning: Family units among the Dagbamba are based on households. Each household is comprised of a cluster of buildings belonging to closely-knit families. Disputes, whenever they arise, are settled within families. A feast usually ends the settlement of issues. The family makes the individual and so they need to help each other in times of need.

Form: Solo and chorus, repetitive form.

Performance Style: This is a simple call and response performance. The lead/main cantor sings the first half or section of the song and then the chorus responds with the second half.

Scale: Pentatonic (five-note).

Melody: Melody follows the tonal inflections of spoken language with some variations.

Rhythm: Rhythmic phrases follow speech rhythms of the spoken text.

Harmony: i. Use of parallel octaves between voices.
       ii. Overlapping of cantor and chorus.

Tonality: *Daani yee daanaa yee, bombala daŋmalgu*
       1 1 1 1   2 3 1   1 1 1 1 2
       Daani yee daanaa yee, bombala daŋmalgu
       1 1 1 1   2 3 1   1 1 1 1 2
       Guŋgona kumsi kuŋan, saa saɣmmiya daŋmalgu
       1   1 1 1 2 3 1 3   3 1 1 1 1 1 2
       Daani yee daanaa yee, bombala daŋmalgu
       1 1 1 1   2 3 1   1 1 1 1 2
       Daani yee daanaa yee, bukana nomal daŋ
       1 1 1 1   2 3   2 1 2 2   2 3

Daŋ Malgu

Family Members

Bla Song as Performed by Sulley Moro
Transcription by Paschal Yao Younge
2010

FIGURE 28.37: *Daani Yee Aaanaa Yee, Bombala Da'malgu*

Daani yee daanaa yee, bombala daŋmalgu
1   1 1 1   2 3   1 1 1 1 1   2

Jɛra Songs

See page 308 for Figure 28.38 (*Buɣili yeei, Buɣili bora bo*)

• Title: *Buɣili Yeei, Buɣili Bora Bo?* •
Lyrics in Dagbaŋli: *Buɣili yeei, Buɣili bora bo?*
Naa zaŋ noo mali Buɣili

Buɣuli Yeei, Buɣuli Bora Bo?

The Gods, What Do The Gods Want?

FIGURE 28.38: *Buɣili Yeei, Buɣili Bora Bo*

                    Buɣili yeei
                    Naa zaŋ noo mali Buɣili
Lyrics in English: The Gods! What do the Gods want?
                    I would have sacrificed a fowl to the Gods
                    The Gods!
                    I would have sacrificed a fowl to the Gods

Cultural Meaning: Dagbamba believe in the supernatural. They strongly believe that their ancestors and all the gods play a role in shaping and guiding their daily lives. Due to the catastrophic famine that brought in the *Baamaaya* dance-drumming in the 18th century, the Dagbamba are always in constant communication with spiritual forces by performing a variety of rituals and sacrifices. The song is a further affirmation of their readiness to seek the help of their ancestors and deities in time of crises.

Form: Solo and chorus, repetitive form.

Performance Style: This is a simple call and response performance. The lead/main cantor sings the first half or section of the song and then the chorus responds with the second half.

Scale: Hexatonic (six-note).

Melody: Melody follows the tonal inflections of spoken language with some variations. Change of tonal center from F to Bb in the second section of the song.

Rhythm: Rhythmic phrases follow speech rhythms of the spoken text.

Harmony: i. Use of parallel octaves between voices.
           ii. Overlapping of cantor and chorus.

Tonality: *Buɣili yeei, Buɣili bora bo?*
1 1 1 2 3 1 1 112 2
Naa zaŋ noo mali Buɣili
1 1 1 1 21 11
Buɣili yeei
1 1 1 2 3
Naa zaŋ noo mali Buɣili
1 1 1 1 21 11

Goo Yaa Yan Go Yoo

We Are Here to Dance

FIGURE 28.39: *Go Yaa Yan Go Yoo*

• Title: *Go Yaa Yan Go Yoo* •

Lyrics in Dagbaŋli: *Go yaa yan go yoo, go yaa yan go*
Go yaa yan go, go yeriga

Lyrics in English: Dancers are here to ask permission to dance
Dancers are here for a serious dance

Cultural Meaning: Exchange of greetings is a ritual among the Dagbamba. A simple "good morning" may sometimes take from ten to 30 minutes to complete. Likewise, honoring the presence of elders, important dignitaries and the community as a whole at social gatherings is expected of all. Dance-drumming ensembles are not excluded from showing this courtesy. *Jɛra* dancers therefore perform this song as a form of greeting and to announce their readiness to dance. This song usually begins the *jɛra tɔra* phase of the performance.

Form: Solo and chorus, repetitive form.

Performance Style: This is a simple call and response performance. The lead/main cantor sings the first half or section of the song and then the chorus responds with the second half.

Scale: Penatonic (five-note).

Melody: Melody follows the tonal inflections of spoken language with some variations.

Rhythm: Rhythmic phrases follow speech rhythms of the spoken text.

Harmony: i. Use of parallel octaves between voices.
  ii. Unison.

Tonality: *Go yaa yan go yoo, go yaa yan go*
      1   1   2   1 2   1 1   2   1
      Go yaa yan go, go yeriga
      1   1   2   1   1 222

TƆRA SONGS

See page 311 for Figure 28.40 (*Daa dam yoo, daa dam yoo*)

• Title: *Daa Dam Yoo, Daa Dam Yoo* •

Lyrics in Dagbaŋli: *Daa dam yoo, daa dam yoo*
Daa dam yoo yaa yi, daa dam yoo
Daa dam bi mi Oyɛn niŋ shɛm ka bi bo lo nira
Bɛ ti yan bo lo nira Dab a yi ko be lo gba li ni

Lyrics in English: Human beings, Oh human beings
Human beings, Yes, human beings
Human beings do not know what to do to be recognized as important people when they are alive
You'll be in the grave by the time you're recognized for your good work

Cultural Meaning: Dagbamba women use songs to reflect on their status, topical issues and other philosophies of life. Particularly in *Tɔra*, the songs focus mostly on how the men, especially their husbands, treat them in society. They most often use proverbial and metaphoric texts to avoid reprimand from their men. In this song, "human beings" are used as a metaphor for men. This song offers the simple advice to men to treat their women with respect.

Form: Solo and chorus, repetitive form.

Performance Style: This is a simple solo and chorus performance. The lead/main cantor sings the whole song and the chorus repeats.

Scale: Hexatonic (six-note).

Melody: Melody follows the tonal inflections of spoken language with some variations.

Rhythm: Rhythmic phrases follow speech rhythms of the spoken text.

Harmony: i. Use of parallel octaves between voices.
  ii. Overlapping of cantor and chorus.

Daa Dam Yoo

Oh Human Beings

Zamandunia Song by Tamale Youth Home Tɔra Group
Transcription by Paschal Yao Younge
2010

FIGURE 28.40: *Daa Dam Yoo, Daa Dam Yoo*

Tonality: *Daa dam yoo, daa dam yoo*
    1   1 3 1   1   3
Daa dam yoo yaa yi, daa dam yoo
    1 1   3 3 3 1 1   3
Daa dam bi mi Oyɛn niŋ shɛm ka bi bo lo nira
    1   1 1 1 2 1   3   3 3 3 2 2 3 3

Bɛ ti yan bo lo nira Da ba yi ko be lo gba li ni
1   1 1 2 1 33 1 1 1 21 2   3 3 3

Oyee
Oh Yes

FIGURE 28.41: *Oyee Oye Ye Oyee*

• Title: *Oyee Oye Ye Oyee* •

Lyrics in Dagbaŋli: *Oyee oye ye oyee*
                    Oyaa yee mmazara gbamma yo yee
Lyrics in English: Oh yes, oh yes
                    Yes, my mother "Azara" handles me with care
Cultural Meaning: Motherhood is celebrated in *Tɔra* songs. As a way of bragging about their
    responsibilities in the household, some of the songs may touch on the love and care women
    give to their children. This song echoes this sentiment through the eyes of Azara's child, who
    is being used metaphorically to represent all children.
Form: Solo and chorus, repetitive form.
Performance Style: This is a simple solo and chorus performance. The lead/main cantor sings
    the whole song and the chorus repeats.
Scale: Hexatonic (six-note).
Melody: Melody follows the tonal inflections of spoken language with some variations. Change
    of tonal center from F to Bb in the second section of the song.
Rhythm: Rhythmic phrases follow speech rhythms of the spoken text.

Harmony: i. Use of parallel octaves between voices.
           ii. Overlapping of cantor and chorus.

Tonality: *Oyee oye ye oyee*
           1 1111 1 11 3
           Oyaa yee mmazara gbamma yo yee
           1 1   3 2   3 2 3 2 2 1   2

29. A Taste of the
Percussion Ensembles

As is true of most African music, there is no standard written notation system for Ghanaian dance-drumming. Rhythmic patterns played on drums and other percussion instruments may be interpreted as verbal texts or mnemonic vocable syllables.

I have decided to use only the mnemonic vocable syllables for my transcriptions in this book even though the verbal basis of some of the patterns may have significant cultural function and meaning.

The verbal texts of instruments will be included in the comprehensive instructional videos in later publications on how to teach all the phases of the dance-drumming types.

Learning African drumming procedures using mnemonic vocable syllables is the best and easiest way to engage and understand the "voices" of the instruments. One should be able to follow, enjoy and feel the percussion scores once the tones for the various instruments are memorized. In addition, the western staff notation rhythmic system has been adapted for the durational values of the syllables.

Southeastern Eυes Percussion Ensembles

Key to the Mnemonic Vocable Syllables of Southern Eυe Instruments

Instruments	Syllables	Key
Gakogui	*Ti*	A strike on top of the lower/bigger bell with a stick for low tone/sound.
	Ko	A strike on top of the smaller/upper bell with a stick for high tone/sound.
Atoke	*Ken*	Hold the instrument loosely in one hand and strike the side of the instrument close to the opening with an iron rod for a high metallic sound.
	Ka	Hold the instrument tightly in one hand and strike the side of the instrument close to the opening with an iron rod for a muted/soft sound.
Axatse	*Pa*	Hit the rattle against the thigh or play downwards.
	Ti	Hit the instrument against the palm or play upwards.
Kagan	*Ke/Ken*	Strike and bounce two sticks at the center of the drumhead for an open/loud sound.
	Kre	The same technique as *ke/ken* but with a grace note or two rapid sixteenth notes played in succession.

Kidi	*Ke/De*	Strike and bounce two sticks at the center of the drumhead for an open/loud sound.
	Ki/di	Hit and press the drumsticks at the center for a muted/stopped/soft tone.
Sogo	*To*	Press the head at the center with one stick and hit almost the same spot with a second stick for a sharp, high tone.
	Ke/De	Strike and bounce two sticks at the center of the drumhead for an open/loud sound, as in *Adzogbo*.
	Ki/Di	Hit, press and stop the drumhead's vibrations at the center for a soft/muted sound with sticks, as in *Adzogbo*.
	Gi/di	Hit and press the drumhead at the rim with the upper portion of the palms.
	Ga	Strike/bounce the full palm at the center of the head for a deep bass tone.
	Te/Ge/De/Ze	Strike/bounce and alternate the hands on the drumhead for an open/loud sound.
Gboba	*Gbla*	Strike the center of the head with one full palm and hit the wooden frame side of the drum simultaneously.
	Go/Do	Strike/bounce two straight sticks at the center of the drumhead for the lowest open sound.
	To	Press the head at the center with one stick and hit almost the same spot with a second stick for a sharp, high tone.
	Gi/Di	Hit, press and stop the drumhead at the center from vibrating for a soft/muted sound.
Atsimevu	*Dza*	Strike the center of the head with one full palm and hit the wooden frame side of the drum simultaneously.
	To/Ta	Press the head at the center with one stick and hit almost the same spot with a second stick for a sharp, high tone.
	Te/Ge/Be/De/Ze	Strike/bounce and alternate the sticks with the hand on the drumhead for an open/loud sound.
	Tre/Gre/Dre	Same as *te/ge/be/de* but with grace notes or a rapid succession of sixteenth notes.
	Gi/Di	Alternate the hand and the stick while hitting, pressing and stopping the drumhead at the center from vibrating for a soft/muted sound.
Agblɔvu	*Tɔ/Kɔ*	Strike/bounce two curved sticks on the center of the drumhead for the lowest open sound.
	Trɔ/Krɔ	The same technique as *tɔ/kɔ* but with a grace note or rapid succession of sixteenth notes.
	Gu	Hit, press and stop the drumhead at the center from vibrating for a soft/muted sound.
Atopani	*Kɔ/Tɔ*	Strike/bounce the center of the male drum, usually positioned on the left with curved sticks for a low, open sound.
	Di	Strike/bounce the center of the female drum, usually positioned on the right with curved sticks for a high, open sound.
Tavugã	*Gɔ/Dɔ*	Strike/bounce the center of the drumhead with straight/curved sticks for the lowest open sound.

Instruments	Syllables	Key
	Grɔ/Drɔ	The same technique as *gɔ/dɔ* but with a grace note or rapid succession of sixteenth notes.
Totodzi Kroboto	*To*	Strike/bounce the center of the drumhead with straight sticks for the lowest open sound.
	Dzi	Hit, press and stop the drumhead at the center from vibrating for a soft/muted sound.

Adzogbo

Atsiawɔwɔ Phase

A Feel of the Adzogbo Percussion Ensemble
Paschal Yao Younge
2010

FIGURE 29.1: *Adzogbo* Percussion Ensemble (continued on page 316)

2

Agbadza

Uutsɔtsɔ Phase

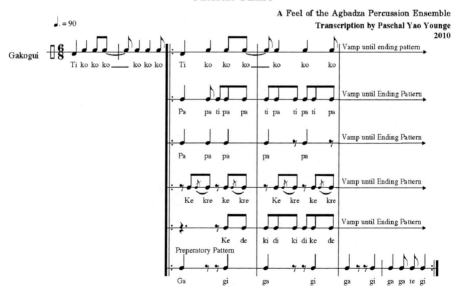

FIGURE 29.2: *Agbadza* Percussion Ensemble (continued on page 318)

2

Atibladekame

Uutsɔtsɔ Phase

A Feel of the Atibladekame Percussion Ensemble
Paschal Yao Younge
2010

FIGURE 29.3: *Atibladekame* Percussion Ensemble (continued on page 320)

2

Atrikpui

Atrilɔlɔ

A Feel of the Atrikpui Percussion Ensemble
Transcription by Paschal Yao Younge
2010

FIGURE 29.4: *Atrikpui* Percussion Ensemble (continued on page 321)

Atsiagbekɔ

Uulɔlɔ Phase

A Feel of the Atsiagbekɔ Percussion Ensemble
Transcription by Paschal Yao Younge
2010

FIGURE 29.5: *Atsiagbekɔ* Percussion Ensemble (continued on page 323)

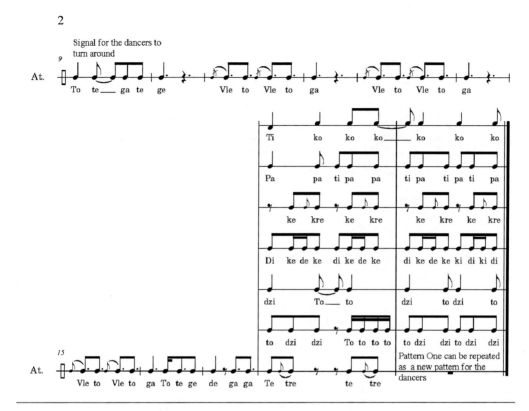

Gadzo

Atsiawɔwɔ Phase

A Feel of the Gadzo Percussion Ensemble
Transcription by Paschal Yao Younge
2010

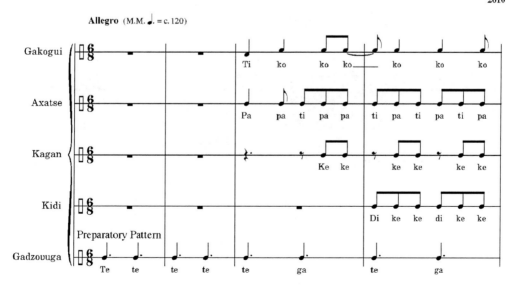

FIGURE 29.6: *Gadzo* Percussion Ensemble (continued on page 324)

2

Gahu
Uutsɔtsɔ

A Feel of the Gahu Percussion Ensemble
Transcription by Paschal Yao Younge
2010

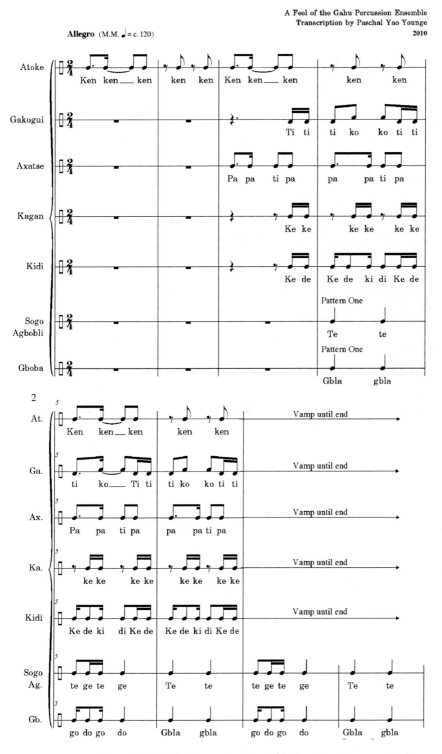

FIGURE 29.7: *Gahu* Percussion Ensemble (continued on page 326)

Central and Northern Eʋes Percussion Ensembles

Key to the Mnemonic Vocable Syllables of Central and Northern Eʋe Instruments

Instruments	Syllables	Key
Tigo	*Ti*	Strike the lower/bigger bell for the low tone/sound.
	Ko	Strike the smaller/upper bell for the high tone/sound.
Kretsiwa	*Ka*	Strike the circular ring against the body of the instrument for a sharp, metallic sound.
Gakogoe	*Ken*	Hold the instrument loosely in one hand and strike the

		side of the instrument close to the opening with an iron rod for a high, metallic sound.
	Ka	Hold the instrument tightly in one hand and strike the side of the instrument close to the opening with an iron rod for a muted/soft sound.
Akaye	*Sa*	Hold the elongated neck and hit/throw the instrument into the second, cupped hand.
	Shekeshe	Hold the instrument in the palms and agitate the beads. This technique is used for a rattle with beads woven outside the gourd, as in *Bɔbɔɔbɔ.*
Uuvi/ Asivui	*Pe/Pem*	Strike the drumhead with a relaxed upper palm and fingers. The root of the fingers should rest on the rim. This technique produces an open sound — the natural voice of the drum.
	Ba	Strike/bounce the full palm at the center of the head for a deep, bass tone.
	Pi	Instead of bouncing off as in *pe/pem,* the drummer presses against the head, producing a dead, muted or closed tone.
	Mada	Strike the same area as *pe/pem,* but with the fingers loose and detached from each other. Fingers must quickly bounce off the head as in *pe/pem* to produce a very high slap or smack tone.
Tamalin	*Du/Dum*	Strike/tap/bounce the palm on the head of the drum held perpendicular to the chest for an open, bass tone.
	Di	Hit but press against the head of the drum for a closed/soft tone.
Krokoto	*Kɔ/Tɔ*	Strike/bounce the center of the drumhead with curved sticks for the lowest open sound.
	Krɔ	The same technique as *kɔ/tɔ* but with a grace note or two rapid sixteenth notes played in succession.
	Gu/Du	Hit, press and stop the drumhead at the center from vibrating for a soft/muted sound.
Uuga/Havana	*Ba*	Strike/bounce the full palm at the center of the head for a deep, bass tone. The drum is sometimes raised from the ground for this tone.
	Be	Strike the drumhead with a relaxed upper palm and fingers. The root of the fingers should rest on the rim. This technique produces an open sound — the natural voice of the drum.
	Bi	Instead of bouncing off as in *be,* the drummer presses against the head, producing a dead, muted or closed tone.
	Pa/Pra	Strike the same area as *be* but with the fingers loose and detached from each other. Fingers must quickly bounce off the head as in *be* to produce a very high slap or smack tone.

Adevu

Adevu Phase

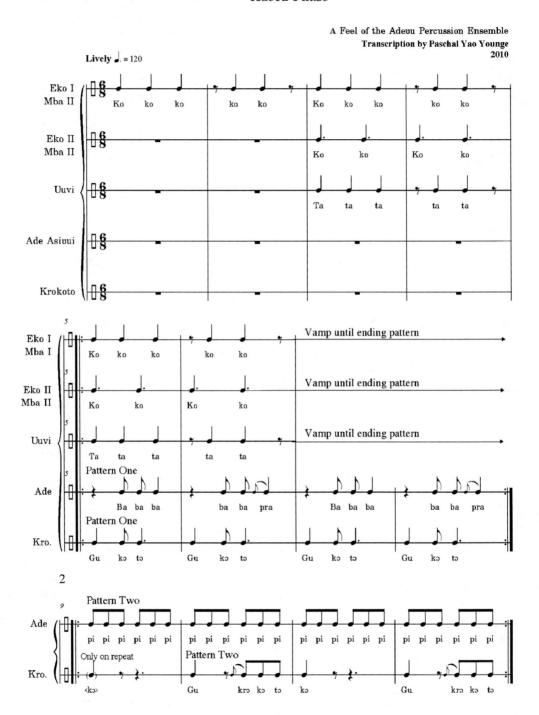

FIGURE 29.8: *Adevu* Percussion Ensemble

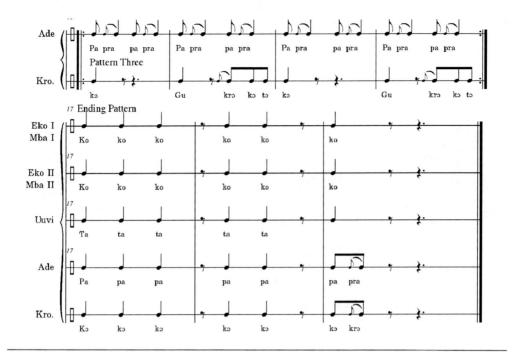

Bɔbɔɔbɔ

Uufofo

A Feel of the Bɔbɔɔbɔ Percussion Ensemble
Transcription by Paschal Yao Younge
2010

FIGURE 29.9: *Bɔbɔɔbɔ* Percussion Ensemble (continued on page 330)

Egbanegba

Egbanegba Phase

A Feel of the Egbanegba Percussion Ensemble
Transcription by Paschal Yao Younge
2010

FIGURE 29.10: *Egbanegba* Percussion Ensemble

Gbolo

Gbolo Akaye

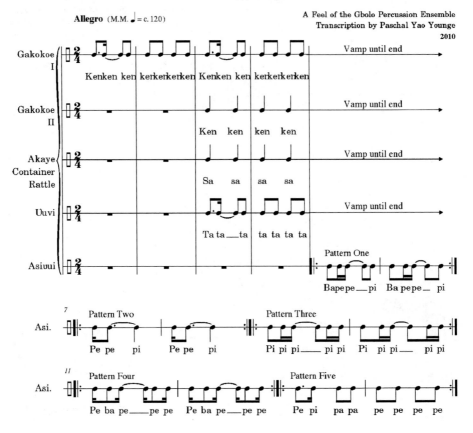

FIGURE 29.11: *Gbolo* Percussion Ensemble

Ga Percussion Ensembles

Key to the Mnemonic Vocable Syllables of Ga Instruments

Instruments	Syllables	Key
Ŋoŋo	Ko	Strike the body of the bell with a straight stick.
Dodompo	Ka	Strike the circular ring against the body of the instrument for a sharp, metallic sound.
Shekeshe	Shekeshe	Hold the instrument supported by a string around the neck and agitate the beads with the palms/fingers.
Maracas	Shekeshe	The rattling sound is produced by shaking and alternating two of the instruments held in both hands.
Kpanlongo Mi Atwreshie	Pe	Strike the drumhead with a relaxed upper palm and fingers. The root of the fingers should rest on the rim. This technique produces an open sound — the natural voice of the drum.
	Pi/Ti	Instead of bouncing off as in *pe*, the drummer presses against the head, producing a dead, muted or closed tone.

	Mada	Strike the same area as *pe* but with the fingers loose and detached from each other. Fingers must quickly bounce off the head as in *pe* to produce a very high slap or smack tone.
	Du/Dum	Strike/bounce the full palm at the center of the head for a deep, bass tone.
Tamalin	**Du/Dum**	Strike/tap/bounce the palm on the head of the drum, which is held perpendicular to the chest for an open bass tone.
	Di	Hit but press against the head of the drum for a closed/soft tone.
Gome	**Pe**	Strike the drumhead with a relaxed upper palm and fingers. The root of the fingers should rest on the rim. This technique produces an open sound — the natural voice of the drum.
	Du/Dum	Strike/bounce the full palm at the center of the head for a deep, bass tone.
	Pi/Ti	Instead of bouncing off as in *pe*, the drummer presses against the head with his/her heel, producing a dead, muted or closed tone.
	Mada	Strike the rim of the drumhead with fingers loose and detached from each other. Fingers must quickly bounce off the head to produce a very high slap or smack tone.

Gome

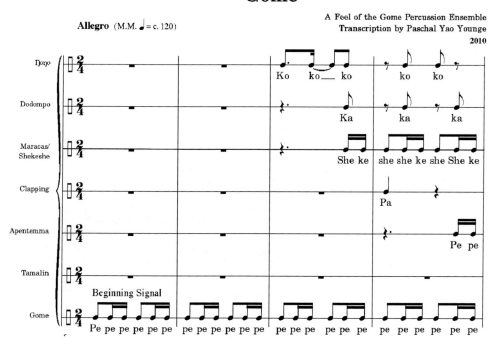

FIGURE 29.12: *Gome* Percussion Ensemble (continued on page 334)

Kolomashie

A Feel of the Kolomashie Percussion Ensemble
Transcription by Paschal Yao Younge
2010

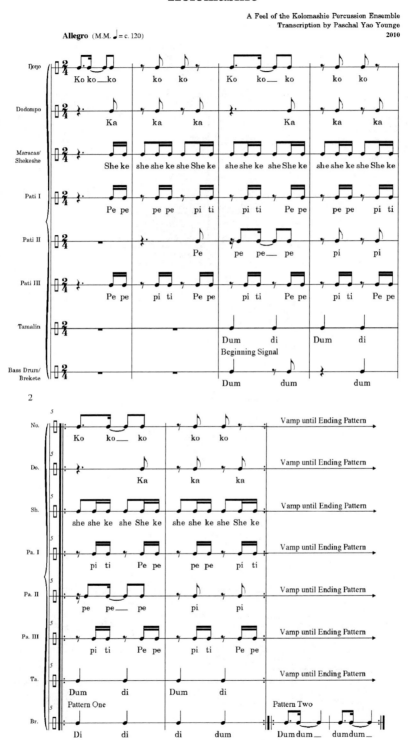

FIGURE 29.13: *Kolomashie* Percussion Ensemble (continued on page 336)

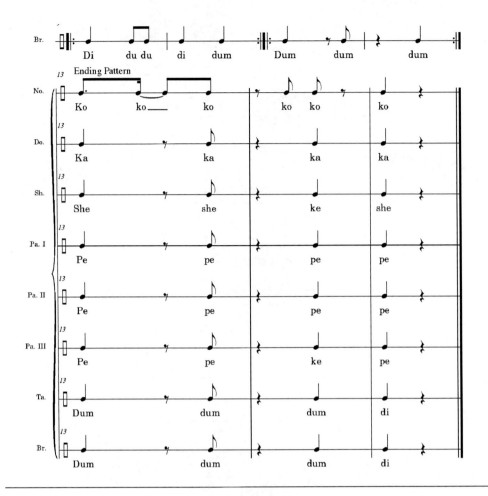

Kpanlongo

A Feel of the Kpanlongo Percussion Ensemble
Transcription by Paschal Yao Younge
2010

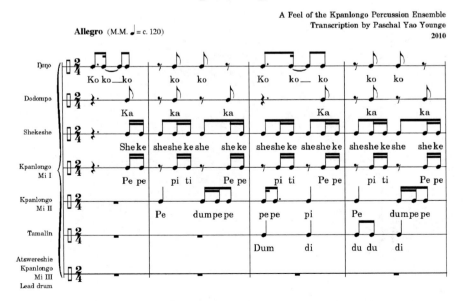

FIGURE 29.14: *Kpanlongo* Percussion Ensemble (continued on page 337)

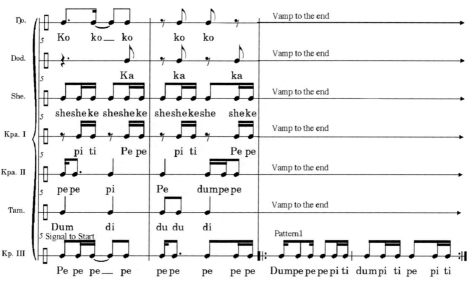

2

Akan Percussion Ensembles

Key to the Mnemonic Vocable Syllables of Akan Instruments

Instruments	Syllables	Key
Firikyiwa	*Ka*	Strike the circular ring against the body of the instrument for a sharp, metallic sound.

Aburukuwa	*De*	Strike and bounce two sticks at the center of the drumhead for an open/loud sound.
	Di	Hit but press the drumsticks at the center for a muted/stopped/soft tone.
Adawura *Kete Dawuro*	*Ken*	Hold the instrument loosely in one hand and strike the side of the instrument close to the opening with an iron rod for a high, metallic sound.
	Ka	Hold the instrument tightly in one hand and strike the side of the instrument close to the opening with an iron rod for a muted/soft sound.
Nnawuta	*Ti*	Strike the lower/bigger bell for a low tone/sound.
	Ko	Strike the smaller/upper bell for a high tone/sound.
Ntorowa	*Sa*	Shake but at the same time rotate the instrument in a circular motion in front of the body.
Tamalee	*Du/Dum*	Strike/tap/bounce the palm on the head of the drum, which is held perpendicular to the chest for an open bass tone.
	Di	Hit but press against the head of the drum for a closed/soft tone.
Petia	*To*	Press the head at the center with one stick and hit almost the same spot with a second stick for a sharp high tone.
	Te/De	Strike and bounce two sticks at the center of the drumhead for an open/loud sound.
Apentemma	*Pa/Ra*	Strike the drumhead with a relaxed upper palm and fingers. The root of the fingers should rest on the rim. This technique produces an open sound — the natural voice of the drum.
	Pi/Ri	Instead of bouncing off as in *pe*, the drummer presses against the head, producing a dead, muted or closed tone.
Sikyi	*Pe*	Strike the drumhead with a relaxed upper palm and fingers. The root of the fingers should rest on the rim. This technique produces an open sound — the natural voice of the drum.
	Pi	Instead of bouncing off as in *pe*, the drummer presses against the head, producing a dead, muted or closed tone.
	Du	Strike/bounce the full palm at the center of the head for a deep, bass tone.
	Mada	Strike the same area as in *pe*, but with the fingers loose and detached from each other. Fingers must quickly bounce off the head, as in *pe*, to produce a very high slap or smack tone.
Donno	*Gon/Goŋ*	A release of the tension produces a low or medium range sound. Glide tones for both the *gon/kon* tones are generated by immediately releasing the strings after a stroke.
	Kon/Koŋ	To generate a high sound, the player must squeeze or tighten the heads by pressing against the strings.
	Bam	The very lowest tone is scarcely used.
Kwadum	*Kɔ/Tɔ*	Strike/bounce the center of the drumhead with curved sticks for the lowest open sound.

	Krɔ	The same technique as *kɔ/tɔ* but with an additional grace note or two rapid sixteenth notes played in succession.
	Gu/Du	Hit, press and stop the drumhead at the center for a soft/muted sound.
Atumpan	*Kɔ/Tɔ*	Strike/bounce the center of the male drum, usually positioned on the left with curved sticks for a low, open sound.
	Krɔ	The same technique as *kɔ/tɔ*, as but with a grace note or two rapid sixteenth notes played in succession.
	Di/Gi	Strike/bounce the center of the female drum, usually positioned on the right with curved sticks for the high, open sound.
	Dri/Gri	The same technique as *di/gi*, but with a grace note or two rapid sixteenth notes played in succession.
	Ta	A gentle tap/stop made by pressing into the drum produces a soft/muted tone on the male drum.
	Ti	A gentle tap/stop made by pressing into the drum produces a soft/muted tone on the female drum.
	Grrr	A roll with two sticks on any of the drum heads.

Adowa

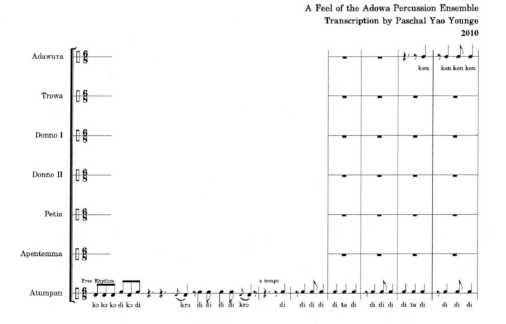

FIGURE 29.15: *Adowa* Percussion Ensemble (continued on page 340)

(continued on page 341)

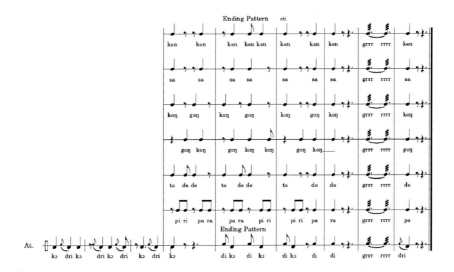

Asaadua

Asaadua Phase

A Feel of the Asaadua Percussion Ensemble
Transcription by Paschal Yao Younge
2010

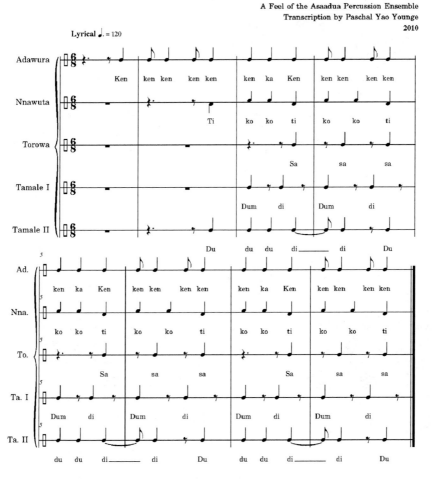

FIGURE 29.16: *Asaadua* Percussion Ensemble

Sikyi

Sikyi Phase

A Feel of the Sikyi Percussion Ensemble
Transcription by Paschal Yao Younge
2010

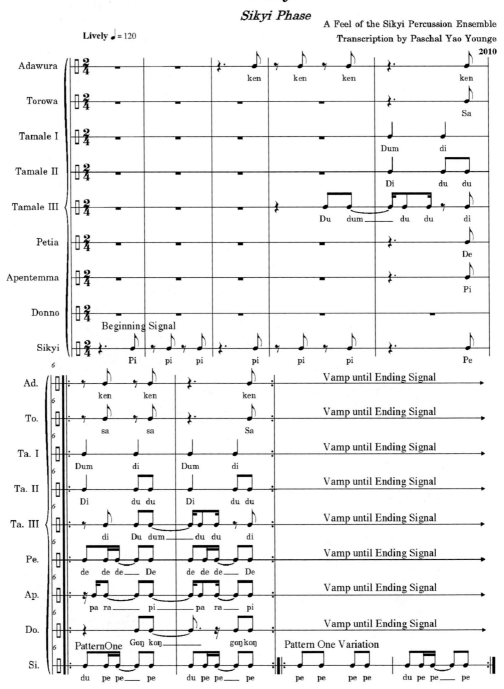

FIGURE 29.17: *Sikyi* Percussion Ensemble (continued on page 343)

Kete Percussion Ensemble

Apɛntɛ

A Feel of Kete Apɛntɛ Percussion Ensemble
Transcription by Paschal Yao Younge
2010

FIGURE 29.18: *Kete* Percussion Ensemble (continued on page 344)

Dagbamba Percussion Ensembles

Key to the Mnemonic Vocable Syllables of Dagbamba Instruments

Instruments	Syllables	Key
Saɣyelim	**Tsi/ki/tsi**	The rattling sound is produced by shaking and alternating two of the instruments held in both hands.
Luŋa	**Goŋ**	A release of the tension produces a low or medium range sound.
	Koŋ	To generate a high sound, the player must squeeze or tighten the heads by pressing against the strings.
	Bam	The very lowest tone is scarcely used.
		NB: Glide tones for both the *goŋ/koŋ* tones are generated by immediately releasing the strings after a stroke.
Guŋgoŋ	**Bam**	Strike/bounce the curved stick(s) at the center of the drumhead for an open bass tone.
	Bi	Hit, press and stop the stick(s).
	Pa	Strike the drumhead above the strings.
	Ta	Strike the drumhead above the snare with loose, cupped fingers.

Baamaaya

Baamaaya – Sochendi Phase

A Feel of the Baamaaya Percussion Ensemble

Transcription by Paschal Yao Younge
2010

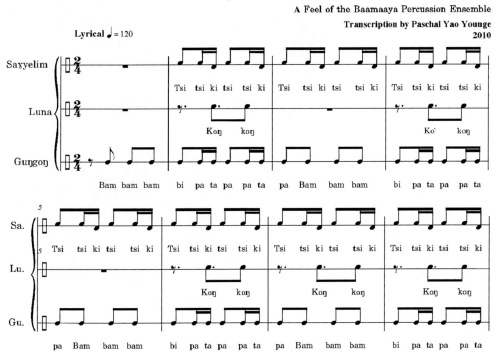

FIGURE 29.19: *Baamaaya* Percussion Ensemble (continued on page 346)

Bla

FIGURE 29.20: *Bla* Percussion Ensemble (continued on page 347)

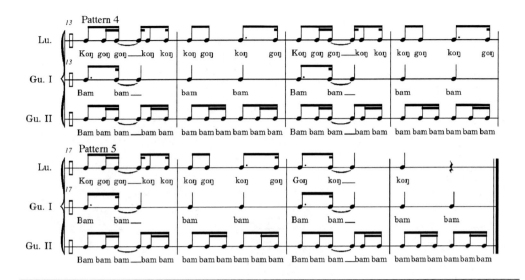

Jɛra

Jɛra - Sochendi Phase

A Feel of the Jɛra Percussion Ensemble
Transcription by Paschal Yao Younge
2010

FIGURE 29.21: *Jɛra* Percussion Ensemble (continued on page 348)

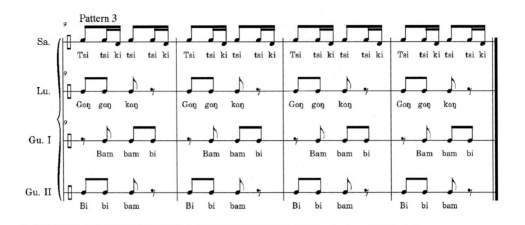

Tɔra

Zamandunia – Processional Phase

A Feel of the Tɔra Percussion Ensemble

Transcription by Paschal Yao Younge

2010

FIGURE 29.22: *Tɔra* Percussion Ensemble (continued on page 349)

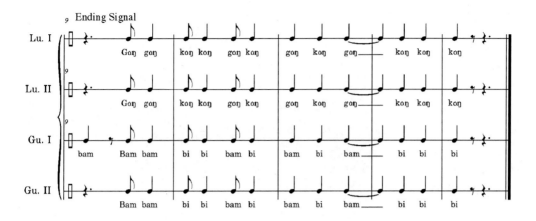

Part Seven.
Teaching African Music and Dance-Drumming

Notes to the Teacher/Educator

Part Seven of this book provides an overview of *Music and Dance Traditions of Ghana*. It discusses curriculum development in detail and also includes a comprehensive list of activities for the classroom. These activities are recommended when teaching any selected African musical type.

Teaching African dance-drumming should be an interdisciplinary endeavor. At different age levels, the selection of curriculum content materials should be guided by the goals and objectives of the teacher, the students, the school and the larger community as a whole.

A teacher may decide to develop a comprehensive curriculum incorporating all of the components discussed in this book to cover an entire academic year or semester. Or, a week or two of a school year may be set aside for investigating African cultures.

Whenever the opportunity is created in the classroom to learn about Africa in general, the performing arts—music in particular—should be the first subject area of choice. Teachers will find the various themes, content, theory, philosophy and processes outlined in this document to be very useful in multicultural music education.

30. Components of an African Music Dance-Drumming Curriculum

In developing materials and strategies for teaching African music, it is important for the teacher to: i. Identify the particular ethnic music culture; ii. know the components of the particular music culture — the ideas about music, music and belief systems, aesthetics of music, contexts of music, history of music, social organization of music, repertoires of music style, genres, texts, transmission, movement, composition, material culture and instruments (Titon 1996, 7–12); and iii. know the student age group and suitability of content material.

A general introduction to and foundation of the African music curriculum should therefore address and discuss in detail some generalizations of the music that identify it as African. Broadly, these features are as follows.

1. Functional and Nonfunctional Uses of Musical Arts

African dance-drumming performances are related to the following events:

life cycle events: birth, outdooring, naming, twin rites, initiation, wedding, marriage, death and funerals, etc.;
economic activities: girls hawking, men fishing, farming, herding, hunting, etc.;
religious activities: private/individual worship, public/communal worship, healing, agricultural rituals, etc.;
ceremonial and political activities: festivals, state assemblies, meetings, installation and destoolment of chiefs, state processions and funerals, etc.; and
recreational and leisure activities: storytelling, games, etc.

2. Organization and Social Control of Musical Events

When Africans come together for any musical event, several factors are involved:

spontaneous and voluntary participation;
obligation to perform due to social inclination, responsibility, or economic activity; and
age and gender groups, musical groups, occupational groups, religious groups, warrior organizations, and royal court associations, etc.

3. Performer-Audience Relationships

In African communities, there is a close relationship between performers and audience, since musical events usually involve a whole community.

When a performance becomes a group activity guided by social, religious or political affiliations, observers are culturally bound to show outward dramatic expression of feeling: shouts, yells, or grunts to show appreciation, singing with chorus, dancing, and clapping if permitted by the group, raising two fingers towards a dancer to show encouragement, and putting a piece of cloth or wiping the face of a dancer to show approval. Negative expressions indicating disapproval may be due to inappropriate costumes, instruments, drumming, singing, and other aesthetic variables.

4. Instrumental Resources

There are five sound sources available for dance-drumming:

idiophones: melodic types include xylophones and hand pianos; non-melodic types include shaken, struck/concussion, scrapped, friction and stamped instruments;
membranophones: closed drums, frame drums, gourd drums, cylindrical drums and open drums;
chordophones: musical bows, zithers, lutes, harps, and lyres;
aerophones: flutes, reed pipes, horns and trumpets (Nketia 1974, pp. 67–107); and
the voice, which remains the most used and most important sound source in African music traditions.

5. Intrinsic Properties of Music

The elements and components of style (organization of sound) vary from ethnic group to ethnic group, including:

the tonal organization: scales, melody, harmony and polyphony;
the rhythmic organization: divisive, additive, hemiola, spacing of parts, cross rhythms, interplay of parts, and use of timeline, strict and free rhythms and syncopation; and
form and structure: binary, ternary, call and response, solo and chorus, declamations, chants, etc.

6. Music and Related Art Forms

The African music aesthetic can be summarized as the interdependency and appropriate use of several art forms. A performance is seen to be a closely knit representation of several artistic variables. Therefore, there is a strong connection between:

music (elements of style) and dance/movement;
music and drama — music and narrative drama, music and ceremonial drama and music and dance drama;
music and language; and
music and visual art forms—costumes, masks, makeup, objects at dance venues, and decorations on musical instruments.

7. Aesthetics in African Music Events

Just what makes African music events unique? What are the aesthetic values in sub–Saharan African cultures that guide the nature of musical performances and norms of beauty? Should non–Africans search for those values and concepts in order to better appreciate and understand the musical traditions? Answers to the above questions are multifaceted.

Levi (1970), discussing the importance of the humanities in school curriculums, reiterates the aesthetic learning and appreciation of the arts as avenues for "communication, creation, continuity, and criticism" (Smith 1992, 54).

Interpretation and understanding of African musical events in order to achieve these above objectives must be guided by the following pedagogical questions as suggested by Smith (p. 54):

— Who made the music (participants)?
— How was it made (organization of music)?
— When was it made (function of music)?
— For whom was it made (audience)?
— What is its message or meaning (symbolism)?
— What is its style (organization of sounds)?
— What is the quality of experience it affords?
— What was its place in the culture in which it was made?
— What is its place in the culture or society of today?
— What peculiar problems does it present to understanding and appreciation?

If African musical events should help in "shaping the self in positive ways and providing humanistic insight" (Smith 56), and also provide "moral education and constitutive powers to the young" (57), then, it is relevant that teachers come to terms with its ways of aesthetic experience.

Aesthetic appreciation and understanding is a cultural phenomenon in which varied cultural elements of a society or group of people determine the models for evaluation. In this direction, western music aesthetic values cannot be used in determining the meaning and nature of so-called African music.

In addition to the "generalizations" of the music discussed in previous paragraphs, there are other conventions of musical practice which are of significant aesthetic value. Any sound, regular or irregular, pitched or unpitched, is musical to the African depending on the context of its usage and cultural location. Also, the selection of materials to make instruments is very important to an African musician. Certain types of wood or trees are preferred over others. This is a cultural phenomenon. The techniques of production or sounds produced on musical instruments are also of great importance and concern to the music-maker.

These sounds have to agree with the accepted tradition as well as the playing technique employed. Instrumentalists may therefore attach objects to their instruments for tone color. Sometimes, broken bells are preferred over unbroken ones.

Techniques of playing drums differ from instrument to instrument. The four techniques generally utilized are: hand technique, stick technique (single or double), stick and hand technique, and stick, hand, and armpit technique. The stick technique, depending on the type of drum, will either use "straight and round sticks with or without a knob at the end, or curved or slightly bent sticks, with weight of the stick depending on the drum" (Nketia 1974). Techniques for using hands in playing may involve using a cupped hand, a palm, palm and fingers or the base of the palm in different positions on the drumhead. The stick, hand, and armpit techniques using the squeeze and release approaches are for drums with strings.

Drums and other instruments are used in three different ways: the signal, speech, and dance modes. The signal mode of drumming is recognized as short, repetitive, nonlinear rhythms or a broken series of drumbeats played at one level of pitch (Nketia 1963b). Usually, this type of drumming is reserved for political systems in Africa.

Some of the signal drums found in the courts of the Akan chiefs of Ghana include the *susubiribi, petepire, adedenkura, nkrawiri,* and *mmidie.* Other instruments are also used for signal purposes. The *gakogui* (double bell) is used among the Eʋe to transmit messages. Before one can interpret signal messages, one might need to already know the text in order to be able to recognize it when played.

Speech drum sounds are interpreted as verbal or burden texts, which are characterized by a steady flow of beats following the rhythm of speech and operating within a two-tone framework. Instrumental sounds recognized as speech utterances are therefore avenues for communication. Some of the principal "talking drums" in Ghana include: the *bata, koso, apinti*, and *dundum* of the Yoruba of Nigeria; the *atumpan* of the Akan; the *gyile* of the Dagarti; and the Eʋe *agblɔvu* and *atsimevu*.

Dance interpretation is by far the most common purpose for drumming. These rhythms are organized both linearly and multi-linearly. Unlike the signal and speech modes, dance-drumming combines a variety of instruments.

The popular practice in West Africa is the employment of a basic rhythmic framework, the timeline, which guides the whole performance (Nketia 1974). Combinations of drums and other instruments for the dance vary from place to place. Generally, however, instruments in dance or dance-drumming take the following roles: master or lead drum, support or response instruments, basic rhythm enforcers, and the basic rhythmic line (timeline). The roles of the master drum and timeline are the most essential in any ensemble.

It is pertinent that the above factors be critically examined in order to understand any musical activity. An omission of even the smallest element may lead to the misinterpretation of the whole performance. African-Ghanaian musical traditions and other facets of the culture can only be understood if the terms, words, and symbols used are mutually understood.

The perception of the above general characteristics and aesthetics may also vary from ethnic group to ethnic group. Each ethnic group prefers their own performance practices that make their musical events unique. In Ghana, for example, the different ethnic groups may have identical traditional perspectives about dance-drumming but may differ in specific organizational structures depending on their own specific situations.

Musical events in Ghana are perceived as performance activities and are interactive and communicative social processes. The musical elements of style, dance and drama are treated as inseparable activities. Several movement centers are inherent in performing art events while polyrhythmic interdependency forms the basis of all dance-drumming performances.

In addition to these perspectives, the shifting of rhythmic relationships is paramount within a given rhythmic cycle and a steady inner pulse is maintained throughout a given performance, especially in dance-drumming or music organized in strict or metered rhythm.

The joy derived from any musical activity stems from the understanding that any performance is a play activity in which improvisation, re-composition, or creative performance is paramount. This creative performance or creativity in any musical event is organized within the concept of melody, text, rhythm, form, polyphony and timbre in order to achieve the desired goals.

To develop a curriculum that reflects the above features of African-Ghanaian "music" is to provide learning situations that recognize music and other performing arts as cultural expressions. Activities should be related to the history, political systems, commerce, and other social and cultural activities.

Drumming, singing, dance and other dramatic enactment, when treated as one phenomenon, are activities that play a key role in cultivation of music in Ghanaian societies. A musical performance as a social event can be justified aesthetically by the integration of these variables.

Generally, drumming in Ghanaian societies is integrated with dance and dramatic gestures or postures. Apart from setting the stage for the release of emotions, drumming can also be used as "a social and artistic medium of communication" (Nketia 1974, 207).

African dance is a "language, a mode of expression, which addresses itself to the mind, through the heart, using related and significant movements which have their basic counterparts in our everyday activities, to express special and real life experiences in rhythmic sequences to musical and poetic stimuli" (Mawere Opoku 1968, 11).

The dance can be used to express certain behaviors such as: social behavior, communicative behavior, educational behavior, religious behavior, corrective behavior, economic behavior, psychological behavior, poetic behavior, political behavior, and artistic behavior. At the same time dance can show a person's level of enjoyment.

Singing in Africa, apart from its purely musical function, serves as an avenue for verbal communication that reflects both personal and social experiences. Africans perform cradle, reflective, historical, philosophical and topical songs in their everyday lives (Nketia 1974, 189–205). Songs may be sung as part of a musical event or to accompany labor.

The African music curriculum will rely on drumming, singing and dance activities. However, to cater to all the concepts, processes and characteristics involved in this multifaceted tradition, the basic components of an integrated African music dance-drumming curriculum should include activities in the following areas:

appreciation, focused or guided listening;
drumming;
singing;
movement and dance;
interactive storytelling;
games and physical education;
social studies;
visual arts; and
drama, pantomime and other theatrical activities.

Topics to be discussed under each component may vary and overlap. Appreciation, focused and guided listening activities provide the foundation for the whole curriculum, and so should precede all other components. Below are suggested topics around which the teacher can organize the various activities. The determination of focus and duration of each lesson or activity is left to the teacher.

Appreciation and Focused and Guided Listening Activities

A general objective underlying these activities will be to expose students to the various features and elements of a particular musical style or type and the people who perform it. Activities should be centered around, but not limited to, the following topics:

i.   Sounds: Introduce students to the sounds of the selected musical type.
ii. Function: Introduce students to the functions of the music among the people.
iii. Relation: Introduce students to the relationship between music, dance, drama and other cognate art forms.
iv. Interaction: Introduce students to the interaction and dialogue between participants—drummers, dancers and singers, etc.
v.   Instruments: Introduce students to the instruments of the ensemble.

Materials required for effective implementation of the above activities should include: maps of Africa and African regions (east, central, west, north and south), maps of the country from which the selected music comes, video and audio recordings of the music in authentic settings, photographs of instruments and costumes, and instruments of the ensemble and other related artifacts.

Drumming Activities

African drumming has been thought by many to be only the manipulation of membranes. Drumming is therefore seen to have no other significant purpose then to create an avenue for motor behavior and personal enjoyment. There are, however, many valuable aspects of African culture and musical concepts that can be learned through in-depth study of African drumming procedures. The focus for drumming activities should include:

i. Instruments: Introduce students to the types of instruments of the ensemble — aerophones, idiophones, chordophones, and membranophones, etc.
ii. Techniques: Introduce students to playing techniques on instruments.
iii. Modes: Introduce students to the three modes of drumming — speech, dance and signal.
iv. Concepts: Introduce students to the rhythmic concepts in African drumming — creative performance, interpolation, staggered rhythms, repetition, timeline, cross-sets, additive and divisive rhythms, hemiola and cross rhythms, etc.
v. Construction: Introduce students to the various methods of constructing instruments.
vi. Substitution: Introduce students to non–African instruments that can be used as substitutes for the traditional ones.

The teaching materials recommended for these activities are the same as those for the appreciation activities, with the addition of transcriptions.

Singing Activities

African folk songs generally relate to the day-to-day occurrences in the lives of the people. It is therefore essential to emphasize the meaning of the lyrics, function of the songs and, especially, the pronunciation of the words.

Activities for teaching songs should be guided by Nketia's observation that "the treatment of the song as a form of speech utterance arises not only from stylistic considerations or from consciousness of the analogous features of speech and music; it is also inspired by the importance of the song as an avenue for verbal communication, a medium for creative verbal expressions which can reflect both personal and social experiences" (Nketia 1974, 189).

Other features of vocal music, such as the themes of songs (historical, philosophical, topical, etc.) should also be addressed. Topics for singing activities should include:

i. Meaning: Introduce students to the various themes and meanings of songs.
ii. Concepts: Introduce students to general musical concepts in vocal music — scales, melody, form, rhythm and harmony, etc.
iii. Singing styles: Introduce students to singing styles specific to Africa — call and response, solo and chorus refrain, declamations, and voice masking, etc.
iv. Pronunciation: Introduce students to appropriate pronunciation of words and terms.
v. Singing: Help students learn and perform the songs.

Materials for the above activities should be those recommended in previous activities in addition to language and pronunciation guides.

Movement and Dance Activities

Activities for movement and dance lessons should incorporate elements that reflect dance as a medium for communication and as a form of motor action. To the African, as observed by

Mawere Opoku, "the dance is a language, a mode of expression which addresses itself to the mind through the heart, using related and significant movements which have their basic counterparts in everyday activities" (Opoku 1968, 11). Focus therefore should include:

i.   Symbolism: Introduce students to understanding the symbolic and proverbial gestures and movements in selected dance forms.
ii. Arrangements: Introduce students to the spatial arrangement of dance rings and dance formations.
iii. Relation: Help students dance to the musical type.
iv. Creation: Help students to create their own dances (choreographies) using the vocabulary of dances learned, etc.

Appreciation teaching materials are also recommended for these activities.

Interactive Storytelling Activities

Stories are imaginative dwelling places where animals, birds, trees, rocks and humans are regarded as the same species. In African stories, rocks may have eyes, ears, mouths and may even talk. Likewise, trees may walk, attend town meetings and install chiefs. Storytelling sessions in African cultures provide opportunities for families to get together. The history and traditions of a particular culture can be learned through stories.

Musical activities are essential components of African stories. Songs in particular serve important functions in stories:

songs emphasize the theme of the story;
songs make the story more interesting;
songs create another avenue for music education; and
songs create opportunity for socialization.

In addition, music in storytelling in general can create avenues for dance, drama and theater education. Important issues to consider when integrating African stories into the music curriculum are:

i.   Situation: Introduction or opening of the story — Do you know how to situate your story? Have you explained the rules to the students?
ii. Telling the story: Are you telling your stories with the help of props? Are you reading the story from a book? Make your story as dramatic as possible.
iii. Interludes: Have you provided opportunities for songs, drumming and dance in your stories?
iv. The recapitulation: The ending or conclusion of the story should become the title of the story; were you able to achieve this goal?
v.   Themes: Through questions students should be able to identify the major themes and lessons from the story.

Games and Physical Education Activities

Games have been a part of many cultures for thousands of years. They have been used to bring whole communities together, to teach history and values and to provide entertainment. Learning African games provides the opportunity to teach traditional and contemporary customs, beliefs, values and culture as a whole.

In an integrated African music curriculum, games help students with their social skills, problem-solving skills and musical development (Orlando 1993, 5). Games provide a means for children to learn social and moral behavior.

Traditional education in Africa, sometimes referred to as "socialization," is a cultural mechanism through which culture is taught. Individuals are prepared to act within what the society accepts as "norms of behavior." African children up to the age of ten have the opportunity to play alone, in groups, and in and around the house. "They may imitate adults' everyday activities in early stages but in later years of childhood create their own games. Most of the games are derived from and lead towards the social, cultural and economic activities" (Egblewogbe 1993, 27).

These activities include: economic —farming, hunting, fishing, building, pottery, and selling; domestic —cooking, caring for children, parenting, and feeding a baby; religious— sacrifices to idols, praying at shrines, performing the role of diviner, and possessing dances; funerary rites— singing funeral songs and imitating funeral rites; drumming; dancing; singing lullabies; and imitating adult dances, etc.

Music in games is very unique and plays an important part in African traditional education. Musical games serve as a means of learning the rules of moral behavior, learning a language, and learning musical skills and dance movements. Any music or dance performance during games creates a "great force of socialization" (Egblewogbe 1975, 42). Important steps to note when integrating musical games into the curriculum are:

i. Identification: Identify the game. Is the game appropriate for the age level of the class?
ii. Description: Describe the games. Do you have sufficient background on the game?
iii. Obeying the rules: Know the rules of the game. Do you know how to start and end the game? Do you know how one wins or loses a game?
iv. Skills: What skills are developed during the games? Are they musical, social, or dance skills?

Social Studies Activities

Social studies is an interdisciplinary and multidimensional approach to teaching about citizenship. Teaching social studies serves four main purposes:

i. Future citizens may learn about cultural heritage.
ii. Future citizens can learn to think and process information skillfully and intelligently.
iii. Future citizens can learn about human behavior.
iv. It develops in future citizens a commitment to act in accordance with what they know and believe (Welton and Mallam 1992, 17).

Citizenship education has been the cornerstone of African oral traditional forms of education. The subject area has grown over the last decade to include "history, geography, economics, political science, anthropology, sociology, psychology, archaeology, cultural anthropology, medicine and law" (Welton and Mallam 1992, 3).

The United States National Endowment for the Arts believes that an integrated arts program:

i. Provides a more complete understanding of civilizations being studied.
ii. Provides opportunities to make critical assessment and evaluation.
iii. Offers students opportunities to express their own creativity.

    iv.   Offers effective alternative means of communicating new verbal and nonverbal thoughts and feelings (Maxim 1995, 398).

Social studies integrates the arts using three complementary perspectives:

    i.   Students examine and respond to creative works already produced.
    ii.   Students reproduce the art product of a culture.
    iii.   Students create art as an expressive or informative medium of communication (Maxim 1995, 399).

Social studies can be another effective subject area in which to teach African performing arts and culture. To the African, music and dance is a normal part of life. Everyday experiences are dramatized through movement, gestures, and organized dance activities.

Exposure to traditional musical situations is perhaps the most fitting vehicle for teaching about the lifestyles and beliefs of various African groups. African heritage and traditions can be learned though various social studies activities that include some sort of music.

Singing activities provide opportunities for creating and recreating new songs. Activities involving instruments emphasize playing and construction of instruments. Movement activities involve creative dances. Dramatic enactment can also include pantomime, poetry and other verbal art forms.

In the African music curriculum, social studies activities include music and dance linked to other subject areas. Instructional themes and activities should be geared towards African human experiences and how these experiences shape Africans' lives and contribute to global education. Cross-cultural or intercultural methods should be encouraged in the classroom.

When discussed in the social studies classroom, the functionality of African music and dance, its purpose in the lives of the people, its concepts and processes, performance practices, instrumental resources, form and structure and related art forms, create another avenue for students to study global issues and diverse human values.

Visual Arts Activities

The famed unity of the arts in African performance suggests a sensible approach in which one medium is never absolutely emphasized over others. Sculpture is not the central art, but neither is the dance, for both depend on words and music and even dreams and divination. Music, dance, and visual objects are all important, separate or together [Thompson 1974, xii].

Although the origin of traditional African visual art and the names of the original creators of the designs and styles are unknown, visual arts remain an integral part of the cultural life of the people. The sophistication of the visual arts produced by the Akans, Dagbamba, Eʋes and Ga-Dangmes has been documented since the 11th century (Anene/Brown 1966, 245). Visual art forms are developed and appreciated today for their functional and aesthetic qualities.

The integration of African performing and visual arts into daily events creates room for its place in the music curriculum. The use of visual art or objects of art in traditional and contemporary African societies depends on three important factors: i. the musical type being performed, ii. the nature of the dance, and iii. the requirement of the dramatic enactment.

There are five categories of visual arts that are generally used during musical performances: i. costumes, ii. masks, iii. makeup, iv. sculpture or molded objects at performance arena, and v. geometric figures or decorations on musical instruments.

COSTUMES. Africans have specific dress for the various musical situations because the dances involved are of a varied nature. The dances are both simple and complex in concept and use such elements as shaking, stamping, stooping, leaping, lifting, and tumbling of the body.

The dances are perceived as cultural behaviors which are used to teach and reinforce cultural patterns, and they call for varied costumes (Lynne Hanna 1973, 165–174).

Some of the dances may be vigorous and might require very tight costumes, while others are graceful and need free-flowing attire. The level of diversity in the dances means that specific costumes are required for the effective realization of the movements.

Ghanaians, for example, conceive of the costume as part of the entire dance mode and as additions to or extensions of the various parts of the body. The appropriate costume enhances or dictates the flow of the dances. The physical requirements of the particular dance thus determine the type of costume.

Costumes generally range from raffia skirts, fiber pants and animal hides to those made from textile materials. Music-making is not limited to musical groups. Occupational groups such as hunters, butchers and fishermen also perform music while wearing their work attire. Costumes in Ghanaian musical situations can also be seen as bodily extensions or appendages. One can identify them as ox tails, whiskers, horsetails, handkerchiefs, wooded or real swords, spears and guns.

Costumes in musical performances, apart from the above functions, can also be used simply as a means of identification or creating a message through the symbolism of colors, shapes or details of design.

MASKS. Originally, masked musical scenes were exclusively religious, as the masks represented gods. Contemporary masks in musical activities represent various features such as ancestral spirits, mythological beings, totems and gods, with nonrepresentational masks, now common in most places.

Masks could be seen from the above as living art forms defined by the crucial presence of music and dance. Understanding the significance and role of each mask at a performance adds to the meaning of the total production.

MAKEUP. Body painting and a variety of stylistic hair designs are used in most music and dances in Ghana. These features may convey a message, maybe a means of identifying or differentiating dramatic roles or characters, or may signify something spiritual (as in religious performances).

In most communities, puberty rites for girls are well celebrated with music. The initiates are usually oiled and painted before the dance performance. In some social musical situations, as in the Eʋe *Adzogbo* and the Akan *Adowa,* there is special makeup for the dancers' hair. Special geometric designs in varied colors (red, white and blue) are painted on the bodies of priests and priestesses of the Ga people of Ghana during their *Homowo* harvest festival celebrations.

SCULPTURE OR MOLDED OBJECTS AT PERFORMANCE ARENA. Other art objects can be seen at musical arenas representing ancestral spirits and gods. In the twin rite celebration, *Eʋewɔwɔ*, of the Eʋe people, two wooden carved replicas of two humans representing the sexes of the twins are seen in the arena of performance. Dance clubs of the Anlɔ Eʋe of Ghana have specific emblems which are displayed in the form of sculptured objects during performances.

GEOMETRIC FIGURES OR DECORATIONS ON MUSICAL INSTRUMENTS. Objects of art can also be seen engraved, attached, or as geometric or sculptured figures on musical instruments. The Akans of Ghana believe the *atumpan* drums are made of *tweneboa*, tree harbor spirits, and so consecrate the drums by giving them "eyes." Each of the "eyes" has two small squares crossed with diagonal lines which mark the spot for offerings. Iron jingles, *akasaa*, are also attached to the male *atumpan* drums.

Musical instruments also wear special cloths. The white cloth seen on most state drums in Ghana symbolizes purity and victory. Other materials, like leaves and palm branches, may also be attached to Ghanaian musical instruments.

It is apparent that in Ghanaian musical situations, complex values form the basis for judgment and appreciation. Music performance analysis, as observed by Regula Burchardt Oureshi (1987, 56–86), should include the following essential requirements: "accessibility to tests of verification, replications and comparison and usability and manipulability in the context of a broader analytical perspective that includes nonmusical variables."

African music, being a contextual organization closely related to the authentic traditional practices of the people, can be understood if viewed along with the visual arts. Objects of art, though not as dynamic as music and dance, are nonetheless significant, meaningful symbols (Nketia 1974, 226–228).

Categories of visual arts in the fine art domain of the music curriculum should include i. pottery art, ii. sculpture, and iii. decorative art and other paraphernalia (Fosu 1994).

Pottery art, which is probably the earliest form of artistic expression, continues to be the most viable creative work of art in Ghanaian traditional society. Pottery is comprised of hand-made domestic, prestige and ceremonial pots.

Domestic pots, which are simple in construction with little or no decoration, are used for storage, cooking, bathing, brewing, drinking and serving. The wealthy upper class and the aristocrats use prestige pots, which may also be used for the same purposes as the domestic pots, but are more elegant. Ceremonial pots are decorated in geometric, abstract and figurative relief motifs. These motifs are often symbolic and range from simple to intricate combinations of linear motifs (Fosu 1994, 4).

Sculpture art includes terra-cotta portrait statues that are symbolic representative images of the deceased. The statues represent rulers, warriors, the elite and nobility. Features of these portraits are a fusion of abstract and naturalistic features that conveys the symbolic relationship between the spirit world and the living.

Other sculptures include commemorative female statues made of wood with characteristic details of the symbolic ideals of physical beauty, fertility and motherhood; and metal sculptures, referred to as "gold weights," which provide commentary on every aspect of life as well as social and political activities. Almost every gold weight is a literal illustration of a popular proverb, a parable or a maxim with some profound interpretations.

Indeed, the full aesthetic appreciation of the authoritative dignity of the traditional ruler is observed within the total interplay of every item displayed at one particular moment of pageantry. These decorative art forms, "glittering weapons, the gilded staffs, the brightly colored costumes, the uniforms, and other royal paraphernalia," in addition to music and dance, enhance the splendor of the royal person (Fosu 1994, 32). Royalty decorations represent the best in the artistic production of traditional Ghana. Most of the motif patterns and colors are for decorative and symbolic purposes.

Fabric decorations are by far the most decorative Ghanaian visual arts. *Batik*, *kente* and *adinkra* cloths are the most common fabrics made in Ghana. According to Fosu (1994), a typical *kente* fabric is woven in narrow strips. Each strip contains a series of bands designed in intricate multicolored geometric patterns alternated with other bands of simple line designs in contrasting coordinated colors for harmonious effect. The result is a smashing display of brilliant colors in joyous combination with abstract patterns of great sophistication.

Adinkra is made up of printed graphic symbols of geometric motifs on a background of white, rust-brown or black fabric. Motifs are arranged in patterns to convey specific messages. Decorative fabrics can also be seen in the diverse traditional dresses worn by the people. These dresses include *fugu* and *binŋmaa* (*batakari*), which are typical of the Dagbamba people of northern Ghana.

Other decorative arts include beads, rattan weaving, ceramics, calabash carving, leather tanning, wooden and raffia toys, rubber toys, metal fabrication, blacksmithing, gold-smithing, sandals, and stools, which are common household furniture and are also used for ceremonial purposes.

Other paraphernalia that enhance the traditional scene are umbrellas for chiefs, saddles for the horses of the chiefs from northern Ghana, traditional boots, ceremonial swords and linguistic staffs. In the above-mentioned visual art forms, when properly used, the meanings of the symbols add to the appreciation, enjoyment and understanding of the music and dance. They symbolize the beauty of the Ghanaian society in which they are found.

See Figure 30.1 on page C-15 of the color insert.

FIGURE 30.2: Traditional *Kente* and printed textile cloths worn by women from Dzodze (2006).

Drama, Pantomime and Other Theatrical Activities

It is evident in all human existence and in the fields of language arts that all cultures communicate some aspect of their social and cultural experiences to audiences in one form or another. This process is called drama and theater (Bame 1991, 61).

Drama is based on several modes of verbal and nonverbal communication. The choice of presentation (gestures, pantomime or a linguistic medium) depends on the nature of the activity and the culture or both. African dramatic and theatrical mediums therefore vary from ethnic group to ethnic group due to the varied nature of African people and their experiences.

Dramatic elements abound in Ghanaian festivals, funeral celebrations, ritual ceremonies, dancing, and storytelling, etc. In each of the above traditional events, dramatic enactments provide enjoyment to the participants and audience in addition to influencing their thoughts, values and attitudes.

Drama is yet another tool used by Ghanaians to teach aspects of their culture. Rediscovery of oneself as a member of a community, as well as the basic way of life, is reinforced through drama and theatrical activities.

The social system, sense of community, and overall attitude of belonging to a particular community is further enhanced through traditional and contemporary forms of drama and theater. Traditional and contemporary Ghanaian drama and theatrical activities come in various forms such as traditional plays, community theater, and folk operas. These forms are exhibited in ceremonial drama, narrative drama and dance drama (Nketia 1974).

Ceremonial drama is associated with social, ritual and ceremonial events, and it follows specific routines. Narrative drama combines dialogue, music, dance and pantomime. Dance drama is by far the most elaborate in Ghana since it also permeates the other forms, especially in ceremonial events.

Dance dramatic enactments are expressed through music (drumming, singing and playing of other instruments), dance, poetry, pantomime, gestures and movements. Speech or verbal dialogue is less emphasized and expressive movement and actions are highlighted.

Nketia identifies three categories of dance drama in Ghana. These categories are found in funeral celebrations and public worship (Nketia 1974). Funeral drama or memorial drama can be seen at the funeral celebration, where episodes from the lives of the dead, their social relations, and their beliefs and values are enacted.

Among the northern Eʋe of Ghana, the *Adeʋu,* hunters' dance, is performed during the funeral celebration of a dead hunter. During this dance, the experiences of hunters are mimed with weapons, skulls and horns of animals used as props. Public and individual religious worship also create opportunities for carefully crafted enactments throughout the phases of worship or ritual.

Traditional and contemporary Ghanaian drama and theater reach across the barriers of time and space, penetrate barriers of race and nationality, and aesthetically promote the emotional needs of the individual (Addo 1997, 58).

In all of the above dramatic and theatrical activities, the pres-

FIGURE 30.3: *Gahu* dancer from Tadzeʋu in full costume (2006).

ence of music, dance and other performing or visual art forms is felt. The interdisciplinary nature of the African arts can be seen at its height during dramatic and theatrical events in Ghana. Because of this, the place of African arts in the music curriculum cannot be overemphasized.

Closely linked with drama are poetry and other language art forms. Poetry is an art form that directly connects representational thinking with language. In traditional Ghanaian societies, poetic forms provide the people with avenues for exploring the environment through song, drama and other language activities.

Through the structuring of words and themes about a particular subject, traditional artists are able to create new riddles, songs, and proverbs which are used in day-to-day encounters. During the recreation and composition stages of dramatic activities in the classroom, opportunities should be given students to construct ideas and themes that can be used in their dramatic enactments.

The organization of music and dance has a dramatic orientation. Focus for classroom activities may include, but are not limited to:

i. Recreation and composition of traditional rituals, festivals, and funerals, etc.

ii. Acting: Students participate in the enactments with specific roles.

iii. Stage design: Students recreate the African stage for their enactments.

iv. Directing: Students each have the opportunity to direct presentations.

v. Comparative analysis: Students analyze traditional stage plays, as well as their own.

vi. Publicity: Students participate in creating publicity for their presentations.

vii. Different modes: Students in all the above aspects of recreating African theater use all the various modes available, such as gesture, movement, dance, music, mime, and other linguistic mediums.

viii. Improvisation and creative drama: Using their personal experiences as material, students should explore roles, moods, music, dance and images through pantomime, gestures and other verbal and nonverbal language arts.

FIGURE 30.4: Nuumo Wolomo Abordai III, chief priest of Kweikuma Tsoshishie, Jamestown, Accra, about to pray before photographs were taken (April 2010).

Seven Steps to Teaching any African Music Type: An Interdisciplinary Approach

The recommended steps below are aimed at fully discussing all the components of the curriculum when any musical type is being studied:

STEP 1 • Select an appropriate musical type.
   • Introduce the selection in context.
   • Students listen to the music from an audio recording.
   • Students view an "authentic" performance on video or film.
   • Students observe a live performance (if available).

STEP 2 • Discuss the historical, geographical, social, and cultural background of the African people who perform the selected music.
   • Discuss the musical and dance activities of the people, and the function of music and dance in everyday life.

STEP 3 • Discuss the historical development of the selection: its origin, distribution, and function.
   • Discuss the mode of organization and performance.

STEP 4 • Systematic instruction on the instruments of the ensemble in this order:
   i.   Introduce instruments playing the timeline (if included).
   ii. Introduce instruments that emphasize or reinforce the timeline.
   iii. Introduce supporting instruments which play basic ostinato patterns.
   iv. Introduce supporting instruments which play in dialogue with the lead or master drum.
   v.   Introduce the master drum.
   vi. Introduce rhythmic concepts as they apply to specific patterns: additive, divisive, hemiola, etc.

STEP 5 • Teach songs if applicable, and:
   i.   Discuss background to the songs.
   ii. Discuss lyrics and key words; emphasize meaning and pronunciation of words.
   iii. Students learn to sing songs to instrumental accompaniment.
   iv. Discuss musical elements: tonal organization, rhythm, harmony, form, and structure, etc.

STEP 6 • Introduce dance movements, gestures or any dramatic enactment.
   • Discuss dance symbolism.

STEP 7 • Introduce students to transcriptions of instrumental parts and "Music Minus One" procedures. (Music Minus One is used for practicing or performing in an ensemble setting with recorded ensemble music. The procedure allows the individual or musician to practice each instrument or part by turning off that particular track from the audio. A similar approach is used with karaoke performance, when the voice track is taken off.)

The above steps should aid teachers in teaching the musical types discussed in these volumes. Percussionists and others who are interested in enriching their knowledge of Ghanaian music should also follow the above steps to benefit from a full understanding of the music and the culture.

31. Activities for Teaching
Bɔbɔɔbɔ Dance-Drumming

The general purpose underlying these activities is to expose students to the main features and elements of *Bɔbɔɔbɔ* music and the culture of the Eʋe who perform this music. Students' interests and level of engagement with this music and the people will be heightened in subsequent content areas if all the activities in this unit are followed. Specifically, students will be introduced to the following topics:

    i.   introduction to the sounds of *Bɔbɔɔbɔ* dance-drumming;

    ii.   functions of *Bɔbɔɔbɔ* among the Eʋe of Ghana;

    iii. *Bɔbɔɔbɔ* music and its relation to dance, drama and other cognate art forms;

    iv. objects of art in *Bɔbɔɔbɔ* performance; and

    v.   instruments of the *Bɔbɔɔbɔ* ensemble and the percussion ensemble.

Overview of Activities

ACTIVITY 1 UNIT ONE.

Focus: The music of *Bɔbɔɔbɔ* and the social and cultural background of the Eʋe of Ghana.

Objectives: Students will:

    1. identify the sounds of *Bɔbɔɔbɔ* dance-drumming; and

    2. view and listen to *Bɔbɔɔbɔ* dance-drumming performance and discuss with the teacher the historical, geographical, anthropological, social, economic, and political background of the Eʋe of Ghana.

Materials: 1. Video *Bɔbɔɔbɔ* DVD 5, MTG by Paschal Younge, 2011.

            2. Audio *Bɔbɔɔbɔ: Ghana Rhythms of the People,* Tr.6 MCM 3018.

            3. Regional maps of Africa and Ghana.

            4. Ethnic map of Ghana.

Background Notes. Legends, folktales, historical songs, and oral tradition suggest that the Eʋe, together with the Ibo, Hausa, Ga, Dangbe, Akwamu, Akan, and other West African people crossing the Sahara from the Far East, set up the mighty Sudanese empires of the 13th century.

The following lyrics from an Eʋe folk song, "We were once near the Kong River in Abyssinia," have been thought to suggest a settlement along the Kong River in present-day Ethiopia (Fianu 1986, 2). Tradition, however, is certain of settlements in Oyo (Ayo) in Nigeria, Ketu in Benin, and Nɔtsie in Togo, from where the Eʋe finally migrated to their present habitations in the late 16th century. The Eʋe were certainly some of the settlers in the Gold Coast (now Ghana) before the Portuguese, who were the first Europeans to arrive in West Africa in 1471.

Presently, the Eʋe are located in the southeastern part of Ghana, the southern half of Togo, Benin — around Aja-Tado, and southwestern Nigeria in West Africa. Despite enough cultural uniformity in all these areas to justify identifying people as one ethnic group, the Eʋe culture is not entirely homogeneous. Apart from dialectical differences, there are differences in religious activities, political systems, and musical styles.

The central and northern Eʋe, described as "Eʋemeawo," on which this study is based, were part of the major Eʋe block who migrated from Ŋɔtsie and live in parts of Ghana and Togo. These people occupy the central and northern Eʋeland in both countries.

In Ghana, where Bɔbɔɔbɔ started, they can be found in the Ho, Peki, Kpando, Hohoe and Awudome traditional areas. Despite the conflicting dialects spoken by the Eʋes in Ghana, the Volta River has united the people into a single ethnic unit and brought the area into a geographical entity with similar customs, beliefs, and habits.

The religious activities of the people center around the One Supreme being, who they refer to as Mawu. Through numerous deities and cults, the people are able to reach their God, who is conceptualized as male, a father and sustainer of the universe. Ancestral worship creates an avenue by which the people link the living with the dead through the pouring of libation and the worship of ancestral stools—*zikpuiza* or *kpukpowawa*.

Ritual officials exist for magic, witchcraft, medicine, divination, and soothsaying. Christian religions, especially the Catholic and evangelical Presbyterian churches, are very prominent among the people today.

The chief and his elders of various degrees rule over the people. Traditional arbitration courts or intermediary spirits and powers are called upon to resolve disputes any time they arise. Succession to chiefship is vested in the royal family through stool elders and is also patrilineal. The basis of social organization is the clan, whose membership passes through the father. Descent of office and inheritance is also within the male line.

The nature of rainfall and the various topographical features that cover the region have given rise to a variety in vegetation. The economic activities of the people, therefore, are influenced by the variety in ecology. The majority of the people are involved in farming, poultry, basketry, mat-making, petty trading, and fishing by those around the Volta River.

Major festivals celebrated are those derived from ancestral harvest festivals. Unlike the past when these celebrations were purposely to thank God for abundant food, contemporary festivals create opportunities for family reunions, and platforms for purification rites and planning of development projects. Then celebration of the annual Yam Festival, *Teduzã*, is by far the most major festival celebrated by these people.

Education among the Eʋe is of paramount importance. Traditional education is through a social mechanism in which the young are trained to become accepted members of the larger society. Through consistent but gradual adult influence and guidance, young children are prepared to be "acceptable" citizens.

To be accepted among the Eʋe means that one follows the rules which govern the physical, spiritual, moral and socio-cultural existence of the people. Respect for parents and elders, honesty, generosity, hospitality, bravery, and patience are virtues promoted in every home.

"Education for the Eʋe is, therefore, the making of a child (*Ame*). Indeed anyone who behaves contrary to the rules of society is referred to simply as an animal, or born-but-not-bred" (Egblewogbe 1975, 21). The overall traditional education is geared towards the success of the society. Acquisition of musical knowledge, which also follows the traditional process, is therefore given special attention. A good dancer, drummer or singer is given a special place in the society.

Music among the Eʋemeawo forms an integral part of everyday life. Music exists for rites of passage, work, political institutions, religion, and leisure. Music associated with chieftaincy, referred to as court music, is only performed during the installation and removal from office of chiefs, state assemblies, state processions, state funerals and annual festivals.

Instruments used on these occasions include *atumpani*, a pair of cylindrical and single-headed drums used as "talking drums"; an *ʋuga*, a single-headed cylindrical drum; a *ladzo*, animal horn; an *ekpo*, single bell; and a *gakpevi*, double bell. Vocal music at the courts includes female praise songs, *osaye*, and male war declamations, *ampoti*. Religious music is simply called *trɔvu* or *dzoʋu*, and can be heard during traditional rituals. Christian worship has introduced the singing of church hymns and anthems among the converted.

Music for occupation groups are mainly *adeʋu*, hunters' music; and *akpi*, music for the warriors. Music for rites of passage include puberty songs, *gbɔtohawo*; *fefehawo*, children's play songs; and *avihawo*, choral lament and funeral dirges.

The majority of musical types are performed during any social event that is a community event. Some of the popular dance-drummingçtypes are *Gbolo, Egbabnegba, Totoeme, Zigi, Asiko, Prampoʋu, Tudzi* and *Bɔbɔɔbɔ*.

Procedure:

1. Play audio of *Bɔbɔɔbɔ*, performance by Taviefe Deme *Bɔbɔɔbɔ* Group from Ghana, and ask students if they can identify or have ever heard such music. Associate this music with any type of music they already know.

2. Tell students the name of this music and where it comes from.

3. Display African maps and help students to identify countries and their capital cities. Discuss with students the major sub-regions: North Africa versus sub–Saharan Africa.

4. Tell students that the type of music they will be working with is from a country in sub–Saharan Africa called Ghana.

5. Display various maps of Ghana: regions and ethnic groups. Discuss some of the important facts about Ghana. Refer to notes provided in Chapter 30. Help students to identify the location of the Eʋe in West Africa. Discuss the cultural background of the Eʋe of Ghana.

6. Show the video of *Bɔbɔɔbɔ* and continue discussion on the social and cultural background of the Eʋe.

ACTIVITY / UNIT TWO

Focus: Function of *Bɔbɔɔbɔ* music and dance among the Eʋe of Ghana.

Objectives: Students will:

           1. view and discuss the features of authentic traditional and theatrical performances of *Bɔbɔɔbɔ*;

           2. discuss the background of *Bɔbɔɔbɔ*: its historical development, mode of performance, and organization of the dance;

           3. discuss the functional and nonfunctional uses of the music and dance: role of religion, family organization and life-cycle events; and

           4. perform some rhythmic patterns to experience *Bɔbɔɔbɔ* music.

Materials: 1. Video *Bɔbɔɔbɔ* DVD 5, MTG by Paschal Younge, 2011.

           2. Audio *Bɔbɔɔbɔ: Ghana Rhythms of the People*, Tr.6 MCM 3018.

Background Notes. *Bɔbɔɔbɔ* is the most popular social music and dance of the central and northern Eʋe of Ghana and Togo in West Africa. This music and dance, also known as *Agbeyeye* (New Life) or *Akpese* (Music of Joy), emerged from a village called Kpando in the Volta Region of Ghana during the independence struggle in the country between 1947 and 1957.

This musical type was derived from an older secular dance called *Konkoma* due to the ingenuity of the late Francis Nuatrɔ. Although this music was initially confined to a few towns and villages in central and northern Eʋeland, it has now spread to all Eʋe-speaking territories in Ghana and Togo. The music can also be heard in some non–Eʋe-speaking communities, including those in the big cities.

Bɔbɔɔbɔ music is harmonious in nature. It is generally seen during all social community events, particularly at funerals and festivals. Although Bɔbɔɔbɔ bands are well established musical groups, it is sometimes difficult to distinguish between audience and performers at a very large and festive occasion.

Procedure:

1. Review activity one to put this lesson in context.

2. Show the video of Bɔbɔɔbɔ. Students should view the performances by the Ho Agbenya Bɔbɔɔbɔ group.

3. Discuss the historical development and mode of performance of Bɔbɔɔbɔ with students.

4. Continue to show the video. Ask students to describe the phases of the performance. They should write their observations.

5. Discuss the functions of Bɔbɔɔbɔ in the society. When the band is hired to perform at special functions, participation is restricted to only members who perform in their costumes. During festivals and funerals, however, everybody can participate in the performance. Choice of songs reflects the context of the performance. At a funeral, for example, the tempo of the music and dance is considerably slow. Songs and dance movements further emphasize the mood of the performance. The mode of performance, however, is the same on all occasions. All Bɔbɔɔbɔ performances commence with a short procession by the band to the dance ring. When the drummers have taken their seats, series of songs are performed to warm up the dancers. The cue to commence or end a performance is given by either the master drum, ʋuga, or the hourglass drum, ɖonno. The performance may sometimes end with another procession.

6. To conclude the activities, play the audio of the Bɔbɔɔbɔ performance and help students to feel the rhythmic flow by clapping some rhythmic motifs relating to the timeline.

7. Students can clap combinations of these patterns with and without the timeline.

Combinations:

1. Exercises 1 and 2	2. Exercises 1 and 3
3. Exercises 1 and 4	4. Exercises 1 and 5
5. Exercises 2 and 3	6. Exercises 2 and 5
7. Exercises 2 and 5	8. Exercises 3 and 4
9. Exercises 3 and 5	10. Exercises 1, 2 and 3
11. Exercises 1, 2 and 4	12. Exercises 1, 2, and 5
13. Exercises 1, 3, and 4	14. Exercises 1, 3, and 5
15. Exercises 1, 4, and 5	16. Exercises 2, 3, and 4
17. Exercises 2, 3, and 5	18. Exercises 3, 4, and 5

Activity / Unit Three

Focus: Music, dance, and drama in Bɔbɔɔbɔ performance.

Objectives: Students will:

1. view and discuss the relationship between music, dance, drama, and other visual elements

Materials: 1. Video Bɔbɔɔbɔ DVD 5, MTG by Paschal Younge, 2011.

2. Audio Bɔbɔɔbɔ: Ghana Rhythms of the People, Tr.6 MCM 3018.

Procedure:

1. Students should view the video of Bɔbɔɔbɔ. Ask them to identify any relationship between the musicians and dancers.

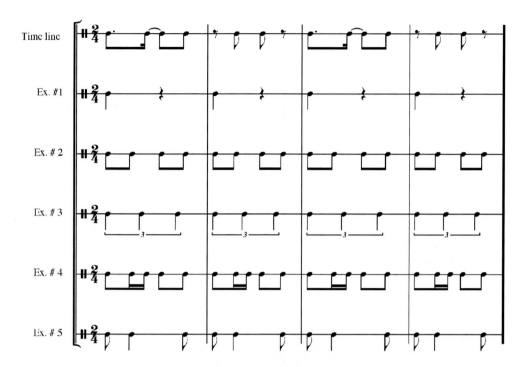

FIGURE 31.1: Rhythmic Exercise One

2. Discuss how African musical events are related to the dance. Musical sound that is integrated with the dance emphasizes and develops rhythms that can be articulated in bodily movement. The rhythmic structure mostly influences the patterns of dance movements.

In *Bɔbɔɔbɔ*, the organization of rhythms both linearly and multi-linearly, resulting in regular or irregular accents and cross rhythms, well placed, guide the dance. Linearly, the rhythms to be articulated in bodily movement are organized in strict time and are grouped into patterns or phrases imparting a feeling of regularity.

Basic dance steps, therefore, relate to the timeline. Multi-linearly, all the different percussion instruments play varied patterns which reinforce the basic pulses. The dancer will take cues from the rhythmic framework to articulate the dance movements.

A close-knit correlation between musical sounds and dance in *Bɔbɔɔbɔ* also occurs when specific songs direct specific dance steps. Depending on the context of performance, musical sounds and dance can be used to express artistic behavior, cultural behavior, psychological behavior, communicative behavior, economic behavior, political behavior, and poetic expression.

3. Help students to identify some of these behaviors from the phases of the performance in the video. Pause video when necessary during this activity.

4. Discuss dramatic enactments seen during the performances. Depending on the context of the performance, *Bɔbɔɔbɔ* can include memorial drama during festivals. Dancers may enact episodes showing social relations, beliefs, and values.

Symbolic gestures by dancers during funerals may relate to sorrow. Social drama at festivals or other social occasions can reflect topical issues. Symbolic gestures may also dramatize joy and happiness.

5. Play the timeline and help students to move around in time. Their steps should correspond to the timeline as shown in the Figure 31.2 exercise.

6. Repeat the same activity as in step six while playing the full performance audio tape by the Taviefe *Bɔbɔɔbɔ* group Tr. 6 MCM 3018: Audio *Bɔbɔɔbɔ.*

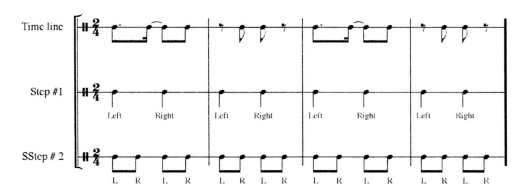

FIGURE 31.2: Movement Activities

Left, FIGURE 31.3: Costume of *Bɔbɔɔbɔ* dance, type one. Zelma Badu Younge (2009). *Right,* FIGURE 31.4: Costume of *Bɔbɔɔbɔ* dance, type two. Ho Agbenya *Bɔbɔɔbɔ* Group (2009).

Activity / Unit Four

Focus: Objects of art in *Bɔbɔɔbɔ.*

Objectives: Students will:

        1. view and discuss costumes, makeup, and appendages used by dancers in *Bɔbɔɔbɔ* performances.

Materials: 1. Video *Bɔbɔɔbɔ* DVD 5, MTG by Paschal Younge.

        2. Two pairs of white handkerchiefs.

Background Notes. Costumes used in *Bɔbɔɔbɔ* vary from band to band. Two are very common in contemporary times: i. The women will wear a designed t-shirt, usually printed with the band's logo, over a cloth tied to the waist. The men will wear the same t-shirt over any pair of knickers or trousers. ii. The most common costume is an *awu,* which is a type of blouse worn over matching cloth. This is the traditional dress of all Eʋe women. The men will wear a shirt made from the same cloth over any pair of knickers or trousers as in the first type. All women dancers in *Bɔbɔɔbɔ* carry a pair of white handkerchiefs as appendages to symbolize joy, victory, and freedom. The spirit of *Bɔbɔɔbɔ* is evidenced in the stylistic waving of the white handkerchiefs.

Procedure:

1. Show pictures of the various costumes to students.

2. Discuss the nature of each costume.

3. Discuss the function of costumes in the *Bɔbɔɔbɔ* performance. The selection of costumes in African dances depends on the type of music being performed, the nature of the dance, and the requirement of dramatic enactment. Costumes in *Bɔbɔɔbɔ* can also be seen as bodily extensions or appendages. The white handkerchief is therefore an extension of the personality of the *dramatis personae.*

4. Assist some of the students to dress in the two *Bɔbɔɔbɔ* costumes if costumes are available.

5. Students can draw some of the dancers and their costumes.

Activity / Unit Five

Focus: Instruments of the *Bɔbɔɔbɔ* ensemble.

Objectives: Students will:

        1. listen to and identify instruments of the *Bɔbɔɔbɔ* ensemble;

        2. categorize instruments according to their acoustical groups: idiophones, membranophones, chordophones, and aerophones;

        3. listen to, analyze, and describe *Bɔbɔɔbɔ* music; and

        4. discuss instruments as historical data.

Materials: 1. Video *Bɔbɔɔbɔ* DVD 5, MTG by Paschal Younge, 2011.

        2. Audio *Bɔbɔɔbɔ: Ghana Rhythms of the People,* Tr.6 MCM 3018.

        3. Instruments of the ensemble (if available).

        4. Pictures of instruments.

        5. Slides of instruments (if available).

Teaching Notes. Instruments of the *Bɔbɔɔbɔ* ensemble have undergone several modifications. Initial instruments used were the *kretsiwa,* finger bell; the *ʋuvi,* small drum; the *asiʋui,* hand drum; the *pati,* tom tom; the *ʋugã,* master drum; and the bugle. Contemporary *Bɔbɔɔbɔ* ensembles are comprised of the following instruments: *kretsiwa,* finger bell (two or three may be used); one *tigo,* double bell, or one *gakokoe,* slit bell (optional for most groups); one *akaye,* rattle; an *ʋuvi* and *asiʋui,* small supporting drums; a *pati,* concert tom which may be used in the absence of the *ɖonno* an hourglass drum; an *ʋugã/Havana,* master drum (two or three may be used); and a bugle/trumpet.

Contrasting rhythmic patterns played on the *kretsiwas* are essential in any performance. Apart from the master drums, no other instrumentalists are required to improvise during a performance. If more than one master drum is played, only the one with the lowest picth may lead the performance. The bugle/trumpet is used to accentuate specific points in the dance.

Procedure:

1. Students should view the video of *Bɔbɔɔbɔ*. Help them to identify each instrument. Pause the video when appropriate.

2. Play the video of *Bɔbɔɔbɔ* and ask the class to identify instrumental parts.

3. Display pictures or authentic instruments and help students to identify them by their traditional and English descriptive names.

4. Help students to categorize instruments:

kretsiwa	idiophone
tigo	idiophone
akaye	idiophone
vuvi	membranophone
asivui	membranophone
pati	membranophone
conga	membranophone
vuga/havana	membranophone
bugle/trumpet	aerophone.

5. Repeat recording of the whole ensemble on the video of *Bɔbɔɔbɔ*. Now play a recording of each instrument. Ask students to identify instruments as they play.

6. Students should play instrumental parts and try to layer all parts. Students should prepare a chart to show these combinations.

7. Students should draw instruments and make a pictorial map of the instruments of the ensemble.

Bɔbɔɔbɔ Instruments

Top right, Figure 31.5: *Kretsiwa. Bottom right,* Figure 31.6: *Tigo. Above,* Figure 31.7: *Akaye*

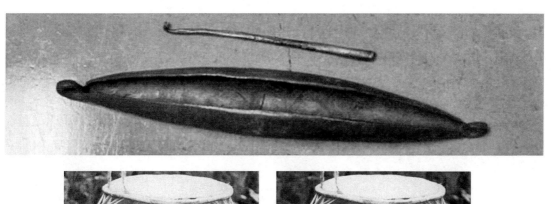

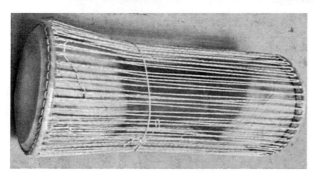

Top, FIGURE 31.8: *Gakokoe. Middle left*, FIGURE 31.9: *Uuvi. Middle right*, FIGURE 31.10: *Asivui. Bottom left*, FIGURE 31.11: *Ɖondo. Bottom right*, FIGURE 31.12: *Uuga/Havana.*

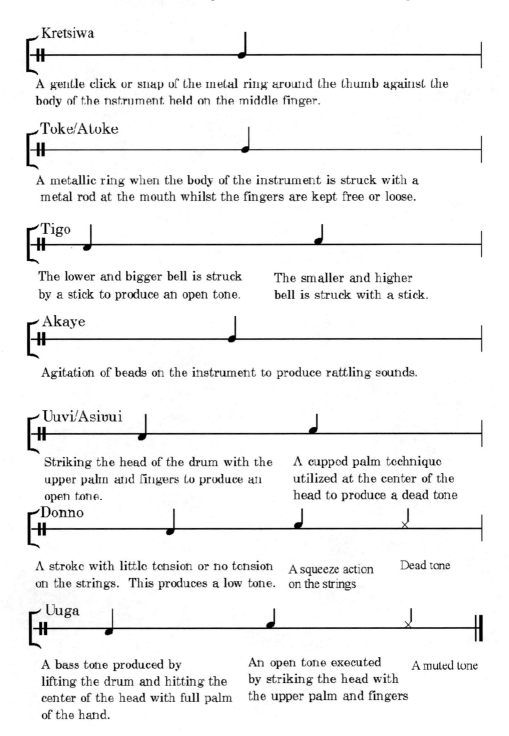

Kretsiwa

A gentle click or snap of the metal ring around the thumb against the body of the instrument held on the middle finger.

Toke/Atoke

A metallic ring when the body of the instrument is struck with a metal rod at the mouth whilst the fingers are kept free or loose.

Tigo

The lower and bigger bell is struck by a stick to produce an open tone.

The smaller and higher bell is struck with a stick.

Akaye

Agitation of beads on the instrument to produce rattling sounds.

Uuvi/Asivui

Striking the head of the drum with the upper palm and fingers to produce an open tone.

A cupped palm technique utilized at the center of the head to produce a dead tone

Donno

A stroke with little tension or no tension on the strings. This produces a low tone.

A squeeze action on the strings

Dead tone

Uuga

A bass tone produced by lifting the drum and hitting the center of the head with full palm of the hand.

An open tone executed by striking the head with the upper palm and fingers

A muted tone

FIGURE 31.13: Key to transcription

Instruments and Basic Rhythmic Patterns

KRETSIWA. This instrument is described as a finger bell or castanet. It is made from a solid metal scrap. The instrument has two parts. The main body is egg-shaped with an opening at one end. The middle finger passes through this opening to support the body of the instrument. The second part of the instrument is a metal ring worn on the thumb. Sound is produced by striking the ring against the body. Two or three of these instruments may be used in the ensemble. Players of these instruments usually perform standing. The lead cantor may occasionally play one of these bells. The timeline pattern played on the first *kretsiwa* can also be played on the *atoke*, a boat-shaped bell.

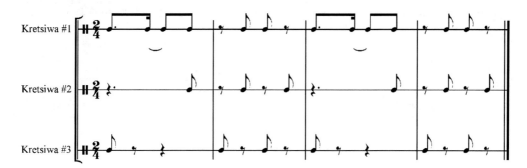

FIGURE 31.14: Basic rhythmic patterns on *kretsiwa*

TIGO. This instrument is described as the double bell. It is adopted from the southern Eʋe people and is a recent addition to the ensemble by some contemporary bands. It is also made from a solid metal scrap. The instrument is made of two bells (small and big) joined together so that the smaller bell rests on the big bell. Sound is produced by either striking on the small or big bell with a straight, foot-long stick. The rhythmic pattern on this instrument can also be played on the *gakokoe* when the second variation of the pattern shown is being played.

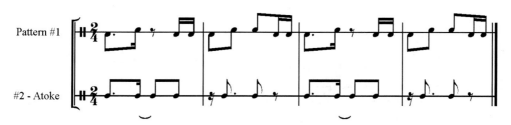

FIGURE 31.15: Basic rhythmic patterns on *tigo*

AKAYE. This is a rattle made by weaving beads around a gourd or calabash. Two smaller maracas can also be used. Sound is made by holding the elongated neck and hitting it against the thigh, or by holding the instrument in the palms and agitating the beads.

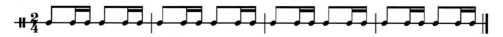

FIGURE 31.16: Basic rhythmic pattern on *akaye*

GAKOKOE. This instrument has four descriptive English names: boat bell, banana bell, slit bell, and taco bell. This is a canoe-shaped bell. Sound is produced by striking the side of the instrument very close to the slit mouth. This instrument may play the timeline or the *tigo*'s supporting part. *Gakokoe* is another southeastern Eʋe instrument added to the *Bɔbɔɔbɔ* ensemble.

UUVI AND ASIVUI. These are single-headed drums with bottle necks at their bases. They are played in sitting position with the drums slightly tilted forward and held between the knees. The *vuvi* and *asivui* may be the same size. You can differentiate between the two by tuning the *#uvi* a little higher in pitch. These drums serve as the basic supporting drums of the ensemble. The hand or palm technique is used on these drums.

FIGURE 31.17: Basic rhythmic patterns on *vuvi*

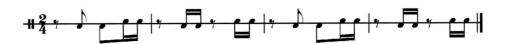

FIGURE 31.18: Basic rhythmic patterns on *asivui*

ĐONĐO. This instrument is referred to as the hourglass-shaped drum. It is a double headed cylindrical drum. The stick and armpit technique is used in realizing the different sonorities on the drum. To generate a high sound, the player must squeeze or tighten the heads by pressing against the strings. A release of the tension will then produce a low sound. Glide tones are generated by immediately releasing the strings after a stroke or vice versa. The *ɖonɖo* may play the starting or ending signal.

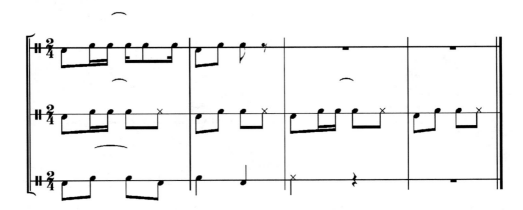

FIGURE 31.19: Basic rhythmic patterns on *ɖonɖo*

UUGĀ. This is the master or lead drum of the ensemble. It is also called *havana*. It is a single-headed drum played upright between the legs. The lifting of the drum with the thighs provides a spectacular visual effect during a performance but, most importantly, produces the desired bass tone. Two or more of these drums can be used in a performance but only one leads.

Techniques used on this drum include the open bounce technique, the smack or slap technique, the bass or deep sound technique and the dead tone technique. This master drum may start or end a performance. This role can also be performed by the *dondo*.

FIGURE 31.20: Basic rhythmic patterns on *Uugā*

FIGURE 31.21: Combination of timeline and supporting instrumental parts

FIGURE 31.22: Combination of *Bɔbɔɔbɔ* timeline and *vugã* patterns

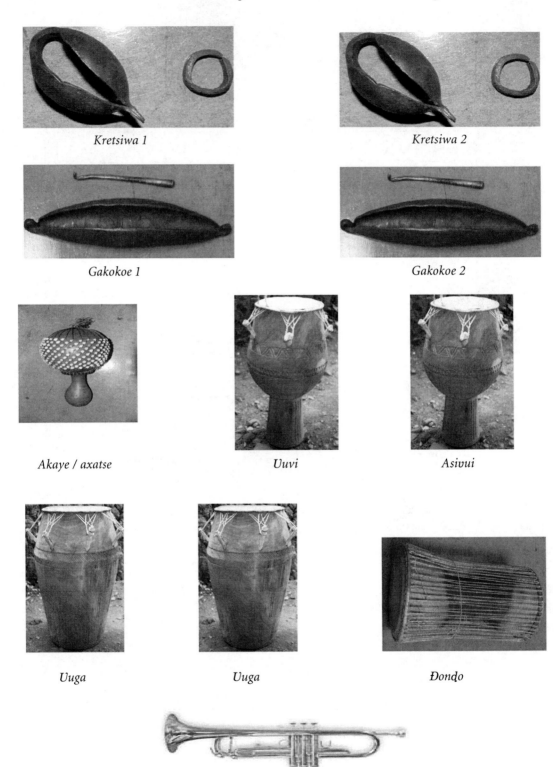

Kretsiwa 1

Kretsiwa 2

Gakokoe 1

Gakokoe 2

Akaye / axatse

Uuvi

Asivui

Uuga

Uuga

Ɖoṇɖo

FIGURE 31.23: Contemporary *Bɔbɔɔbɔ* ensemble organization

Bɔbɔɔbɔ Drumming Activities

There are many important aspects of the Eʋe people that can be learned through the study of *Bɔbɔɔbɔ* drumming procedures. The set of activities under this unit are designed to teach these aspects:

a. instruments of the *Bɔbɔɔbɔ* percussion ensemble;
b. development of playing techniques on *Bɔbɔɔbɔ* instruments;
c. modes of drumming in *Bɔbɔɔbɔ* music;
d. rhythmic concepts in *Bɔbɔɔbɔ* drumming; and
e. construction of *Bɔbɔɔbɔ* instruments.

ACTIVITY / UNIT ONE

Focus: Instruments of the *Bɔbɔɔbɔ* percussion ensemble.
Objectives: Students will:
         1. listen to and identify the tone color of *Bɔbɔɔbɔ* instruments; and
         2. classify instruments according to their roles in the ensemble.
Materials: 1. Video *Bɔbɔɔbɔ* DVD 5, MTG by Paschal Younge, 2011.
         2. Audio *Bɔbɔɔbɔ: Ghana Rhythms of the People,* Tr.6 MCM 3018.
         3. Wall pictures of authentic *Bɔbɔɔbɔ* instruments.
         4. Traditional authentic instruments, if available.

Procedure:

1. This activity should follow Unit Five.
2. Show the video of *Bɔbɔɔbɔ:* section on making instruments.
3. Discuss with students the tones or pitch levels of instruments of the ensemble. Show and play the different instruments:

> *Kretsiwa #1:* Due to the way this instrument is played, the sound produced is short and sharp. Different sizes can be used if three are being played.
> *Gakokoe:* Produces a sharp, metallic, ringing sound.
> *Tigo:* Distinguished by the two different tone levels.
> *Akaye:* Produces a rattling sound.
> *Ɖonɖo:* Produces two contrasting delayed sounds of high and low tones.
> *Ʋuvi:* Higher in pitch when compared with the *asiʋui.*
> *Asiʋui:* Lower in tone when compared with the *ʋuvi.*
> *Ʋuga:* Produces the lowest tones in the ensemble. It can also be identified by its variations.

4. Play the audio of *Bɔbɔɔbɔ.* Students should be able to differentiate between the instruments.
5. Show the video of *Bɔbɔɔbɔ* again and discuss the functions or roles of individual instruments in the ensemble:

> *Kretsiwa #1:* Plays the timeline. This pattern guides the whole ensemble. It provides entry cues to the rest of the ensemble.
> *Kretsiwa #2 and 3:* These instruments emphasize the pattern of the timeline.
> *Tigo:* Supports the timeline. This part may be omitted. It is not utilized by all *Bɔbɔɔbɔ* bands.
> *Akaye:* Supports the timeline.
> *Ɖonɖo:* Supporting drum but may start or end a performance.
> *Ʋuvi:* Supporting drum.
> *Asiʋui:* Supporting drum. This instrument plays an interlocking pattern with the *ʋuvi.*

Uuga: Master drum. This drum may start and end a performance. It serves as the conductor of the ensemble.

6. Students should prepare a chart as below. This will show the names of instruments and their functions in the ensemble.

Instrument	Function
Kretsiwa #1	Timeline
Kretsiwa #2	Emphasizes timeline
Kretsiwa #3	Emphasizes timeline
Tigo	Supports and plays timeline
Akaye	Supports timeline
Uuvi	Supports master drum
Asivui	Supports master drum
Ðonḍo	Supports master drum
Uugā	Master or lead drum

ACTIVITY / UNIT TWO
Focus: Developing playing techniques on *Bɔbɔɔbɔ* instruments.
Objectives: Students will:
            1. practice playing techniques on *Bɔbɔɔbɔ* instruments: hand and palm technique, stick technique, and armpit and stick technique; and
            2. play simple rhythmic patterns using each technique.
Materials: 1. Authentic *Bɔbɔɔbɔ* instruments.
            2. Conga drums.
            3. Cow bells.
            4. Maracas.
            5. Any available hand drum.
            6. Video *Bɔbɔɔbɔ* DVD 5, MTG by Paschal Younge.

Procedure:

1. Students should view the video of *Bɔbɔɔbɔ.*

2. Help students to hold and produce sounds on the various instruments or their substitutes. Refer to notes on description of instruments provided at the beginning of this unit.

3. Students should practice the various techniques using the rhythmic exercises that follow. The teacher should select exercises that are appropriate for each instrument.

See Figure 31.24 (Rhythmic Exercises Two) on page 385.

ACTIVITY / UNIT THREE
Focus: Modes of drumming in *Bɔbɔɔbɔ* music.
Objectives: Students will:
            1. view a traditional performance and discuss the different modes of drumming: dance, speech, and signal; and
            2. perform some of these modes.
Materials: 1. Authentic *Bɔbɔɔbɔ* instruments.
            2. Conga drums.
            3. Cow bells.
            4. Maracas.
            5. Any available hand drum.
            6. Video *Bɔbɔɔbɔ* DVD 5, MTG by Paschal Younge, 2011.
            7. Audio *Bɔbɔɔbɔ: Ghana Rhythms of the People,* Tr.6 MCM 3018.
Procedure:

FIGURE 31.24: Rhythmic exercises two

1. Discuss the three modes of instrumental music in African societies. Refer to Chapter 30, subsection on "Aesthetics in African Musical events."

2. Show Video *Bɔbɔɔbɔ* and help students to identify some of the modes used: dance, speech, and signal.

3. Discuss with students the tonal nature of the Eʋe language. Help students to understand that the tonal inflection of syllables in spoken language determines the meaning of words.

4. Help students to pronounce the following Eʋe words and phrases. Refer to pronunciation guide and orthograpghy.

Word	Pronunciation	Meaning
Mawu lolo	— –	God's great
	– –	
Ame sia ame	–	Everybody
	– – –	
Va midzo	– –	Come let's go
	–	
Dzodofe	– –	Kitchen
	–	
Bɔbɔɔbɔ	–	Name of a dance
	– –	

Word	Pronunciation	Meaning
Asime	–	Palm
Asime	– – –	Market
Dzó	–	Go
Dzò	–	Fire or fly

5. Teach students to play the texts on the master drum. They can use a conga or any hand drum on which different tones can be realized.

Activity / Unit Four

Focus: Rhythmic concepts in *Bɔbɔɔbɔ* dance-drumming.

Objectives: Students will :
1. identify rhythmic procedures in dance-drumming; and
2. perform on individual instruments and in groups in ensemble situations. NB. Refer to Chapter 29, "A Taste of the Percussion Ensembles."

Materials: 1. Authentic *Bɔbɔɔbɔ* instruments.
2. Conga drums.
3. Cow bells.
4. Maracas.
5. Any available hand drum.
6. Video *Bɔbɔɔbɔ* DVD 5, MTG by Paschal Younge, 2011.
7. Audio *Bɔbɔɔbɔ*: *Ghana Rhythms of the People*, Tr.6 MCM 3018.

Procedure:

1. Teach students the rhythmic patterns of instruments of the ensemble in this order: *kretsiwa* #1, *kretsiwa* #2, *kretsiwa* #3, *tigo, akaye, vuvi, asivui, dondo,* and *vuga*. Refer to Unit Five.

2. They should clap and vocalize the patterns. They should construct their own verbalization of the patterns. For example, the timeline can read: "Taco bell is good."

3. Students should combine various instrumental parts with the timeline as illustrated at the beginning of this unit. The teacher should construct more combinations. For example:

4. *kretsiwa* 1 and *kretsiwa* 2; or

5. *kretsiwa* 1 and *tigo*, etc.

6. Discuss with students African rhythmic procedures found in *Bɔbɔɔbɔ* dance-drumming, e.g., divisive, hemiola, additive and cross rhythm.

Figure 31.25: Divisive rhythm

FIGURE 31.26: Hemiola pattern

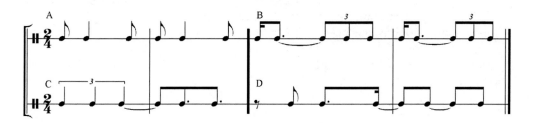

FIGURE 31.27: Additive pattern

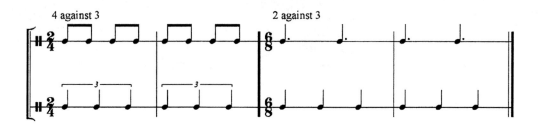

FIGURE 31.28: Cross rhythm

FIGURE 31.29: Divisive and additive patterns in vertical motion

ACTIVITY / UNIT FIVE

Focus: Construction of Bɔbɔɔbɔ drums.

Objectives: Students will:

     1. learn about the construction of Bɔbɔɔbɔ drums; and

     2. find substitutes for traditional instruments and perform with them.

Materials: 1. Traditional authentic Bɔbɔɔbɔ instruments.

     2. Conga drums.

     3. Cow bells.

     4. Maracas.

     5. Any available hand drum.

     6. Video Bɔbɔɔbɔ DVD 4, MTG by Paschal Younge (2011).

Procedure:

1. Show Video DVD 4: section on construction of *Bɔbɔɔbɔ* instruments. Discuss the process as outlined in the video.

2. Divide students into seven groups. Each group should be assigned an instrument which will then be substituted with another. Tell students that in the absence of the real African instruments, they should find substitutes to be used in the performance of the music. Divide the class as follows: Group A: *kretsiwa,* Group B: *tigo,* Group C: *akaye,* Group D: *ḍonḍo,* Group E: *vuvi* and *asivui,* and Group F: *vuga.* Allow students to use their own creativity and judgment as much as possible.

3. Students should perform with these instruments.

Bɔbɔɔbɔ Singing Activities

Folk songs from sub–Saharan Africa reflect daily occurrences in the lives of the people. An African song as observed by Nketia (1984) should be treated not only as a form of speech utterance but as a medium that recounts the experiences of the people. *Bɔbɔɔbɔ* songs can be understood and interpreted if the lyrics are treated as such. Activities in this unit will therefore address the analogous features of music and speech and lyrics as creative verbal expressions:

1. themes and cultural meaning of *Bɔbɔɔbɔ* songs.
2. musical concepts in *Bɔbɔɔbɔ* songs: form, melody, rhythm, harmony, and singing styles, etc.

Activity / Unit One
Focus: Themes and meaning of *Bɔbɔɔbɔ* songs.
Objectives: Students will:
       1. listen to and discuss lyrics of songs—
         historical themes
         religious themes
         topical themes
         social themes
         beliefs/value themes
         death and afterlife
         human relations;
       2. learn and and perform songs with and without the ensemble; and
       3. sing songs with expression and technical accuracy.

Teaching Notes. The repertoire of any *Bɔbɔɔbɔ* band is very wide. The changes in style and form depend on the mood and context of performance. Tempo is the main distinguishing factor in the various styles. The choice of songs during a particular performance is also guided by the function taking place. Generally, songs relate to every aspect of community life. Religious and funeral themes are by far the most common themes used in *Bɔbɔɔbɔ* songs. Other themes may relate to human issues, praise and ridicule, topical issues, death and afterlife, history, and the social and cultural beliefs of the people. It can be said that the dance mirrors the song in any performance, as the dance gestures dramatize the song text. A change in song results in a change in dance movement.

Tonal arrangements in *Bɔbɔɔbɔ* songs are based on the heptatonic (seven tone) scale, an arrangement that lends itself to the use of Western hymnal-style harmonic arrangements. Melodic lines usually follow the word contour and rhythm of speech patterns.

Harmony is realized when the chorus sings in unison with the use of sporadic or consequent thirds, fifths, sixths, octaves, or a combination of all of the techniques. The advent of Christianity has resulted in the use of *Bɔbɔɔbɔ*-derived songs in the church. *Bɔbɔɔbɔ* songs are performed in call and response and in solo and chorus form. One soloist is the ideal but sometimes two or more may introduce a song before the chorus enters.

Procedure:

1. Help students to understand the importance of song texts in African cultures. Discuss the function, background, and texts of songs to be studied.

2. Work on pronunciation of words with students.

3. Teach students to sing the song with and without the timeline and full ensemble accompaniment. Use this procedure for teaching all songs.

ACTIVITY / UNIT TWO

Focus: Musical concepts in *Bɔbɔɔbɔ* songs: form, rhythm, melody, harmony and singing styles.

Objectives: Students will:
  1. identify repetitions, call and response, solo and chorus refrain in songs;
  2. identify and perform harmonic devices in song — singing in unison, singing in thirds, fifths, sixths, octaves, two-part singing, etc.; and
  3. identify the use of speech and rhythmic properties as they relate to the melodic shape and rhythm of songs.

Materials: 1. Song transcriptions.

Procedure:

1. The teacher should review songs intended to be used in explaining musical concepts. Each song should be performed at least three times.

2. Discuss the musical concepts as used in each song.

Melody	Follows speech intonations
	Scalic passages and sequences
Rhythm	Syncopations and anacrusis
	Speech rhythm
Scales	Tetratonic, pentatonic,
	Hexatonic and heptatonic
Form	Call and response
	Solo and chorus refrain
	Repetitions
Harmony	Singing in unison and singing in octaves
	Singing in thirds, fifths, sixths and octaves
	Two-part, three-part, and four-part singing.

3. Discuss the impact of spoken language on the melodic contour of songs. This information is provided under the brief analysis of each song. Use this process for each song.

Analysis of *Bɔbɔɔbɔ* Songs

See Figure 32.30 (*Manɔ Efe Ɖusime*) on page 390.

• Title: *Manɔ Efe Ɖusi Me* •

Lyrics in Eʋe: *Manɔ efe ɖusime*
            Manɔ efe ɖusime
            Manɔ efe ɖusime
            Matsɔ miabɔ, da ɖe efe kɔ me, ɖusime

FIGURE 31.30: *Manɔ Efe Ɖusime*

Lyrics in English: I will be at your right-hand side
                    I will be at your right-hand side
                    I will be at your right-hand side
                    And place my left arm on your neck, at your right-hand side

Cultural Meaning: This song reflects on the virtues of love and care. As with many Eʋe folk songs, the meaning of *Manɔ efe ɖusime* should not be understood for its literal translation. Rather, its proverbial meaning is that perfect love should be made available in times of good and bad. This song can be performed at all social functions.

Form: Solo and Chorus. A:B form: The main cantor sings the song through once, and the chorus repeats in parts.

Performance style:
    1. Cantor sings melody alone.
    2. Cantor and chorus sing melody in unison.
    3. Cantor repeats melody alone.
    4. Chorus sings with cantor in parts.

Scale: Heptatonic

Melody: Scalic descent of pitches. Melody follows the tonal inflections of spoken language in most cases.

Rhythm: Rhythmic phrases follow speech rhythms of the spoken text. Dotted rhythm.

Harmony: Use of parallel thirds and sixths, overlapping of solo and chorus, and two- and three-part harmony.

Pronunciation: There are seven significant vowels in Eʋe: a, e, ɛ, i, o, ɔ, u and 23 consonants, excluding the English c, j and q, in addition to ɖ, ƒ, ɣ, ŋ, ʋ and x. Diagraphs include: ts, tsy, dz, gb, and ny. Refer to the Eʋe Orthography in Part One.

Tonality: *Ma nɔ efe ɖusi me, Ma tsɔ miabɔ da ɖe fe kɔ me*
           1   3 11 31 3   3 1 2   1 2 1 1 3 3

NB: I have come across three versions of this song. The variations are in the fourth line: *Ma tsɔ miabɔ da ɖe fe kɔme.* One version is, *Matsɔ miabɔ da ɖe fe dɔ me,* which means, "I will place my left arm on your stomach." Another version reads, *Matsɔ miabɔ da ɖe fe dzime,* which means, "I will place my left arm on your back." The philosophical meaning of the song, however, is the same for all the versions.

FIGURE 31.31: *Ayelevinɔ Ku Lo*

• Title: *Ayelevi Nɔ Ku Lo* •

Lyrics in Eʋe: *//Ayelevinɔ ku lo*
                    Mido baba na Ayele
                    E! mido baba n'a Ayele//
                    //Ayele, Ayele
                    E! mido baba na Ayele//

Lyrics in English: //Ayelevi's mother is dead
                    Let's mourn with Ayele
                    Yes, let's mourn with Ayele//

//Ayele Ayele
Yes, let's mourn with Ayele//

Meaning: This is a choral lament to mourn the death of Ayelevi's mother. Ayelevi is the name of a young lady, though in this composition, it can refer to any bereaved person. This song would be heard exclusively at funerals.

Form: Solo and chorus refrain. //A: B// //C : B//

Scale: Heptatonic

Melody: Scalic patterns. Melody follows speech tones.

Rhythm: Follows speech rhythms. Anacrusis and dotted rhythm.

Harmony: Use of parallel thirds and sixths with occasional crossing of parts. Two-part singing.

Pronunciation: Refer to notes on *Ma Nɔ Efe ɖusi Me* for guide to the pronunciation of vowels, consonants, and diagraphs.

Tonality: *Ayelevinɔ kulo Mi do ba ba na, Aye le*
            2 11 1 2 11 1 2 1 3 3 2 2 1 1

Bɔbɔɔbɔ Dance and Movement Activities

Movement is an essential part of sub–Saharan musical events. It serves as an avenue for creative response and aesthetic appreciation. The main factor that generates movement is rhythm. Rhythmic organization in any instrumental or vocal music is seen as movement. The dance, therefore, is an outward manifestation of movement in African dances.

African dances serve as a form of reaction to music and medium for communication. The dance is "a language, a mode of expression, which addresses itself to the mind, through the heart, using related, relevant, and significant movements which have their basic counter-parts in our everyday activities, to express special and real life experiences in rhythmic sequences to musical and poetic stimuli" (Opoku 1968, 11).

Activities for teaching movement and dance will include:

1. symbolism in *Bɔbɔɔbɔ* movement and dance; and
2. dancing to *Bɔbɔɔbɔ* music.

ACTIVITY / UNIT ONE

Focus: Symbolism in *Bɔbɔɔbɔ* movement and dance.

Objectives: Students will:
1. view and discuss meaning of symbolic movements and gestures in *Bɔbɔɔbɔ* performance; and
2. learn and perform these symbolic movements and gestures.

Materials: 1. Video *Bɔbɔɔbɔ* DVD 5, MTG by Paschal Younge, 2011.
2. Audio *Bɔbɔɔbɔ: Ghana Rhythms of the People*, Tr.6 MCM 3018.
3. Pictorial representation of symbolic gestures and movements.

Teaching Notes. *Bɔbɔɔbɔ* is organized as a circular dance into which the dancers come after a short procession. This dance requires great flexibility and fluidity in movement, and is therefore performed by women who are considered in Africa to be more flexible than men. The specific dance movements and gestures are symbolic. The *ritornello* dance movement, the basic dance steps known as the "cutting move," symbolizes a clearing of the pathway towards a happy future, devoid of oppression. In this basic movement, the leg placement of the dancer divides the timeline into four or multiple beats if the music is going very fast. The right leg moves forward on the strong beat and the left follows on the second. This is repeated for the third and fourth beats. Other gestures which are illustrated in this activity relate to social, religious, and human issues.

The dance ring can vary depending on the function of performance. In a communal performance such as during a funeral or festival when participation is not restricted, the instrumentalists will be positioned in the middle and surrounded by dancers who move around in a circular direction. This formation is shown in Figure 31.32.

In a theatrical arrangement, where only members of the band are allowed to perform, the dancers will dance in front of the instrumentalists and a small chorus standing at the rear. This arrangement is shown in Figure 31.33.

A performance starts with a short procession. Before the actual dance begins, there are songs led by the lead singer as a warm-up. This section can be in free rhythm or accompanied by only bells and rattles. When the mood is set, the master drum, the *vugā* or *dondo*, will play a signal to begin the whole performance. The end of the performance is also signaled by any of the two drums mentioned earlier.

Procedure:

1. Show MTG DVD 5, section on *Bɔbɔɔbɔ*, and discuss symbolic movements and gestures.

    a. Movement One: Figure 31.34, processional movement. This movement reminds us that as we journey through this life, it is important that we pause and reflect on our actions. As the dancers turn to the left and then to the right, they are being reminded of this aspect of their lives.

    b. Movement Two: Figure 31.35, the basic movement. This movement reminds us that we have to work hard to become successful in life. Literally, this movement means "cutting a path to the future."

    c. Movement Three: Figure 31.36. When dancers take a step to the right and wave their handkerchiefs in the air and then to the left while moving forward, it means, "When we travel this world, the Almighty God above is looking over us. His name should be praised."

    d. Movement Four: Figure 31.37. When the dancers take a step forward while rolling their handkerchiefs in front and then take a step backwards while looking behind, still rolling their handkerchiefs on the side, it means, "Whatever we do, we must not forget the past. Our past experiences should always guide our decisions."

    e. Movement Five: Figure 31.38. When the dancers move their arms in a circular motion

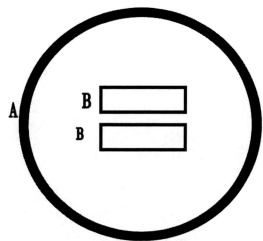

FIGURE 31.32: Traditional spatial arrangement for *Bɔbɔɔbɔ* performance. A: chorus and dancers; B. drummers.

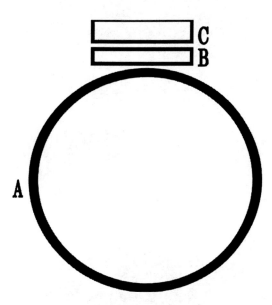

FIGURE 31.33: Theatrical arrangement for *Bɔbɔɔbɔ* performance. A: dancers; B: drummers; C: chorus.

with their eyes focused on the handkerchiefs, it means, "Whatever problems we face today, we will one day be free. "This movement reminds the Eʋe of the independence of Ghana and that we should never despair in this life.

    f. Movement Six: Figure 31.39. When dancers take three steps to the right while waving their handkerchiefs and then turn to face the opposite direction, it means, "When the going gets tough in this life, we are advised to seek wisdom from our elders."

    g. Movement Seven: Figure 31.40, contrast and release motion. This is an adaptation from the southern Eʋe *Agbadza* dance. This movement means, "Open your heart to everybody. Treat everybody as your own."

    h. Movement Eight: Figure 31.41, recessional movement.

2. Teach students to perform these movements and gestures with and without the music.

3. Guide students to match pictoral representations of symbolism with their meanings.

Pictorial Representation of Dance Movements and Symbolism

Beat 2 — Step 1   Beat 1—Step 2   Beat 2—Step 1   Beat 1—Step 2

FIGURE 31.34: Movement One (processional movement).

Beat 1— Step 1   Beat 2—Step 2   Beat 3—Step 3   Beat 4—Step 4

FIGURE 31.35: Movement Two (basic movement —four steps illustrated)

Beat 1— Step 1   Beat 2 — Step 2   Beat 3 — Step 3   Beat 4 — Step 4

Beat 1— Step 1   Beat 2 — Step 2   Beat 3 — Step 3   Beat 4 — Step 4

FIGURE 31.36: Movement Three (eight steps illustrated)

Beat 1 — Step 1   Beat 2 — Step 2   Beat 3 — Step 3   Beat 4 — Step 4

FIGURE 31.37: Movement Four (four steps illustrated)

Beat 1 — Step 1   Beat 2 — Step 2   Beat 3 — Step 3   Beat 4 — Step 4

FIGURE 31.38: Movement Four (four steps illustrated)

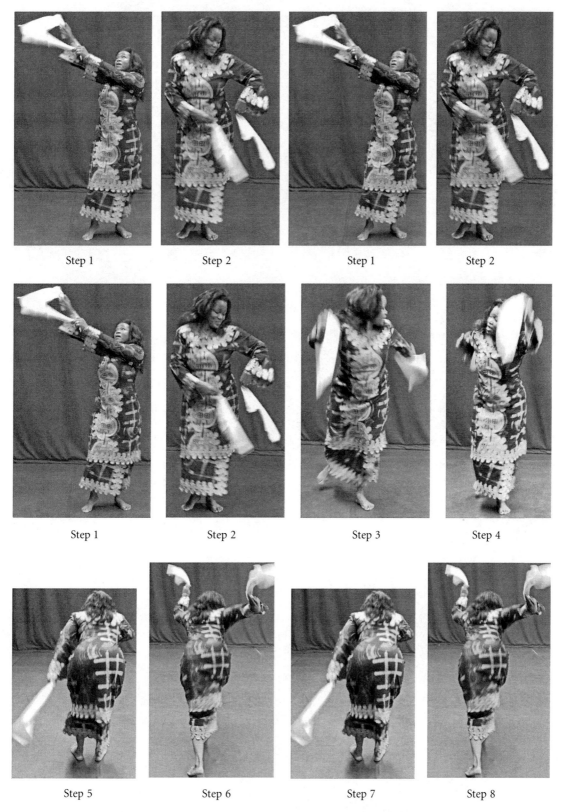

Step 1 Step 2 Step 1 Step 2

Step 1 Step 2 Step 3 Step 4

Step 5 Step 6 Step 7 Step 8

FIGURE 31.39: Movement Six (12 steps illustrated) (continued on page 398)

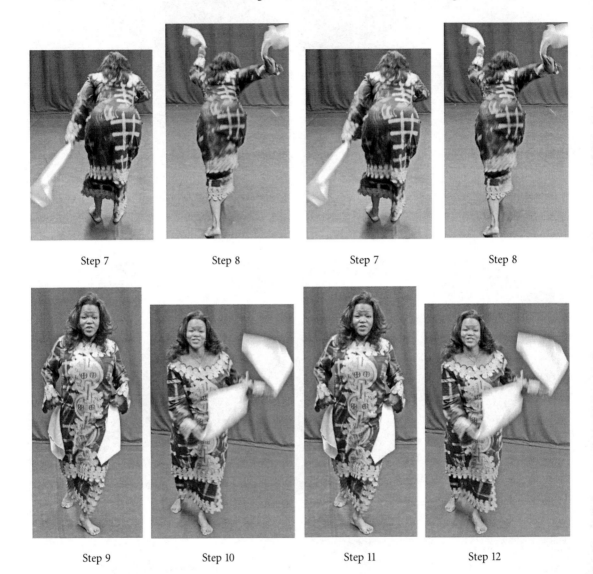

Step 7   Step 8   Step 7   Step 8

Step 9   Step 10   Step 11   Step 12

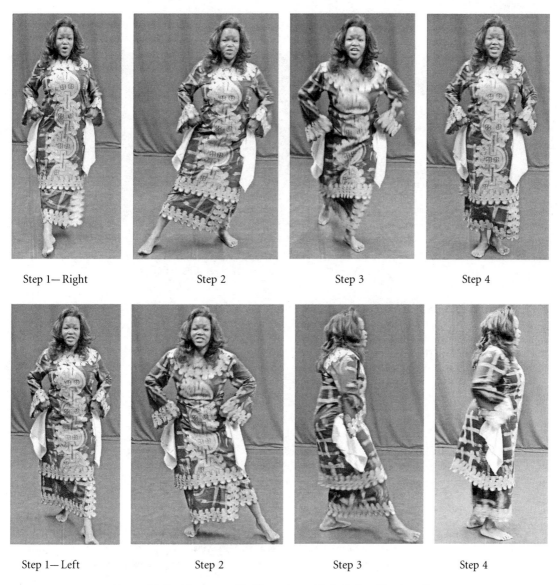

| Step 1— Right | Step 2 | Step 3 | Step 4 |

| Step 1— Left | Step 2 | Step 3 | Step 4 |

FIGURE 31.40: Movement Six (four steps with both legs illustrated)

Step 1— Right　　　　Step 2 — Right　　　　Step 3 — Left　　　　Step 4 — Left

FIGURE 31.41: Movement Six (four steps illustrated)

ACTIVITY / UNIT TWO

Focus:　　　Dancing to *Bɔbɔɔbɔ* music.

Objectives:　Students will:
1. learn and perform basic dance steps in *Bɔbɔɔbɔ*;
2. dance to the *Bɔbɔɔbɔ* timeline; and
3. perform the dance with a full instrumental ensemble.

Materials:　1. Video *Bɔbɔɔbɔ*, DVD 5 MTG by Paschal Younge (2011).
2. Audio *Bɔbɔɔbɔ*, TR. 6, MCM 3018 by Paschal Younge.

Procedure:

1. Show MTG DVD 5, section on *Bɔbɔɔbɔ*. This demonstrates the dance movements.

2. Teach students the basic steps of the dance. Students move around the classroom to counts one, two, three, and four. Each leg movement or foot placement should take a count. This movement will divide the timeline into four equal steps.

3. Add the timeline while students perform the basic step.

4. Repeat the same activity but add the arms. Move both arms across the body to the right and left to correspond with feet placement. Repeat this movement with the upper body slightly bent forward. Activities from step two to four describe the basic processional dance steps in *Bɔbɔɔbɔ*.

5. Use MTG DVD 5, section on *Bɔbɔɔbɔ* to teach other movements.

6. Students should perform the dance with all instrumental parts. The teacher can rearrange the different movements in any order. A concert can be organized at the end of the semester or year to perform for the whole school.

Evaluation of Procedures, Materials, and Student Achievement

The *Bɔbɔɔbɔ* dance-drumming teaching unit would be incomplete without an evaluation. The evaluation, to be carried out by both teachers and students, should focus on the effectiveness of instructional procedures, validity and appropriateness of subject matter, student participation, understanding, and development in the arts and culture of Africa.

Since the *Bɔbɔɔbɔ* teaching unit is tied to the needs and capabilities of the middle school learner, their artistic, aesthetic, and global understanding could be evaluated through cumulative assessment of each student's growth and development and criterion reference tests.

Skills that are to be examined should be categorized according to the specific objectives of the curriculum content. Each student's progress during independent practice and rehearsals should also be noted. Some of the progress charts to be considered for students' cumulative assessment are illustrated in charts 1 to 3, which follow (Younge 1998).

Chart 1:   Student's Record of Musical Development

Content Area: _____   Name of Student _____

Skills	Comments
1. Listening	_____
2. Social	_____
3. Analytical	_____
4. Classification	_____
5. Aural	_____
6. Construction	_____
7. Kinesthetic	_____
8. Imagination	_____
9. Creative	_____
10. Drawing	_____
11. Leadership	_____
12. Picture interpretation	_____
13. Pronunciation	_____
14. Performance	_____
15. Singing	_____

Chart 2:   Student Record of Drumming Competency

Name of Student _____

Instrument	Comment
1. *Kretsiwa #1* timeline	_____
2. *Kretsiwa #2*	_____
3. *Kretsiwa #3*	_____
4. *Tigo*	_____
5. *Akaye*	_____
6. *Uuvi*	_____
7. *Asivui*	_____
8. *Ɖondo*	_____
9. *Uugā*	_____

Chart 3:   Criteria for Evaluation of Instructional Activities

Content Area   _____

Activity (Unit)   _____

Evaluation Scale   (1   2   3   4   5   )

1 — Not appropriate for students
2 — Just below students' ability and scope
3 — Average content for student ability
4 — Appropriate for students
5 — Excellent material for students: suitable and relevant.

Constructive comments given to students can serve as great motivation and encouragement. Apart from the above records, teachers should organize aural and written tests regularly to evaluate subject matter and students' understanding and achievement. Teachers should design their own tests. The format of these tests can include multiple choice questions, short answers, true and false questions, and short essays. Specific areas to be tested in some of the activities under appreciation and drumming units are shown below:

Test One   Focus: the music of Bɔbɔɔbɔ and the Eʋe of Ghana
            1. Facts about Africa and Ghana
            2. Historical background of the Eʋe
            3. Geography of Ghana and the Eʋe
            4. Religious beliefs, customs, and habits of the Eʋe
            5. Education among the Eʋe
            6. Musical activities of the Eʋe

Test Two   Focus: function of Bɔbɔɔbɔ and dance among the Eʋe
            1. Historical development of Bɔbɔɔbɔ
            2. Distribution of Bɔbɔɔbɔ
            3. Functional and nonfunctional uses of Bɔbɔɔbɔ
            4. Mode of performance of Bɔbɔɔbɔ

Test Three   Focus: music, dance, and drama in Bɔbɔɔbɔ
            1. Relationship of music and dance
            2. Relationship of music and drama
            3. Symbolism and dance

Test Four   Focus: instruments of the Bɔbɔɔbɔ ensemble
            1. Categorization of instruments
            2. Description of instruments
            3. Functions of instruments in the ensemble
            4. Basic rhythms of instrumental parts
            5. Holding of instruments
            6. Playing techniques for instruments
            7. Modes of drumming — speech, dance, and signal
            8. Aesthetics in drumming

Test Five   Focus: rhythmic concepts in *Bɔbɔɔbɔ* drumming
          1. Definitions of the following terms:
             divisive rhythm
             additive rhythm
             hemiola
             cross rhythm, etc.

The main purpose of the above tests is to ascertain the validity of subject matter and to determine whether students have mastered a topic or unit well enough to proceed to the next topic or unit. The tests must therefore reflect the objectives of every focus area. It is also important for teachers to regularly give feedback to students.

Teachers can also document their involvement with the curriculum and students by keeping journals after each activity or unit. An example of such journal is provided below.

Chart 4: Teacher's journal — African dance-drumming curriculum

Name of Teacher: _____
Musical Background: _____
School: _____
Week: _____

Date	Time	Activity	Unit	Grade	Class	Size
____	____	____	____	____	____	____

Class Period _____
Materials _____
Extent to which materials are used

_____
_____

Comments about students' and teacher's reaction to activities

_____
_____
_____

Very Good	Good	Average	Poor	Very Poor
____	____	____	____	____

Other comments and suggestions to improve future lessons

_____
_____

The attainment of set goals and objectives should be seen as the overall success of this African music curriculum (Younge 1998).

NOTES. "The Organization of Teaching Activities: Outline of Activities for Teaching *Bɔbɔɔbɔ* Music*,*" originally appeared in the author's "Enhancing Global Understanding through Traditional African Music and Dance: A Multicultural African Music Curriculum for American Middle Schools," an unpublished dissertation submitted to the College of Human Resources and Education at West Virginia University in partial fulfillment of the requirements for the degree of doctor of education in curriculum and instruction, 1998.

Appendix: Performing Groups and Notes on DVDs

Music and Dance Traditions of Ghana MTG DVD 1

Adzogbo Ritual Dance-Drumming Ceremony

Date of performance and field recording: July 11, 2006
Venue of performance: Aflao
Phase One: *Tsifofofdi*, pouring of libation
Phase Two: *Kadodo*, women's show-off dance-drumming phase
Phase Three: *Atsiawɔwɔ*, main dance-drumming phase (male dancers only)
Phase Four: *Kadodo*, women's round-off dance-drumming phase

Group: Aflao Mauwulikplimi *Adzogbo*

Agbadza Funeral Dance-Drumming Ceremony

Date of performance and field recording: July 13, 2006
Venue of performance: Dzodze
Phase One: *Banyinyi*, tribute to the ancestors and gods
Phase Two: *Avɔlunyanya*, tribute to the musicians who died
Phase Three: *Uutsɔtsɔ*, main dance-drumming phase
Phase Four: *Hatsiatsia*, joining of songs or song cycle
Phase Five: *Uutsɔtsɔ*, main dance-drumming phase

Group: Anlɔ Afiaɖenyigba Agbadza (2006)

Music and Dance Traditions of Ghana MTG DVD 2

Atibladekame Women's Funeral Dance-Drumming Ceremony

Date of performance and field recording: July 13, 2006
Venue of performance: Dzodze
Phase One: *Uulɔlɔ*, the procession
Phase Two: *Adzotsotso*, tribute to the ancestors and gods
Phase Three:
    Uutsɔtsɔ, main dance-drumming phase Aƒeteƒe Atsigo
    Uutsɔtsɔ, main dance-drumming phase Dafɔnyami Anyanui
    Uutsɔtsɔ, main dance-drumming phase KpɔɖoaveAkpalu
    Uutsɔtsɔ, main dance-drumming phase Fiagbedu Aɖidokpui Nyawuame
    Uutsɔtsɔ, main dance-drumming phase Fiagbedu Agbikpɔnu Ɖegbato
    Uutsɔtsɔ, main dance-drumming phase Fiagbedu Aƒegame Ɖekɔenu

Group: Dzodze *Atibladekame* (2006)

Atrikpui Warriors' Dance-Drumming Ceremony

Date of performance and field recording: July 13, 2006
Venue of performance: Dzodze
Phase One: *Asafosetsotso*, a prewar ritual to warm up the participant
Phase Two: *Atrilɔlɔ*, processional dance-drumming phase
Phase Three: *Asafosetsotso*, a prewar ritual to warm up the participant
Phase Four: *Hatsiatsia*, joining of songs or song cycle
Phase Five: *Atrikpui*, main dance-drumming phase
Phase Six: *Asafosetsotso*, a prewar ritual to warm up the participant

Group: Dzodze Afetefe *Atrikpui* Group (2006)

Music and Dance Traditions of Ghana MTG DVD 3

Atsiagbekɔ Warriors' Dance-Drumming Ceremony

Date of performance and field recording: July 11, 2006
Venue of performance: Dzogadze
Phase One: *Uulɔlɔ*, processional dance-drumming
Phase Two: *Adzo*, a tribute to the old warriors
Phase Three: *Hatsiatsia*, joining of songs or song cycle
Phase Four: *Atsiawɔwɔ*, main dance-drumming phase
Phase Five: *Uulɔlɔ*, processional dance-drumming

Group: Dzogadze *Atsiagbekɔ* (2008)

Gadzo Warriors' Dance-Drumming Ceremony

Date of performance and field recording: July 12, 2006
Venue of performance: Anlɔ Afiaɖenyigba
Phase One: *Misego*, tribute to the ancestors
Phase Two: *Uulɔlɔ*, processional dance-drumming
Phase Three: *Atsiawɔwɔ*, main dance-drumming phase
Phase Four: *Hatsiatsia*, joining of songs, song cycle
Phase Five: *Atsiawɔwɔ*, main dance-drumming phase
Phase Six: *Uulɔlɔ*, processional dance-drumming

Music and Dance Traditions of Ghana MTG DVD 4

Gahʋ Recreational Dance-Drumming Ceremony

Date of performance and field recording: July 11, 2006
Venue of performance: Tadzeʋu
Phase One: *Hatsiatsia*, joining of songs or song cycle
Phase Two: *Ayoɖeɖe*, greetings and prayers to the ancestors
Phase Three: *Atsiawɔwɔ*, warm-up and preparation for *Uutsɔtsɔ*
Phase Four: *Uutsɔtsɔ*, main dance-drumming phase

Group: Anlɔ Afiaɖenyigba *Gadzo* (2006)

Group: Tadzeʋu *Gahu* (2006)

Music and Dance Traditions of Ghana MTG DVD 5

Adeʋu Hunters' Dance-Drumming Ceremony

Date of performance and field recording: July 12, 2006
Venue of performance: Alavanyo Uudidi

Phase One: *Adezɔlizɔzɔ*, procession
Phase Two: *Adekaka*, dramatization of a hunting expedition
Phase Three: *Adevu*, hunters' main dance-drumming phase
Phase Four: *Adevu*, hunters' main dance-drumming phase
Phase Five: *Adevu*, hunters' main dance-drumming phase
Phase Six: *Adevu*, hunters' main dance-drumming phase
Phase Seven: *Adevu*, hunters' main dance-drumming phase
Phase Eight: *Akpi*, warrior's dance-drumming phase
Phase Nine: *Adevu*, hunters' main dance-drumming phase

Group: Alavanyo Uudidi *Adevu* (2006)

Group: Ho Agbenya *Bɔbɔɔbɔ* Group (2008)

Bɔbɔɔbɔ Recreational Dance-Drumming Ceremony

Date of performance and field recording: July 12, 2008
Venue of performance: Ho
Phase One: *Azɔlizɔzɔ*, procession
Phase Two: *Ahomu*, warming up the voice
Phase Three: *Uufofo*, main dance-drumming phase
Phase Four: *Uufofo*, main dance-drumming phase
Phase Five: *Azɔlizɔzɔ*, processional dance-drumming

Music and Dance Traditions of Ghana MTG DVD 6

Egbanegba Recreational Dance-Drumming Ceremony

Date of performance and field recording: July 12, 2006
Venue of performance: Alavanyo Uudidi
Phase One: *Gbemefofo*, warming up the voice
Phase Two: *Egbanegba*, main dance-drumming phase
Phase Three: *Adzomadɔalɔe*, lovers' dance-drumming phase
Phase Four: *Dzeḍoḍo*, conversational dance-drumming phase
Phase Five: *Egbanegba*, main dance-drumming phase

Group: Alavanyo Uudidi *Egbanegba* (2008)

Gbolo Recreational Dance-Drumming Ceremony

Date of performance and field recording: July 12, 2006
Venue of performance: Alavanyo Uudidi
Phase One: *Gbemefofo*, warming up the voice
Phase Two: *Gbolo Akaye*, main dance-drumming phase
Phase Three: *Gbolo Akaye*, main dance-drumming phase
Phase Four: *Gbolo Akaye*, main dance-drumming phase
Phase Five: *Gbolo Akaye*, main dance-drumming phase

Group: Alavanyo Uudidi *Gbolo* (2007)

Music and Dance Traditions of Ghana MTG DVD 7

Gome Recreational Dance-Drumming Ceremony

Date of performance and field recording: December 1, 2006
Venue of performance: Accra
Phase One: *Oshwe*, warm-up singing phase
Phase Two: *Gome*, main dance-drumming phase

Group: Abɔdzen Etse *Gome* (2006)

Kolomashie Recreational Dance-Drumming Ceremony

Date of performance and field recording: June 23, 2001
Venue of performance: Accra
Phase One: *Oshwe*, warm-up singing phase
Phase Two: *Kolomashie*, main dance-drumming phase

Group: Emashie *Kolomashie* (2001)

Kpanlongo Recreational Dance-Drumming Ceremony

Date of performance and field recording: June 23, 2001
Venue of performance: Accra
Phase One: *Oshwe*, warm-up singing phase
Phase Two: *Kpanlongo*, main dance-drumming phase

Group: Emashie *Kpanlongo* (2001)

Music and Dance Traditions of Ghana MTG DVD 8

Adowa Funeral Dance-Drumming Ceremony

Date of performance and field recording: July 2009
Venue of performance: University of Ghana, Legon
Phase One: *Anyanee*, the awakening of the dance arena
Phase Two: *Ayan, atumpan* drum poetry/messages
Phase Three: *Atene*, setting the stage for the dancers
Phase Four: *Ahuri*, climax and main dance-drumming phase
Phase Five: *Anyanee*, the awakening of the dance arena
Phase Six: *Atene*, setting the stage for the dancers
Phase Seven: *Ahuri*, climax and main dance-drumming phase funeral performance
Phase Seven: *Adowa Kete, adowa* highlife fast dance-drumming phase

Group: National Dance Company of Ghana, University of Ghana, Legon (2009)

Asaadua Recreational Dance-Drumming Ceremony

Date of performance and field recording: July 2009
Venue of performance: University of Ghana, Legon
Phase One: *Aho*, warm-up singing phase
Phase Two: *Asaadua*, main dance-drumming phase

Group: National Dance Company of Ghana, University of Ghana, Legon (2009)

Sikyi Recreational Dance-Drumming Ceremony

Date of performance and field recording: July 2009
Venue of performance: University of Ghana, Legon
Phase One: *Aho*, warm-up singing phase
Phase Two: *Agorɔ*, setting the stage for the dancers
Phase Three: *Sikyi*, main dance-drumming phase
Phase Four: *Aho*, warm-up singing phase
Phase Five: *Agorɔ*, setting the stage for the dancers
Phase Six: *Sikyi*, main dance-drumming phase

Group: National Dance Company of Ghana, University of Ghana, Legon (2009)

Kete Royal Dance-Drumming Ceremony

Venue of performance: University of Ghana, Legon
Phase One: *Abɔfoɔ*, hunters dance-drumming phase
Phase Two: *Adamuabua*, slow dance-drumming phase
Phase Three: *Srɛsrɛbidi/Akatape*, tribute to the chief "Majestic Walking"
Phase Four: *Akuadum*, royal dance-drumming phase
Phase Five: *Kwekwenisuo*, slow
dance-drumming phase

Phase Six: *Frimpong Manso*, tribute to Alexander Ata Yaw Keremanteng
Phase Seven: *Wɔfa Ata*, tribute to
founder of the youth wing of
Amammereso Agofomma
Phase Eight: *Apɛntɛ*, processional
dance-drumming phase
Phase Nine: *Akɔkono Bɛtɛɛ*, royal
dance-drumming phase

Right: Group: National Dance
Company of Ghana, University
of Ghana, Legon (2009)

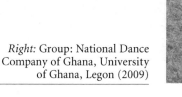

Music and Dance Traditions of Ghana MTG DVD 9

Baamaaya Recreational Dance-Drumming Ceremony

Date of performance and field recording: July 2009
Venue of performance: Tamale
Phase One: *Baamaaya Sochendi*, processional dance drumming
Phase Two: *Baamaaya Valiŋa*, fast dance-drumming phase
Phase Three: *Sikoro*, prevention from entering peoples' homes
Phase Four: *Nyaɣboli*, main dance-drumming phase
Phase Five: *Kondoliya*, tribute to water
Phase Six: *Dakolkutooko*, mockery at bachelors
Phase Seven: *Abalimbee*, the beauty of *Baamaaya* dance-drumming
Phase Eight: *Baaŋa*, song cycle, singing of praise songs
Phase Nine: *Baamaaya Valiŋa*, fast dance-drumming as recessional dance

Group: Tamale Youth Home Cultural *Baamaaya* (2009)

Group: Jakpahi Dang Maligu *Bla* (2009)

Bla Religious Dance-Drumming Ceremony

Date of performance and field recording: July 2009
Venue of performance: Jakpahi
Phase One: *Bla*, main dance-drumming phase as procession
Phase Two: *Bilje*, honoring the dead around the grave
Phase Three: *Yila*, song cycle, praise and historical songs
Phase Four: *Sagali*, procession to honor the dead
Phase Five: *Damba*, festival dance drumming of Damba
Phase Six: *Zem*, tribute to warriors dance-drumming phase
Phase Seven: *Yila*, song cycle, praise and historical songs
Phase Eight: *Bla*, main dance-drumming phase as procession
Phase Nine: *Yaawum*, tribute to grandchildren

Music and Dance Traditions of Ghana MTG DVD 10

Jɛra Religious Music and Dance

Date of performance and field recording: July 2009
Venue of performance: Kpegu
Phase One: *Jɛra-Sochendi*, processional dance-drumming phase
Phase Two: *Jɛra-Tɔra*, preparatory dance drumming phase
Phase Three: *Jɛra-Lura*, main dance dance-drumming phase
Phase Four: *Baaŋa*, song cycle, praise and historical songs
Phase Five: *Jɛra-Tɔra*, preparatory dance-drumming phase
Phase Six: *Lelba*, tribute to the *Jɛra* costume
Phase Seven: *Jɛra-Sochendi*, processional dance-drumming phase

Group: Kpegu *Jera* (2009)

Tɔra Women's Recreational Dance-Drumming Ceremony

Date of performance and field recording: July 2009
Venue of performance: Tamale
Phase One: *Zamandunia*, processional dance-drumming phase
Phase Two: *Tɔra*, main dance-drumming phase
Phase Three: *Nyaɣboli*, tribute to *Baamaaya*
Phase Four: *Ŋundanyuli*, creating a name for yourself
Phase Five: *Damduu*, rebuke of those who instigate trouble
Phase Six: *Anakuliyela*, mockery at talkative persons
Phase Seven: *Ŋumalpieŋ*, those with power are always right
Phase Eight: *Tɔra yiɣera*, celebration of joy through jumping
Phase Nine: *Ŋunkpelimkpe*, patience — he who remains last always gets the best and succeeds
Phase Ten: *Bangumaŋa*, self protection
Phase Eleven: *Kookali*, teaching the virtue of goodness
Phase Twelve: *Kondoliya*, recessional dance-drumming phase

Group: Tamale Youth Home Cultural Group (2009)

Glossary

Eʋe Terms

Abebubuwo Eʋe proverbial and symbolic actions and gestures.

Abrase Gbemefofo, warm-up singing in *Adevu* that starts every phase of the Eʋe *Adevu* dance-drumming. Performed in a recitative or declamatory style.

Abuḍu See *tavuga*

Adasasa Preparatory dance movement in dance-drumming ceremonies. Also, a preliminary warm-up movement in the Eʋe dance-drumming *Atrikpui* involving arms and legs. The master drummer also uses it to usher dancers into action.

Adegba An Eʋe word for "the hunters' god," and a shrine representing the spirits of the hunters, warriors and ancestors who have died.

Adekaka Dramatization of a hunting expedition in the *Adevu* dance-drumming ceremony.

Adekotoku A hunting pouch used by hunters.

Adekplɔvi Eʋe word for apprentice hunter.

Adekpoeza An Eʋe festival.

Adekpui Dagger, an implement used by the Eʋes in wars and hunting.

Ademega The chief or headhunter. This title would only be bestowed on a hunter who was able to hunt one of the following animals: lion, leopard, buffalo, elephant, tiger or hyena.

Adetre An Eʋe word for a calabash normally filled with *wɔtsi* in the hunters' ceremony.

Adevu A dance-drumming ceremony for *adelawo*, hunters, which originated among the Eʋes during their settlement in Ŋɔtsie. Also, it refers to the hunters' main dance-drumming phase.

Adewu Eʋe word for hunter's dress made from the bark of gboloba or logo azagu, a species of the cedar tree, which is also used in drum-making.

Adezɔlizɔzɔ The procession phase in *Adevu* dance-drumming.

Adoḍeḍe See *adasasa*.

Adodo An Eʋe instrument, idiophone, multiclapper bell.

Aḍondo See *Ɖondo*.

Adzo Eʋe word for war god. Also represents a phase in *Atsiagbekɔ* dance-drumming.

Adzogbo One of the religious dance-drumming ceremonies introduced to Ghana in the late 19th century by the Eʋe from Benin. Other names used today for the same dance are *Adzogbe*, meaning "Let us go to war"; and *Dogbo*, used by the Wheta people of Ghana.

Adzotsotso An Eʋe prewar dance-drumming ritual.

Adzɔka Eʋe word for bush rope used to fasten skin onto the drumheads.

Adzovu An Eʋe religious dance-drumming ceremony.

Afa An Eʋe divination order or cult, its dance-drumming is called *Afavu*.

Afla Eʋe word for species of thatch, *Imperetus cylindrical*.

Aflawu-Godigbezā An Eʋe festival.

Agbadza Eʋe funeral dance-drumming. Also refers to a war girdle used for carrying war implements.

Agbazo A "possessed" member of an *Adzogbo* dance-drumming group, usually the spiritual head/medicine man.

Agbeyeye Another name for the *Bɔbɔɔbɔ* recreational dance-drumming ceremony.

Agblɔvu Serves as a speech surrogate, in addition to its function as a supporting drum in most Eʋe percussion ensembles.

Agbobli A master drum of an Eʋe ensemble, a name of a war dance-drumming ceremony of the Aves of Ghana and also another name for the *sogo* drum.

Agbomlɔanyi A membranophone or drum used in Yeʋe religious ceremonies and other ancient dance-drumming ceremonies. It resembles a smaller version of the *atimevu*.

Agbozume-Sometutuzā An Eʋe festival.

Ahiavu An Eʋe love or courtship dance-drumming performance during which young men would display their love charms.

Ahomu Preparation of the voice phase of the Eʋe dance-drumming, *Bɔbɔɔbɔ*.

Akadodo Eʋe word for trial by ordeal.

Akatsi-Denyazā An Eʋe festival.

Akaye An Eʋe instrument classified as a shaken, non-melodic idiophone. It is made of beads or seeds placed in a hollowed gourd. Women (solely) in all northern Eʋe musical events use it. It is also used to describe the southern Eʋe *axatse*, rattle.

Akoge See *kretsiwa*.

Akpe An Eʋe term for hand clapping.

Akpese Another name for *Bɔbɔɔbɔ* dance-drumming.

Akpi Central and northern Eʋe warriors' dance-drumming ceremony.

Akplɔ See *hlo*.

Ala An Eʋe woven raffia skirt tied over the dancers' knees in the *Adzogbo* dance-drumming ceremony.

Alivoe A two-yard piece of cloth worn around the waist by women in central and northern dance-drumming performances.

Amawuwu The sprinkling of spiritual herbs during an Eʋe dance-drumming ceremony.

Amaze A pot filled with medicinal herbs and water for Eʋe dance-drumming ceremonies.

Ameɗiɖi An Eʋe burial ceremony.

Ampoti Songs of exhilaration usually performed by the Eʋe warriors' song during the Akpi phase in *Adeʋu*. Performed in a recitative or declamatory style.

Amuti Eʋe word for a typical lagoon tree, *Avicennia germinanus*.

Anecho-Tugbazā An Eʋe festival.

Anl-Hogbetsotsozā An Eʋe festival.

Asafohawo Eʋe songs of valor.

Asafosetsotso See *adzotsotso*.

Ashiawɔ An Eʋe term for harlots or prostitutes.

Asiʋui See *kidi* and *Uuvi*.

Atamkahawo Eʋe songs of oath.

Atamugā An Eʋe word literally meaning "the great oath"; also the previous name for *Atsiagbekɔ*, when it was used as a prewar dance ritual. The name was changed to *Atsiagbekɔ* or *Agbekɔ* in the absence of wars.

Atibladekame An Eʋe philosophical thought: "United we stand; divided we fall," literally meaning, "trees tied together." It is the name for six distinct women's dance-drumming groups which come together to sing choral laments, dirges, recite eulogies and dance at funerals for loved ones and relatives in Dzodze.

Atible The original costume for the *Atibladekame* dance-drumming ceremony.

Atiɖeke Eʋe terms for individual dance sections or self-expression.

Atifu Northern Eʋe dress similar to *atible* of the southern Eʋes.

Atimeʋu A membranophone or drum is one of the largest and tallest drums in any Eʋe percussion ensemble. Modeled after *agbomlɔanyi*, a similar drum used in Yeʋe religious ceremonies, it is mostly featured as a lead drum.

Atinua Eʋe title for the disciplinarian of dance-drumming ensembles.

Atoke An Eʋe instrument, which is an idiophone. It is a boat-shaped or slit bell.

Atopani An Eʋe membranophone or drum believed to be of Akan origin, it is featured mostly at the courts of chiefs and in limited dance-drumming performances such as *Atrikpui*, *Afli*, *Uugā*, and *Kete*.

Atrikpui Southern Eʋe dance-drumming for warriors.

Atrilɔlɔ An Eʋe processional dance-drumming during funerals, ceremonies for state gods, and state festivals. It is also a phase in *Atrikpui* dance-drumming.

Atsaka A special type of knee-high dancing shorts used by the Eʋe in most dance-drumming ceremonies.

Atsiadotɔ See *lebiala*.

Atsiagbekɔ An Eʋe war dance-drumming ceremony.

Atsiawɔwɔ A phase in *Adzogbo*, *Gadzo*, *Atsiagbekɔ* and *Gahu* dance-drumming ceremonies when the dancers perform stylistic movements.

Atsiayɔla See *lebiala*.

Atsokla See *kadodo*.

Avadadawo Military commanders of the Eʋes.

Avaʋu A war dance of the Eʋes.

Avlaya A type of skirt made up of several layers of cloth with different designs as used in *Adzogbo* and *Yeʋe* dance-drumming ceremonies.

Avernopedo-Agbelizā An Eʋe festival.

Avɔlunyanya A phase in southeastern Eʋe dance-drumming ceremonies that pays tribute to musicians who have died.

Awɔmefia The paramount chief of the southern Eʋes who lives in Aŋlɔgā.

Awu Eʋe word for blouse.

Axatse An Eʋe instrument which is an idiophone. It is a rattle made of beads woven around a hollowed gourd or a gourd wrapped in strings of seeds or beads.

Ayoɖeɖe A phase in the *Gahu* dance-drumming ceremony.

Ayoo See *ayoɖeɖe*.

Azagunɔ Eʋe master/lead drummer.

Azagunɔkpewo Eʋe word for players of supporting instruments.

Banyinyi A phase of Eʋe dance-drumming ceremonies that pays tribute to the ancestors and gods.

Be See *afla*.

Biglo An Eʋe name for the western bugle.

Blēmaʋuwo Eʋe ancient dance-drumming ceremonies.

Bɔbɔɔbɔ The most popular recreational dance-drumming of the central and northern Eʋes.

Brekete An Eʋe religious order or cult, its dance-drumming is called *Brekete*. This is also the name for the Dagbamba *guŋgoŋ* drum.

Dabawu An Eʋe shirt made from the bark of the logo tree. Similar to the present-day northern Ghanaian smock.

Ɖonɖo See *Ɖonno*.

Ɖonno An Eʋe hourglass-shaped drum.

Du Eʋe word for a town.

Dufiawo Eʋe title for a town chief.

Dumegāwo Elders among the Eʋes.

Dzatsi A mixture of corn flour and water used for pouring libations.

Dzeɖoɖo Fourth phase in the *Egbanegba* performance, which expresses friendship and happiness. *Dzeɖoɖo*, which means a conversation between lovers, shows the climax of the ceremony.

Dzidefohawo Eʋe songs of courage.

Dzimeŋeŋe The main dance movement in Eʋe dance-drumming ceremonies.

Dzimewu A blouse worn over cloth in most Eʋe dance-drumming ceremonies.

Dzoka Eʋe protective talisman or charm.

Dzoʋu An Eʋe ritual dance-drumming ceremony.

Egbanegba Northern Eʋe dance-drumming ceremony that started as *Gabada*, a courtship or love dance.

Efɔ See *logo*.

Eko See *ladzo*.

Eʋegbe The Eʋe language.

Eʋedomeawo See *Eʋemeaw*.

Eʋemeawo Refers to the central and northern Eʋes of Ghana and Togo.

Fianɔfe Eʋe word for the chief's palace.

Gadzo One of the oldest traditional war dance-drumming ceremonies of the southern Eʋes.

Gagbleve See *gakogui*.

Gahu Eʋe recreational dance-drumming ceremony.

Gakogoe Northern Eʋe boat-shaped or slit bell similar to the *atoke* used by the southeastern Eʋe.

Gakogui An Eʋe instrument, idiophone, double bell.

Gakpevi See *gakogui*.

Gazo See *gadzo*.

Gbemefofo Eʋe word for clearing of the voice. *Gbemefofo* in *Bɔbɔɔbɔ* is referred to as *ahomu*.

Gbleke Eʋe word for short grass, *Paspalum vaginatum*.

Gboba Eʋe instrument, membranophone or drum, originally called *gbagba* because of its wide playing area or head. *Gboba* is a low-pitched, single-headed drum with an opening at one end mainly used for the dance-drumming types *Kinka* and *Gahu*.

Gbolo Literally meaning the "loved one," *Gbdo* is principally an Eʋe women's recreational dance-drumming performance.

Go See *axatse*.

Glitoto Eʋe word for the telling of folktales.

Hādzidzi Eʋe term for the art of singing, also stands for the vocal form of music.

Hadzitɔ Eʋe word for lead singer or cantor.

Hāglā See *hadzitɔ*.

Hakpala Composer of songs among the Eʋes.

Halo Eʋe songs of ridicule.

Hatsiatsia The joining of songs or song cycle in Eʋe dance-drumming ceremonies.

Hatsola Eʋe word for the special assistant to the *henɔ*.

Hatsovi Assistants to the *henɔ* and *hatsola*.

Havana See *Uuga*.

Hawuwu Eʋe song cycle in free rhythm.

Henɔ See *hadzitɔ*.

Hlo Spear, an implement used by the Eʋes in war.

Hūsago See *misego*.

Kadaa See *atinua*.

Kadodo Women's dance "show off" section or round off in the *Adzogbo* dance-drumming ceremony.

Kagan An Eʋe instrument, a membranophone or drum, it is the smallest and highest-pitched drum in Eʋe percussion ensembles.

Kaganu See *kagan*.

Kaleawoe Eʋe warriors.

Kaleseye See *asafohawo*.

Kaleʋu See *Atrikpui*.

Kidi An Eʋe membranophone or drum. It is single-headed, closed and has all the features of a *sogo* except for its size, timbre and function in the percussion ensemble. It functions mainly as a supporting drum and plays in dialogue with or doubles the *sogo*.

Kini See *Gadzo*.

Kɔfe An Eʋe village.

Kɔku An Eʋe religious order or cult, its dance-drumming ceremony is called *Kɔkuʋu*.

Kpakpanu See *kagan*.

Kpe An Eʋe aerophone or horn.

Kpetsi See *kidi*.

Kpetsigo See *kagan*.

Kpo A club used in Eʋe war dance-drumming ceremonies.

Kpɔnkuitɔwo Special assistants to the *Uumega* and *Uudada* in Eʋe dance-drumming ensembles.

Kretsiwa Finger bell or castanet used by northern Eʋes.

Kroboto Eʋe membranophones or drums—the main instruments used as signal drums during wars. The *kroboto* functions as the male principle and *totodzi* as the female principle in the *Atsiagbekɔ* dance-drumming ceremony.

Krokoto An Eʋe instrument used both as a signal and speech drum. This instrument is reserved exclusively for the chief and the hunters' and warriors' associations.

Lādzo The horn from a buffalo or other big game or animals is used as a side-blown wind instrument reserved solely for the chief. A smaller horn from the antelope or deer functions as a bell in the *Adeʋu* dance-drumming ceremony.

Le/Atsia "Style" or "display" or pre-choreographed

steps or phrases of movement/dance routines in the *Adzogbo* dance-drumming ceremony.

Lebiala Male lead dancer in the *Adzogbo* dance-drumming ceremony.

Lega See *lebiala*.

Lēgba Eʋe name for an idol.

Loglo A camouflage hat worn in warriors' dance-drumming ceremonies.

Logo Special species of the cedar tree used to carve Eʋe drums.

Logobo The bark of the logo tree used for making dabawu.

Mafi An Eʋe word for a small scarf or towel.

Mawu The Eʋe word for the Almighty God or Supreme Being.

Mawu Aɖanuwɔtɔ Eʋe phrase meaning the Blessed Trinity, which is omnipotent, omnipresent and omniscient.

Mawu Kitikata Eʋe phrase meaning "God is the source of life."

Mawuenyega An Eʋe word meaning "God is the greatest one."

Mawuli An Eʋe word meaning "God is near/exists."

Mawunyo An Eʋe word meaning "God is kind."

Mawu Segbolisa An Eʋe word for God the Father.

Mawusi An Eʋe word meaning "in the hands of God."

Mba Wooden clappers made from bamboo strips used in central and northern Eʋe dance-drumming ceremonies.

Misego An Eʋe dance-drumming ceremony performed as a tribute to the ancestors. It highlights their migration from Ŋɔtsie in the Republic of Togo to their present settlements. It is one of the phases in Yeʋe ritual performance.

Modzakadeʋu Eʋe word for a recreational dance-drumming ceremony.

Nkɔmɔ See *dzeɖodo*.

Nukpɔkpɔ Eʋe word meaning a public spectacle.

Nyatse A local hardwood often used for drum pegs by Eʋe drum-makers.

Ŋudɔdɔ Eʋe word for wake-keeping.

Ŋutsuʋu See *Atrikpui*.

Pati A small tom tom. Adaptation of the western military field drum.

Sanku Eʋe name for a western instrument, the harmonica.

Sebe/Badua Eʋe word for animal tail.

Sogo An Eʋe membranophone or drum. It is a single-headed, closed drum symbolizing the "father" with *kidi* and *kagan* as "mother" and "child" respectively, in Eʋe percussion ensembles.

Sokpe-Tɔtsotsozā An Eʋe festival.

Sɔshi Eʋe word for horsetail or switch used in dance-drumming ceremonies.

Taku See *mafi*.

Tavugā A membranophone or drum. It is the Eʋe version of the Akan *bɔmma* or *fɔntɔmfrɔm*; like *atopani*, it is reserved solely for political institu-

tions and events. It is usually dressed in white cloths as a symbol of sacredness and purity.

Televi A secondary rattle/bell worn by dancers in the *Adzogbo* dance-drumming ceremony.

Tigo See *gakogui*.

To Eʋe word for ward/division of a town.

Toke See *atoke*.

Tokɔmefiawo Clan heads among the Eʋes.

Totodzi See *kroboto*.

Tsafulegede An Eʋe chordophone, or bow-harp.

Tsi fo fodi Purification rites or libation in Eʋe societies.

Tsyɔga Grand funeral celebration among the Eʋes.

Tsyɔlɔlɔ Final funeral rites of the Eʋes.

Tu Gun, an implement used by the Eʋes in wars and for hunting expeditions.

Tɔgbuizikpui kɔklɔ The cleansing or pacification of Eʋe ancestral stools.

Tɔgbuizikpuiwo Eʋe ancestral stools.

Trɔnuawo Spiritual heads/leaders of the southeastern Eʋes.

Trɔwo Lesser gods or deities of the Eʋes.

Vewɔwɔ Celebration of twin rites among the Eʋes.

Viheheɖego Naming or outdooring ceremony for newborns among the Eʋes.

Voga-Adzinukuzā An Eʋe festival.

Uudada The female leader or queen mother of Eʋe dance-drumming ensembles.

Uubabla The most common method of constructing drums among the Eʋe. The process involves cutting wooden staves to special sizes, fastening the individual staves together and then attaching the membrane of an antelope or deerskin to the head.

Uudeti See *Uuglātsi*.

Uugā An Eʋe instrument used as the master or lead drum in the *Bɔbɔɔbɔ* percussion ensemble.

Uugbe An Eʋe term for interpreting the tones of instruments as mnemonic vocable syllables or texts.

Uuglātsi Eʋe names for a stand used to support large/long drums like the *atsimeʋu*, which is played tilted forward.

Uulɔlɔ The processional phase in most Eʋe dance-drumming ensembles.

Uumegā The male patron of Eʋe dance-drumming ensembles.

Uukpo See *krokoto*.

Uutoto Eʋe method of constructing drums by carving from solid wood of a special species of the cedar tree.

Uutsɔtsɔ The main phase of most southern Eʋe dance-drumming ceremonies.

Uuvi Single-headed drums with bottle necks at the base which may be carved to the same size. *Uuvi* is a little higher in pitch. The *asiʋui* or *ade-asiʋui* leads in most percussion ensembles while the *Uuvi* serves as the main supporting drum in northern Eʋe ceremonies.

Uɔnu A designated assembly ground in all Eʋe communities which is used for state assemblies, meetings, and dance-drumming performances or other social events in the community.

Wɔtsi See *dzatsi*.

Xotutuwo The historical tales/stories of the elders among the Eʋes.

Yelu See *Gadzo*.

Yeʋe The traditional god of Xebieso, Hũ or Tɔhonɔ, is a thunder god. He has historical relations to the Yoruba Shango and Xevioso of Benin. The cult is one of the most powerful and most secretive in West Africa.

Yi Cutlass, an implement used in Eʋe war dance-drumming ceremonies and for farming activities.

Zizihawo Eʋe songs that proclaim the presence of chiefs.

Ga Terms

Abɛibe Ga word for April, when butterflies and moths are plentiful and found around fruit-bearing trees. It is considered to be mango season.

Accra The capital city of Ghana.

Adaawe lala Ga term for songs sung during puberty or maiden rites.

Aklama Ga words for hunters' dance-drumming and songs performed by fishermen during expeditions.

Adebɔɔ Shia Ga word for one's house of origin.

Adesa lala Ga term used for songs performed as interludes during storytelling sessions.

Agbeona Ga word for the rainy season from May to July.

Agbieɛnaa Ga word for May, in which the rains begin. It is known as the end of the Ga year.

Aharabata Ga word for January, the harmattan cold season — mid–December to early February.

Alemele Ga word for the cold and dry season with little sunshine — November.

Asafotufiam Ga festival that unites the Ga-Dangme of today.

Atswereshi Ga word for a conga-type drum —*kpanlongo mi*.

Ayawa Ga term for bragging with the drum or performing slap tones on the drum.

Dadefoɔkye Ga word for master drummer.

Dodompo Ga word for castanets.

Donno Ga hourglass-shaped drum.

Fume Fume Ga recreational dance-drumming ceremony.

Ga-Maŋtsɛ See *Ga maŋtsɛ-nukpa*.

Ga Maŋtsɛ-nukpa Ga paramount chief.

Gamashi Ga area, Jamestown and Usher Town.

Gamɛi Ga people.

Gbatsu Ga word for shrines and animals.

Gbla mii Ga term for tearing up the drum.

Gbo Ga word for the rainy season from the last half of September to December.

Gome Ga word for box drum or a Ga recreational dance-drumming that uses the drum as its lead instrument.

Haaji lala Ga word for a type of song used for twin rituals.

Hɔmɔwɔ Ga word for "hooting at hunger," the main harvest festival.

Jama Ga name for *Kolomashie*. Used by the youths living along the coastal areas, who perform it at sporting events.

Jemawɔnii Ga word for deities.

Kolomashie Ga recreational dance-drumming ceremony.

Kpa One of the traditional Ga deities.

Kpanlongo Ga recreational dance-drumming ceremony.

Kple Main traditional deity for the Gas.

Kyen kyen Ga word for cymbal.

Lala Ga term for categories of songs, song types, or function, or a song or the act of singing.

Lalatsɛ Ga word for "the father of songs" or the conductor of dance-drumming ensembles.

Lala woɔlɔ Ga word for caller of songs.

Maawɛ Ga word for the name of a cool breeze experienced in July. Believed to be responsible for increased diseases and deaths, especially of the elderly.

Maa Ga word for stick clappers.

Maawɛ Ga word for the cold season from early August to the first halo of September.

Mankralo Ga word for elders.

Maŋtsesi Ga word for matches.

Maŋtsɛwe Ga word for palaces.

Manyawale The intermittent rains that fall during August.

Me Ga word for deity, small gods or lieutenants of the Almighty God.

Mi Ga word for drums.

Milɛ gbeeŋ Ga term for the original sound of the drum.

Miishi mɔ Ga word for the pounding of the drum.

Miyilɔ Ga word for drummer.

Miyilɔkye See *dadefoɔkye*.

Mulatofoi A word used to describe Gas/Africans of "mixed race."

Nkpai Ga word for pouring of libation.

Ŋoŋo Ga word for single bell.

Ŋoŋonta Ga word for double bell.

Nyɛmɔ Ga word for pressing of the drum.

Nyɔŋmɔ Ga word for Supreme Being.

Oflɔ Ga word for the name of a flower that guides farmers. The flower grows in the hinterland in February.

Oge Ga recreational dance-drumming.

Otso Kilikli Ga word for the hot season — late February to April.

Otsokriki Ga word for warm and sunny March —
suitable for fishing and outdoor activities.

Oshwe Ga term for the first phase of every dance-
drumming ceremony when *Oshwebɔɔ Lala* is performed. Warm-up songs in speech rhythm.

Oshwebɔɔ Lala Ga term for an introductory singing
or prelude to invoke the spirit of the deities to
guide a performance and also to warm up or prepare the voices for performances.

Oshi Ga word for the special *Hɔmɔwɔ* dance-drumming ceremony.

Otu One of the Ga deities.

Papa Ga word for fan.

Pati Ga word for concert tom.

Samfee Ga word for key.

Sɛy Ga word for sacred stools.

Shekeshe Ga word for rattle made with beads woven
outside the gourd.

Tagologo Ga word for the plains of Accra, near
Kpong.

Tamalin See *tamalee*.

Tamalee Ga word for frame drum, a reconstruction
of the tambourine.

Tigare Ga religious deity and dance-drumming ceremony.

Tokata Ga word for sandal.

Tsɛ Ga word for the head or father of the family.

Tu Ga word for gun.

Webii Ga word for members of the family.

Wulɔmɔ (*Wulɔmɛi*, pl.) Ga word for traditional
ruler, high chief, or priest.

Yɛlɛ Ga word for yam.

Akan Terms

Abeɛ Lyrical singing in speech rhythm at the beginning of most Akan dance-drumming ceremonies.
Used as a warm-up exercise.

Abofoɔ Akan hunters' association; also refers to one
of the phases of *Kete* royal and *Akɔm* ritual dance-
drumming ceremonies.

Abosom Name for Akan deities.

Adae The major festival celebrated by the Akan, instituted for remembering their ancestors and for
renewing the spiritual and political bonds that
allow for continued participation of the dead in
the affairs of the living.

Adampa One of the phases of *Kete* dance-drumming, this is one of the pieces also used in *Adowa*.

Adawura Akan name for a boat-shaped or slit bell.

Adefe Modern style of *Adowa*, played very quickly.

Adenkum Gourd stamping tube played by the Akan
women of Ghana; also the name of the musical
type performed to the accompaniment of this instrument.

Adewa See *Adzewa*.

Adinkra Symbolic tie-dyed cloth; also one of the
phases of *Kete* dance-drumming.

Adowa Women's funeral dance-drumming.

Adowahemmaa The queen of the *Adowa* dance-
drumming ensemble.

Adowapa An old style of *Adowa* in a moderately
slow tempo.

Adzewa The Fante equivalent of *Adowa*; this dance-
drumming is lighter, and is made of voices, rattles,
bells, and one drum, *apentemma*.

Afirikyewa An Akan term for castanet or finger bell.

Agorɔhemaa Female patron of Akan performing
ensembles.

Agorɔhene Male patron of Akan performing ensembles.

Agyegyewa A small open drum used in *Asafo* percussion ensembles.

Aho Choral chants performed at the beginning of

most Akan dance-drumming ceremonies to awaken
the performance arena.

Akan The largest ethnic group in Ghana.

Akapuma One of the oldest pieces in *Adowa* music.

Akatape Akan term used generally for any form of
light, gay and leisurely drumming. It is used in
Adowa and *Kete* dance-drumming.

Akatem A piece played in *Adowa*.

Akom Religious dance-drumming of the Akan. It
is a possession dance.

Akukua A small high-pitched drum common in
many Akan ensembles.

Anantuhwɛneɛ See *Adefe*.

Apentemma A small *ɔperenten*. It is a fairly small
sonorous drum used as an intermediary drum in
many Akan ensembles. Plays a corresponding role
in the *Adowa* ensemble and uses the hand technique.

Apirede A drum orchestra found in the courts of
Akan paramount chiefs.

Asaadua An Akan recreational dance-drumming
ceremony.

Asafo Warrior organization of the Akan; also a term
used for their music.

Asafohene An elder, councilor, or leader of the
Asafo company.

Asafotwɛne The lead/master drum of the warrior
associations. It is used as a musical instrument
and also as a "talking drum."

Ashanti The largest of the Akan ethnic groups in
Ghana.

Asɔkɔre One of the largest traditional towns of the
Akan in Manpong.

Asɔnkɔ See *Asafo*. This is the same organization, but
it had different dance-drumming in the 1950s.

Atɛntɛ Music of double-headed drums and bamboo
flutes.

Atɛntebɛn Bamboo flutes used in the *Atɛntɛ* ensemble.

Atona See *Mpreh.*

Atumpan A pair of drums used in Ghana and some other parts of West Africa for playing speech texts. The pair is referred to as talking drums."

Baasankye One of the female costumes used for the *Adowa* dance.

Bɔmma Used as a synonym for *fɔntɔmfrɔm*; also the name of the two lead drums in the ensemble.

Bragorɔ Puberty rites for Akan girls. Also refers to the song and dance incorporated into these ceremonies.

Brakune A religious music of the Akans.

Dangme An ethnic group in Ghana.

Dawuro A hand-held bell. There are three variations among the Akan: a small slit bell, *adawura*, as used in *Adowa*; a conical bell as used in *Asafo*; and the double bell, *nnawuta*.

Densinkran Special head/hair makeup used by female dancers in *Adowa*.

Dɛnte One of the state deities of the Akan.

Donno/Dondo Hourglass-shaped drum; played by stick and armpit technique. Also see *Luŋa.*

Fante One of the matrilineal clans of the Akan; the word also represents the dialect of the Twi language spoken by the people.

Firikyiwa See *afirikyiwa.*

Fɔntɔmfrɔm Royal and warrior dance of the Akan courts. Also refers to the largest and tallest royal drums.

Kente Handwoven Ghanaian cloth with symbolic designs.

Kete Music of the royal court of the Akans. Drums used in this ensemble are covered with black and red cloth.

Krumuu Choral response at the end of *abeɛ.*

Kumasi The second largest city in Ghana, the regional capital of the Ashanti Region, and also the political, cultural, and commercial center of Akans.

Kwadum Lead drum of the *Kete* percussion ensemble.

Mpanyinfo Elders of the Akan.

Mpintin A drum orchestra at the courts of Akan chiefs. It consists of hourglass drums, gourd drums, *impintintoa*, and a cylindrical drum —*gyamadudu.*

Mpreh A lighter form of *Adowa* similar to *Adzewa.* Performed without the percussion ensemble.

Nana, pl. *Nananom* Title for Akan chiefs, kings, queens or elders.

Nnawuta Akan double bell.

Nsamanfoo Refers to the ancestors.

Ntehera Ensemble of ivory horns played at the courts of Akan chiefs.

Ntoa One of the state deities of the Akan.

Ntoro See *Ntoa.*

Ntorowa Container gourd rattle.

Nyame The Akan name for the Almighty God.

Odurugya End-blown Akan flute made from the bark of cane.

Offin A river in Ghana.

Onyame See *Nyame.*

Onyankopɔn One of several attributes of the Supreme God as head of the universe.

Ɔkyeame Linguist; the official spokesman for the chief.

Ɔkyerɛma Akan court drummer, usually plays the *atumpan.*

Ɔkyerɛma Panin Master drummer in Akan communities.

Ɔbosom An Akan deity.

Ɔdomankoma One of the attributes of the Almighty God as the creator of the universe.

Ɔperenten See *apentemma.*

Ɔtwe bedi mprem One of the pieces in *Adowa* music. It means, "The antelope will swallow bullets."

Petia The smallest drum of the *Adowa* percussion ensemble.

Pra A river in Ghana.

Seperewa An old Akan harp.

Sikyi Recreational dance-drumming of the Akan.

Tano One of the rivers in Ghana, it is worshipped as a state deity by the Akans.

Tekyiman One of the major commercial towns of the Akan; also refers to a piece in *Adowa* dance-drumming.

Tigare Possession religious dance-drumming ceremony of the Akan, Eʋe and Ga ethnic groups.

Torowa Same as ntorowa.

Dagbamba Terms

Abalimbee Seventh of the nine phases in the Dagbamba *Baamaaya* dance-drumming. The beauty of the dance is shown as the dancers take the opportunity to show their enjoyment. This section leads to a break for refreshments.

Agbatoro See *mukuru.*

Anakuliyela A phase in *Tɔra* dance-drumming.

Baamaaya Was derived from two Dagbamba words: *baa* (valley) and *maaya* (coolness). It literally means, "Because the rain has come." This is the name for the most popular recreational dance-drumming of the Dagbamba.

Baamaaya Sochendi The processional phase in *Baamaaya.*

Baamaaya Valiŋa The final phase in *Baamaaya.* The dancers recess quickly back to the dressing room.

Baaŋa Eighth of the nine phases in the *Baamaaya* and the fourth phase of the *Jɛra* dance-drumming ceremonies. A period of singing historical and praise songs during the refreshing of the performers and adjustment of costumes by dancers.

Baga The Dagbamba word for the soothsayer or diviner who reveals to every family sacrifices to be made for the well-being of households.

Bangumaŋa The tenth phase of the *Tɔra* dance-drumming ceremony. *Bangumaŋa* is also a praise name for one of the chiefs of Dagbɔŋ.

Batani A Dagbamba gourd drum.

Bia A Dagbani word for child.

Biegu A Dagbamba three-stringed plucked lute.

Bil Maŋa A word from the Dagbamba ethnic group which literally means "to roll around." *Bil Maŋa* was later changed to simply *Bla* or *Bila* as the name for this dance-drumming ceremony.

Bilje A phase of the Bla dance-drumming ceremony, during funerals this phase honors the dead and takes place around the grave. It is used to drive away evil spirits.

Bina A Dagbamba word for ankle beads.

Binchara A piece of cloth on the legs, on top of which the dancer ties secondary rattles. Used in most Dagbamba dance-drumming ceremonies.

Bindili A Dagbamba gourd drum.

Binŋmaa A Dagbamba word for smock, often referred to as *batakari*.

Bla The first and original phase of the *Bla* dance-drumming ceremony.

Bla Guŋgɔŋ laa A double-headed cylindrical drum; supports the lead drum; two may be used as supporting drums for the *Bla* dance.

Bla Guŋgɔŋ nyaŋ A Dagbamba double-headed cylindrical drum; serves as the lead drum in *Bla* dance-drumming.

Bɔbga Dagbamba word for head scarf.

Bodisi Dagbamba word for bra or brassier.

Boduwa Dagbamba word for the towel worn around one's neck to clean sweat during performances.

Buga Dagbamba name for sacred shrines.

Bugum Fire Festival, a non–Islamic–derived festival of the Dagbamba, which is celebrated to reactivate the spiritual powers of the people.

Chaɣla Dagbamba word for secondary rattles worn around the ankles to emphasize dance movements.

Chinchina Costume used for the *Bla* dance which is made with six six-yard cloths tied in a special way on the waist. The cloths are looped around on an additional waist sash and tied, allowing each cloth to hang down.

Chinchini maga The local woven cloth of the Dagbamba.

Dagbaŋli The language of the Dagbamba.

Dakolkutooko The sixth of the nine phases in *Baamaaya*. This section provides comic relief and pokes fun at bachelors in the community.

Damba The sixth phase of *Bla*. It is used as a festival or celebration during a funeral. Originally an exclusively Islamic festival used to honor the birth

and naming of the prophet Mohammed. Also a New Year's festival.

Damduu The fifth of the 12 phases of *Tɔra* dance-drumming. It is a phase for reflecting on the evils of society — particularly about those individuals who cause problems at home.

Dawule A Dagbamba double bell.

Eid-ul-Adhai An Islamic-derived festival of the Dagbamba marking the Feast of Sacrifice.

Eid-ul-Fitr An Islamic-derived festival of the Dagbamba marking the end of Ramadan.

Feinŋa A Dagbamba self-sounding idiophone; a castanet.

Gbuɣunli Dagbamba word for lion, the animal in charge of *Yendi*; also a symbol of kingship.

Gondanaa Dagbamba word for chief of the kapok tree.

Gonje Dagbamba word for the one-stringed fiddle.

Guŋgɔŋ A Dagbamba cylindrical, laced drum.

Guŋgɔŋ bila *Guŋgɔŋ* with a high voice.

Guŋgɔŋ titali *Guŋgɔŋ* with a low voice.

Gurim (guru) A Dagbamba word for talismans covering most parts of the upper body — the arms, wrists and shoulders of dancers.

Jɛra A Dagbamba word literally meaning "fools dance," it is a religious and warrior dance-drumming ceremony.

Jɛra-Lura Third and main phase of the *Jɛra* dance-drumming ceremony.

Jɛra-Sochendi First of six phases in *Jɛra*. After brief preparation at the head hunter or chief's house, the dancers, led by the drummers, file in to the dance area. It is also the seventh and final phase of *Jɛra*. In this recessional phase, the lead singer calls the recessional song "Nanjaa," which is a tribute to the founder of this celebration.

Jɛra-Tɔra The second of six phases in *Jɛra*. This section begins after a circle is completed and the lead dancers give a signal. Moving at a faster pace, the dancers, as if charging on an animal or an enemy, move forward and back.

Kafina A Dagbamba fan used in the kitchen to fan the chiefs and dancers.

Kafini See *kafina*.

Kalamboo A Dagbamba side-blown wind instrument; a cane flute.

Kani Dagbamba word for the armband used by dancers.

Kanton See *Kondoliya*.

Kondoliya Fifth of the nine phases in *Baamaaya*. *Kondoliya*, meaning "There lies the water," reminds the Dagbamba of the value of water. It is also a recessional and the last of the 12 phases in *Tɔra*.

Kookali The 11th of 12 phases of *Tɔra* dance-drumming.

Kpakoto See *binŋmaa*.

Kpari The original name for *Tɔra*.

Kpini Guinea fowl festival — a non-Islamic-derived harvest festival of the Dagbamba.

Kpukpuli Set of cowries woven on four strands of rope and worn around the waist on top of *laɣmihi* as part of the *Jɛra* costume.

Krugu/Kurugu A large long baggy pant used in most Dagbamba dance-drumming ceremonies.

Kuntunji A Dagbamba three-stringed plucked lute.

Laɣmihi A bulging bag made of cloth tied around the waist. It hangs directly in front of the dancer in *Jɛra* dance-drumming.

Lelba Sixth and final phase in *Jɛra*. This section pays tribute to the *kpukpuli*. Each strand of the cowries represents a child — therefore, this section pays tribute to children.

Luŋa (-*si* pl.) A Dagbamba hourglass drum. Also refers to the drummer(s) who play this drum.

Luŋsi See *luŋa*.

Mukuru A type of skirt used in *Baamaaya* that highlights the rapid twist of the hips.

Muɣuri A Dagbamba word for leather boots.

Naawuni Dagbamba word for the Supreme Power, or God.

Nema A Dagbamba word for costume/clothes.

Ŋmani Dagbamba word for calabash or gourd.

Ŋumalpieŋ One of phases of the *Tɔra* dance-drumming ceremony.

Ŋundanyuli The fourth phase in *Tɔra* dance-drumming. It literally means "creating a name for oneself"; it also means that a man who buys yams for a woman "takes her buttocks"; or, "You will get a beautiful wife if you behave well in society."

Ŋunkpelimkpe The ninth phased in *Tɔra* dance-drumming. It means, "He who remains last always gets the best." This is a philosophy of life taught during *Tɔra* performances.

Nyaɣboli Fourth of the nine phases in the *Baamaaya* and third in the *Tɔra* dance-drumming ceremonies.

Pabo One of the two most powerful deities throughout Dagbɔŋ.

Saboniba A Dagbamba word for rainmaker.

Sapani The Dagbamba word for the thunder god who operates during the night.

Sariga A Dagbamba word for shawl worn around the neck.

Saɣyali A Dagbamba self-sounding idiophone; a container rattle played in pairs.

Shilmalibu shee Special clothing for dancers among the Dagbamba.

Sikoro Third of the nine phases in *Baamaaya*.

Takai A Dagbamba royal dance-drumming ceremony for men.

Tamanaa Dagbamba name for chief of the shea butter tree.

Tendamba See *tindamba*.

Tikpara Dagbamba word for earrings.

Tindambaa Dagbamba word for land or earth priests.

Tiyanima Dagbamba word for ancestral spirits who are worshipped through heads of families.

Tɔra The main Dagbamba women's dance-drumming ceremony.

Tɔra yiɣera The eighth phase of the *Tɔra* dance-drumming ceremony.

Tubankpeli A Dagbamba word literally meaning, "Unless you are satisfied, you cannot take part in the dance." It is also the preferred traditional dish made of beans and groundnuts (peanuts). Also the original name for the *Baamaaya* dance-drumming ceremony.

Tunaa Dagbamba word for chief of the baobab tree.

Wɔliɣa A Dagbamba word for a hat made from a black monkey's fur used in *Baamaaya*.

Yaawum The last phase of the *Bla* dance-drumming ceremony, created for children.

Ya Naa Traditional supreme head of the Dagbamba.

Yanderi One of the two most powerful shrines throughout Dagbɔŋ.

Yaneli See *Yanderi*.

Yɛvili See *binŋmaa*.

Yila/Baaŋa The third phase of the *Bla* dance-drumming ceremony which includes praise-singing, storytelling and a period of refreshing.

Yua A Dagbamba wooden notched flute.

Zamandunia The first of the 12 phases of the *Tɔra* dance-drumming ceremony.

Zem The fifth phase of the *Bla* dance-drumming ceremony. It is performed as tribute to the warriors or hunters who founded this dance-drumming.

Zule Dagbamba name for horsetail.

Zupuliga Dagbamba word for head turban, hat or head scarf.

General terms

Aerophones Classification of wind instruments.

Benin Formerly called Dahomey, Benin is a country in West Africa.

Burkina Faso Formerly Upper Volta, this is a country that lies to the north of Ghana in West Africa.

Chordophones Classification of string instruments.

Chiefship Traditional African institution of political authority.

Choral lament Organized funeral song performance by groups of women in Africa. May sometimes be accompanied by one or two musical instruments.

Clan Members of an ethnic group bonded together by blood relationship who are legally held to one another. It is believed that all members of the clan descend from one ancestor or ancestress.

Côte d'Ivoire A country in West Africa (Ivory Coast).

Dirge Unorganized solo performance of funeral

songs in speech rhythm; non-stazaic and full of declamations.

Durbar Ceremonial gathering of chiefs and the people amid dance-drumming to pay homage to their paramount chiefs.

Harmattan Dry season in Ghana and other parts of Africa.

Hausa The largest ethnic group in Nigeria, West Africa.

Ibo An ethnic group in Nigeria.

Idiophones Self-sounding instruments, meaning that sound is made by agitating their bodies. There are two main categories: non-melodic and melodic idiophones. The non-melodic group includes bells and rattles; the melodic group includes wooden xylophones, slit drums and hand pianos.

Matrilineal Inheritance, succession, and/or status determined through the female line. Clans may be patrilineal or matrilineal.

Membranophones Classification of instruments with parchment heads (drums).

Niger River Largest and longest river in West Africa.

Queen mother She appoints the chief of the Akans. She is regarded as the *kra*, which means the life-giving soul of the land. She therefore becomes the head of state and final arbiter in disputes which cannot be solved by the chief.

Stools Symbol of authority of Akan and many Ghanaian chiefs. They are usually carved from wood.

Togo A small country to the east of Ghana.

Volta The largest and longest river in Ghana; also refers to one of the administrative regions of the country, mostly occupied by the Eʋe-speaking people.

Yoruba One of the largest ethnic groups next to the Hausa in Nigeria; they occupy most of the southern parts.

Bibliography and Further Reading

Ackah, C.A. (1959). An ethical study of the Akan of Ghana. Ph.D. diss., University of London.

Acquah, John H. (1987). Neo traditional music among the Ga of Accra. Ph.D. diss., University of Ghana.

Adu-Asare, Michael. (1992). Extinct Akan dance from the Akuapem traditional area. Diploma thesis, University of Ghana.

Aduama, E.Y. (1966). Ewe traditions. *Northern Ewes of Have* 17, Legon IAS.

Adzenyah, Abraham K., Dumisani Maraire, and Judith Cook Tucker. (1986). *Let your voice be heard! Songs from Ghana and Zimbabwe*. Danbury, CT: World Music Press.

Affour, E.A. (1992). The role of dance in the Daa Festival of the people of the Tongo. Diploma thesis, University of Ghana.

Agawu, Kofi. (Winter 1986). "Gi Dunu," "Nyekpadudo," and the study of West African Rhythm. *Ethnomusicology, 30* (1): 64–83.

_____. (1995). *African rhythm: A Northern Ewe perspective*. Cambridge: Cambridge University Press.

Agbodeka, Francis. (1972). *Ghana in the twentieth century*. Accra: Ghana University Press.

Akuffo-Amoabeng, Betty. (1989). *Ghana: The land, the people, and the culture* (tourist guide). Accra: Ghana Tourist Development Company Limited.

Akufu, S.N.K. (1983). Kpatsa: A recreational musical type of the Dangmes. Ph.D. diss., University of Ghana, Legon.

Allotey, Seth N.M. (2005). *Ganyo bi tete (a book on Ga proficiency)*. Vol. 1. Legon: Language Centre, University of Ghana.

Amoaku, W.K. (1971). *African songs and rhythms for children*. New York: Schott Music Corporation.

_____. (1982). Parallelism in traditional African systems of music education and Orff Schulwerk. *African Music, 6* (2): 116–119.

_____. (1985). Toward a definition of traditional African music: A look at the Ewes of Ghana. In *More than Drumming*, edited by Irene Jackson, 31–40. Westport, CT: Greenwood Press.

Ampofo, Doudo. (1980). *Symbolic movements in*

Ghanaian dances. Legon: School of Performing Arts at the University of Ghana.

Anafu, M. (1983). *The northern region, Ghana*. Vol. 1, *A descriptive overview*. Ghana: Northern Region Rural Integrated Program Technical Unit.

Anderson, L. (1990). A rationale for global education. In *Global Education: From Thought to Action*, edited by Kenneth A. Tye, 13. Alexandria, VA: Association for Supervision and Curriculum Development.

Anderson, W., ed. (1991). Teaching music with a multicultural approach. Music Educators National Conference, Reston, VA.

_____. (May 1992). Rethinking teacher education: The multicultural imperative. *Music Educators Journal*, 52–55.

_____, and S.P. Campbell. (1989). Teaching music from a multicultural perspective. Multicultural Perspectives in Music Education, Music Educators National Conference, Reston, VA, viii–ix, 1–7.

Anene, Joseph C., and Godfrey N. Brown, eds. (1966). *Africa in the nineteenth and twentieth centuries*. Ibadan, Nigeria, and London: Ibadan University Press & Nelson Press.

Anku, William Oscar. (1988). *Procedures in Akan-/Ewe traditions and African drumming in Pittsburgh*. Ph.D. diss., University of Pittsburgh.

Anning, B.A. (1964). Adenkum: A study of Akan female bands. Ph.D. diss., University of Ghana.

_____. (1977). *Atumpan drums: An object of historical and anthropological study*. New York, NY: Town House Press.

Annyon, Jean. (Summer 1994). The retreat of Marxism and socialist feminism: Postmodern and poststructural theories in education. *Curriculum Inquiry, 24* (2): 115–133.

Anyidoho, Kofi. (1982). Death and burial of the dead: Ewe funeral folklore. Master's thesis, Indiana University.

Avorgbedor, D. (1986). Modes of musical continuity among the Anlo-Ewe of Accra: A study in urban ethnomusicology. Ph.D. diss., Indiana University.

_____. (March 1994). Freedom to sing, license to insult: The influence of halo performance on social violence among the Ewe-Ewe. *Oral Tradition,* 9 (1): 83–112.

Awuku, R.S. (1991). Agbekor Dance of Anlo Afiadenyigba. Ph.D. diss., University of Ghana-Legon.

Azu, Diana Gladys. (1974). *The Ga family and social change.* Leiden: Afrika-Studiecentrum.

Azu, N.A.A. (1926). Adangbe (Adandme) History. 3 parts. *Gold Coast Review,* 2, 239–270; 3, 89–166; and 4, 3–30.

Badu-Younge, C.M. (2002). Ewe culture as expressed in Ghana West Africa: The development of a tool for teaching culture through Adzogbo dance ceremony, using interactive multimedia technology. Ph.D. diss., McGill University.

_____. (2010). *Descriptive notes on Bamaaya dance movements of the Dagbamba of Ghana.* Unpublished manuscript, Ohio University, Athens.

_____. (2010). *Descriptive notes on Bla dance movements of the Dagbamba of Ghana.* Unpublished manuscript, Ohio University, Athens.

_____. (2010). *Descriptive notes on Jera dance movements of the Dagbamba of Ghana.* Unpublished manuscript, Ohio University, Athens.

_____. (2010). *Descriptive notes on Tora dance movements of the Dagbamba of Ghana.* Unpublished manuscript, Ohio University, Athens.

Balmer, William T., and C.M. Welman. (1925). *A history of the Akan people of the Gold Coast.* London: Atlantis.

Bame, K.N. (1991). *Profiles in African traditional popular culture: Consensus and conflict: Dance, drama, festival[s] and funerals.* Bronx, NY: Clear Type Press Inc.

Banks, James A. (1996a). Multicultural education: Characteristics and goals. In *Multicultural Education: Issues and Perspectives,* edited by James A. Banks & Cherry A. McGee Banks, 2–3. Newton, MA: Allyn & Bacon.

_____. (1996b). *Teaching strategies for ethnic studies.* 6th ed. Needham, MA: Allyn & Bacon.

Barker, Peter. (1986). *Peoples, languages and religion in northern Ghana.* Asempa Publishers for Ghana Evangelism Committee.

Bascom, W. (1969). *The Yoruba of southwestern Nigeria: Case studies in cultural anthropology.* New York, NY: Holt, Rinehart and Winston.

Beane, J., P.S. George, C. Stevenson, and C. Thomason. (1992). *The middle school and beyond.* Alexandra, VA: Association for Supervision and Curriculum Development.

Beecham, John. (1841). *Ashantee and the Gold Coast.* London.

Benedict, Ruth. (1934). *Patterns of culture.* Boston, MA: Houghton Mifflin. Reprint, New York: New American Library, 1950.

Bening, Raymond B. (1973). Indigenous concepts of boundaries and significance of administrative stations and boundaries in northern Ghana. *Bulletin of the Ghana Geographical Association, 15,* 7–20.

_____. (1975a). Colonial development policy in northern Ghana, 1898–1950. *Bulletin of the Ghana Geographical Association, 18,* 15–34.

_____. (1975b). Foundations of the modern native states of northern Ghana. *Universitas (Ghana), 5* (1): 116–138.

_____. (1975c). Location of district administrative capitals in the northern territories of the gold coast (1897–1951). *Bulletin de l'IFAN, 37,* series B (3): 646–667.

_____. (1976). Land tenure system and traditional agriculture of the Sissala. *Bulletin of the Ghana Geographical Association, 17,* 65–79.

_____. (1977). Administration and development in northern Ghana, 1898–1933. *Ghana Social Science Journal, 4,* 58–76.

_____. (1983). The administrative areas of northern Ghana, 1898–1951. *Bulletin de l'IFAN, 45,* series B (3–4): 325–356.

_____. (1990). *A history of education in northern Ghana, 1907–1976.* Accra: Ghana University Press.

Bennett, C.I. (1995). *Comprehensive multicultural education: Theory and practice.* 3rd ed. Needham Heights, MA: Allyn and Bacon.

Beyer, A.E. (1982). Ideology, sociology efficiency, and curriculum inquiry: An essay response to Franklin's "the social efficiency movement." *Curriculum Inquiry, 2* (3): 305–316.

Boahen, A.A. (1966). *Topics in West African history.* London: Longman.

Boateng, E.A. (1960). *A geography of Ghana.* Cambridge: Cambridge University Press.

Botwe-Asamoah, G.K. (1979). *The study of Gabada music and dance among the northern Ewes of Ghana.* Unpublished African dance thesis, University of Ghana.

Brown, S.C. (1974). *Philosophy of psychology.* New York: Barnes and Noble.

Bruce-Meyers, J.M. (1928). The origin of Gas. *Journal of the African Society, 27.*

Burchardt, R.O. (1987). Musical sound and contextual input: A performance model for musical analysis. *Journal of the Society for Ethnomusicology, 31* (1).

Bureau of Ghana Languages (1986). *Language guide: Ewe version.* Accra: Author.

_____. (1986). *Language guide: Ga version.* Accra: Author.

Busia, K.A. (1954). *The Ashanti, African worlds.* Oxford: Oxford University Press.

_____. (1968). *The position of the chief in modern political system of Ashanti.* London: New Impression, Frank Cass.

Campbell, E.D. (1996). *Choosing democracy: A guide to multicultural education.* Englewood Cliffs, NJ: Prentice Hall.

Campbell, P.S. (1991). *Lessons from the world: A cross-cultural guide to teaching and learning.* New York: Schirmer Books.

_____. (1996). *Music in cultural context: Eight views on world music education.* Reston, VA: Music Educators National Conference.

Cardinall, A.W. (1921). Customs at the death of a king of Dagomba. *Man, 21,* 52.

_____. (1925). *The natives of the northern territories of the Gold Coast.* London: Routledge.

Carleton, I.L. (1974). Music in culture: a practical introduction to African music. *Music Educators Journal, 50.*

Chernoff, John. (1979). *African rhythm and African sensibility.* Chicago: University of Chicago Press.

_____. (1985). The drums of Dagbon. In *Reflections: A Celebration of African-American Music,* edited by Geoffrey Haydon and Dennis Marks. London: Century Publishing.

Cherryholmes, C.H. (1987). A social project for curriculum: A post-structural perspective. *Journal of Curriculum Studies, 19* (6): 569–573.

Christaller, J.B. (1933). *Dictionary of the Ashante and Fante languages.* Basel, CH: Basel Evangelical Missionary Society.

Christian, Angela. (1976). *Adinkra oration.* Accra: Catholic Book Center, Accra Catholic Press.

Clark, K.B. (1988). The Brown decision: Racism, education, and human values. *The Journal of Negro Education, 2,* 125–132.

Clottey, V.M. (1968). Music and dance of Oshie ceremony in the Homowo Festival among the Gas. Ph.D. diss., University of Ghana.

Collins, John. (1992). *West African pop roots.* Philadelphia: Temple University Press.

Colon, C.J. (May 1992). Explore the world in song. *Music Educators Journal, 78* (9): 46–51.

Coull, G.C. (1929). Foodstuffs in the Dagomba district of the northern territories. *Bulletin of the Department of Agriculture of the Gold Coast, 16,* 203–215.

Cruz, C. (1954). Les instruments de musique du Dahomey. *Etudes Dahomeennes, 11,* 15–36.

Cudzoe, S. (1963). *The technique of Ewe drumming and the social importance of music in Africa.* Rlylon.

Darkwa, A. (Year Unknown). *Music and dance of the Turkana of Kenya in socio-cultural profile of the Turkana district.* Edited by R.C. Soper.

Davis, Art. (1994). Midawo Gideon Foli Alorwoyie: The life and music of a West African drummer. Master's thesis, University of Illinois, Urbana-Champaign.

Davordzi, F. (1989). *The Ewe recreational music of the people of Dzodze Ablorme.* Unpublished African dance thesis, University of Ghana, Legon.

Danquah, J.B. (1928). *Akan laws and customs.* London: G. Routledge.

_____. (1945). *The Gold Coast Akan.* London: United Society for Christian Literature.

_____. (1968). *The Akan doctrine of god.* 2nd ed. London: Frank Cass.

Deese, James. (1972). *Psychology as science and art.* New York: Harcourt Brace, Jovanovich Inc.

Der, Benedict. (2001). The traditional political systems of northern Ghana reconsidered. In *Regionalism and Public Policy in Northern Ghana,* edited by Yakubu Saaka, 35–65. New York: Peter Lang.

Devereux, Stephen. (1993). "Observers are worried": Learning the language and counting the people in northeast Ghana. In *Fieldwork in developing countries,* edited by Stephen Devereux and John Hoddinott, 43–56. Boulder, CO: Lynne Rienner.

Dewey, J. (1996). *Democracy and education: An introduction to the philosophy of education.* New York: Free Press. First published 1916 by Macmillan.

Dickson, Kwamina B. (1971). *A historical geography of Ghana.* Cambridge: Cambridge University Press.

Dieterien, Germaine. (1971). Les ceremonies soixantaires du Sigui chez les Dogon. *Africa, 16:* 1–11.

DjeDje, J.C. (1978). The one-string fiddle in West Africa. Ph.D. diss., University of California–Los Angeles.

_____. (1980). *Distribution of the one string fiddle in West Africa.* Los Angeles: Program in Ethnomusicology, University of California.

_____. (1982). The concept of patronage: An examination of Hausa and Dagomba one-string fiddle traditions. *Journal of African Studies, 9* (3): 116–127.

Doll, W.E., Jr. (1993). *A post-modern perspective on curriculum.* New York, NY: Teachers College Press.

Dor, G.W.K. (1986). The Alavanyo orchestra: A legacy of Europe on indigenous musical cultures of Africa: A case study. Ph.D. diss., University of Ghana, Legon.

_____. (2004). Communal creativity and song ownership in Anlo Ewe musical practice: The case of havolu. *Ethnomusicology, 48* (1): 26–51.

Dorvlo, J.K. (1987). *Agbadza music of the southern Ewes.* Unpublished African dance thesis, University of Ghana, Legon.

Dowoeh, W.I.C. (1980). *Gbolo, a northern Ewe musical type.* Ph.D. diss., University of Ghana, Legon.

Duncan-Johnstone, A.C., et al. (1931). *Enquiry into the constitution and organization of the Dagomba kingdom.* Accra: Government Printer.

Edwards, L.C. (1997). *The creative arts: A process approach for teachers and children.* 2nd ed. Upper Saddle River, NJ: Merrill.

Egblewogbe, E.Y. (1967). *Songs and games as an aspect of socialization in Eweland.* MA thesis, University of Ghana, Legon.

_____. (1975). *Games and songs as education media: A case study among the Ewes of Ghana.* Accra: Ghana Publishing Corporation.

Ekweme, L.U. (1988). Nigerian indigenous music as basis for developing creative music instruction for

Nigerian primary schools and suggested guidelines for implementation. Ph.D. diss., Columbia University Teachers College.

Ellis, A.B. (1887). *The Twi-speaking peoples of the Gold Coast.* London: Chapman and Hall.

Engmann, E.V.T. (1975). Migration and population pressure in northern Ghana: A note on methodology. *Bulletin of the Ghana Geographical Association, 17*: 38–55.

Euba, Akin. (January 1975). The dichotomy of African music. *Music Educators Journal, 61* (5): 54–56.

Eyre-Smith, S.J. (1933). *A brief review of the history and social organization of the people of the northern territories of the Gold Coast.* Accra: Government Press.

Fage, J.D. (1959). *Ghana: A historical interpretation.* Madison: University of Wisconsin Press.

_____. (1964). Reflections on the early history of the Mossi-Dagomba group of states. In *The Historian in Tropical Africa*, edited by J. Vansina, R. Mauny, and L.V. Thomas, 177–191. London: Oxford University Press for the International Africa Institute.

Fiagbedzi, N.S. (1966). *Sogbadgi songs: A study of Yeve music.* Legon: Institute of African Studies at the University of Ghana-Legon.

_____. (1977). The music of the Anlo: Its historical background, cultural matrix and style. Ph.D. diss., University of California, Los Angeles.

_____. (1979). *Religious music traditions in Africa: A critical evaluation of contemporary problems and challenges.* Accra: Ghana Universities Press.

Fiawo, D.K. (1959). The influence of the contemporary social changes on the magico-religious concepts and organization of southern Ewe-speaking people of Ghana. Ph.D. diss., University of Edinburgh.

Field, M.J. (1937). *Religion and medicine of the Ga people.* London: Oxford University Press.

_____. (1940). *Social organization of the Ga people.* London: Crown Agents.

Flanagan, Owen. (1984). *The science of the mind.* Cambridge, MA: MIT Press.

Fortes, M. (1948). The Ashanti social survey: A preliminary report. *Rhodes-Livingstone Journal, 6.*

_____. (1950). Kinship and marriage among the Ashanti. In *African systems of kinship and marriage*, edited by A.R. Radcliffe-Brown and Cyril Daryll Forde. Oxford: Oxford University Press.

_____. (1954). A demographic field study in Ashanti. In *Culture and Human Fertility*, edited by Frank Lorimer. Paris: Unesco.

Fosu, K. (1994). *Traditional art of Ghana.* Kumasi, Ghana: Dela Publications & Design Services.

Franklin, B.M. (1982). The social efficiency movement reconsidered: Curriculum change in Minneapolis, 1917–1950. *Curriculum Inquiry, 12* (1): 9–13.

Gadzekpo, B.S. (1952). Making music in Eweland. *West Africa Review, XIII,* 299.

Gatewood, Thomas E., and Charles A. Dilg. (1975).

The middle school we need: A report from the A.S.C.D. working group on the emerging adolescent learner. Washington, DC: Association for Supervision and Curriculum Development.

Gbeho, P. (1951). African drums are more than tom-tom. *West Africa Review, XXIII,* 289.

George, L.A. (1983). African music through the eyes of a child. *Music Educators Journal, 5,* 47.

_____. (1987). *Teaching music of six different cultures.* Danbury, CT: World Music Press.

Ghana Tourist Board. (1989) *Ghana: The land, the people, and the culture, a tourist guide.* London: WICFF Limited.

Glazer, N. (1988). Education for American citizenship in the 21st century. *Education and Society, 12:* 5–10.

Goldstein, D.L. (1988). *Multicultural education: A transformative approach.* Florida: Development Associates International, Educational Materials and Service Center.

Goodkin, D. (1994). Diverse approaches to multicultural music. *Music Educators Journal, 81, 1* (July): 39–43.

Goody, J.R. (1954). *The ethnography of the northern territories of the Gold Coast, west of the White Volta.* London: Colonial Office. Mimeo in Archaeology and Anthropology Library, University of Cambridge.

_____. (1969). "Normative," "recollected" and "actual" marriage payments among LoWiili of northern Ghana, 1951–1966. *Africa, 39:* 54–60.

Gunther, S. (1990). The influences of jazz on concert music. New perspectives on jazz, edited by David Baker, 23–24. Report on a National Conference held at Wingspread, Racine, Wisconsin, 8–10 September, 1986.

Gyekye, Kwame. (1996). *African cultural values: An introduction.* Philadelphia, PA: Sankofa Publishing, 7, 135.

Haberman, M. (1987). *Recruiting and selecting teachers for urban education.* New York: Teachers College Press.

Hall, Edward. (1983). *Ghana languages.* Accra: Asempa Publishers for Christian Council of Ghana.

Hans, Cory. (1936). Ngoma ya shetani: An East African native treatment for psychological disorders. *Journal of the Royal Anthropological Institute, LVI,* 206.

Hartoonian, M.H., and M.A. Laughlin. (1991). Designing a social studies scope and sequence for the 21st century. In *Renewing the social studies curriculum*, edited by Walter C. Parker. Alexandria, VA: Association for Supervision and Curriculum Development, 115.

Hazlett, J.S. (1979). Conception of curriculum history. *Curriculum Inquiry, 9* (2): 129–135.

Henderson-Quartey, D.K. (2002). *The Ga of Ghana: History and culture of a West African people.* London: Book-in-Hand.

Hernández, H. (1989). *Multicultural education: A teacher's guide to content and process.* New York: Macmillan.

Hilton, T.E. (1960). *Ghana population atlas.* London: Thomas Nelson.

———. (1961). Population and emigration in the northern territories of Ghana. Proceedings of the 6th International West African Congress.

———. (1962). Notes on the history of Kusasi. *Transactions of the Historical Society of Ghana, 6,* 79–86.

Hodgkinson, H. (1985). *All one system.* Washington, DC: Institute for Educational Leadership, Inc.

Hopton-Jones, P. (November 1995). Introducing the music of East Africa. *Music Educators Journal, 82* (3): 26–30.

Horton, T., and P. Raggat. (1982). *Challenge and change in curriculum: A reader.* London: Hodder & Stoughton with Open University.

Hunter, J.M. (1965). Regional patterns of population growth in Ghana, 1948–1960. In *Essays in Geography for Austin Miller,* edited by J.B. Whittow and P.D. Woods, 272–290. Reading, UK: University of Reading.

———. (1967). The social roots of dispersed settlement in northern Ghana. *Annals of the Association of American Geographers, 57:* 338–349.

———. (1968). The clans of the Nangodi. *Africa, 38* (4): 377–412.

Husserl, E. (1931). *Ideas.* New York: Macmillan.

Iannone, Ron. (1995). *The missing community voice in the phenomenological perspective of curriculum.* Morgantown: University of West Virginia.

———, and P. Obenauf. (May 1984). A set of criteria for curriculum theorizing. *Curriculum Perspectives, 4* (1): 61–65.

Information Services Department, Ghana. (1977). *An official handbook.* Accra: New Times Corporation.

Jones, A.M. (1959). *Studies in African music.* London: Oxford University Press.

Jones, W.J.A. (April 1938). The northern territories of the gold coast. *Crown Colonist,* 193–195.

Joseph, Rosemary. (1973). Zulu women's music, Africa and music. *Journal of the International Library of African Music, 6* (3): 53–89.

Kilson, Marion. (1967). *Excerpts from the diary of Kwaku Niri, 1884–1918.* Legon: Institute of African Studies.

———. (1968–1969). The Ga naming rite. *Anthropos, 63/64:* 904–920.

———. (1971). *Kpele lala: Ga religious songs and symbols.* Cambridge, MA: Harvard University Press.

———, ed. (1974). *African urban kinsmen: The Ga of central Accra.* New York: St. Martin's Press.

———. (1979). Ritual portrait of a Ga medium, the new religions of Africa. *Journal of African Studies, 2* (3): 395–418.

Kindred, L.W., R.T. Wolotkiewicz, J.M. Mickelson, L.E. Coplein, and E. Dyson. (1976). *The middle school curriculum: A practitioner's handbook.* Boston, MA: Allyn and Bacon.

Kinney, Sylvia. (1970). Drummers in Dagbon: The role of the drummer in the Damba Festival. *Ethnomusicology, 14* (2): 258–265.

Koetting, James. (1970). Analysis and notation of West African drum ensemble music. In *Selected Reports in Ethnomusicology,* vol. III, edited by J.H. Kwabena Nketia and Jacqueline Cogdell DjeDje, 115–146. Los Angeles: Institute of Ethnomusicology, University of California.

———. (1984). Hocket concept and structure in kasena flute ensemble music. In *Selected Reports in Ethnomusicology,* vol. V, edited by J.H. Kwabena Nketia and Jacqueline Cogdell DjeDje, 161–172. Los Angeles: University of California.

———. (1992). Africa/Ghana. In *Worlds of Music: An Introduction to the Music of the World's People,* 2nd ed., edited by Jeff Todd Titon. New York: Schirmer.

Kole, Nene Azu Mate. (1955). The historical background of Krobo customs. *Transactions of the Gold Coast and Togoland Historical Society, 1* (4): 133–140.

Kovey, J.S.A. (1998). *Togbui Evemega akpa gbato.* Accra: Bureau of Ghana Languages.

Krige, E.J. (1954). *The lovedu of the Transvaal.* London: African Worlds, Oxford University Press.

Kwakwa, Patience A. (1974). Dance and drama of the gods. Master's thesis, Institute of African Studies, University of Ghana-Legon.

Kyerenmanten, A.A.Y. (1965). *Panoply of Ghana: Ornamental art in Ghana traditions and culture.* Accra: Ghana Information Services.

Labdouceur, Paul A. (1979). *Chiefs and politicians: The politics of regionalism in northern Ghana.* London: Longman.

Ladzekpo, Kobla. (1971). The social mechanics of good music: A description of dance clubs among the Anlo Ewe-speaking people of Ghana. *Africa Music, 5* (1): 6–22.

Lentz, Carola. (1997). Creating ethnic identities in north-western Ghana. In *The Politics of Ethnic Consciousness,* edited by Cora Govers and Hans Vermeulen, 31–89. London: Macmillan.

———. (2000). Of hunters, goats and earth-shrines: Settlement histories and the politics of oral tradition in northern Ghana. *History in Africa, 27:* 193–214.

Lever, J. (1970). Mulatto influence on the Gold Coast in the early nineteenth century: Jan Niese of Elmina. *African Historical Studies, 3:* 253–261.

Levi, A.W. (1970). *The humanities today.* Bloomington: Indiana University Press, Chapter 1.

———. (July–October 1976). Literature as a humanity. *Journal of Aesthetic Education, 10* (3–4): 45–60.

———. (Winter 1977). Teaching literature as a humanity. *Journal of General Education, 28* (4): 283–289.

Levtzion, Nehemiah. (1968). *Muslims and chiefs in West Africa*. Oxford: Oxford University Press.

Locke, D. (1978). The music of Atsiagbekor. Ph.D. diss., Wesleyan University.

_____. (1982). Principles of offbeat timing and cross-rhythm in southern Ewe dance drumming. *Ethnomusicology, 26* (2): 289–314.

_____. (1987). *Dance Gahu*. Tempe, AZ: White Cliffs Media.

_____. (1988). *Drum Gahu*. Tempe, AZ: White Cliffs Media.

_____. (1990). *Drum Damba*. Tempe, AZ: White Cliffs Media.

_____. (1992). *Kpegisu: A war drum of the Ewe*. Tempe, AZ: White Cliffs Media.

Locke, David, and K. Agbeli Godwin. (1980). A study of the drum language in Adzogbo. *African Music, 6* (1): 32–51.

Lovlie, L. (1992). Post modernism and subjectivity. In *Psychology and post modernism*, edited by S. Kvale, 119–134. Newbury Park, CA: Sage.

Lundstroom, Hakan. (14–17 October 1993). The role of ethnomusicology in the training of music teachers. In *Teaching Musics of the World: The Second International Symposium, Basel*, edited by Margot Lieth-Philip and Andreas Gutzwiller, 96–102.

Lynn, C.W. (1946). Land planning and resettlement in the northern territories of the Gold Coast. *Farm and Forest, 7* (2): 81–83.

Lynne, J.H. (1973). African dance, the continuity of change. *Yearbook of the International Folk Music Council*, 165–174.

MacDonald, J. (1977). *Value bases and issues in curriculum theory*. Washington: Association for Supervision and Curriculum Development.

_____. (1982). Curriculum and human interest. Virgil E. Herrick Memorial Lecture, University of Wisconsin.

Maicom, Tait. (April 1975). World music: Balancing your attitudes and strategies. *Music Educators Journal, 61*: 29–32.

Mallan J.T., and D.A. Weldon. (1992). *Children and the world: Strategies for teaching social studies*. 4th Edition. Boston, MA: Houghton Mifflin.

Malm, W.P. (1972). Teaching rhythmic concepts in ethnic music. *Music Educators Journal, 10*: 95.

Mamattah, Charles M.K. (1976). *The Ewes of West Africa: The Anlo-Ewes and their immediate neighbours*. Vol. 1. Accra: Volta Research Publications.

_____. (1978). *History of the Ewes of West Africa*. Legon: University of Ghana.

Manoukian, M. (1952). *Tribes of the northern territories of the Gold Coast*. London: Oxford University Press for the IAI.

Mawere, Opoku. (1971). *Descriptive notes on selection of African dances*. Legon: Institute of African Studies, University of Ghana.

Maxim, G.W. (1995). *Social studies and the elementary school child*. 5th Edition. Englewood Cliffs, NJ: Prentice Hall.

McCaskie, Tom C. (1983). R.S. Rattray and the construction of Asante history: An appraisal. *History in Africa, 10*: 187–206.

Mendonsa, Eugene L. (1975). Traditional and imposed political systems among the Sisala of northern Ghana. *Savanna, 4* (2): 103–115.

_____. (1976a). Aspects of Sisala marriage presentations. *Research Review, 9* (3): 23–56.

_____. (1976b). Elders, office-holders and ancestors among the Sisala of northern Ghana. *Africa, 46*: 57–65.

_____. (January 1976c). The value of children in Sisala society: Implications for demographic change. Paper presented at the 15th International Seminar on Family Research, Lome, Togo.

_____. (1977a). The explanation of high fertility in Sisala-land, northern Ghana. In *The persistence of high fertility: Population prospects in the Third World*, edited by J.C. Caldwell, 223–258. Canberra: Australian National University Press.

_____. (1977b). The soul and sacrifice among the Sisala. *Journal of Religion in Africa, 8*: 1–17.

Mensah, A.A. (1958). Professionalism in the musical practice of Ghana. *Music in Ghana, 1* (1): 28–35.

_____. (1971). *Folk songs for schools*. Accra: Ghana Publishing Corporation.

Mereku, C.K. (2000). The music and dance of the Fante-Akan of Ghana. Lecture Presented at the Sixth Annual Summer course in African Music and Dance on the Theme: Experience the Authentic Rhythms of Africa. Freedom Hotel, Ho, Volta Region of Ghana.

Merriam, A.P. (1964). *The anthropology of music*. Evanston, IL: Northwestern University Press, 258–269.

Meyerowitz, E.L.R. (1949). *The sacred state of the Akan. Concepts of the soul among the Akan of the Gold Coast*. Vol. XXI. London: Faber and Faber.

_____. (1950). *Akan traditions of origin*. London: Faber and Faber.

_____. (1958). *The Akan of Ghana*. London: Faber and Faber.

Ministry of Food and Agriculture. (1958). *East Dagomba agriculture and livestock survey*. Tamale, GH: Author.

Music Educators National Conference. (1972). Music in world cultures. *Music Educators Journal, 10* (October).

_____. (1983). Multicultural imperatives. *Music Educators Journal, 5* (May).

_____. (1994). *Dance, music, theater, visual arts: National standards of the arts*. Reston, VA: MENC.

Naughton, C. (14–17 October 1993). Samba project '93: An example of world music in teacher training courses at the University of Exeter. In *Teaching Musics of the World: The Second International Sym-*

posium, Basel, edited by Margot Lieth-Philip and Andreas Gutzwiller, 109–117.

Nayo, N.Z. (1964). *Akpalu and his songs*. Legon, GH: Institute of African Studies, University of Ghana, Legon.

Neimeyer, R.A. (1995). Constructivist psychologies: Features, foundations, and future directions. In *Constructivist Psychotherapy*, edited by Robert A. Neimeyer and Michael J. Mahoney, 11–38. Washington, DC: American Psychological Association.

Nettl, Bruno. (November 1992). Ethnomusicology and the teaching of world music. *International Journal of Music Education, 20*, 3–7.

Nkansa-Kyeremateng, K. (1999). *Akan Heritage*. Accra, GH: Sebewie Publishers, 76–84.

Nketia, J.H.K. (1949). *Akanfoo nnwom bi*. London: Oxford University Press.

_____. (1955). *Funeral dirges of the Akan people*. Achimota, GH: Uden Forlag.

_____. (1958a). The ideal in African music: A note of Klama. *Universitas, 3* (2): 40–42.

_____. (1958b). The organization of music in Adangme society. *African Music, 2*(1): 28–30).

_____. (1958c). Traditional music of the Ga people. *Universitas*, 3 (3): 76–81. (Also printed in *African Music, 2* [1]: 21–27).

_____. (1959). African gods and their music. *Universitas, 4* (1): 3–7.

_____. (1962). The problem of meaning in African music. *Ethnomusicology, 6* (1): 1–7.

_____. (1963a). *African music in Ghana*. Evanston, IL: Northwestern University Press.

_____. (1963b). *Drumming in Akan communities of Ghana*. New York: Thomas & Sons, on behalf of University of Ghana, Legon.

_____. (1963c). *Preparatory exercises in African rhythm*. Legon, GH: Institute of African Studies, School of Music and Drama.

_____. (1964a). *A calendar of Ghana festivals*. Legon, GH: Institute of African Studies.

_____. (1964b). *Continuity of traditional instruction*. Legon, GH: Institute of African Studies, University of Ghana.

_____. (1964c). Historical evidence in Ga religious music. In *The Historian in Tropical Africa*, edited by J. Vansina, R. Mauny, and L.V. Thomas. London: International African Institute.

_____. (1965). *Music, dance, and drama: A review of the performing arts of Ghana*. Accra: Ghana Information Services.

_____. (1966). *Music in African cultures: A review of meaning and significance of traditional music*. Legon, GH: Institute of African Studies, University of Ghana.

_____. (1968a). *Our drums and drummers*. Tema, GH: State Publishing Corporation, Publishing Division.

_____. (1968b). The poetry of Akan drums. *Black Orpheus, 2* (2): 27–35.

_____. (1970). *Ethnomusicology in Ghana*. An inaugural lecture delivered on 20 November 1969 at the University of Ghana, Legon. Accra: Ghana University Press.

_____. (1971a). History and the organization of music in West Africa. In *Essays on Music and History in Africa*, edited by Klaus Wachsmann, 3–25. Evanston, IL: Northwestern University Press.

_____. (1971b). Surrogate languages of Africa. *Current Trends in Linguistics, 7*: 699–732.

_____. (1972). *Sources of Historical Data on the Musical Cultures of Africa*. Legon: Institute of African Studies, University of Ghana.

_____. (1973a). *Folk songs of Ghana*. Accra: Ghana University Press.

_____. (1973b). The musician in Akan society. In *The Traditional Artist in African Societies*, edited by Warren L.O. Azevedo. Bloomington: Indiana University Press.

_____. (1974). *The music of Africa*. New York: W.W. Norton.

_____. (1983). *New perspectives in music education*. Legon: Institute of African Studies, University of Ghana.

_____. (1990). Contextual strategies of inquiry and systematization ethnomusicology. *Ethnomusicology 34* (1): 75–97.

_____. (1991). Music and cultural policy in contemporary Africa. In *Music in the Dialogue of Cultures: Traditional Music and Cultural Policy*, edited by Max Peter, 77–94. Wilhelmshaven, DE: F. Noetzel Verlag.

_____. (1994). Generative processes in Seperewa music. In *To the Four Corners: A Festschrift in Honor of Rose Brandel*, edited by Ellen Claire Leichtman, 17–151. Harmonie Park: Detroit Monograph Series.

_____. (2005). *Ethnomusicology and African Music: Collected Papers. Volume One, Modes of Inquiry and Interpretation*. Accra, GH: Afram Publications.

Nukunya, G.K. (1969). *Kinship and marriage among the Anlo Ewe*. London: Athlone Press.

Oberg, K., ed. (1940). *The kingdom of Ankole, African political systems*. London: M. Fortes and E.E. Evans-Pritchard.

Odotei, Irene. (1976). The Ga-Dangme. In *Proceedings of the Seminar on Ghanaian Historiography and Historical Research*, edited by J.O. Hunwick, 20–22. Legon, Ghana.

_____. (1989). What is in a name? The social and historical significance of Ga names. *IAS Research Review (New Series) 5*: 34–51.

_____. (1991). External influences on Ga society and culture. *IAS Research Review (New Series) 7*, 61–71.

Ofei, Ahwireng K. (1992). Kpanlongo-Gome fusion, a marketable potential. Ph.D. diss., School of Performing Arts, University of Ghana, Legon.

Ofori, E.A. (1980). Egbanegba: A traditional musical type of northern Eweland. Ph.D. diss., University of Ghana, Legon.

Ombiyi, M.A. (1972). A model of African music curriculum for elementary schools in Nigeria. Ph.D. diss., University of California, Los Angeles.

Onwubiko, K.B.C. (1982). *School certificate, history of West Africa AD 1000-1800.* Book One. Onitsha, NE: Africana-Fep Publishers Limited.

Opoku, Kofi Asare. (1978). *West African traditional religion.* Jurong, SG: FEP, International Private Limited.

Opoku-Ampomah, J.K. (May-August 1961). Introducing an Ashanti girl into womanhood. *Ghana Notes and Queries, 2.*

_____. (1964). Thoughts of the school of music and drama. *Okyeame, 2.*

_____. (1968). *The Ghana dance ensemble.* Ibadan, NE: Abiobum Printing Works for Mbari Ibadan.

Oppong, Christine. (1973). *Growing up in Dagbon.* Accra-Tema, GH: Ghana Publishing Corporation.

Orfield, G. (July 1991). School desegration needed now. *Focus,* 5–7.

Orlando, L. (1993). *The multicultural game book: More than 70 practical games from 30 countries.* New York: Scholastic Professional Books.

Oureshi, R.B. (1987). Musical sound and contextual input: A performance model for musical analysis. *Journal of the Society of Ethnomusicology, 31* (1): 56–86.

Ozanne, Paul. (1962). Notes on the early historic archaeology of Accra. *Transactions of the Historical Society of Ghana, 6,* 51–72.

Parker, John. (1995). Ga state and society in early colonial Accra 1860–1920. Ph.D. diss., London School of Economics.

_____. (1998). Makraloi, merchants, and mulattos: Carl Reindorf and the politics of "race" in early colonial Accra. In *The Recovery of the West African Past: African Pastors and African History in the Nineteenth Century,* edited by Paul Jenkins, 31–37. Basel, CH: Basler Afrika Bibliographien.

_____. (2000). *Making the town, Ga state and society in early colonial Accra: Social history of Africa.* Portsmouth, NH: Heinemann.

Parrinder, E.G. (1949). *West African Religion.* London: Epworth Press.

Patterns in our fabric are changing. (1986). *Education Week,* Number 35 (14 May): 16.

Peterson, S. (1996). World cultures through the arts. Proposal for undergraduate international studies & foreign language program. Morgantown, WV: West Virginia University. CFDA # 84.0–16: 4.

Philips, J.B. (1962). *Social and religious symbolism in certain Akan chiefdoms.* Ph.D. diss., Oxford University.

Pinar, William, ed. (1973). *Search for a method in curriculum theorizing: The re-conceptualists.* Berkeley, CA: McCuchan Corporation.

Plange, Nii-K. (1984). The colonial state in northern Ghana: The political economy of pacification. *Review of African Political Economy, 31:* 29–43.

Poppi, Cesar. (1986). *The Vagla of northern Ghana: Notes towards an ethnography.* Cambridge Anthropology, 11 (2): 40–69.

Puplampu, D.A. (1951). The nation epic of the Adangme. *African Affairs, 1,* 50: 200, 236–241.

Quarcoo, A.K. (1967). The lakpa principle and deity of labadi. *IAS Research Review, 5:* 2–43.

Quarcoopome, Samuel. (1980). Political activities in Accra 1924–1945. Master's thesis, University of Ghana, Legon.

_____. (1993). The impact of urbanization on the socio-political history of the Ga Mashie people of Accra: 1877–1957. Ph.D. diss., University of Ghana, Legon.

Quarty-Papafio, A.B. (1924). Apprenticeship among the Gas. *Journal of the African Society, 13,* 416.

Quaye, Irene. (1972). The Ga and their neighbours 1600–1742. Ph.D. diss., University of Ghana, Legon.

Rattray, R.S. (1923). *Ashanti.* Oxford: Oxford University Press.

_____. (1927). *Religion and art in Ashanti.* Oxford: Oxford University Press.

_____. (1932). *The tribes of the Ashanti hinterland.* 2 vols. Oxford: Clarendon Press.

Reindorf, G.C. (1950). *The history of the Gold Coast and Asante: Based on traditions and historical facts comprising a period of more than three centuries from about 1500–1860.* Basel, CH: Mission Book Depot.

Sackeyfio, Godfrey (1968). *Music and dance of Otu gods of Ga Mashi.* Ph.D. diss., University of Ghana, Legon.

Sarpong, Peter. (1971). *Sacred stools of the Akan.* Kumasi, GH: Ghana Publishing Corporation.

_____. (1974). *Ghana in retrospect.* Tema, GH: Ghana Publishing Corporation.

Schott, Rudiger. (1977). Sources for a history of the Builsa in northern Ghanai. *Paideuma 39:* 145–168.

Schubert, William. (1984). Curriculum theorizing. *Curriculum Perspectives, 4* (1).

Seshie, L.K.M. (1991). *Akpalu fe hawo.* Accra, GH: Sedco Publishing Limited.

Shore, H.L. (March 1964). African drama today. *AMSAC Newsletter, 6* (7).

Smith, B.O., W.O. Stanley, and J.H. Shores, eds. (1957). *Fundamentals of curriculum development.* Yonkers-on-Hudson, NY: World Book.

Smith, P.G. (1992). Transcription of a keynote address at the First General Session of the Second Annual Conference for Multicultural Education in Orlando, Florida, 6–7.

Smith, R.A. (1992). Towards perception: A humanities curriculum for arts education. In *The arts, education, and aesthetic knowing: Ninety-first yearbook of the National Association of Education,* edited by Bennett Reimer and Ralph A. Smith. Chicago, IL: University of Chicago Press.

Staniland, Martin. (1975). *The lions of Dagbon: Political change in northern Ghana*. Cambridge: Cambridge University Press.

Steier, F. (1991). *Research and reflexivity*. Newbury Park, CA: Sage.

Stone, Ruth. (2000). *Garland handbook of African music*. New York: Garland.

Tait, David. (1961). *The Konkomba of northern Ghana*. London: Oxford University Press for the International Africa Institute.

Takaki, R. (1993). *A different mirror. A history of multicultural America*. Boston: Little, Brown.

Tamakloe, Emmanuel Forster. (1931). *A brief history of the Dagamba people*. Accra, GH: Government Printer.

Tashijian, Victoria B. (1998). The diaries of A.C. Duncan-Johnstone: A preliminary analysis of British involvement in the "native courts" of colonial Asante. *Ghana Studies, 1*: 135–150.

Thime, P.V. (1973/74). Some preliminary notes on the music of the Cwezi cult in Ankole. *African Music, 3* (1): 55–56.

Thomas, Roger. (1975). Education in northern Ghana, 1906–1940: A study in colonial paradox. *International Journal of African Historical Studies, 7*: 427–467.

Thompson, R.F. (1974). *African art in motion*. Berkeley: University of California Press.

_____. (1966) An aesthetic of the cool: West African dance. *African Forum, 2* (2): 85–102.

Trimillos, R.D. (1972). Expanding music experience to fit today's world. *Music Educators Journal, 10*: 91.

Trowell, M., and K.P. Waschman. (1953). *Tribal crafts of Uganda*. London: Oxford University Press, Amen House.

Turnbull, C.M. (1962). *The forest people, a study of the pygmies of the Congo*. New York: Simon & Schuster.

Tuury, Gabriel. (1982). *An introduction to the Mole-speaking community*. Wa, GH: Catholic Press.

Tyler, R.W. (1949). *Basic principles of curriculum and instruction*. Chicago, IL: University of Chicago Press.

Vars, G.F. (1996). *Interdisciplinary teaching: Why & how*. Columbus, OH: National Middle School Association.

Volk, T. (Summer/Fall 1993). The history and development of multicultural music education as evidenced in the *Music Educators Journal* 1967–1992. *Music Educators Journal, 41* (2): 137–155.

Ward, William Ernest. (1927). Music in the Gold Coast. *Gold Coast Review 3* (2): 199–223.

Watherston, A.E.G. (1907–1908). The northern territories of the Gold Coast. *Journal of the African Society, 7*, 344–373.

Wiles, J., and J. Bondi. (1979). *Curriculum development: A guide to practice*. Columbus, OH: Charles E. Merrill Publishing.

Wilks, Ivor. (1959). Akwamu and Otublohum: An eighteenth-century Akan marriage arrangement. *Africa, 29* (4): 391–404.

Williamson, S.G. (1965). *Akan religion and the Christian faith*. Legon: Ghana University Press.

Wolz, C. (1972). Understanding ethnic music through movement. *Music Educators Journal, 10*: 100.

Yamoah, Felix (1971). Installation ceremony of an Ashanti chief. Ph.D. diss., University of Ghana, Legon.

Yankah, Kwesi. (1983). To praise or not to praise the king: The Akan Akpae in the context of referential poetry. *Research in African Literatures, 14* (3): 381–400.

Younge, Paschal Yao. (1991, 1992). *Musical traditions of Ghana: A handbook for music teachers and instructors of West African drumming*. Revised ed. Legon, GH: School of Performing Arts, University of Ghana.

_____. (1996). Enhancing global understanding through African music and dance at West Virginia University: A transformative, interdisciplinary, and multidimensional pedagogy. Paper Presented at a Conference on the Music and Dance of Africa and the Diaspora: The Present State and Potential in the United States. April 5, 1997, University of Michigan, Ann Arbor.

_____. (1998). Enhancing global understanding through traditional African music and dance: A multicultural African music curriculum for American middle schools. Ph.D. diss., College of Human Resources and Education at West Virginia University, Morgantown.

Zais, Robert. (1976). *Curriculum: Principles and foundations*. New York: Harper & Row.

DVDs: Contact WWW.DANCE-DRUMMING.COM

Index

This alphabetization of all the languages used in the book combined was used when crafting the index.

Aa Bb Cc Dd Ɖɖ Ee Ɛɛ Ff Ƒƒ Gg Ɣɣ Hh Ii Jj Kk Ll
Mm Nn Ŋŋ Oo Ɔɔ Pp Qq Rr Ss Tt Uu Vv Ʊʊ Ww Xx Yy Zz

439